AF327810

30 Years of Climbing Magazine

Origins

It's all different, it's all the same

Harvey T. Carter published the first issues of *Climbing* in 1970. In them you could find the details on the new Bill Forrest route in the Mystery Towers, read about big adventure on El Cap or in the Himalaya, get educated on access issues that threatened to strangle the sport. Back then you probably knew all those articles' authors (they were your climbing partners), and could soundly harangue them for leaving out some crucial detail. If you were really worked up you might even write a letter to the editor, and expose yourself to a barrage of letters directed at your own shortcomings.

It is this sharing of our adventures and back and forth of ideas that has kept *Climbing* alive since before many of its current readers could tie their shoelaces.

Compiling an anthology such as the one you hold is always tricky business, for it taxes a democratic process designed for simpler projects, like lawmaking. The task is doubly vexing when you have 30 years worth of material and only 352 book pages to operate with. How do you do it? Our first attempt left us with three books' worth of stories. Since you can only cram so many words on a page, hard decisions were made and worthy articles put aside. Let us apologize in advance for those left out.

The best thing about putting this book together was that it caused us to reread gems all the way back to 1970, when Vietnam was a war, Nixon was in his first term, and pitons were our primary protection. What struck us throughout all that page turning is how, though the voices and issues change (remember when chalk was controversial?), the passion for climbing never wavers. Climbers of three decades ago lived out of rusty vans, took jobs scrubbing dishes in between climbing seasons, and never pulled punches with opinions — or fists, as was sometimes the case. Climbers back in the Golden Era endured thirst, hunger, cold, heat, crowds, bureaucracy. They asked themselves why bother, cursed the sport, and vowed never to return. Only to return. Today, we still share many of the same challenges.

Happily, climbers are a talented lot and there has never been a shortage of those who could put their thoughts down on paper, and do a lively job of it. Some of these writers only wrote one piece, then went back to their nine-to-five flipping burgers or pounding nails or setting broken bones, but some also became regular writers. A few even broke through into mainstream and today make livings at their craft. Regardless, large and small they are here, and we climbers have the good fortune of relating to their stories, and being able to insert our names into their plots.

Reliving so many close calls on paper (and through living a few in real life) reminds us that climbing can be a game with tragic consequences. Indeed, it is shocking to look back and see how many of our friends have come up short racing the weather on an alpine route or chasing a dream in some unpronounceable mountain range halfway around the world. Losses such as these always come as terrible blows, but so long as there are climbers there will be writers, and so long as there are writers there will be words that will not let us forget. We have these writers past and present to thank for the wealth of articles that made this book possible.

— Climbing Magazine

Introducing the Writers

Jeff Achey is a long-time climber, photographer, and writer, and is *Climbing's* Editor at Large. He won Nike's the Nike Earthwrite Award for his "Turning Green," which appeared in *Climbing* No. 164.

Michael Benge is the Editor of *Climbing*. He co-authored *Climbing's Rock: Tools and Technique.*

Jim Bridwell has been pioneering visionary climbs for over 35 years, including the first ascents of Alaska's Kichatna Spire and *Zenyatta Mondatta* on El Capitan, and the first one-day ascent of the *Nose* in 1975 with John Long and Billy Westbay. He founded Yosemite's high-angle search and rescue team.

Andy Cave lives below the gritstone edge of Stanage, England. He works as a UIAGM mountain guide and is also researching dialect and folklore at Sheffield University. Since his ascent of Changabang, he has attempted a hard mixed route on Guillamet, Patagonia, and climbed ice in Scotland and long rock routes in Norway and the Outer Hebrides.

Geoffrey Childs lives in Mazama, Washington. He guides for Mazama Mountain Guides and is a representative for Wild Country/Charlet Moser. He has been writing for the climbing press for 25 years. The Mountaineers Books is to publish a collection of his writings in autumn 2000.

Greg Child has been thrilling readers of *Climbing* with his stories since 1982. A Senior Contributing Editor for *Climbing* and author of its Postcards from the Edge column, Child has also written several books, *Postcards From the Ledge, Mixed Emotions,* and *Thin Air: Encounters in the Himalayas.* His work also regularly appears in *Outside* magazine.

Yvon Chouinard made the first ascent of El Capitan's *North America Wall* in 1964 with Tom Frost, Royal Robbins, and Chuck Pratt. At the time it was the hardest big-wall route in the world. Chouinard is the owner of Patagonia clothing company, and his writings include the classic how-to book, *Climbing Ice.*

John Climaco, since his encounter with the "liaison officer from hell," has gone on to work for Quokka Sports, a digital sports-entertainment company. He just returned from the remote, rarely visited north (Chinese) side of the Karakoram, where his team made the first ascents of two previously unclimbed peaks.

Bill Donahue of Portland, Oregon, has written for the *New Yorker,* the *New York Times Magazine, Double Take, George,* and *Outside,* for whom he is a correspondent. Once the pogo-sticking champion of the world (for one day, in 1974), he is now the inventor of a for-sale parlor game, Spiel.

Dick Dorworth is a staff reporter and columnist for the *Idaho Mountain Express,* Ketchum, Idaho. He also guides for Exum Mountain Guides and Shasta Mountain Guides. He has written for *Ski, Skiing, Powder, Wild Duck Review,* and the venerable *Mountain Gazette* (for which he wrote the classic "Night Driving"). He skis every day all winter, and climbs regularly.

Jeff Jackson is a Contributing Editor for *Climbing,* and also works as a mountain guide. He has won the James Michener Scholarship for creative writing.

Mark Jenkins is a well-traveled climber and writer, who was a member of the 1986 U.S. Everest North Face Expedition. He is author of *Off the Map: Bicycling Across Siberia* and *To Timbuktu,* which is about the first descent of Africa's Niger River in 1993. He now writes a regular column for *Outside* magazine called The Hard Way.

Alan Kearney is a climber, photographer, and author living in the Northwest, and a longtime *Climbing* contributor. He wrote *Mountaineering in Patagonia.*

Michael Kennedy is the former Publisher/Editor in Chief of *Climbing,* and now President of the Access Fund. In between his former magazine duties, he squeezed in, among many others, the first ascents of the Northeast Face of Ama Dablam in Nepal (with Carlos Buhler) and the *Infinite Spur* on Mount Foraker, Alaska (with George Lowe).

Andy Kirkpatrick is a world-ranging British alpinist with a mysterious penchant for the long, the cold, and the difficult.

Jon Krakauer's account of soloing the Devils Thumb also appears in his first book *Eiger Dreams,* a collection of his climbing stories. He is a frequent contributor to *Outside* and many other magazines, and the best-selling author of *Into The Wild* and *Into Thin Air.*

Lance Leslie survived nine years in Alaska as a mountain guide, and subsequently served a stint as *Climbing's* Photo and Copy Editor.

Jeff Long is a novelist, journalist, historian, and screenwriter living in Boulder, Colorado. His novel *The Ascent* won both the Boardman-Tasker Award and the American Alpine Club Literary Award. His screenplays for *The Ascent* and *Angels of Light* have been employed by Sylvester Stallone and Steven Seagal. The film rights to his latest novel, *The Descent,* have been purchased by Warner Bros.

John Long is Senior Contributing Editor for *Climbing,* and writes a regular column, Living Large. His instructional book *Advanced Rock Climbing* won the 1997 Banff Mountain Book Festival award for Best Mountain Exposition, while one of his most entertaining climbing books is his *Rock Jocks, Wall Rats, and Hang Dogs,* about his days in Yosemite.

John Middendorf founded A5 equipment and is the author of *Big Walls: How to Rock Climb.* His pioneering first ascents include the grade VII *The Grand Voyage* on Great Trango Tower, Pakistan, and *Atlantic Ocean Wall* on El Capitan.

Alison Osius is the senior editor for *Climbing,* president of the American Alpine Club, and author of *Second Ascent: The Story of Hugh Herr.* In the 1980s-90s Osius won three National championship titles in sport climbing. She has written for many anthologies and publications including the *Wall Street Journal,* the *London Independent,* and the *Washington Post Sunday Magazine.*

Dave Pagel is a Contributing Editor for *Climbing.* Despite his everyman's persona, he has climbed such tough classics as the North Face of the Eiger, of which he writes in this volume.

Dave Pegg is a Senior Associate Editor for *Climbing.* Since writing "What's Your Problem?" he has found himself in the embarrassing position of being out-climbed by Americans wherever he goes.

Duane Raleigh is the Publisher and Editor in Chief of *Climbing,* and was a 1998 National Book Award winner for his *Knots and Ropes for Climbers.* He has also authored *Ice: Tools and Technique* and co-authored *Rock: Tools and Technique.*

David Roberts is a long-time climber and writer, and is a Senior Contributing Editor for *Climbing.* He is the author of nine books, including *Deborah, and the Mountain of My Fear* and *Moments of Doubt.* He is also a Contributing Editor for *Men's Journal* and *Outside.*

Audrey Salkeld is a highly acclaimed mountaineering writer and historian. She won the Boardman-Tasker Award for Mountain Literature in 1996 for her book *A Portrait of Leni Riefenstahl*. She also wrote *The Mystery of Mallory and Irvine* (with Tom Holzel) and has edited the excellent large-format books *Great Climbs* and *World Mountaineering* (both with Chris Bonington).

Matt Samet is a Contributing Editor for *Climbing,* and supplies regular doses of vitriol and self-deprecating humor by writing its Sporting Life column.

John "Vermin" Sherman is a Senior Contributing Editor for *Climbing,* and author of *Stone Crusade, Verm Exposed, Better Bouldering,* and *Hueco Tanks Climbing and Bouldering Guide.*

Tyler Stableford is the Photo and Copy editor at *Climbing* and an outdoor photographer for The Image Bank.

Mark Synnott is a contributing editor for *Climbing.* Beginning with his cave-dwelling days in Yosemite, "Scrappy" (so named for his grungy lifestyle) has gone on to establish several difficult wall routes in the remote corners of the world, from Polar Sun Spire in Baffin Island to Shipton Spire in Pakistan.

Pete Takeda is a Senior Contributing Editor for *Climbing,* writing the regular column Pete's Wicked Tales, recollections from his 18 years of climbing around the world from big walls to ice falls. A collection of his tales is due out from *Climbing* in 2000.

John Thackray of New York, New York, is a freelance writer whose work has appeared in the *New York Times,* the *New Republic, New York, Appalachia, Forbes* and (in England) *Mountain,* the *Observer,* the *New Statesman,* and the *Financial Times.* For over a decade he was book-review editor of the *American Alpine Journal.*

Mark Twight, aka Doctor Doom, is a longtime contributor to *Climbing,* and author of the recently published *Extreme Alpinism: Climbing Light, Fast, and High.* He has also authored many alpine desperates, such as *Deprivation* on Alaska's Mount Hunter, *Fuck 'em, They're All Posers Anyway* on Bolivia's Pico del Norte, and *The Gift (that keeps on giving)* on Mount Bradley in Alaska (included herein).

Wills Young is a Senior Associate Editor for *Climbing.* He tries not to take himself as seriously as the fictional narrator of his story featured herein.

The Big Easy
Everest the weird way

By Greg Child

Fifty feet ahead of me and a hundred feet below the summit of Everest, a Sherpa named Ang Babu grunts and pushes at the butt of some French geezer who pulls up with all his might on an old hank of bootlace-thick rope hanging off a cliff. With a mighty heave the Sherpa shoulders his client onto the summit ridge, then they begin the easy home stretch to the top of the world.

It's a windless, cloudless morning near the apex of the North Ridge. On one side of this 2.5-mile fin of ice and rock, starkly backlit clouds lap at Nepalese peaks; on the other, tawny Tibetan hills stretch into a soft, heliotropic haze. I pause to take in the view. Realizing that in a few minutes I'll be on the highest place on earth, I start sniffling with emotion. Or is it that bloody cold that's been dogging me for weeks?

Wiping frosted goggles and freeing my oxygen mask of a golf ball-size ice-cube of drool, I look up at the Frenchman and his Sherpa guide. They move side by side, until after a few paces the Sherpa inadvertently overtakes his client by a stride — and is sternly stopped by a mitten backhanded against his chest. The Frenchman has paid a bundle of cash to be escorted up Everest, and he'll be damned if anyone else is going to beat him to this most coveted summit.

This display of inverted camaraderie and neo-colonialism squeezes a weary laugh out of me. When I share a glance with Karsang, the Sherpa beside me, I detect an expression that crosses the borders of language to say, "Can you believe that arsehole?" But we humor the Frenchman, who creeps ahead with excruciating slowness, and the six members of our polyglot summit party fall into rank behind the imaginary line he has drawn in the snow.

I share those last steps with Bob Hempstead, a Nebraskan who ropes steers for a hobby, and who, like the Frenchman, is a member of a commercial Everest trip. Bob is just happy to be where he is. His summit fantasy includes twirling a lariat to become the highest roper in history. When we'd passed through Lhasa, he'd done tricks on a street corner, jumped in and out of the lariat, and lassoed a cheering Tibetan bystander — until Chinese soldiers broke up the crowd. Yeah, Bob is a nice guy, which is why I find it particularly upsetting when he slips on the skating-rink-hard slope, pivots upside down when he tries to self-arrest, then slides 40 feet to disappear over the 10,000-foot north face.

It happens lightning quick, a blur to the eyes and the imagination. Aside from my lame shout of "Stop!" he is gone without a sound. I turn toward Karsang, partly to gauge from his expression whether I have hallucinated all this, but he too gapes toward the claw marks of Bob's slide to oblivion.

I gather what wits I can muster at nearly 29,000 feet and crampon toward the precipice. I foolishly call Bob's name. What's the point? He's a croaker for sure. Then I hear his weak-lunged cry for help.

"Dammit," I think to myself, imagining the epic of extricating a mangled Bob from the cliffs below the Big One's crown. "Looks like I won't climb this tit of a hill after all."

Doing Everest became possible for people with disposable incomes in the 1990s when a few climbers started guiding the mountain. A cheaper alternative to the guided ascent emerged with the advent of the commercial trip, where a team of lead climbers and Sherpas outfit the mountain with camps, oxygen, and fixed ropes, then let the punters have it without a guide. This is the ultimate high-adventure package tour, and the ultimate blind date, as you don't meet your partners until you reach the mountain. To me, letting inexperienced people loose on an 8000-meter peak is like giving a drunk an Uzi with a full clip, but it is astonishing how many people have gotten to the top, guided or in a commercial group, and have enjoyed the experience.

I'd always sneered at Everest, snubbed invitations to join expeditions to it, pooh-poohed it as an over-rated, over-climbed status symbol. "Just because it is the biggest shitpile on earth doesn't mean it is the best shitpile on earth," I used to say. But this year I went to the mountain Tibetans call Goddess Mother of Earth. Maybe because I was tired of making excuses as to why I had climbed so much in the Himalaya, but never on Everest. Maybe a crack at Everest is just inevitable for anyone silly enough to dub themselves a Himalayan climber. Whatever the reason, as the departure date for Tibet neared I did feel a growing fascination — OK, call it a dose of Everest fever — with the idea of standing on the earth's highest point. Mostly though, I just wanted to get the bloody mountain off my back.

I justified selling out my no-Everest principles because I had a project up there: to make a film about climbing the North Ridge with an old friend who was an amputee. Tom Whittaker is a loquacious Brit I met in Yosemite in 1978 while I was crawling out of a dumpster with an armful of pop cans stamped with the magic nickel deposit seal. He was crawling in. He had two legs back then, and he talked me into doing the *Nose* on El Cap with him. Seventeen years later, and after he'd lost his right foot in a car crash caused by a drunk driver on Thanksgiving night in 1979, he phoned me to suggest another climb. This time I would help him become the first amputee up Everest. "Why would I want to climb with a one-legged man, Tom?" I asked him bluntly. "Because it will make us both very sexy," he replied.

To launch the expedition we needed capital, and the best leverage for capital in this case was to make a documentary of Tom's attempt. I faxed Leo Dickinson, the British adventure filmmaker who had made 70 films, including one in which he ballooned over Everest and crashed in Tibet. Leo took my bait and persuaded a British TV station to finance the film. Armed with a film deal, we persuaded sponsors to help underwrite the expedition, then we bought places for Tom, me, and a four-person film crew on a commercial trip to Everest's Tibetan side.

Soon we were at basecamp, along with about 500 other people. Half were support members, cooks, bottlewashers, and Chinese liaison officers for the 11 expeditions whose camps dotted the snout of the East Rongbuk Glacier. The rest had their eyes on the summit of Everest. Aside from a behemoth Japanese/Sherpa team on the Northeast Ridge, the bulk of the traffic was on the North Ridge.

Why the North Ridge? Because it was a climber's bargain with a peak fee of $15,000 and no limit on team size, as opposed to the $50,000 minimum royalty demanded by the Nepalese team of five climbers. It also allowed the four commercial operators on the North Ridge to offer middle-class Everest wannabes a package priced between $18,000 and $25,000. In contrast, a guided ascent of Nepal's South Col route — the domain of the filthy rich — sported the tony price tag of $65,000.

Everesting has always been a separate sport to the rest of climbing. For a certain breed of climber, it is the only mountain they'll ever try, and they'll pay big bucks for the big tick. As David Breashears, who has climbed Everest twice, says, "Everest is the ultimate feather in the pseudo-mountaineer's cap."

Altitude-addled from the drive to basecamp at 17,000 feet, I almost fell out of the jeep. Everest loomed in the distance. The long sweep of the North and Northeast Ridge routes formed the left skyline, the West Ridge the right, and the Great Couloir and Hornbein Couloir formed gashes up the center. I was surprised at how rocky the mountain was — "black as a snake's arse," Australian climber Jon Muir had quipped when we'd flown past it, en route to Lhasa.

Through binoculars I scoped the landmarks of the North Ridge route. Above the highest campsite at 27,000 feet were the crumbling cliffs of the Yellow Band. I'd read that around there the British climber Frank Smythe, in 1933, had been so discombobulated by altitude he had offered a bite of his lunch to a non-existent partner. Above that, protruding from the ridge, were two rocky humps, the First Step and the Second Step. The Second Step, a stack of rocks culminating in a 15-foot vertical cliff, was the technical crux of the route. It was here that the Englishmen George Leigh Mallory and Andrew Irvine were last sighted during a summit bid on June 8, 1924. Some climbers believe they beat Ed Hillary and Tenzing Norgay to Everest's first ascent by nearly three decades, but until their bodies are found and the film in the cameras they carried is restored, the matter of whether or not they summitted will always be conjecture. The Second Step was also where Chinese climbers, on the second ascent of the North Ridge in 1975 (the Chinese made the first ascent in 1960), erected a 10-foot aluminum ladder.

Rumor had it that in 1994 some wiseguy had cut the ropes securing this rickety old ladder to the wall and hurled it off the mountain. Some climbers in camp looked forward to the challenge of climbing the Second Step by "fair means." Others were mortified that the aid move had been eliminated.

Also on the slopes below the curve of the North Ridge, Reinhold Messner made his tour de force in 1980, by soloing a new route without oxygen. He had been the only climber on the entire Tibetan side of Everest. His sole companion at basecamp was his girlfriend. Never again would a climber experience solitude on Everest.

By early May all the expeditions had marched the 15 miles up the East Rongbuk Glacier to establish Advance Basecamp, a 200-tent ghetto jammed onto a moraine strip at 21,000 feet, below Everest's bleak northeast wall. It is well-known by biologists that while a few lab rats in a cage can co-exist as a harmonious community, when the population gets out of control and the cage gets overcrowded, the rats get strange, go crazy, and eat their young. The first sign of anti-social behavior on Everest came when a few expeditions got territorial and encircled their camps with rope fences to keep trespassers out. Then on a foul, windy day in mid-April, while I stood below the North Col at 21,500 feet watching snow plumes stream over the ice-blue crest 2000 feet above, I met The Man With An Attitude.

All around me, climbers were setting out, then abandoning their journeys to the tent village of Camp I on the North Col, driven back by the gale and signs of impending storm. Wind swirled about in a vortex, occasionally sweeping breathable air away and leaving a momentary vacuum that left one with an awful suffocating feeling. While I zipped up my suit to keep spindrift out, I noticed Leo locked in conversation with a climber from another team, then watched them march purposefully toward me.

"This fellow says he's going to cut our tents loose from the North Col and toss them off the mountain," said Leo. After an introduction I learned that The Man With An Attitude was the climbing leader of his expedition; he held a dim view of commercial groups and people like me who are part of them. He'd been on Everest a month longer than me and he didn't like our intrusion on his ridge. He'd placed all the fixed ropes himself; if I wanted to use his ropes I had to ask his permission. Anyway, it was too late to ask permission to use his ropes, as he intended to cut them free, and, as Leo said, he planned to slash the guy ropes of our tents and let the wind devour them.

It took but a second to identify this character as a dangerous alpine psycho in need of a mega-dose of Thorazine. Leo prescribed different treatment. His heritage was of British barroom brawls and the use of Don Whillans-style fisticuffs to settle climbing disagreements. While Leo shadowboxed in the background whispering, "Hit him, hit him," I pretended to be a U.N. negotiator trying to arrange a cease-fire.

After a heated discussion in the cold, I negotiated safe passage for us to the North Col, and threatened sanctions and reprisals if The Man With An Attitude touched our tents. His threat to destroy our camp was, in his words, "A non-life threatening protest to our presence." It was the first time I'd heard that one in 11 Himalayan expeditions. As we parted company I wondered how anyone was going to summit with kooks like him around.

On May 10 a thick, warm fog rolled up the glacier. For climbers like Russell Brice, a New Zealander who was our expedition leader and who, during four expeditions to the north side, had known only winds that flatten tents and send rocks frisbeeing through the sky, it was a perplexing omen. "This either means the worst storm in history is about to hit," he said, "or we're about to get perfect weather." After 24 hours it was clear the latter was true.

First to summit were six members of a Japanese/Sherpa team on the Northeast Ridge, on May 11. This was the first time this immensely long route had been climbed in its entirety, though Russell and Harry Taylor had climbed the ridge to its junction with the North Ridge in 1988, alpine style.

After the Japanese success the gauntlet was down. Between May 11 and 17, about 50 more people summitted by the North Ridge. There were first national ascents for Taiwan, Turkey, Latvia, and Rumania. Russian, American, British, Austrian, and Italian climbers succeeded as well. Italian Reinhard Patsheider set a north side speed record, covering the 8000 feet from Advance Basecamp to the summit in a 21-hour, oxygenless blitz. Britain's Alison Hargreaves made a seemingly effortless oxygenless ascent in "unsupported" style, meaning that although she was always surrounded by other climbers and had radio contact with basecamp, she carried her own gear, established her own camps, and had no Sherpa help (as opposed to climbers like me who were vying for bad-style ascents, and who happily paid Sherpas to carry their junk, sucked the guts out of oxygen bottles, and hauled themselves up fixed ropes). So independent and style-conscious was Alison that she wouldn't even accept a cup of tea from me while on the mountain, lest it be construed as "support."

Though hers was the best ascent of the season, her publicity machine in Britain got carried away afterward, variously claiming hers as the first-ever female ascent, first female oxygenless ascent, and that it was all done solo. In fact, Junko Tabei of Japan made the first female ascent in 1975, Lydia Bradey was the first woman up without oxygen in 1988 (though Lydia's claim was disputed at the time of her climb, all but misogynists and Luddites credit her ascent now), and on her summit day Alison was seldom more than 50 feet behind two Italians.

Others were gunning for firsts too. There were contenders for the youngest ascent (age 15) and the oldest ascent (age 63). And then there was The Man Who Would Bivy Highest. A member of a guided expedition, this guy hit the spotlight one morning when a team going for the summit found him shivering below the Second Step, at 28,100 feet. He had survived the night dressed only in his climbing suit. Fearing he'd be frostbitten, two Sherpas gave up their summit bids — and the $300 bonus they stood to earn for helping their clients to the top — to assist. Radios buzzed as a rescue was mounted, people moved up the ridge to help, and yaks were assembled for a full-scale evacuation down the glacier.

When The Man Who Would Bivy Highest passed my tent at 25,600 feet, he was verbally abusing his Sherpa rescuers from behind an oxygen mask. When I saw his gloves dangling from strings on his wrists I suggested he put them on his dead-fish-colored hands. This prompted him to launch into a tirade about how everyone on the mountain was over-reacting to his plight. "I'm in control. I don't need rescuing." Later, Leo would hand His Bivouacship a cup of tea at the North Col, only to have it thrown back at him because there wasn't sugar in it.

During April and May, Tom and I and several score of summit hopefuls reached the wind-ravaged site of Camp II at 25,600 feet. For anyone with two feet this section of climb up firm 40-degree snow and scree was easy, but not for Tom with his spatula-footed carbon-fiber-ankled, Terminator-like, crampon-adapted, Flexfoot prosthesis. Though he could saunter down a city street with a gait that hinted nothing of a disability, his footing was sketchy on rocky terrain. He couldn't just kick a foot into snow or edge up on rock; he had to eyeball the jet-black appendage his stump was slotted into, place it carefully, and ease onto it. He had no ankle rotation, no calf muscle, no toe to spring off, and two trick knees.

His leg was sensitive to cold. He combated this with a battery-powered warming device taped to his stump. After a month, he was running out of feet, having damaged two of his four prosthesis on the slog between basecamp and

Advanced Basecamp. Still, he was going.

With his strange foot Tom was easily the most conspicuous, but George Mallory, the grandson of the late George Leigh Mallory, was no less intriguing. After young George summitted on May 14, there was little doubt in his mind that his grandfather was the first man up Everest. He based his belief on the fact that in 1924 their teammate, Noel Odell, saw Mallory and Irvine crest the Second Step, 900 vertical feet and a horizontal half mile before the summit, at about 1 p.m. "After that, the route is easy," young George said enthusiastically. "There is nothing to stop you from climbing to the top."

Indeed, the weather on June 8, 1924, was good though cloudy. Mallory and Irvine were strong climbers and they were using oxygen. Although young George had found the Chinese ladder intact, he'd checked out the ladderless variation and he felt grandpa could have flashed it, or at least stood on Irvine's shoulders.

Though nothing concrete is known about Mallory and Irvine's last hours, they left some tantalizing clues, like the ice axe found midway between the First and Second Steps by a 1933 British expedition. Did it signify their high-point, the site of a fall, or was it just dumped because it was useless on the rocky ridge? One of their bodies seems to have been found in 1975 by a Chinese porter, Wang Hung-bao, who went for a 20-minute stroll from his camp at 26,600 feet, and returned with the tale of finding "an English dead." Wang's tentmate on the day of the grisly discovery, Zhang Jun Yan, later confirmed Wang's tale. In 1979 Wang revealed his story to Japanese climbing leader Ryoten Hasegawa, but before they could relocate the corpse, Wang was killed in an avalanche below the North Col.

As the season wore on, thievery raised its ugly head. It began with allegations that precious oxygen bottles stashed at high camp had been stolen. Tents on the glacier were pilfered, then uprooted and stolen altogether by Tibetan yak men. Even my ice axe disappeared from beside a tent at the North Col. But most disturbing to our team was the disappearance of 60 liters of rum, spirited away from basecamp.

Was nothing sacred on Everest? Lawsuits were threatened by clients against guides, fax machines spewed out messages to constantly remind us of the real world, and the concrete blockhouse toilets at basecamp filled with shit.

The infamous jet stream winds returned to sandblast the summit on May 18. It occurred to me then that I had missed the good weather, and I probably would not climb the mountain. I tried to take this in stride but the threat of failure became a wart on my psyche that I scratched and scratched like a mangy, ill-tempered dog. Punters, who I'd helped into their crampons, had summitted. I was supposed to be a climber, and these people were — tourists. What was wrong?

The timing was wrong, and getting wrapped up in a film project was wrong, and being trapped in a heavyweight expedition where management decreed when you could climb the mountain and when you could not was wrong. I'd failed on about half of my 11 Himalayan expeditions, but the failures were always more or less on my terms, an amicable agreement between me and the mountains. Slow learner that I am, I realized that my self-image is defined to an unhealthy degree by mountaineering, and I resolved to lighten up, get into the Zen of failure. But before I could get into any of that feel-good bullshit the weather cleared.

On May 25, Tom, Russell, Sherpas Karsang and Lobsang, and I hunkered down for the night in Camp III. The summit stood 2100 feet above and a horizontal mile southwest of us. At midnight we woke, plugged into ill-fitting Russian oxygen masks, and set off into the moonless night.

We followed a trail of decrepit ropes anchored to the even more decrepit rock of the Yellow Band. The bulbous muzzles made it impossible to see our feet. Cold killed our headlamp batteries. We probed about like blind men. It wasn't easy for Tom but he forced himself on, pulling on the ropes that snaked up a seemingly endless flow of ramps and cliffs. To speed Tom's progress the rest of us took his load. The weight was ridiculous. Each of us carried three oxygen bottles. I also lugged along a video camera, a radio, a still camera, and a liter of water.

At the first glow of sunrise at 4:30 a.m., we stopped at 27,200 feet to assess our progress. We had not even reached the crest of the Northeast Ridge. At this speed we could get to the summit, but not until very late, and we'd run out of oxygen. Although it was an agonizing moment for Tom, it signaled the end of the road for him — at least this year. He returned to the high camp with Russell, while I continued with Karsang and Lobsang.

The sun was rising when we hit the ridge crest. Makalu, the world's fifth highest peak, appeared as a massive molar in the east. In the oblique sunlight, Nepal seemed an endless succession of parallel ridges and cloud-filled valleys, of steaming jungles and iced peaks. Tibet's horizon was a sheet of brown velvet, the foreground a swirl of porcelain-white glaciers.

We passed the First Step, then sidled across a wall of limestone festooned with tattered rope tied to pitons that at times I could remove by hand. Sometimes a tricky free move had to be made to connect the series of footpath-wide ramps that the route followed. I blew a sequence at one point, got off route, and found myself poised on small crumbling holds in muzzle, mittens, and Frankenstein boots. I looked between my legs at a huge drop leading to the glaciers, and saw a pinkish dot about 500 feet down — the body of Michael Rheinberger, an Australian who'd summitted in 1994 on his seventh attempt on Everest, then died after bivouacking on the descent.

At the Second Step we encountered the Chinese ladder, flanked left and right by an overhanging offwidth and a tricky arete. I deduced that the ladder was the most expeditious alternative, and I wondered if Mallory and Irvine had overcome this obstacle, with their heavy steel oxygen tanks, hobnailed boots, and wool tweed jackets. Only the Chinese in 1960 were known for certain to have climbed this cliff. The book of their ascent says it took three hours to overcome it, and that they climbed with the power of Mao Ze Dong Thought.

Even though I was on oxygen I'd been gasping desperately for the last hour. Scaling the ladder nearly made me faint. At the top of the Second Step I checked the pressure gauge on my bottle. It registered zero. No wonder I felt so wasted. How long it had been empty I didn't know. I switched onto another bottle, dumped the spent one in a cluster of abandoned orange torpedoes, and joined the ranks of the world's highest litterbugs.

An easier quarter-mile of ridge and we caught up with Bob, the Frenchman, and three Sherpas. They had set off an hour earlier that morning.

"Hi, Greg," said Bob. "Hi, Bob," said Greg. It was then that Bob fell off Mount Everest.

I still don't understand what stopped him from taking the big dive. When I got to him he was lying on a steeply tilted, coffee-table-sized slab of rock, on his back, head pointed down the mountain. Seeing his legs and arms waving about reminded me of the character in Franz Kafka's story The Metamorphosis, the guy who turns into a beetle and who, when he tries to walk like a man, falls over and lays on his back wriggling around pathetically.

"Don't move an inch!" Bob was just out of reach, and I was damned if I was going to risk reaching over the cliff and being catapulted over the North Face. I needed a rope but didn't have one. Bob's face was turning red as blood flowed to his head and his eyes pleaded for fast action. I was about to remove my harness and drag him up with that, when I looked at my feet and saw an old hank of rope lying on the slope.

This discovery didn't give me religion, but it may have converted Bob. I hacked the rope out of the ice, tied a loop, and cast it to him. He grabbed it. Then Ang Babu arrived, dug out more rope and tossed it down. When we hauled Bob up I asked him what had caused his fall.

"I was day dreaming," he answered.

The summit, which I reached at 9:45 a.m., was a busy spot. For the seven of us up there, there were hands to shake, radio broadcasts to make, photos to take. Cameras were exchanged in a confusing number of permutations to ensure everyone had their photo taken with everyone else. The apex of the mountain bristled with a forest of metal poles decorated with red, yellow, and blue prayer flags. One object up there, a scientific instrument, appropriately resembled a traffic light.

Bob spun his lariat, then left with the mob. I spent a few minutes on top alone. Quiet at last. Just the flapping of prayer flags and the sound of my lungs and heart. No clouds. A curving horizon. Somewhere out there in the great southern distance the monsoon was rolling toward the Himalaya, pushing aside the jet stream winds like a cosmic bulldozer to create this freakish spell of calm. I pocketed a few small ancient rocks from a scree patch 30 feet below the top then headed down.

There were 67 ascents of Everest from Tibet that spring. Nobody died. Mine was the 736th ascent of the mountain. Been there, done that.

First published in Climbing *No. 155, 1995.*

Notes from the Thunderbird

Desert highways, granite walls, and other necessities of life

By Jeff Achey

Should have stopped in Ely. Gas tank way past E now as my car labors up a shoulder of the Hot Creek Range toward Black Rock Summit. I crest the hill and turn the key; the engine dies suddenly into a white-noise quiet of hot wind. I coast down, past dark boulders and ravens perched like thunderbirds on a signpost, toward shimmering dry basins and scattered mountains rising out of the mirages like piles of charred debris. Miles later I hit the flats. Roll to a dusty stop by a lone ranch, hop a fence and approach a wind-chapped house set among carelessly fenced yards, rusting tanks, and trailers. There's an ancient Ford pickup listing to one side, a Beware of the Dog sign. No one in sight except the boot-kicked dog, eyeing me. Not a breath of wind. Whine of gnats. Faint smell of oil and baked sage. Huge, blinding sky. A faded thermometer outside the kitchen window reads 108 degrees. A yelled "Hello" vanishes as if never uttered. Dog between me and the front door. Back to the road to run out of gas in peace.

"Warm Springs (site)." The map of southern Nevada is full of "sites" — Adven, Nyala, Tempiute. Mining-bust names. "Sites" are never useful to the traveler low on fuel. Sure enough, at Warm Springs there is an ancient ruin of a roadhouse, tumbleweeds visible inside through broken-out windows. A rusting historical marker full of bullet holes. Nothing else.

Though I fear getting stranded I like the desolation, the mind bleaching of crossing a big desert. You forget the color green. You have strange thoughts, then no thoughts, then strange thoughts. You pull over just to hear the silence. Passing an abandoned shack a half-mile out in the sand, I conjure faces for those who spent enough time here to give places names. Twisted visages appear — hermit miners and fugitives — their lives as mysterious as this landscape, where eagles appear out of nowhere in the middle of the night, and boulders leave mile-long skid marks across level salt flats. The faces mingle with other images — granite walls, cammed Hexentrics, corduroy knickers.

With only a mirage left in the tank I top one last hill into the bleak mining town of Tonopah, and stop at the first convenience store. Slot machines flank the magazine racks. Heading out of town I am suddenly elated not to be 30 miles back in the desert trying to flag down a lone Winnebago or renegade Manson disciple on a grocery run. This tank will get me to Bishop, California, and the Sierra Nevada range.

"Clean is climbing the rock without changing it: a step closer to organic climbing for the natural man ..." My windows are open at the Thunderbird Motel in Bishop. It's almost dark outside. I'm reading an essay by Doug Robinson from the 1972 Chouinard Equipment catalog, which has, in a way, inspired this trip. On the same page is a black-and-white photo of the author, bearded, in silhouette with only a few nuts and carabiners and the creases in his cord knickers highlighted, climbing the Grandma Peabody Boulder. The catalog was the first piece of climbing literature I ever read, and everything in it, including those boulders, became mythical to me. Today I had beheld the Peabodies for the first time: massive egg-like rocks reaching up out of the sand into the blue sky of a deliriously hot afternoon.

Above my laptop and through the motel curtains I can see the red and blue blinking of neon: an arrow and thunderbird, compelling and significant. It's the heat. My mind drifts.

I remember sitting in my room in New Jersey, planning my first rack, re-reading every word of the catalog, whose cover is a Chinese landscape painting. Its clean-climbing essays inspired my first leads in the Gunks, steep 5.4s with abundant fixed pitons, which I dutifully avoided in favor of precarious arrangements of opposing Hexes. Many would tumble out with a clink-clank as I moved up — sometimes whole pitches would come undone. Finally my partner refused to climb with me unless I clipped the pins. I dreamt images from the catalog, Anglesey sea-cliffs and Cerro Torre, always climbing ever-so-clean on the rock, and with French technique and bamboo-shafted *piolet* on the ice.

" *...perfection is finally attained not when there is no longer anything to add, but when there is no longer anything to take away, when a body as been stripped down to its nakedness.*" — Antoine de Sainte Exupery (from the catalog)

The Peabody boulders *felt* even higher than they were. The heat made me weak, so I picked just one route on each boulder, being careful to scout the downclimbs, some of which could be five-bolt sport routes. Starting up was like stepping into my adolescent climbing fantasies. There was a sense of being in church, I set hands and feet as meticulously as chalices on the alter, tiptoeing up climb after climb until, after two hours, I realized that epiphany never comes to an insistent mind; I was taking it all way too seriously. Time to visit the high country.

Mount Whitney, about 50 miles south of the Peabodies, is the highest mountain in the 48 contiguous states. Rising 10,000 feet above the Owens River Valley, it is christened — in good American fashion — after a forgettable 19th-century functionary. Josiah Whitney was a Harvard professor and one-time head of the California Geological Survey. The only other thing I know of him is his condescending rebuke of John Muir's theory of glacial sculpting, a radical geological concept at the time, now universally accepted. Whitney the mountain I know for its spectacular eastern cirque, the main summit flanked by a series of impressive needles, all laced with alpine rock climbs. The peak is a classic example of glacial sculpting.

I sit below Whitney's east face, by a blue pool full of icebergs at 12,500 feet. My partner, Karen Tracy, who has come north out of the desert to climb with me, has just jumped in. In a past life she was a rollerblade performer on Venice Beach, then a dentist; now, at 45, she's an ambulance nurse and climber of five years. A year ago she broke her back in a climbing fall in Joshua Tree. We are just down from the East Buttress of Whitney, her first "alpine climb," an impressive eight-pitch line first done in 1937. She had never used an ice axe before our thousand-foot glissade descent. Between hiking and climbing we have started at dawn and reached camp at dusk two days in a row; Karen decides she has recovered from her injury.

" *... the motions of climbing, the sharpness of the environment, the climber's reactions, are still only themselves, and their dividends of joy personal and private.*" — Doug Robinson (from the catalog)

"Tonight I get to sleep in my waterbed with my kitty cats," Karen says before heading home.

I am pounding up the trail west of Bishop, trying to get a look at the high basins, trying to chase down the innocent mind of my first foray into these mountains 20 years ago. The images are still strong: Banner Peak, north of here near the Minarets, my first mountain ... my first time ever on a snowfield. Fin Dome, near Kearsarge Pass, a solo climb ... a sensation of granite under my worn mountain boots still vivid, a body memory from another life.

Though I'm now capable of casual ascents of those days' dream climbs, the feelings of accomplishment alternate with a sense of loss. I keep hiking, looking for signs and symbols: in the clouds and trees, in the quality of light.

I round a corner and see a strange plant, stop-sign red, weird asparagus-shaped stalks pushing up from beneath pine needles. The plant is red because it lacks chlorophyll; botanists call it a saprophyte — a plant that can't live on sunlight but must gain its sustenance from decaying remains on the forest floor. A sign aimed at the nostalgic.

"*Lose your dreams and you'll lose your mind ...*" — a Rolling Stones quote printed over a picture of Cerro Torre on the last page of the catalog. *Back then* ... that was the beginning of "clean climbing." What an enduring trend that proved to be. Back then ... what a powerless state of mind. A trap. Nostalgia is just a romanticized form of giving up. A way of not learning. Some say learning to climb is essentially becoming comfortable in the mountains. But comfort is mostly just the onset of ignorance.

Above me is the *Sun Ribbon Arete,* a long and dramatic knife-edge leading to the top of 13,000-foot Temple Crag, a half-day's hike in from the East Side of town of Big Pine. After three false starts I am back where I started, barely 50 feet off the snow, looking at the same bad crack I backed off 20 minutes ago. Vertical rock, even my small pack pulling me off balance. Flexible hand holds. A lapse of patience. *Fuck getting turned around on another solo ... then, Whoa ... balance ... rashness will kill you.*

Rashness subsides but another wave of desire comes. I grip harder and step up, suddenly stripped of that comfortable sensation of "scrambling" that lingers with the soloist up to a certain level. Squeezing the jams harder than needed, serenaded now by a chattering internal monologue: ... *squeeze, like a trigger, man ... anchor that hand inside the Earth ...* Brain sputtering out banal mixed metaphors and unburned thought-fragments like a cold car engine revving up. Undercling flakes at an overlap — pause here to work out another steep sequence — then the wall easing back, easy ground. Was I really on route? Scrambling again, for long enough to relax and get into it, warming up by covering four hundred feet without needing to stop. Then onto the Ribbon, one of the features that Don Jensen, an early climber and guide, named the "Celestial Aretes." I bypass a Tyrolean traverse with some face moves and a steep finger crack, and find an old hollow carabiner, circa 1977.

A dozen pitches' worth and it still keeps going — up, down, and around. Views of peaks and the Palisade glaciers opening up. Glimpsing the Owens Valley for the first time in two days. The color of ashes. Looks hot down there.

In Temple Crag's summit register I find cryptic messages, snapshots from a rich climbing history. One is by Gordon Wiltsie and Andy Selters, arriving with a prayer flag and memorial stones for their mentor Smoke Blanchard, a legendary Sierra guide killed on a desert highway in 1989. Another entry is by Peter Croft, who summitted at 10:30 a.m. one summer day via *Dark Star* (5.10-

something and over 30 pitches if you're wearing a rope): "... clouds already building, may have to winge ..." He had planned to continue up two other peaks that day. Reassuring somehow, the presence of a *real* soloist.

An eagle flies by the summit, riding the updrafts. Winge-ing. Craggy 14,000-foot peaks all around. Norman Clyde Peak to the south, named for another real soloist, who hiked these mountains for over 30 years with a hundred pounds of cast-iron cookware and hardbound books in his rucksack, and died in 1972 after thousands of first ascents.

On the descent I link turns down the steep snow in my hiking boots, jumping suncups, comically fearless now. Clattering down talus into the sudden scent of pine, sweet and startling after hours amid rock and melting snow.

Camp overlooks a lake. Distant waterfall sounds. View of the Temple and a slow purple sunset. It's an inexplicably hot night, full of restless, malarial visions. Mosquitoes' whine becomes incoming rockfall ... images of a sunlit knife edge dropping away into blackness like night sky, of the Big Dipper turning, of a chamber of a revolver coming around.

Certain sects of ascetic monks in northern India develop a power called the Mystic Heat. After years of meditation and training, a monk declares his readiness and is escorted to an icy cave high in the Himalayas, and left there naked, with seven bed sheets soaked in glacial runoff. At nightfall the monk wraps himself in a sheet, then summons the Mystic Heat, which he radiates from the heart chakra out through his body, thawing and then drying the cloth. He removes the dry sheet and wraps himself in the next. In the morning, when the other monks return, seven dry sheets lie neatly folded next to the naked monk, who sits clear-eyed in lotus position.

In the morning I sit up in my down bag and make a second cup of coffee. In their ritual, the monks show their mastery just once, then renounce the power, which they consider a distraction on the spiritual quest. I wonder how much is merely clinging. I wonder ... what peak to climb next?

A couple of teenage girls sit near my car humming a tune by the Crash Test Dummies. Beyond them is Yosemite Valley's Camp Curry, a shantytown of tent cabins inhabited by tourists and park employees. Beyond the tourist enclave there are neighborhoods — the Terrace, Camp Six, Boys Town — basketball hoops, ethnic quarters, stereos playing.

Mid-afternoon in the parking lot. My car is in direct sun and there's a welt on my arm from touching the metal seatbelt clip. I can hear the sizzle of someone frying pork chops behind a nearby camper, the sharp aroma drowning the usual Valley bus exhaust-campfires-tourist cologne.

I'm just down from Half Dome, a summit unusual to begin with, and so frequently photographed that it has become unnatural, more like a huge 3-D postcard than a mountain. From the valley floor the monolith looks formal, a classical bust, but from the backside, where Melinda Carillo and I climbed, it has the oblong form of a Henry Moore sculpture. An impressive Park Service ladder is its easiest route, cables and stairs up fifth-class friction slabs. Hikers linger on the spacious top for hours, exploring, peeking down over the Visor at climbers coming up the Northwest Face, or striking out in random directions until coming to the place where they finally stop walking because the stone starts to roll away too steeply, like water pouring off the edges of the earth on a medieval map. On top we talk to a hiker who says he taught Dave Shultz, Valley legend, to climb.

In the mountains north of Tuolumne, I hesitate on a ridge above Mount Conness' southwest cirque, overlooking one last climb I'm thinking of trying before heading home. Rockfall just before I start down from the ridge — big, flying boulders, smoke from the release zone. I ignore the omen, in favor of a found raven feather. Gifts from the thunderbirds.

I have talked to a couple of guys who backed off the icy approach gully early in the morning, wishing they'd brought crampons. Later now, snow much softer. I kick steps backward down the gully in my rock shoes, resting my calves when I reach the deeper suncups. Ice crystals melt inside my shoes. At the base of the Harding Route is a memorial plaque for Don Goodrich, killed when he pulled a block onto himself during the first attempt on this beautiful silver wall, visible from all over Tuolumne Meadows, in the late 1950s. This is an ambitious climb for me.

Weird head trips as I begin: half-purposely conjuring a sort of fog to obscure the sensation of being unroped. Trying to visualize: free movement on a warm tapestry of granite. Searching my brain for that feeling — elusive, until I forget about it — of solidity at the point of contact between hand and rock. Keeping the mind's eye from looking down.

I am sketchy on the first pitch off the snow. With a strange detachment and disdain I watch myself pull a flared fist jam down almost to my waist, and with a gritty sidepull swap it for a foot. Really poorly done. *You better climb better than that, dude, or you're going down.* Mind going through ritual solo images — of Derek and the sight of Sentinel from the Valley floor, of my kids' faces. The next steep thin-hands crack, supposedly the crux, goes perfectly, and from that sensation comes confidence — a sharp, double-edged sword. Rounded laybacking above, shoes picking up bits of grit. A chockstone chimney and overhanging hand crack into an offwidth and squeeze. Fantastic crack climbing.

"Personal qualities — judgment, concentration, boldness — the ordeal by fire, take precedence, as they should, over mere hardware." — Robinson (from the catalog)

Higher is a traverse to cracks on the right wall of a dihedral. Steep up there. Good hand holds, but still takes two forays. Seven hundred feet of air now. A few more strange moves to the last hard section, a good finger crack. Then, mostly hands.

From the summit I can see Half Dome, the Cathedral group, and — yeah, there it is — Banner Peak, my first-ever mountain, climbed with my high-school pal Bob Palais last time I was in the High Sierra, before my first rope had even lost its middle-marker, the summer after he approached me in the hall because I was wearing a "Go Climb a Rock" T-shirt I'd gotten as a tourist kid in Yosemite. Today I made a two-hour round trip up a thousand-foot route hard enough to be called a "free climb." Feeling proud, and glad right now for what 20 years of practice has given me. But also humble, wondering about the difference between good luck and skill. About illusion. About clinging and letting go, in all their senses.

Clouds are building, for the first time since day one of my trip. Feels like the opening and closing of venetian blinds, through which I was supposed to see something.

Trip's end, in Death Valley, a kind of symbolic gesture. Sitting on a stained picnic table next to Furnace Creek. The highway is swimming in mirages; I later hear that temps topped 130. Behind me is a huge National Park Service palm grove, which hides a golf course. Suspicious-looking facilities, probably all a front for some mega Nevada Test Site, where technicians disguised as park rangers commute to dust-proof labs by underground nuclear monorail.

Ravens, dozens of them, are hanging out by the small creek, which runs in a man-made channel full of minnows. All around this green oasis with the gurgling water is a landscape bleached and barren as Hades. The ravens stand mostly still, occasionally side-stepping an inch or two, their mouths open to inhale the cool moisture. I pull out the feather I carried with me on Mount Conness.

Traffic going by. Only one other car stopped, way down on the other end of the parking lot. Ravens within eight feet of me, knowing I'm harmless when I'm writing, like a drunk vomiting in an alley.

My descent from Conness took me past the two climbers' camp, where the urge to stop in and talk about the climb came over me, as predictable as a hangover. What part of me needed something from them? Where does it come from? When will it go away? Dropping over the ridge with just a wave felt like a triumph. A true expert would not have been challenged.

I can see 20 ravens without moving my head.

Tourist cars pull up; a caravan from Michigan, with flags on their antennae. Manicured poodle in a front seat. It's cooler now, less than 120 F in the shade. Think I'll move on a few miles down the road to Badwater, low point of the hemisphere.

Really bad water, hot and toxic. I can still taste it a hundred miles later. Farewell, Sierras. Wonder if I can make it to Las Vegas on this tank ...

First published in Climbing *No. 160, 1996.*

Empty Handed on Devils Thumb

An enlightening Alaskan solo

By Jon Krakauer

y the time I reached the interstate I was having trouble keeping my eyes open. I'd been OK on the winding two-lane blacktop between Fort Collins and Laramie, but when the Pontiac eased onto the smooth, unswerving pavement of I-80, the soporific hiss of the tires began to gnaw at my wakefulness like ants in a dead tree.

That afternoon, after nine hours of humping 2-by-10s and pounding recalcitrant nails, I'd told my boss I was quitting: "No, not in a couple of weeks, Steve; right now was more like what I had in mind." It took me three more hours to clear my tools and other belongings out of the rust-stained construction trailer that had served as my home in Boulder. I loaded everything into the car, drove up Pearl Street to Tom's Tavern, and downed a ceremonial beer. Then I was gone.

At 1 a.m., 30 miles eat of Rawlins, the strain of the day caught up to me. The euphoria that had flowed so freely in the wake of my quick escape gave way to overpowering fatigue; suddenly I felt tired to the bone. The highway stretched straight and empty to the horizon. The night was cold, and the stark Wyoming plains glowed in the moonlight like Rousseau's painting of the sleeping gypsy. I wanted very badly just then to be that gypsy, conked out on my back beneath the stars.

I shut my eyes — just for a second, but it was a second of bliss. It seemed to revive me, if only briefly. The Pontiac, a sturdy behemoth from the Eisenhower years, floated down the road on its long-gone shocks like a raft on an ocean swell. The lights of an oil rig twinkled reassuringly in the distance. I closed my eyes a second time, and kept them closed a few moments longer. The sensation was sweeter than sex.

A few minutes later I let my eyelids fall again. I'm not sure how long I nodded off this time, it might have been for five seconds, maybe 20, but when I awoke it was to the rude sensation of the Pontiac bucking violently along the dirt shoulder at 70 miles per hour. By all rights, the car should have sailed off into the rabbitbrush and rolled. The rear wheels fishtailed wildly back and forth, but I eventually managed to wrest the machine back onto the pavement without so much as blowing a tire, and let it coast gradually to a stop. I loosened my death-grip on the wheel, took several deep breaths to quiet the pounding in my chest, then slipped the shifter back into drive and continued down the highway.

Pulling over to sleep would have been the sensible thing to do, but I was on my way to Alaska to change my life, and patience was a concept well beyond my 23-year-old ken.

Sixteen months earlier I'd graduated from college with little distinction and even less in the way of marketable skills. In the interim an off-again/on-again four-year relationship — the first serious romance of my life — had come to a messy, long-overdue end; nearly a year later, my love life was still zip. To support myself I worded on a house-framing crew, grunting under crippling loads of plywood, counting the minutes until the next coffee break, vainly scratching at the sawdust stuck in perpetuum to the sweat on the back of my neck. Somehow, blighting the Colorado landscape with condominiums and tract houses for $3.50 an hour wasn't the sort of career I'd dreamed of as a boy.

Late one evening I was mulling all this over on a barstool at Tom's, picking unhappily at my existential scabs, when an idea came to me, a scheme for righting what was wrong in my life. It was wonderfully uncomplicated, and the more I thought about it, the better the plan sounded. By the bottom of the pitcher its merits seemed unassailable. The plan consisted, in its entirety, of climbing a mountain in Alaska called the Devils Thumb.

The Devils Thumb is a prong of exfoliated diorite that presents an imposing profile from any point of the compass, but especially so from the north: its great north wall, which had never been climbed, rises sheer and clean for 6000 vertical feet. Twice the height of El Cap, the north face of the Thumb is one of the biggest granitic walls on the continent.

I would go to Alaska, ski across the Stikine Icecap, and make the first ascent of this notorious nordwand. It seemed, midway through the second pitcher, like a particularly good idea to do all of this solo.

Writing these words more than a dozen years later, I find that it is no longer entirely clear just how I thought soloing the Devils Thumb would transform my life. It had something to do with the fact that climbing was the first and only thing I'd ever been good at. My reasoning, such as it was, was fueled by the scattershot passions of youth, and a literary diet overly rich in the works of Nietzsche, Kerouac, and John Menlove Edwards — the latter a deeply troubled writer/psychiatrist who, before putting an end to his life with a cyanide capsule in 1958, had been one of the preeminent British rock climbers of the day.

Dr. Edwards regarded climbing as a "psycho-neurotic tendency" rather than sport; he climbed not for fun but to find refuge from the inner torment that characterized his existence. I remember, that spring of 1977, being especially taken by a passage from an Edwards short story titled "Letter From a Man:"

So, as you would imagine, I grew up exuberant in body with a nervy, craving mind. It was wanting something more, something tangible. It sought for reality intensely, always as if it were not there ...

But you see at once what I do. I climb.

To one enamored of this sort of prose, the Thumb beckoned like a beacon. My belief in the plan became unshakable. I was dimly aware that I might be getting in over my head, but if I could somehow get to the top of the Devils Thumb, I was convinced, everything that followed would turn out all right. And thus did I push the accelerator a little closer to the floor and, buoyed by the jolt of adrenaline that followed the Pontiac's brush with destruction, sped west into the night.

You can't actually get close to the Devils Thumb by car. The peak stands in the Boundary Ranges on the Alaska-British Columbia border, not far from the fishing village of Petersburg, a place accessible only by boat or plane. There is regular jet service to Petersburg, but the sum of my liquid assets amounted to the Pontiac and $200 in cash, not even enough for one-way airfare, so I took the car as far as Gig Harbor, Washington, then hitched a ride on a northbound seiner that was short on crew. Five days out, when the Ocean Queen pulled into Petersburg to take on fuel and water, I jumped ship, shouldered my back-pack, and walked down the dock in a steady Alaskan rain.

Back in Boulder, without exception, every person with whom I'd shared my plans about the Thumb had been blunt and to the point: I'd been smoking too much pot, they said; it was a monumentally bad idea. I was grossly overesti-mating my abilities as a climber, I'd never be able to hack a month completely by myself, or I would fall into a crevasse and die.

The residents of Petersburg reacted differently. Being Alaskans, they were accustomed to people with screwball ideas. Most of the local residents I met, if they reacted at all, simply asked how much money there was in climbing mountains.

Petersburg sits on an island, the Devils Thumb rises from the mainland. To get myself to the foot of the peak I first had to cross Frederick Sound. For most of a day I walked the docks, trying without success to hire a boat to ferry me across. Then I bumped into Bart and Benjamin.

The two were pony-tailed constituents of a Woodstock Nation tree-planting collective called the Hodads. We stuck up a conversation. I mentioned that I too had once worked as a tree planter. The Hodads allowed that they had chartered a floatplane to fly them to their camp on the mainland the next morning. On May 3, a day and a half after arriving in Petersburg, I stepped off the fortuitous Cessna, waded onto the tidal flats at the head of Thomas Bay, and began the long trudge inland.

The Devils Thumb pokes up out of the Stikine Icecap, an immense, labyrinthine network of glaciers that hugs the crest of the Alaskan panhandle like an octopus, with myriad tentacles that snake down to the sea from the craggy uplands. In putting ashore at Thomas Bay I was gambling that one of these frozen arms, the Baird Glacier, would lead me safely to the bottom of the Thumb, 30 miles distant.

An hour of gravel beach led to the tortured blue tongue of the Baird. I turned my back to the sea, donned crampons, and scrambled up onto the glacier's broad, lifeless snout. After three or four miles I came to the snowline and exchanged crampons for skis. Putting the boards on my feet cut 15 pounds from the awful load on my back and made the going much faster. But now that the ice was covered with snow, many of the glacier's crevasses were hidden, making solitary travel extremely dangerous.

In Seattle, anticipating this hazard, I'd purchased a pair of stout 10-foot aluminum curtain rods. Now I lashed the rods together diagonally, strapped them to the hip-belt of my backpack so that they extended like landing gear, and hoped they would arrest a fall into a crevasse. Staggering up the glacier with my overloaded backpack, bearing the queer metal cross, I felt like some kind of strange penitente.

The first climbers to venture onto the Stikine Icecap were Bestor Robinson and Fritz Wiessner, who spent a stormy month in the Boundary Ranges in 1937 but failed to reach any major summits. Wiessner returned in 1946 with Donald Brown and Fred Beckey to attempt the nastiest-looking peak in the Stikine, the Devils Thumb. Wiessner was injured during fall on the hike in and was forced to limp home in disgust, effectively ending the trip. But Beckey went back that same summer with Bob Craig and Cliff Schmidtke. On August 25, after several aborted tries and some exceedingly hairy climbing on the peak's east ridge, Beckey and company sat on the Thumb's wafer-thin summit tower in a tired, giddy daze. Theirs was by far the most technical ascent that had been done in Alaska, an important milestone in the history of American mountaineering.

In the ensuing decades three other teams also made it to the top of the Thumb, but all steered clear of the big north face. Reading accounts of these expeditions,

I had wondered why none of them had approached the peak by what appeared, from the map at least, to be the easiest and most logical route, the Baird. I wondered a little less after coming across an article by Beckey in which he cautioned, "Long, steep icefalls block the route from the Baird Glacier to the icecap near Devils Thumb." But after studying aerial photographs I decided that Beckey was mistaken, that the icefalls weren't so big or so bad. The Baird, I was certain, really was the best way to reach the mountain.

For two days I slogged steadily up the glacier without incident, congratulating myself for discovering such a clever path to the Thumb. On the third day I arrived beneath the Stikine Icecap proper, where the long arm of the Baird joins the main body of ice. Here the glacier spills abruptly over the edge of a high plateau, dropping seaward in a phantasmagoria of shattered ice; at close range it made a different impression than the photos had. As I stared at the tumult from a mile away, for the first time the thought crossed my mind that maybe this Devils Thumb trip wasn't the best idea I'd ever had.

The icefall was a maze of crevasses and teetering seracs. From afar it brought to mind a bad train wreck, as if scores of ghostly white boxcars had derailed at the lip of the icecap and tumbled down the slope in a chaotic heap. The closer I got, the more unpleasant it looked. My 10-foot curtain rods seemed a rather feeble defense against crevasses that were 40 feet across and 250 feet deep. Before I could finish figuring out a course thorough this maze, the wind came up, hurling snow that stung my face and reduced visibility to almost nothing.

In my impetuosity, I decided to carry on anyway. For the better part of the day I groped through the labyrinth in a whiteout, retracing my steps from one dead end to another. Time after time I'd think I had found a way out, only to wind up in a deep blue cul de sac, or stranded atop a detached pillar of ice. My efforts were lent a sense of urgency by the noises emanating underfoot. A madrigal of creaks and sharp reports served as a reminder that it is the nature of glaciers to move, of seracs to topple.

As much as I feared being flattened by a wall of collapsing ice, I was even more afraid of falling into a crevasse, a fear that intensified when one ski punched through a snow bridge spanning a slot so deep that the bottom was beyond view. A little later I broke through another bridge to my waist; the rods kept me out of the 100-foot hole, but after extricating myself I doubled over with dry heaves at the thought of lying in a pile at the bottom of the crevasse, waiting for death to come, with nobody even aware of how or where I'd met my end.

Night had fallen by the time I emerged onto the empty, wind-scoured expanse of the high glacial plateau. In shock and chilled to the core, I skied far enough past the icefall to put its rumblings out of earshot, pitched the tent, crawled into my sleeping bag, and shivered myself to a fitful sleep.

Although my plan to climb the Devils Thumb didn't fully hatch until the spring of 1977, the mountain had been lurking in the recesses of my mind for about 15 years — since April 12, 1962, to be exact. The occasion was my eighth birthday. When it came time to open presents, my parents announced that they were offering me a choice of gifts. They would either escort me to the new Seattle World's Fair to ride the Monorail and see the Space Needle, or give me a taste of mountain climbing by taking me up the third-highest peak in Oregon, a long-dormant volcano called the South Sister that, on clear days, was visible from my bedroom window. It was a tough call. I thought the matter over at length, then settled on the climb.

To prepare me for the rigors of the ascent, my father handed over a copy of *Mountaineering: The Freedom of the Hills,* the leading how-to manual of the day, a thick tome that weighed only slightly less than a bowling ball. Thenceforth I spend most of my waking hours poring over its pages, memorizing the intricacies of piton-craft and bolt placement, the shoulder stand and the tension traverse. None of which, as it happened, was of any use on my inaugural ascent, for the South Sister demanded nothing more in the way of technical skill than energetic walking, and was in fact ascended by hundreds of farmers, house pets, and small children every summer.

Which is not to suggest that my parents and I conquered the mighty volcano; in the middle of a 20-degree snow slope that would be impossible to fall from if you tried, I decided that I was in mortal jeopardy and burst into tears, bringing the ascent to a halt.

Perversely, after the South Sister debacle, my interest in climbing only intensified. I resumed my obsessive studies of *Mountaineering.* Something about the scariness of the activities portrayed in those pages just wouldn't leave me alone. The book contained black-and-white plates of notable peaks in the Pacific Northwest and Alaska, and though all the photographs were striking, one was much, much more than that: it made my skin crawl. An aerial photo by the noted geologist Maynard Miller, it showed a singularly sinister tower of ice-plastered black rock. Not one place on the entire mountain looked safe; I couldn't imagine anyone climbing it. The caption identified the peak as the Devils Thumb. On hundreds of occasions over the years that followed I returned, with almost pornographic fascination, to that dark and threatening image.

I had planned on spending between three weeks and a month on the Stikine Icecap. Not relishing the prospect of carrying a four-week load of food, heavy winter camping gear, and a small mountain of climbing hardware all the way up the Baird on my back, before leaving Petersburg I paid a bush pilot $150 — the last of my cash — to airdrop six cardboard cartons of supplies when I reached the foot of the Thumb. I showed the pilot exactly where, on his map,

I intended to be, and told him to give me three days to get there; he promised to fly over and make the drops as soon thereafter as weather permitted.

On May 6 I set up a basecamp just northeast of the Thumb and waited for the plane's arrival. For the next four days it snowed, nixing any chance for a flight. Too terrified of crevasses to wander far from camp, I occasionally went out for a short ski to kill time, but mostly I lay silently in the tent with my thoughts, fighting a rising chorus of doubts.

As the days passed, I grew increasingly anxious. I had no radio, nor any other means of communicating with the outside world. It had been many years since anyone had visited this region, and would likely be a long time before anyone did so again. I was nearly out of fuel and down to a single chunk of cheese, my last package of Ramen noodles, and half a box of Cocoa Puffs. This, I figured, could be stretched for three or four more days, but that would be it. A two-day ski would take me back down the Baird to Thomas Bay, but then a week or more might pass before a fisherman happened by who could give me a lift back to Petersburg.

When I went to bed on the evening of May 10 it was still snowing and blowing hard. I was vacillating on whether to head for the coast in the morning or stick it out on the icecap, gambling that the pilot would show before I starved or died of thirst, when, just for a moment, I heard a faint whine, like a mosquito. I tore open the tent door. Most of the clouds had lifted, but there was no airplane in sight. The whine returned, louder this time. Then I saw it: a tiny red-and-white speck, high in the western sky, droning my way.

A few minutes later the plane passed directly overhead. The pilot, however, was unaccustomed to glacier flying and had badly misjudged the scale of the terrain. Worried about winding up too low and getting nailed by sudden turbulence, he flew a good thousand feet above me, believing all the while that he was just off the deck, and never saw my tent in the flat evening light. My waving and screaming were to no avail; from his altitude I was indistinguishable from a pile of rocks. For the next hour he circled the icecap, scanning its barren contours without success. But to his credit, the pilot appreciated the gravity of my predicament and didn't give up. Frantic, I tied my sleeping bag to the end of one of the crevasse poles and waved it for all I was worth. When the plane banked sharply and began to fly straight at me, I felt tears of joy.

The pilot buzzed my tent three times in quick succession, dropping two boxes on each pass, then the airplane disappeared over a ridge and I was alone. As silence again settled over the glacier, I felt abandoned, vulnerable, lost. I realized that I was sobbing. Embarrassed, I halted the blubbering by screaming obscenities until I grew hoarse.

I awoke early on May 11 to clear skies. Startled by the good weather, mentally unprepared to commence the actual climb, I hurriedly packed a rucksack nonetheless and began skiing toward the base of the Thumb. Two previous Alaskan expeditions had taught me that, ready or not, you simply can't afford to waste a day of perfect weather if you expect to get up anything.

A small hanging glacier extended out from the lip of the icecap, leading up and across the north face like a catwalk. My plan was to follow this line to a prominent rock prow in the center of the wall, executing an end-run around the ugly, avalanche-swept lower half of the face.

The catwalk turned out to be a series of 50-degree icefields blanketed with knee-deep powder snow and riddled with crevasses. The going was slow and exhausting; by the time I front-pointed up the overhanging wall of the upper-most bergschrund, some three or four hours after leaving camp, I was whipped. And I hadn't even gotten to the "real" climbing yet. That would begin immediately above, where the hanging glacier gave way to vertical rock.

The rock, exhibiting a dearth of holds and coated with six inches of crumbly rime, did not look promising, but just left of the main prow was a shallow, steep dihedral glazed with frozen meltwater. This ribbon of ice led straight up for 300 feet, and if it proved substantial enough to support the picks of my tools, the line might go. I hacked out a small platform in the snow slope and stopped to eat a candy bar and collect my thoughts. Fifteen minutes later I shouldered my pack and inched over to the bottom of the corner. Gingerly, I swung my right axe into the two-inch-thick ice. It was solid, plastic — a little thinner than I would have liked but otherwise perfect. I was on my way.

The climbing was steep and spectacular, so exposed it made my head spin. Beneath my boot soles, the wall fell away for 3000 feet to the dirty, avalanche-scarred cirque of the Witches Cauldron Glacier. The prow soared authoritatively up to the summit ridge, a vertical half-mile above. Each time I planted a tool, that distance shrank by another 20 inches.

The higher I climbed, the more comfortable I became. All that held me to the mountainside, to the world, were six thin claws of metal stuck half an inch into a smear of frozen water, yet I began to feel invincible, weightless, like one of those lizards that cling to the ceilings of cheap Mexican hotels.

Early on a difficult climb, especially a difficult solo climb, there is a hyper-aware-ness of the abyss pulling at your back. You constantly feel its call, its immense hunger. To resist takes a great conscious effort; you don't dare let your guard down for an instant. Your movements begin tentative and clumsy, but as the climb goes on you grow accustomed to the exposure, and come to believe in the reliability of your hands and feet and head. You learn to trust your self-control.

By and by, your attention becomes so intensely focused that you no longer notice the raw knuckles, the cramping thighs, the strain of maintaining nonstop concentration. A trance-like state settles over your efforts and the climb becomes a clear-eyed dream. Hours slide by like minutes. Everything outside of this immediate sphere is temporarily forgotten, crowded from your thoughts by an overpowering clarity of purpose and the seriousness of the task at hand.

At such moments, something like happiness actually stirs inside, but it isn't the sort of emotion you want to lean on very hard. In solo climbing the whole enterprise is held together with little more than chutzpa, not the most reliable adhesive. Late in the day on the north face of the Thumb, the glue disintegrated with a single swing of an ice axe.

I'd gained nearly 700 feet since stepping off the hanging glacier, all of it on unrelenting and technical ground. The ribbon of ice had ended 300 feet up, followed by a fragile armor of frost. Though just barely substantial enough to support body weight, the rime was plastered over the rock to a thickness of two or three feet, so I kept plugging upward. The wall, however, had been steepening imperceptibly, and as it did the coating became leaner. I'd fallen into a slow, hypnotic rhythm — swing, swing; kick, kick; swing, swing; kick, kick — when my left axe pierced through the thinning rime and slammed into rock.

I tried left, then right, but kept striking rock. The veneer holding me up, it became apparent, was maybe five inches thick and had the structural integrity of stale cornbread. Below was 3700 feet of air. Waves of panic rose in my throat. My eyesight blurred, I began to hyperventilate, my calves started to shake. I shuffled a few feet farther to the right, hoping to find thicker ice, but managed only to bend a pick on the rock.

Awkwardly, stiff with fear, I started working my way back down. The rime gradually thickened, and after descending about 80 feet I got back on reasonably solid ground. I stopped for a long time to let my nerves settle, then leaned back on my tools and stared up at the face above, searching for a hint of solid ice, for some variation in the underlying rock, for anything that would allow passage over the frosted slabs. I looked until my neck ached, but nothing appeared. The climb was over. The only place to go was down.

Heavy snow and incessant winds kept me inside the tent for most of the next three days. The hours passed slowly. In the attempt to hurry them along I chain smoked for as long as my supply of cigarettes held out, and read. When I ran out of things to read, I was reduced to studying the ripstop pattern on the ceiling. This I did for hours on end, flat on my back, while engaging in an extended and very heated inner debate: Should I leave for the coast as soon as the weather broke, or stay put long enough to make another attempt on the mountain? In truth, my little escapade on the face had left me badly shaken, and I didn't want to go up on the Thumb again at all. On the other hand, the thought of returning to Boulder in defeat — of parking the Pontiac behind the trailer, buckling on my tool belt, and going back to the same brain-dead routine I'd so triumphantly walked away from just a month before — was even less appealing. Most of all, I couldn't stomach the thought of enduring the smug expressions of condolence from all those who were certain I'd fail anyway.

By the third afternoon of the storm, I couldn't stand it any longer: the lumps of frozen snow poking me in the back, the clammy nylon walls brushing against my face, the incredible smell drifting up from the depths of my sleeping bag. I pawed through the mess at my feet until I located a small green stuff sack, in which was a film can containing the makings of what I had hoped would be a sort of victory cigar. I'd intended to save it for my return from the summit, but now it wasn't looking like I'd be visiting the top any time soon. I poured most of the can's contents onto a leaf of cigarette paper, rolled it into a crooked, sorry-looking joint, and promptly smoked it down to the roach.

The reefer, of course, only made the tent seem even more cramped, more suffocating, more impossible to bear. It also made me terribly hungry. I decided a little oatmeal would put things right. Making it, however, was along, ridiculously involved process. I'd gotten the stove going and was melting a pot of snow when I smelled something burning. A thorough check of the stove and its environs revealed nothing. Mystified, I was ready to chalk it up to my chemically enhanced imagination when I heard something crackle directly behind me.

I whirled around in time to see a bag of garbage, into which I'd just tossed a match, burst into flames. Beating on the fire with my hands, I put it out in a few seconds, but not before a large section of the tent's inner wall had vaporized before my eyes. The built-in rainfly remained intact, however, so the tent was still more or less waterproof; only now it was approximately 30 degrees cooler inside. My left palm was stinging and showed the pink welt of a burn. What troubled me most, though, was that the tent wasn't even mine — brand-new and expensive, it had been a reluctant loan from my father. For several minutes I sat dumbstruck amid the acrid scent of singed hair and nylon, staring at the wreckage of the shelter's once-graceful form. You had to hand it to me, I thought: I had a real knack for living up to the old man's worst expectations.

The fire sent me into a funk that no drug known to man could have alleviated. By the time I'd finished cooking the oatmeal my mind was made up — the moment the storm was over, I was breaking camp and booking for Thomas Bay.

Twenty-four hours later, I was up on the Thumb, huddled inside a bivouac sack under the lip of the bergschrund. It was snowing hard, probably an inch every hour. Spindrift avalanches hissed down from the wall above and washed over me like surf, completely burying the sack every 20 minutes.

The day had begun well enough. When I emerged from the tent, clouds still clung to the ridgetops, but the wind had calmed down and the icecap appeared a shifting patchwork of sun breaks. A shaft of sunlight, almost blinding in its brilliance, slid lazily over the camp. I put down a foam pad and sprawled on the glacier in my longjohns. Wallowing in the radiant heat, I felt the gratitude of a prisoner whose sentence had just been commuted.

As I lay there, a narrow chimney curving up the east half of north face, well to the left of the route I'd tried before the storm, caught my eye. I twisted a telephoto lens onto my camera, and through it could make out a smear of shiny gray ice snaking up the back of the cleft. The alignment of the chimney made it impossible to discern whether the ice continued in an unbroken line from top to bottom. If it did, the chimney might well provide a line through the rime-covered slabs that had foiled me earlier.

Lying there in the sun, I began to think about how much I'd hate myself a month hence if I threw in the towel after a single try, if I scrapped the whole expedition on account of a little bad weather. Within the hour I was geared up and skiing toward the base of the wall.

The ice in the chimney did in fact prove to be continuous, but it was very, very thin — just a gossamer film of verglas. Worse, the cleft was a natural funnel for debris sloughing off the wall above; scratching my way up the narrow groove I was continuously hosed by a stream of powder snow, ice chips, and small stones. The last remnants of my composure evaporated 120 feet up, and I turned around.

Instead of descending all the way to basecamp, I decided to spend the night in the *schrund* beneath the chimney, on the off chance that my head would be more together the next morning. The fair skies that had ushered in the day, however, turned out to be but a momentary lull in a five-day gale. By mid-afternoon the storm was back in full blow, and my bivouac became a grim vigil. The ledge on which I crouched was continually swept by small spindrift avalanches. Five times, snow buried my bivy sack up to the breathing slit. After digging myself out the last time, I threw all my gear in the pack and made a break for basecamp.

The descent was terrifying. Engulfed in the storm, I couldn't tell earth from sky, nor the angle of the slope. I worried that I might step blindly off the top of a serac and end up at the bottom of the Witches Cauldron, a half-mile below. Finally arriving on the horizontal plain of the icecap, I found that my tracks across the featureless expanse had long since drifted over. Impotently, I skied in circles for an hour or so, hoping I'd get lucky and stumble across the tent, until I broke through a small crevasse and realized this was idiocy.

I dug a shallow hole, wrapped myself in the bivy bag, and sat on my pack in the swirling snow to wait out the storm. Drifts piled up around me. My feet grew numb. A damp chill crept down my chest from the base of my neck, where spindrift had gotten inside my parka and soaked the shirt. If only I had a cigarette, I thought, a single cigarette, I could summon the strength of character to put a good face on this fucked-up trip. I pulled the bivy sack tighter around my shoulders. The wind ripped at my back. Beyond shame, I cradled my head in my arms and embarked on an orgy of self-pity.

I had known that people sometimes died climbing mountains. But before I'd come to the Thumb, personal mortality — the idea of my own death — had been largely outside my conceptual grasp; it had always been as abstract a notion as non-Euclidean geometry or marriage. The events of the previous two weeks had seemed to rectify this particular failing of intellect, and one or two others as well.

When I decamped from Boulder that spring, my head swimming with visions of glory and redemption on the Devils Thumb, it didn't occur to me that I might be bound by the same cause-effect relationships that governed the actions of others. I'd never heard of hubris. Because I wanted to climb the mountain so badly, because I had thought about the Thumb so intensely for so long, it seemed beyond the realm of possibility that some minor obstacle like the weather or crevasses or rime-covered rock might ultimately thwart my will.

At sunset the wind died and the ceiling lifted slightly off the glacier, enabling me to locate basecamp. I made it back to the tent intact, but could no longer ignore the fact that the Thumb had made hash of my plans. I was forced to acknowledge that volition alone, however powerful, was not going to get me up the north wall. I saw, finally, that nothing was.

There still existed an opportunity for salvaging the expedition, however. A week earlier I'd skied over to the southeast side of the mountain to take a look at the route Fred Beckey had pioneered in 1946 — the route I'd intended to descend after climbing the north wall. During that reconnaissance, I'd noticed an obvious unclimbed line to the left of the Beckey route — a patchy network of ice angling across the southeast face — that struck me as a relatively easy way to achieve the summit. At the time, I'd considered this route unworthy of my attentions. Now, on the rebound, I was prepared to lower my sights.

On the afternoon of May 15, when the blizzard finally petered out, I returned to the southeast face and climbed to the top of a slender ridge that abutted the upper peak like a flying buttress on a gothic cathedral. I decided to spend the night there, on the airy knife-edge, 1600 feet below the summit. The evening was cold and cloudless. I could see all the way to tidewater and beyond. At dusk I watched, transfixed, as the lights of Petersburg blinked in the west. The closest thing I'd had to human contact since the airdrop, the distant lights set off a flood of emotion that caught me completely off guard. I imagined people watching the Red Sox on the tube, eating fried chicken in brightly lit kitchens, drinking beer, making love. When I lay down to sleep I was overcome by a soul-wrenching loneliness. I'd never felt so alone, ever.

That night I had troubled dreams, of cops and vampires and a gangland-style execution. I heard someone whisper, "He's in there. As soon as he comes out, waste him." I sat bolt upright and opened my eyes. The sun was about to rise. The entire sky was scarlet. It was still clear, but wisps of high cirrus were streaming in from the southwest, and a dark line was visible just above the horizon. I pulled on my boots and hurriedly strapped on crampons. Five minutes after waking up, I was front-pointing away from the bivouac.

I carried no rope, no bivy gear, no hardware save my ice axes. My plan was to go ultralight and ultrafast, to hit the summit and make it back down before the weather turned. Pushing myself, continually out of breath, I scurried up left across small snowfields linked by narrow tunnels of verglas and short rock bands. The climbing was almost fun — the rock was covered with large, incut holds, and the ice, though thin, never got steeper than 70 degrees — but I was anxious about the clouds racing in from the Pacific, covering the sky.

In what seemed like no time (I hadn't brought a watch on the trip) I was on the distinctive final icefield. By now the sky was completely overcast. It looked easier to keep angling to the left, but quicker to go straight for the top. I opted for the direct route. The ice steepened to 75 degrees, then to 85, and grew appallingly thin. I swung my left ice axe and struck rock. I aimed for another spot, and once again glanced off unyielding diorite with a dull, sickening clank. And again, and again: it was a reprise of my first attempt on the north face. I stole a glance between my legs at the glacier, more than 2000 feet below. My stomach churned. I felt my poise slipping away like smoke in the wind.

Forty-five more feet above me the wall eased back into the sloping summit shoulder. Forty-five more feet, half the distance between third base and home plate, and the mountain would be mine. I clung stiffly to my tools, paralyzed with fear and indecision. I looked down at the dizzying drop again, then up, then scraped away the film of ice above my head. I hooked the pick of my left axe on a nickel-thin lip of rock, and weighted it gingerly. I pulled my right axe from the ice, and twisted the pick into a crooked half-inch crack above until it jammed. Barely breathing now, I scrabbled my crampon points up and across the verglas. Reaching as high as I could with my left arm, I flicked the axe gently at the shiny, opaque surface, not knowing what I'd hit beneath it. The pick went in with a heartening THUNK! A few minutes later I was standing on a broad rounded ledge. The summit proper, a series of slender fins sprouting a grotesque meringue of aerated ice, stood 20 feet directly above.

Those last 20 feet remained hard, onerous, scary. But then, suddenly, there was no place higher to go. It wasn't possible, I couldn't believe it. My cracked lips stretched into a huge, painful grin. I was on top of the Devils Thumb.

Fittingly, the summit was a surreal, malevolent place, a slender fan of rock and rime no wider than a filing cabinet. It did not encourage loitering. The north face fell away beneath my left boot for 6000 feet; below my right boot the south face presented a 2500-foot drop. I took some pictures to prove I'd been there, and spent a few minutes trying to straighten a bent pick. Then I stood up, carefully turned around, and headed for home.

Five days later I was camped in the rain beside the ocean, marveling at the sight of green moss and willows. Two days after that, a small skiff motored into Thomas Bay and pulled up on the beach not far from my tent. The man at the tiller introduced himself as Jim Freeman, a timber faller from Petersburg. It was his day off, he said, and he'd made the trip to show his family the glacier, and to look for bears. "You been huntin', or what?" he asked.

"No," I replied sheepishly. "Actually I just climbed the Devils Thumb. I've been here over 20 days."

Freeman kept fiddling with a cleat on the boat, and didn't say anything for a while. Then he looked at me hard and spat, "You wouldn't be givin' me double talk now, wouldja, friend?" Taken aback, I stammered out a denial. Freeman, it was obvious, didn't believe me for a minute. Nor did he seem wild about my snarled, shoulder-length hair or the way I smelled. When I asked if he could give me a lift back to town, however, he offered a grudging, "I don't see why not."

The water was choppy, and the ridge across Frederick Sound took two hours. The more we talked, the more Freeman warmed up. He still didn't believe I'd climbed the Thumb, but by the time he steered the skiff into Wrangell Narrows he pretended to. When we got off the boat, he insisted on buying me a cheeseburger. That night he even let me sleep in a derelict step-van parked in his backyard.

I lay down in the rear of the old truck for a while but couldn't sleep, so I got up and walked to a bar called Kito's Kave. The euphoria, the overwhelming sense of relief, that had initially accompanied my return to Petersburg faded, and an unexpected melancholy took its place. The people I chatted with in Kito's didn't seem to doubt that I'd been to the top of the Thumb, they just didn't much care. As the night wore on the place emptied except for an Indian at a back table and me. I drank alone, putting quarters in the jukebox, playing the same five songs over and over, until the barmaid yelled angrily, "Hey! Give it a rest, kid!" I mumbled an apology, quickly headed for the door, and lurched back to Freeman's moldering step-van. There, surrounded by the sweet scent of old motor oil, I lay down on the floorboards next to a gutted transmission and passed out.

It is easy, when you are young, to believe that what you desire is no less than what you deserve, to assume that if you want something badly enough it's your God-given right to have it. Less than a month after sitting on the summit of the

32

Thumb I was back in Boulder, nailing up siding on the Spruce Tree Townhouses, the same condos I'd been framing when I left for Alaska. I got a raise, to $4.00 an hour, and at the end of the summer moved out of the job-site trailer to a studio apartment on West Pearl, but little else in my life seemed to change. Somehow, things didn't add up to the glorious transformation I'd imagined in April.

Climbing the Devils Thumb, however, had nudged me a little further away from the obdurate innocence of childhood. It taught me something about what mountains can and can't do, about the limits of dreams. I didn't recognize that at the time, of course, but I'm grateful for it now.

First published in Climbing *No. 118, 1990.*

Hide the Women and Children
Yabbo's soloing, again

By John Long

Of the many do-or-die madman I knew from my formative years, John "Yabbo" Yablonski had few peers. Perhaps 5 feet 9 inches tall, lean as a skinned rabbit, Yabbo had an atomic-caliber energy that could take hold of him like a possession. If such a conniption seized him near a crag he was certain to risk his life doing something crazy. On the rock he was strictly rash; on the deck his life was marked by blinding contrasts.

Yabbo dug the odd ditch and washed windows here and there, but he never held a regular job and seemed to survive with mirrors and blind luck.

He'd go days without eating, then would suddenly wolf down 10 hamburgers and a gallon of ice cream — if you were buying. Yabbo loved "shrooms," and flourished on adrenalin, coffee, and Camel straights. A right-brained "feeler," he was generous to a fault, wonderfully childlike, and so naive you'd swear he'd just stumbled from Mother Hubbard's boot. His heart was solid gold. Europeans who visited the Valley and bore witness to Yabbo were simultaneously astounded by his free soloing and revolted by his scruffy, primitive lifestyle. Yet his innocence drew the hospitality out of many around him who craved the strange, spiritual grace one received while in the presence of the "chosen one." For the closeness of his shaves, Yabbo was matched only by the legendary Tobin Sorenson. Both Tobin and Yabbo are now dead. Both, I believe, would be 40 this year.

Tobin's exploits are documented, though not in their full majesty. Yabbo's equally ghastly epics live on in oral history, but I've never once read one in print. As a fellow Californian and Yosemite regular, I climbed on and off with

Yabbo for nearly 10 years, and cringe to remember his countless narrow escapes during that time.

It was a blazing summer day when Yabbo found himself at Suicide Rock — without a partner. This was a dangerous situation for Yabbo's person, for he was a soloing fool. Yabbo spent all of 90 seconds trying to dragoon a partner (he had no rope or rack), then the energy swelled inside him. He set off jogging along the "Buttress of Cracks," searching for an immediate adrenalin blast. Yabbo stalked up to *Frustration* (5.10), a precarious medley of fingertip layaways and beveled flutes that had hosted roughly 25,000 ascents since the last rains, and sported grease enough to lube the fittings of the USS Midway. It was a cloudless, midsummer day. The mountain sun beat down like a sledgehammer. Nevertheless, Yabbo chalked, shuddered, and started climbing. Several gallons of espresso sloshed around his otherwise empty gut, adding a marked urgency to his habitually frantic style.

The crux initial stretch of *Frustration* seemed to ooze suet. Yabbo jittered up the first 30 feet on brute strength, which he had in spades. Just above, the route transitioned from borderline pinches into a bottoming gash that you climbed by smearing a toe on nothing whatsoever while yarding on a wet bar of Palmolive. Yabbo smeared his toe, clasped the greased hold, started to yank — and realized he was buttering off toward the Land of Harps. Had a witness not been standing by, nobody would have believed the sequence that followed.

Just as Yabbo's toe blew off the holds, he torqued his body round to face outward, thrust off the wall with his legs, and dove into open space, Spiderman style. As Yabbo arced through the air, freezing Strawberry Valley with a mortal wail, the stunned witness knew she was watching the act of a man gone mad.

Yabbo had vaulted perhaps 10 feet away from the wall and fallen the same distance when his arms shot out and his hands snatched the quick of a pine bough drooping from a nearby tree. Death-gripping the branch, Yabbo continued his plummet. The branch bowed, popped alarmingly, and, just as Yabbo's decelerated weight touched ground, snapped in two.

"Shucks!" Yabbo scoffed. He pitched the branch aside and, noticing the astonished witness, said, "Hey, you want to do a climb?"

For several more years during the late 1970s, Yabbo continued to dazzle and terrorize spectators with his free solos. Shortly after the *Frustration* debacle, Yabbo free soloed *Leave it to Beaver* (5.12) at Joshua Tree. Unhappy with that performance, where he'd bungled half of the route's moves and compensated with reckless, cross-armed dynamics, Yabbo was no sooner on the deck when he started up the *Beaver* a second time, hoping to improve his style. Sapped from the first lap, Yabbo literally fell up the climb with horribly shaking limbs, typhoon breathing, and troubling grunts, his hands slapping for holds 50 feet above the boulders. The spectacle was so traumatic to behold that one witness jogged behind a boulder and puked. Such episodes were not the exception with Yabbo, rather the rule. Yet for all his near-fatal solos, I never knew him to suffer more than a sprained ankle. In his strange and tragic quest he was able to squeeze more juice from the rock than anyone I've ever known.

Yabbo climbed and lived on the razor's edge, and it surprised no one when he eventually fell. The "normal" world rejected Yabbo from the cradle, but the rock never would. Somewhere in the basement of Yabbo's psyche he wanted to die. Throughout, the rock remained his staunchest ally and refused to make good on that wish. Ultimately, Yabbo had to jump off himself. Into the void went a rogue prince and a strand of memories I'll laugh, cry, and tremble about for the rest of my life.

First published in Climbing *No. 182, 1999.*

Leviathan
The legendary route on the legendary Eiger

By David Pagel

To travel halfway around the world to see or do something is considered a pilgrimage, and falls well within the range of normal behavior. To make such a journey twice is still acceptable; after all, who among us has not nostalgically yearned to revisit the site of some memorable experience from our youth? To go a third time begins to arouse suspicions — it hints at obsession. As I stared up at the North Face of the Eiger, it was through the eyes of a modern-day Ahab; for the third time in my life I stood shivering in the shadow of my whale. Yet I considered myself lucky; I have a friend who has been here eight times and has yet to tie into the rope. If ever a mountain had the power to influence lives and empty bank accounts, this was it.

As I gazed once more upon the infamous rock bands and icefields, my brain, which houses neurons that are normally hard pressed to retrieve the memory of my last meal, amazed me by graphically recalling all the glory details of every Eiger horror story I had ever encountered. Images of iced ropes, hurtling bodies, and fatal stonefall assailed me, threatening to buckle my knees and pitch me headlong into the edelweiss.

Yet my most vivid impression was not from one of the classic "Wall of Death" disasters that are commemorated with tiny crosses on Eigerwand bath towels and other macabre souvenirs found in gift shops throughout the Swiss town of Grindelwald. Instead, my thoughts focused on a smoky tavern in Zermatt and an encounter with a glowering Frankenstein monster who muttered in a heavy Scottish dialect. The man's head suggested a shattered pumpkin that had been clumsily reassembled. From the extent of his injuries, I grimly deduced that he had either been crushed by a truck or struck with a maul.

In fact, he had been struck with the Eiger, repeatedly. His tale was of a routine bivouac gone dreadfully wrong: a sudden lightning storm bursting from the clouds with the explosive violence of an airliner ramming the face. The turbulent energy literally picked him up and hurled him from this ledge, leaving him suspended in space, dangling like a broken puppet from a single anchor peg. Even before he could react, the electricity had grasped him again and savagely slammed him back into the mountain. Then the process was repeated. Like a monstrous paddle-toy the Eiger storm bounced the unfortunate Scotsman against the stony surface again and again. Miraculously, he escaped with his life, but the deep scars etched like the tracks of a switching yard across his face made it plain that he would never be truly free of the Eigerwand.

Now, as I cowered beneath the hulking, familiar outline of the very culprit, the memory of this cruel attack had a profound effect upon me. I felt like throwing up.

What I did have going for me was the perfect Eiger partner. A physical description of Roger can be taken directly from the pages of Mary Shelley: "A being which had the shape of a man, but apparently of gigantic stature." He also possesses two of the most crucial mental attributes of a successful mountaineer: he is as stubborn and tenacious as a rusted bolt. As a result, Roger is a bold, gifted climber — and a weather-god to boot. Sunshine follows him around like a puppy. This had first come to my attention when he departed for the *Cassin Ridge*. In the weeks prior to his trip, the Alaska Range had been pummeled by a storm. Even as I bid him farewell and wished him success, I privately doubted whether he would get an opportunity even to touch the mountain. Roger arrived in Talkeetna with the sunshine licking at his heels. His is probably the only expedition to Denali never to encounter a single cloud. And after two weathered-out trips to the Eiger, I resolved that the next time I went to the Alps, this guy was coming along.

It was beginning to look as though Roger's puppy had run off however. We had been lured from the sunny south of France to the Bernese Oberland by an overly optimistic weather forecast. We arrived in Grindelwald to find the face in good, dry condition, the sky clear, and the barometer steady. In defense of the Bureau de Meteorologie in Chamonix and in keeping with Eiger legend, the prolonged storms that arrived the next day really did seem to come out of nowhere.

Like so many Eiger hopefuls before us, we killed time any way we could: movies in Interlaken, reading, sightseeing. Roger took a day trip to Zermatt. He drove out of Grindelwald at 3 a.m. in the pouring rain. After hiking up the lower flanks of the Matterhorn in a fog and steady drizzle, he proceeded to the summit in an icy whiteout. He bought a postcard on the way back so he could see what the mountain actually looked like. Anyone like myself who has been to the top of the Matterhorn will understand my skepticism upon his return; this is an immense and devious mountain, and any claim to have simply wandered up it in a storm must be regarded as suspect. But Roger described the huge iron cross that marks the summit with perfect accuracy. Personally, I could not imagine a more hideous outing.

And as fate seems to dictate in the valley of the Eiger, the storms dragged on until the time that remained before the return dates stamped on our airline tickets could be measured in days rather than weeks. I was resolving myself to yet another trip to Europe when suddenly the clouds lifted and the whale showed itself. Naturally, it was white.

There was snow — too much snow — on every ledge that could hold it; and where the face couldn't hold it, the snow was coming off. The wall was alive with avalanches, pouring like rivers of granulated sugar down the tentacled gullies and arcing off the icefields. If the Second Icefield was indeed a thousand feet across, then the continuous plume of snow streaming directly down the first half of our route was at least a hundred feet wide. The only part of the Eiger that wasn't plastered with fresh snow was the lower third of the wall which lay below the freezing level. This section was stained a ghastly black by a deluge of running water.

In all my storm-plagued trips to Europe, I had never seen the Eiger so hopelessly out of condition. Any attempts at climbing the face would obviously have to wait at least several more days, and the morning weather bulletin prophesied only one more day of clear weather, and then the storms were predicted to return.

Once again, it appeared as though the great whale had eluded me. Climbing the Eiger simply wasn't in the cards, and to my surprise, Roger was actually the first to voice it: "Let's go," he murmured. With some reluctance I nodded agreement, but I also admit to feeling relieved that, at least for this trip, there would be no opportunity for me to end up as yet another cross on an Eiger ashtray. Imagine then, my horror when I realized the true meaning of my companion's words: I turned to find the man readying his climbing pack!

"Look here," I stammered. "You can't possibly be thinking about going up there. It's madness suicide ... and I won't go!"

He looked at me with a penetrating gunfighter squint and said just about the last thing I expected to hear: "You are a chicken."

I think it's a safe bet that no matter how fiercely Lachenal and Terray disagreed over the prospects of a particular route, the one never resorted to calling the other "chicken." It seems unimaginable that Hillary could have goaded Tenzing to the top of Everest with scornful cries of "wimp." And although Whymper is reputed to have tumbled rocks from the summit of the

Matterhorn to attract the attention of his rivals, he almost certainly did not stick out his tongue. I was genuinely wounded. Gentlemanly behavior is a code that is fundamentally rooted in mountaineering and gentlemen do not open a dialogue by hurling insults.

Roger, however, is not a mountaineer. He is an alpinist. Worst yet, he is an extreme alpinist. The difference is that to an extreme alpinist, the only acceptable ends to an expedition are the summit or the grave, and any means necessary to achieve these ends is fair game, including aggressive coercion. This he now pursued.

He bullied; I protested. He threatened; I stood my ground. He questioned my manhood, and I pronounced him a menace. We held little back — although he refrained from calling me "tubby" or making similar references to my robust Whillans-like morphology, or I think it might have come to blows.

Eventually we ran out of things to call each other, and we arbitrated the only possible compromise I would agree upon: we would return to the weather bureau in the evening, and if the forecast extended the period of settled weather by even a single day, I would attempt the climb. We brooded through the long afternoon, each of us anticipating our respective definitions of bad news.

So when at last the evening forecast went up, we were both surprised, to say the least. At first we wondered if there had been some mistake; surely, the bureau must have swapped forecasts with the Bahamas or some other tropical locale. But there was the map of central Europe and, beside it, perhaps the best Eiger area weather forecast ever seen — something to this effect: "Perfect sunshine and no precipitation for as long as it is possible to see into the future. Perhaps a week. No kidding." Roger's puppy had finally come home.

We were actually going to get a crack at the Eiger. I didn't know whether to laugh or cry. It was with mixed feelings of excitement and foreboding that I sorted my clothing, packed my sack, and sharpened my harpoons.

Morning found us trudging up to the base of the wall from the tiny rail station at Alpiglen. With little difficulty we made our way around the initial snowfields and stepped into the mouth of the whale.

It is an unnerving fact that before you have climbed more than a few hundred feet up the dreaded North Face of the Eiger, you are suddenly confronted by metal plaques commemorating the demise of many of those who have preceded you. It made me want to turn tail and run, and perhaps that's the point: to weed out the sissies. I hoped these markers had not been placed everywhere on the face where some luckless soul had perished. The place was going to be spooky enough without headstones.

After third-classing the hair-raising wet slabs and terraces of the lower wall, we finally roped up below the Difficult Crack, which was not really a crack at all but a flaky corner filled with a waterfall, old fixed lines, and, astonishingly, four other climbers. We were surprised to see these other people, since we had neither seen nor heard anyone in front of us on our long scramble up the lower section of the wall.

"Howdy!" I shouted. Roger frowned at me and I couldn't tell if he was bothered by the unexpected company or by my lack of sophistication — this was the Eigerwand, after all. The other climbers voiced or gurgled some reply, depending upon where they happened to be positioned relative to the torrents that were cascading down the route, but there was no mistaking the fact that everybody seemed to be speaking the same language — although an admittedly more cosmopolitan version than myself.

Some hours later, we all bottlenecked at the start of the Hinterstoisser Traverse. The pair engaged in negotiating the snow-plastered slabs were fellow Americans — Coloradans to be precise — and the other two were Scots, who graciously allowed us to pass in front of them. They were moving more slowly than expected. Being Scots, they had anticipated an ice climb; unfortunately for them, it had become apparent that underneath all the fresh snow the exceptionally dry year hadn't produced enough ice to chill a tumbler of Glenfiddich.

Across the traverse we discovered our compatriots bedding down in the Swallow's Nest bivouac. The Scots were also intending to sleep on this tiny perch, and so, with no room left in the inn, Roger and I climbed a long pitch up the First Icefield and hacked an ice ledge under a rock overhang. We brewed a liquid meal and snuggled into our bags.

The next morning dawned bright and clear, just as predicted. What a joy to awaken on the Eiger to a sky that would not be out of place framing a placid Caribbean lagoon. I was actually beginning to relax. I was totally unprepared then, when the very first obstacle of the day almost killed me. The Ice Hose is a problematic runnel that links the First and Second icefields. The warm summer had reduced the hose to a slabby, verglased rock groove, and the recent storms had packed the chute with a two-foot icing of vertical corn snow. Ten feet up the situation was already critical: the dry snow crumbled away wherever I touched it and threatened to send me tobogganing into the abyss. Imagine a watermelon hurtling down a gigantic, near-vertical bobsled run that empties out over the edge of a 2000-foot cliff. I did.

A hundred feet out I finally gave up trying to get protection; tunneling through the snow in desperate hopes of finding one of the 10 billion fixed pins that everybody says are on the Eiger had repeatedly revealed only blank slabs of limestone. As I flailed up an increasingly precarious house of cards, my mind began to work it all out. If I came off, I would crash like a wrecking ball on to the First Icefield; the impact would undoubtedly break a lot of bones but the steep angle and the cushion of fresh snow would probably keep me from being killed. To my mind, the important thing was that Roger was still anchored to a rock-solid belay, so no matter how you cut it I was not going to become one of those detached bodies that tourists glimpse through the telescope. Believe it or not, this thought calmed me, and just as I was starting to get a handle on things again, I risked a glance downward in order to judge my progress.

What I saw sent my breakfast dashing for the exits; the rope had long since run out between us and instead of alerting me to this fact, Roger, to my absolute horror, had simply unclipped from the anchors and was climbing up behind me. If either of us slid off now we would both be flying home in a body bag. Perhaps the thought of sharing a sack with chunks of Roger is what I needed to propel me up those last few feet. I do remember that as I finally gripped the knot of tattered slings at the base of the Second Icefield, I seriously considered tying my end of the rope to a loose block and trundling it off. Since I couldn't bring myself to actually murder the father of two children — especially since there was no way we really could have done the pitch any differently — I sought some small revenge the only way I knew how; I belayed him with a lot of slack. I doubt if he even noticed.

After such an ordeal, the thought of front-pointing sideways for a thousand feet across the face of the Second Icefield seemed a cruel joke, so I cramponed to the top of the slope in hopes of finding a bergschrund or a level crest that might allow us to dash across in comfort. No such luck: the *schrund,* if it ever existed, had been smoothly caulked with ice and neatly feathered into the vertical rock face. Worse yet, an enticing line of fixed pins (the first I remember seeing) shot horizontally across the rock band in a long chain of absolutely inaccessible protection — the shriveled icefield now placed the old pitons at least 20 feet over our heads. When I pointed this out to Roger, he shrugged. "Screw it," he said.

And so screw it we did, making sure at least one ice screw protected us at all times during the interminable shuffle across the face of the Second Icefield. I insisted upon it.

My calves were veal by the time we reached the foot of the projecting rock buttress known as the Flatiron. We had also arrived at ground zero with respect to the Eiger's notorious stonefall hazard, but so far the only projectiles we had witnessed were a few minor chunks of ice rattling down gullies. It was an eerie and disconcerting silence that we observed in the heart of such a notorious battlefield, but it was vastly preferable to being under siege.

We could see where we needed to go. The Death Bivouac was plainly visible several hundred feet above, but the best way to get there was not obvious. Some weathered fixed ropes dangled suggestively back to our right, but a complex little rock band in front of us seemed to offer a shorter and more direct route. Roger scrutinized both options and then, as I knew he would, chose the road less traveled. The two Coloradans came around the corner just in time to see him take a 30-foot fall. They made a beeline for the fixed ropes.

Remarkably, Roger was unhurt. His huge pack probably cushioned the fall and kept his spine in one piece. Undaunted, he brushed himself off and moved up the rock again. It was an amazing spectacle, the picture of futility — like watching a mountain sheep that has just rammed one of his compatriots shakily pick himself up and head back for more. This time, however, after Roger regained his high point, he moved slightly left and began poking about beneath a grim little overhang. "Ah-ha!" he announced triumphantly. He had uncovered an old piton at the lip of the roof that apparently gave the line just the legitimacy he had been looking for. My amazement turned to disbelief as I watched him clip a sling into the ancient peg and then reach over the roof, pull himself up on tiny downsloping edges and put one cramponed foot into the loop. Scabs of rust flaked from the flexing pin as he committed his full weight to the makeshift aider. His hands scrabbled for purchase on the snowy ledges above the overhang, and finally he stepped up, trusting his front points to the same beveled edges that had miraculously supported his fingertips. Teetering in his bulky pack, Roger manteled onto the snow-packed ledges.

I suddenly noticed one of the Scottish climbers standing beside me. He was staring up at the empty loop of webbing that beckoned like a hangman's noose from the lip of the overhang. "There is no God," I heard him whisper. They also elected to go with the fixed ropes.

Roger's variation got us on top of the Flatiron several hours in front of the other climbers. The Death Bivouac was a weird place, full of strange vibes. No matter where you sleep on the Eiger you share a ledge with a ghost or two, but I was particularly glad we weren't going to be spending the night here. We wasted no time traversing left across the Third Icefield and into the long diagonal cleft of the Ramp.

I had been looking forward to the Ramp. Almost all the Eiger accounts describe it with friendly adjectives like "sheltered," and "protected." We hadn't seen a falling rock, but just the same, it felt good to be climbing somewhere where a lot of people hadn't died. We managed to tick off three long pitches, just over half the Ramp, before the setting sun dictated that we find a good place to set up camp. Those glowing descriptions of the Ramp had not included "loaded with excellent bivouac possibilities" — for good reason. Everything sloped. Luckily, the afternoon sun had softened the thick layer of snow into moldable clay from which we were able to fashion elaborate terraces for sleeping and cooking. We were quite proud of our accommodations, glued to the angled walls of the Ramp like a miniature Machu Picchu.

As we settled in for the night, I heard a puzzling rumble in the distance. A jet, I thought, optimistically. The noise, however, soon became recognizable as the menacing growl of thunder. Sure enough, a cloud as black as a cave was moving up the valley from the direction of Interlaken. I couldn't believe it. The forecasters had blown it. A killer storm was poised to engulf us. The whale was sounding with us locked in its belly — we were going to die.

I peered from beneath my bivouac tarp at Roger, who was making mashed potatoes. He glanced up at me and smiled knowingly. "Don't sweat it," he said coolly.

The storm cruised right up the valley, Kleine Scheidegg got nailed, Alpinglen was blasted, and the folks in Grindelwald must have thought that all hell had broken loose. But the stars never went out over the Eiger. Something very strange was going on here. This relationship between Roger and the elements was starting to unnerve me. His uncanny ability to repel storms struck me as being almost ... supernatural. I spent the rest of the night with one wary eye on the sky and the other trained on Roger.

The first obstacle of the new day was the infamous "Waterfall Pitch." The late September weather had transformed it into a steep wall of spotty ice smears. Oh, man, I thought as I watched Roger scratch away with his front points, the Scottish guys are going to love this.

The next pitch would suit the highlanders even better: the "Ice Bulge." This 10-foot blue-green mushroom blocks the final chimney leading out of the Ramp. It was trivial in modern ice gear, but in deference to the pioneers, it must have been a horror in golf shoes.

The Ramp lay behind us, and we now began the long horizontal traverse back into the heart of the face. But after only a short distance we were confronted by a truly ugly looking vertical step that our route descriptions called the "Rotten Crack." A number of fixed pins were visible in the snowy fissure, and this gave me the confidence I needed to move up it. But the next time someone scornfully tells me that the technical climbing on the Eiger is only 5.7, I'm going to hand them a set of mountain boots, crampons, gloves, strap a full rucksack to their back, and, after loosening a few key holds, point them toward Eldorado Canyon's *Bastille Crack*. That was the "Rotten Crack."

The Traverse of the Gods was next, and it did not meet with our expectations. We anticipated casual sidestepping across highly exposed ledges festooned with old pitons. There was exposure alright — 5000 feet of it — but any fixed pins were buried treasure and the climbing was positively gripping. Everything was downsloping and booby-trapped with thick snow. A slip here meant dangling over a mile above the ground with no way to regain the traverse. I finally reached the lower appendages of the spider, and should have gotten a cigar for the hammer blow with which I drove a screw into the firm ice.

The nefarious White Spider: legend holds that this multi-tentacled icefield is perched like a fat arachnid on the upper reaches of the Eigerwand, patiently waiting for tiny insects to blunder into its pale lair. Two Spaniards had once been trapped in its clutches — their bodies had to be chopped from icy cocoons. We moved tentatively onto the gleaming web; the ice conditions were perfect. The Spider slept, its malice suspended. Like tiny spiders ourselves, we tiptoed furtively up the creature's broad spine. We were nearing its top and congratulating ourselves on such a stealthy escape, when the Spider suddenly moved. Our tiny vibrations triggered a small powder avalanche. Fresh snow streamed around our legs and down the icy gullies. Although we were not in any real danger of being swept from the face, we knew we had been detected.

For the first time in the course of our climb, we encountered objective danger. Ice chunks were breaking away from the upper edges of the face and being funneled down on top of us. A thick cloud also materialized and shrouded us in grey mist. The whole situation was taking on a decidedly more Eiger-like atmosphere. I supposed it had been asking too much for the whale to just roll over and submit to us, but I had hoped.

We doggedly threaded our way up the gullies of the Exit Cracks and past various minor Eiger landmarks. The "Quartz Crack" was a revelation; for some reason, I had always imagined a horizontal vein. Instead, we found a vertical offwidth crack lined with a smooth frosting of the mineral. Eventually we arrived at a cul-de-sac, and the point where all the route descriptions disagree. Some describe a pendulum to the left from this point, others an abseil. Roger found his own alternative. He simple clipped into a horizontal fixed rope that was so rotted that not a thread of sheath was left on it — and slid off into space. A muffled shout through the fog confirmed that he had actually ended up alive and in some desirable location. I attached myself to the remains of what had once been a rope, took a deep breath, and stepped into the void. A terrifying slide down and around a projecting corner deposited me alongside my companion on the top of an airy pulpit. I almost gagged when I saw the bent piton that anchored the other end of the fixed line.

Roger led off up a shallow box-like chimney. The flak was getting serious — looking up the chimney was like trying to stare down a snowblower that is chewing up a frozen pond — and the fog was bordering on a drizzle. These were the monster's last gasps, however; our hooks were in deep. We still couldn't relax. Better men than us had gotten the chop above this point, and the ice bombardment was relentless. But even I had to admit that the thing was almost in the net.

The chimney lasted several pitches, until we found ourselves at the top of an abrupt shoulder. Around the corner we discovered an ice slope angling up through small rock outcrops. Then, just ice. And finally, as the last bit of daylight faded out of the cloud, there was only cloud.

Roger and I spent the night on the summit of the Eiger, and the great cetacean of my dreams was the finest bed I have ever known.

The day after our climb dawned fine and clear. The two Coloradans reached the summit just as we were preparing to descend the western flank, and we all went down together. The two Scotsmen had mysteriously disappeared. The Americans had spent a second night with them in the Death Bivouac, and then rapidly outdistanced them in the steep rock of the Ramp. It was the last any of us ever saw of them. We scanned the face at Scheidegg with telescopes so powerful that we could easily discern our own footprints in the Exit Cracks, but the Scots had vanished without a trace. Perhaps the sustained rock climbing in the Ramp had finally discouraged them to the point of retreat. Perhaps they were still climbing, hidden from our scrutiny in some dark corner or gully. This was our fervent hope.

Roger missed his plane. While he was battling across the thin ledges of the Traverse of the Gods, it left for home without him. It's the first bit of bad luck I think he has ever run into, but he took it well, forking over the three hundred dollars for a new ticket with typical grim determination.

I've got plans for that boy. I've never considered myself much of an extremist, but with a genuine weather-god lashed to the other end of the rope, who can say? The possibilities are tantalizing: Gasherbrum IV without a storm, Cerro Torre in shirt sleeves ...

There are, after all, other fish in the sea.

First published in Climbing *No. 131, 1992.*

A Stone's Throw
Treading the edge in Canyonlands

By Duane Raleigh

The bright winter sun illuminated the minarets of stone rising in oblivious rebellion to the flat, sand-swept floor. Two hundred feet up, I rested below a large corner system, tenuously bound to one of the spires proliferating across the dry Canyonlands of Utah.

The desert is a pious, subdued place — a wilderness of banishment, solitude, and beauty — a monastic mien for the soul. Above me the corner shot straight up before bending right, going out at a roof and out of sight. Its tight angles threw a short, distinct shadow across the dark-red sandstone, chiseling the geometric planes.

It was the shadows that had first caught my eye. As a climber, I was attuned to the nature of shadows. They reveal the subtle overhangs, cracks and dihedrals in a rock; therefore, shadows can be climbed. I pulled a piton off my rack and drove it deeply into the shadow.

The climb began simply enough: a wide crack that abused me, then a vanishing seam, then a swing left into an incipient trough that took me to the base of a massive arete.

The arete was the tower's most prominent feature. It had lured me to the wall, it and the fact that the route stood unclimbed and unspoiled. I was looking for adventure and adventure can only be found in the unknown. Once a route is done, it loses its mystery, its weaknesses and faults become known — it holds no secrets. Would this tower let me in? I wondered.

The pin rang solid at the base of the prow. I nailed upwards, bashing steel into the ancient wall. The rock broke under my hammer, spilling debris down onto the temple floor. Several pins later the crack opened wide enough to accept less damaging cam nuts. I drove one more pin for good measure, then set off on nuts. If I weren't soloing, I would free climb you, I said to the shadow.

I pulled up, weighting the cams, then gave myself an excessive amount of lead rope. I let out the slack largely to speed things up, but also perhaps to keep things interesting ...

Just below the top of the pillar, the corner deepened to form an alcove capped by a horizontal roof. Fortunately, the roof was imperfect — fractured from end to end, making for exhilarating, albeit easy, climbing. Even now, five years later, I can still hear the rush of air and feel the heat of the rock as I moved, swinging from one placement to the next with an exuberance and satisfaction that is rare in life.

I remember looking down the wall to the desert floor where my dog and rusting van awaited me. I looked across the desert to other towers that held steadfast in mute vigilance over the immensity of time. I wondered what scenes of diverse consequence the stone guardians had watched, and what I would have to say for myself if suddenly I was taken before a tribunal of the gods on charges of wanton sacrilege.

"Well you see, sir," I envisioned saying in feigned respect. "I have to climb ... I can't explain why." I could feel the futility of my defense as I stammered, groping for existential words. I imagined the scowl on the face of Zeus or Pluto or whichever deity before whom I was prostrate. I could see him shake his fist as he fed me to the Minotaurs. I thought this, then moved out over the roof.

The prow ended in a small, flat ledge 100 feet below the tower's true summit. From below, I could see no ready faults in the section above the ledge. But I arrived to discover a small cavern winding surreptitiously within the spire.

Squirming through the slot, I was deposited on a narrow ledge beneath the final headwall. The exposure was unnerving; below me, the evening light transfused both rock and sand crimson. It was a disquieting space, but at the same time I relished the freedom.

The ropes hung off the ledge, straight down. A wind buffeted them. "Better hurry," I told myself. "It's supposed to storm tonight."

Leading off from the ledge was a narrow, loose, and typically dusty blade crack that proved to be the crux of the route. The first few placements shifted, creaking in a steely cold language that told their true character. But soon I was standing on the broad summit plateau where, no longer protected by the shield of the wall, I caught the full brunt of the winds that had been massing all day. I gathered my equipment, chucked it in my backpack and scurried to the rappel anchors.

50

As I rigged the ropes through the anchors, the sun set, casting long reflective shadows of the various rocks across the desert. I basked in the solitude of the sunset, then berated myself for not bringing a headlamp. In haste and brashness, I had thought that I could complete the route in an easy day.

Leaning over the edge, I lowered into the darkening night. "I hate rappelling," I said to myself. "It's too mechanical. It has no soul." I tightened my grip on the rope. "But what else can you do?"

I rappelled slowly, straining to keep from capsizing from the weight of the pack. A hundred feet down the wall I looked around for the next set of bolt anchors. I didn't see any, so kept going. At 150 feet, more blank rock told me one thing: I had rappelled off the wrong way.

This put me in a predicament. I had set the ropes through the top anchors so that they could only be used for descent. It hadn't occurred to me that I might need to go back up them. Now it did, and to salt the wound, the wind began singing a shrill tune across the tower rim.

It was an uncomfortable predicament, but some of my previous escapades had been worse. Once, as I'd retreated from El Capitan's *Aquarian Wall,* both ends of my rappel rope had blown out of reach, stranding me 1000 feet up the wall. Tying a set of hooks onto some slings, I had thrown them at the rope, grappling-hook fashion. It had worked. Then there was the time I was trapped on El Cap in a freezing rainstorm, wearing only a T-shirt and jeans. And, as if twice wasn't enough, I was later marooned, alone and without bivy gear, on an ice ridge in the Alps during a storm.

I knew there must be a way to get back up the ropes. "If only I could think," I thought. "My mind has never been strong — some day it will be my undoing." Tipped backwards by the pack, I wrapped both arms around the rope, cradling it in the crook of my elbows to steady my thoughts and conserve strength.

"How, what, huh?" I muttered incoherently. "Yes, of course!" I said with improved syntax. I had decided to hook a jumar onto each rope; with them opposing each other, I could jumar, counter-weighted.

The method was inefficient and tiring, but after an hour or so of penitential struggling, I regained the summit. At the anchors I flipped the ropes to set them on the correct course and started down again. The rope burned into my sore hands.

"Pain is good, it reminds you that you're still alive," I thought grimacing. "But I have to be more careful from now on."

With renewed awareness, I stopped on a small pedestal 50 feet below the top, and gave the ropes a cursory tug to see if they would be retrievable.

I pulled. They didn't move. They were jammed. I slumped over, flopping onto the ledge — an upended turtle. I felt like weeping. I said to the cord, "Jam all you want. I'll get you loose, I'll get down!" My sudden outburst startled me. I was weakening. I pulled again. Nothing. I would have to go back up the ropes and re-set them. Seeing no need to climb with the pack on, I unbuckled it, setting it on the ledge.

Again on the summit, I resolved to get things right the third time around. I looked at the ropes; they were stuck because of the acute angle formed where they bent over the edge of the cliff. The wind blew, I shivered, the sky turned violently gray and blue. Under the circumstances I decided to tie only one rope to the top, rappel down and then leave it behind, and finish the descent with the remaining line.

I strapped the rope vehemently to the bolts. "I'll come back and get your later," I said to it. I lied. I knew that I wouldn't return — the rope was old and worn. It had seen its use.

When rappelling, I always coil and pack away any spare ropes to prevent them from tangling with the rappel line. This time, I made an exception. Cold, and with the weather closing in, I left the extra rope hanging free, clipped to an equipment sling around my neck.

Squatting low to get out of the wind, I grabbed the rappel rope and lowered to the ledge where I stepped sideways a few paces to get the pack. I shouldered it wearily then leaned back to continue. Just as I placed my weight against the rope, a queer sensation came over me. Something was wrong. I couldn't put my finger on it, but something was definitely wrong. Suddenly I knew what it was. In the darkness, in the wind and in the confusion, I had come unclipped from the rappel line. Just as I realized it, it was already too late. The weight of the pack and the steepness of the wall made it impossible for me to keep my balance. With a despairing cry, I pitched over backwards into the night sky.

Luck is ineffable. It rides the wind. Luck is a word and nothing more ... or is it? Maybe luck is just the aftermath of events that are commonplace, occurring every second of every day, events that we only notice when they are extraordinary.

At first, I fell in a line parallel to that of the rope. I reached out in a vain effort to grab it, struggling at the last. I meekly brushed the rope and then it was gone.

The feelings that came over me next were crystalline fear, disbelief, and hopelessness — feelings of the condemned just as the bullet hits the skull.

Detached from the rope, I plunged down the wall, free falling towards the ground, 400 feet below. I turned slowly through the air and knew that I was about to die.

As I fell, I accepted death, and when I did a great curiosity replaced my fears. For here we are on earth in absolute dominion; we think we are so superior, yet the one thing that we have no clue about, the one thing that holds our greatest fear yet is unavoidable, is death. Man is the only animal that can't accept death. For all of his intelligence, man has never learned how to die — we think we can outsmart it. Falling, I realized this and I knew that the great mystery was about to be revealed. I would be dead in an instant, and it may sound crazy, but in a way I was grateful. I resigned myself to fate and waited for the impact.

It came quickly. A sharp jolt and then nothing. I felt and saw nothing. I heard nothing, yet I could still think. My racing brain said: "This is it. I'm dead ... where is the light?" Senseless, I wondered, "My body must be shattered, but my brain is still intact. If it is, it will only be a moment before the oxygen burns away ..."

Slowly, lucidity returned. I felt pain, and with pain, life. I was alive, but strangely ... felt cheated. I thought that after having gone through the vicissitudes of death, I deserved the answer. I felt cruelly mocked, and wanted life to be over.

But man cannot go easily; he must fight to the end for life. To do anything less is to wrong nature. The rope held me by the neck, the gear sling pinned by the pack straps, strangling me. Instinctively, I reached up, feeling the scorched remnants of the rope. "What?" I shuddered. "It wasn't tied to anything, what's holding it?" Dazed, I conjured up the image of a Dantean beast holding my life-leash in grinning jaws; as I climbed up to free it, the jaws would open to devour me. The noose tightened, and I couldn't breath.

In the dark, I tore through my equipment, fumbling for jumars. I found them, snapped them onto the rope, released the hangman's grip, and breathed. With each breath death retreated, taking with it the manifestations. With each breath life returned, bringing with it the enigma. I reached out and touched the rock. It felt solid and warm.

Swaying on the tattered fray of rope, I had no choice but to climb it and see if there was enough left to get to the ground. For the third time that night, I went up the rope. This time, however, was quite different. The jumar's teeth clogged with rope fibers, forcing me to pause every few feet and clear the parts. In some places the sheath broke loose, sending me skidding down the rope until the ascenders regained their purchase.

As I jumared, the outward pull on the rope increased. This worried me. I worried that whatever specter was holding the rope might not be strong enough to hold both a downward and an outward pull. But I didn't worry too much, for there was nothing I could do about it.

I made it to the top of the rope, and what I found surprised me. Evidently, in my earthward drop, I had towed the spare rope behind me like a kite tail. By wind or fate, the tail had twisted, jamming into a small crack like a cork in a bottle. The cork caught after I had fallen over 150 feet. If I had fallen a foot to the right or left, or if the wind hadn't been blowing ... the twist of rope that had held was melted, fused together from the impact.

Do events really turnout the way they do because of a collision of happenstance? Or is the outcome always dictated by preceding events, which in turn were the outcome of an even more complex order? Are there really accidents, or does everything turn out the way it does because it would be impossible for it to culminate any other way? Does a falling stone land on a specific point of chance, or because it has to and when it narrowly misses, we call it luck?

I didn't know if the rope would hold together long enough to get me down, but I had to try. I placed several cams in the crack to replace the rope, which I then dislodged with a quick tug. My hands shook as I forced the melted strands apart. Using what was left, I continued the descent.

First published in Climbing *No. 121, 1990.*

The Dance of the Woo-Li Masters
The First Ascent of the East Face of the Moose's Tooth

By Jim Bridwell

A jet ... yes, I was sure it was a jet. The sound was uniquely different from the roar of avalanches thundering down everywhere around us. It was probably headed for Oslo or some such place, and would arrive in the morning (or evening?). I couldn't figure it out, but that's the way jets are; you're never sure what time it is. My thoughts started to race on into the relationships of time and its necessity for place, but I was harshly interrupted by the sudden realization that I was looking down 3000 feet to our tent. The spacious North Face dome looked like heaven, and we were in hell. What was I doing in this inhuman zone? Was it choice, happenstance, or fate, or possibly some combination of these that brought me to meet my climbing partner Mugs Stump?

Only four months ago we had been strangers, meeting in an outdoor cafe in Grindelwald. We drank strong coffee and shot the bull about the Eiger and similar experiences on the North Face. One cup of coffee equals about one hour of bullshit, and before three cups were gone we were both jawing each other about the East Face of the Moose's Tooth. We had both failed on the 5000-foot face, along with a large contingency of other climbers. At least we were in good company; we figured that the face had been attempted over 10 times by different parties, all very competent. We made plans, not for the Moose's Tooth, but maybe that's where fate came into play.

In early March, Doug Geeting flew us toward the Great Gorge, but when we looked for our objective it wasn't there. Conditions were bad indeed. All the faces were in the worst possible condition; no good ice where we'd hoped, just a thin veneer or aerated ice with a light dusting of spindrift, overhangs bulging with snow clinging incredibly to their undersides. It wasn't just bad, it was inhuman. What could we possibly do in these conditions? We had to think of something quick — Doug's a good guy, but he wouldn't fly us around forever. The Moose's Tooth was close, so we decided to have a look. The East Face looked equally horrendous, but we couldn't impose on Doug's patience any more. It would have to do; these were our cards, and we'd have to play them.

The landing was fine, but getting Geeting aloft took some digging and pushing. As the plane sped away we gazed at the hoary specter before us. Just thinking about it made my bones brittle and my spirit fragile. My imagination balked at more inquest and I set about erecting the tent. At least home on the glacier would be luxurious and the ogre above could wait for inspection when my courage was well braced.

The next day was clear and oh so cold; in March, Alaska still doesn't really feel the sun, it passes but doesn't touch. I remembered my hand freezing white like a burn when I touched the metal on the Cessna the day before, and it felt the same as I adjusted the ring on the spotting scope. The face looked impregnable, and the invaders were armed with slingshots.

We thought that just maybe we could pull off the ol' David and Goliath sketch, and decided on a route to the right of our previous attempts. These technical aid routes were hideously plastered with ice and out of the question. Our new choice was a more perilous passage, but the only reasonable possibility. A lightweight alpine-style approach would be the key.

We were bluffing with only a pair. It would be like grabbing a tiger by the tail — you couldn't let go or you'd be eaten. The lower half of the climb consisted of avalanche chutes and faces fed by the whole upper wall, and if a storm came in while we were on the climb, retreat would be suicide. The only way down was to go to the top; conquest or death, so to speak. It sounded ridiculous, but was true. Retreat in good weather would be very difficult, but you probably wouldn't be retreating in that case anyway. Unless, of course, there was something up there we couldn't climb.

The barometer rose but the storms came without caring. We didn't mind; it gave us time to psyche up and sort out the gear. The minimum would be the rule: four days of food and fuel could be stretched to six or seven. Food was an austere allotment of gorp, coffee and sugar, and two packets of soup. The hardware rack was skeletal; we had trimmed away the fleshy bolt kit and second set of Friends, leaving the bones — 10 ice screws, 15 rock pitons, six wired nuts, a set of Friends, and the essential hook. We planned to rappel mainly off slings around horns for the descent. We opted for a technical and swift descent, hopefully not too swiftly down a 1500-foot rock face into the East Couloir. This of course would also be suicidal in a storm, as two huge faces on either side fed the couloir lethal doses of snow. But it did lead directly to the homeless Ruth Amphitheatre. We would choose what fate decreed.

Clear skies came, but the first day was spent watching the face and timing avalanches, trying to feel for some intuitive glimpse at the secret of its pulsating rhythms. The night was spent deliberating on whether to wait another day while consuming large quantities of whiskey. Something inside told me to go in the morning, perhaps the whiskey. It wields a strong opinion indeed.

We agreed, and in the morning found ourselves trudging to the base, laboring under our packs and hangovers. I didn't want to give myself a chance to know what I was doing until it was too late. Needless to say, Mugs did the leading and I did the motivating.

A steep snow slope led to the Cauldron, a steep, narrow venturi 250 feet long that collected minute spindrift sloughs and amplified them into a blinding, freezing torrent of misery. I was appalled and impressed as Mugs led difficult 75 to 85 degree ice without protection through waves of gushing spindrift, a 35-pound pack tugging at his shoulders. It was my turn and I secretly hoped for some respite, but knew I would get my justice, the justice I had already chosen like we all have. I was frozen when I reached the belay, fingers wooden as I fiddled with the camera and attempted to feed the rope out.

After another pitch we climbed together to the first traverse. It was steep powder snow covering sugar snow over rock. Scratchy to say the least, with imaginary belay anchors. Both leader and follower were in fact leading, each responsible for the other's life. Mistakes weren't allowed. The first traverse was three pitches long and led to a three-pitch calf-burning ice slope, then onto another horrid traverse.

This was worse than the first one and longer. Near its beginning we heard a shout. Our minds must be askew, but it wasn't an alcoholic illusion. Some fellow mountaineers were ski touring up the Buckskin to the Ruth Amphitheatre; we shouted back and carried on. The climbing was tenuous, thin powder snow laid over hidden patches of ice and steep rock. Protection was nearly non-existent and the belays were the same. In places we were climbing three to five inches of snow over 60- to 65-degree rock; much to my distress, these pitches would often start with a downward traverse of 40 or 50 feet before going horizontal or upward.

Near the end of the day we reached a snow slope where it was just possible to dig a platform for sleep. Mugs fixed a pitch above for better anchors and we precariously nestled in.

The morning was supremely frigid and we dared not move from our cocoons until the sun's rays gave some hope for life. Frostbite was our eminent host should we dare break the house rules, so we regulated our desires accordingly.

A steep chimney choked with ice rose up and out of our field of vision, and tested our abilities for the rest of the day. From below I judged it to be about five pitches long, but it turned out to be seven instead. This chimney and the headwall above would constitute the main difficulties of the route.

I led the first and least steep of these pitches before the white ribbon bulged abruptly so as to obscure our inquisitive gaze. Mugs pressed the attack up the 80- to 85-degree slippery gouge. In places he would encounter overhanging bulges which the cold, dry winter had turned to airy unconsolidated granola. A desperate struggle ensued at these overhangs: ice axes and hammers became useless, and we would be forced onto tiny edges for our crampons and shaky pitons for hand holds.

Many times I had to use my ice-tool picks as cliff hangers on edges, or wedged in cracks nut-fashion. The Forrest Saber hammer was especially useful for this and quickly gained favor on these pitches. This assault continued on through the day and into the failing light of evening. I started to become weak and nauseous from dehydration, as our daily consumption of water had been less than six cups per man. In those temperatures, man's devices cease to function as they are designed; the stove was by now an ineffectual nuisance which would only boil water after an hour of coaxing and shaking. We had penetrated the inhuman zone and were paying the price.

Mugs had fixed the last pitch, and I swung around a corner onto a small 65-degree ice slope, the only possible site for a bivouac. We produced a precarious perch after hours of ice sculpturing in the dark. It was nearly 1 a.m. before we collapsed exhausted in our sleeping bags. The morning of the third day started with a tedious struggle for liquids and ascending the fixed rope to our high point. Vertical ice reached upward, and once again Mugs valiantly met the challenge. He led two pitches up the icy serpent, then exited onto an easy 330-foot snow slope that extended to a formidable headwall. Even with the telescope we had been unable to probe the secrets of this section of the climb. Intuition lured us to the right, up an ice runnel and onto a snow rib. I poked my head around the corner to be confronted by a steep rock wall. Its thin cracks were well armored with ice and presented a chilling spectre of extreme difficulty.

I tensioned off a nut I'd chopped a slot for; thinly-gloved hands search for usable rugosities while crampon claws scratched at scaly granite. I laybacked a steep flake to find its top closed with ice. In quiet desperation I clung with one hand, perforating the ice overhead with the hammer, probing for a secure stick. Standing on the shelf of ice I caught my breath and looked for a possible route up the wall now confronting me.

I decided to move right into a groove, where mixed free and aid led to a point where it was possible to swing left onto my ice axe and climb up to a small ice ledge. I got some anchors in and brought Mugs up. Only a portion of the next lead disclosed itself, but things didn't look promising. Mugs moved off hooks onto the fragile thinness of precipitous ice; after 40 feet of slow, begrudging difficulties, he shouted down that it was blank above. The sky had clouded and snow began to fall.

To retrace our steps would be disastrous, we needed a bivy site and there was none below us for many pitches. We had to push on now, and quickly, for a night spent exposed and standing would be devastating to our bodies in their present weak and dehydrated condition.

"Are you sure there is no possible way?" I queried.

"Let me take a good look, I gotta figure this out," he replied. Mugs moved only occasionally, but some progress was being made.

What was he doing? I could only imagine the worst. He called down for the #3 Friend, so I took out the belay anchor and sent it up. I hung in slings off a tie-off draped over a nubbin of rock, and continued my frigid vigil. The Friend went into a shallow hole, then a hook to a knifeblade behind a half-inch flake, and it was working out. Several more technical aid moves, and after two hours of nerve-grinding climbing Mugs reached an ice tongue that led to easier ground.

I got to the belay and started the next pitch as quickly as possible. It was already late in the day, and we had to find some place to bivouac soon. The snow was coming down heavily now, and spindrift cascaded over us with increasing punctuality. The climbing was marginal; a traverse crossed a slab covered with four inches of snow. I had hoped that there wold be ice, but no such luck. I splayed my feet duck style to attain the maximum surface area. I couldn't believe they held; it was like climbing a slate roof covered in snow. Once past this I entered a trough filled with bulletproof ice. By this time I was extremely sick. Mugs came up and found me slumped over, weak and nauseous from dehydration. He led the next two pitches of steep mixed rock and ice, but it was all I could do to follow. It was dark and I had to use my headlamp to follow the last rope length, but we had found a place to dig a snow cave. A gift from heaven! After two hours the cave was completed, and we began brewing tea and coffee, two of the worst drinks possible for dehydration. At 1:30 a.m. we collapsed in our sleeping bags, secure from the storm.

Life came slowly the next morning. From my vantage point near the cave entrance I could see that the storm was breaking up, but I kept the vision secret from Mugs as I wanted to rest just a little longer. Soon the sun was shining into the cave, and it was no longer possible to hide the obvious fact that the weather was turning beautiful. We crawled out from the cave and commenced climbing at 11:30. The problems were mainly in route finding. Picking the easiest but not always obvious way is a talent born of experience and oftentimes luck. We were lucky and by 3:30 we stood on top of the Tooth.

The vantage point was spectacular; it seemed that I took one photograph after another until two rolls disappeared. Soon it was 4:30 p.m. and Mugs asked coyly if I'd like to start down. The weather was clear in all directions; it was also fairly late and I was tired, but secretly I had been having subtle intuitions of forboding about the descent. For you see, I had been thinking of the descent for quite some time. In reply to Mugs, I said a quick no. I felt a possible ordeal ahead, and wanted a full day to cope with any eventuality. Bypassing my suspicions, I offered a further explanation: the descent would be technical and potentially difficult, and we should give ourselves a full day as there would be no place to stop once we had started. We agreed and returned to photography.

Darkness came sneaking over the mountains while our stove begrudgingly produced two cups of hot tea without sugar. Our supplies were nearly finished so getting down was imminently important. We burrowed deep into our survival cells as the cold became increasingly bitter. Temperatures plummeted to minus 30 degrees that night, and the wind decided to continue and wait for some exposed skin in the morning. It was truly torturous packing and getting ready to go. All manmade gadgets ceased to work, just another wonderful quality of the inhuman zone. But the stove did manage one full cup of cold water each before it died.

We climbed down a snow slope and began rappelling over discontinuous snow and rock bands. As we descended rappel after rappel, the snow disappeared, leaving bare, flaking rock, the kind for which the Moose's Tooth is famous. Crumbling and rotten, the face steepened so that it disappeared below us, making it impossible to see where we were going or what we were going to do. I kept angling leftwards as the couloir came upwards towards our left. The rock had become blank of cracks, but there were a few scabs of very flexible rotten flakes.

The alarms went off in my head, activating my whole being into survival mode. I rappelled, passed an overhang and tension-traversed left to a flake-like ledge, pounded two pitons into the compressed gravel behind it, and began wondering what to do next. Looking down I could see nothing to go for. I wished I had brought the bolt kit; Mugs had wanted to, but I had insisted that it wouldn't be necessary, and besides it was too heavy. Alpine style, you know: too much weight, count every match and all that jive. My mind raced in all directions at once, as cat might behave trapped in a corner by salivating Alsasians. The word frantic would best describe my reactions.

Computer-like I made a decision and yelled up instructions to Mugs. I asked him to tie off one rope to his anchors and to send the other down so I could check things out. If I saw nothing, I would have to jumar 300 feet to Mugs, then we would have to climb back to the summit, 10 pitches or more, and look for another way down. It was a devastating course of action that would require the rest of the day and part of the next.

I tensioned left again, and then climbed up and left, my crampons screeching on the rotten granite as I searched for tiny holds. Putting a #3 Stopper in

60

the only place available, I clipped in and continued rappelling. Near the end of the rope, a small but solitary flake came into view. I stopped and stared at it, hanging on the rope as a sad, sweet rhapsody of emotion washed over me. I remained there motionless with visions of people I loved and owed love to. It's sad that we don't appreciate the commonplace yet wonderful and beautiful trivial duties of life, like saying hello or washing the dishes. I guess that you don't miss the water until your well runs dry.

These thoughts rustled over my mind, and I emerged slowly from the reverie, realizing that this was what we in California call a "heavy scene." My intuition had been correct; we had come to meet our ordeal. I looked up and saw clouds beginning to prey the sky, then started back up the rope, turning for one last look at the flake.

Reaching the nut, I unclipped, swung back right, and continued up to the anchors. I yelled to Mugs to come down, waking him, as he had fallen asleep from the excitement. He could tell there was uncertainty in my voice. When he reached me, I explained the situation before we pulled the ropes so that he could partake in the decision. Once the ropes were down, we'd have no choice. He had an easy way of boosting my confidence while accepting my course of action, whatever I might choose.

Casino time: one roll of the dice for all the marbles. I said a prayer and started down. Retracing my traverse, I reached the Stopper I'd previously fixed and brought Mugs down to a minimal stance. He surveyed the anchor briefly, and then looked at me with wonder that was broken off by doubt. I shrugged my shoulders and said, "That's it." My heart was trying to escape from my mouth for the next 150 feet, until I secured a #1 Friend behind the small flake I'd seen. I placed another nut while Mugs duplicated the rappel; he later told me that he almost unclipped from the anchor, but quickly decided and realized that a fast death was more appealing than a slow and agonizing, yet inevitable, one.

After descending half the rope, I gave thanks to the merciful one. For, wonder of wonders, the ropes reached a snow-covered ramp. The chilling grip of death relaxed and a calming peace soothed my quaking soul. The descent became routine and within two hours we were galloping down steep snow toward the security of the tent.

Everything there was frozen. We immediately fired up the stove, and began guzzling brew after brew of hot liquid. We laughed and joked until late in the night. We'd had five days of intense experience, and required some time to unwind. The cards were played and we had drawn aces. Finally I collapsed into prone paralysis; just before unconsciousness, the memorable words of French climber Jean Afanasief came to mind, "This is the fucking life, no?"

First published in Climbing *No. 69, 1981.*

Arctic Education
Learning the ropes on Baffin Island's new frontier

By Mark Synnott

The Illauq family's home buzzed with the commotion of climbers, Inuit men and children, and husky pups. While Beverly tended to a steaming pot of polar bear meat, I jockeyed to get a better look at the map, spread below Jushua's feet, of Baffin Island's eastern fjords. Gesturing with a hand-rolled cigarette, he drew my attention to an obscure fjord: "This one here, it got real big cliffs. You would like this one." Jushua's uncle Iqaqrialuq and brother Joannasie both grinned, nodding in consent. Within minutes the map was covered in markings, and Jushua had yet to even mention the newly discovered climbing region of the Sam Ford Fjord.

We had been on Baffin Island for less than an hour, but already I never wanted to go home. My friends and I had often felt that we'd missed out on climbing's heyday, when first ascents were all that existed. Now I knew that we had been wrong. Most of the 26 major fjords on Baffin Island's east coast contain formations similar to that of the Sam Ford Fjord; the amount of undiscovered rock in this area will be a bonanza to wall climbers for generations.

As we got acquainted with our hosts over a late dinner in their home in the tiny Inuit village of Clyde River, we came to realize that the Inuit, in addition to holding doctorates in survival, are some of the most outgoing and friendly people in the world. They had no hesitations about making fun of my partners' and my greenness, but their good humor was so contagious that we were always laughing. We also greatly respected the combined strength of their experience; our three guides from Qullikkut Outfitters Jushua, Joannasie, and Iqaqrialuq had all grown up as nomads wandering from fjord to fjord, following the caribou, polar bears, seals, fish, and narwhal that fed their families.

My partners for this adventure were two people I hardly knew. I first met Warren Hollinger hanging out in "Bum's Row" at the lodge in Yosemite. Tall, with a shaved head and mean-looking goatee, he seemed to be constantly entertaining gumby climbers with Beta on the routes he had done. A few days later I ran into him again at Warren Harding's 70th birthday party, and we had such a good time drinking together that we decided to do a wall. We ended up suffering an epic 23 hours on the *Nose,* running out of water at the Great Roof on a 100-degree day. Warren climbed six El Cap routes back to back that trip, including *Lost in America, Space,* and *Sea of Dreams.*

Jerry Gore, on the other hand, was from England, and I didn't even know what he looked like. He turned out to be short, very stocky, and full of jokes and stories. Though he had not done a lot of big walls, Jerry had been on a major expedition every year since 1977, including several trips to the Himalaya. In life stages, he was in a very different position than Warren and I: three months prior to our departure his wife had given birth to their first child, Beth.

Only when he took off his shirt did I remember a special bond he and Warren held. Both were badly scarred last summer from a lightning strike on the summit of North Howser Spire in the Bugaboos.

I had kept in touch with Warren since Yosemite, knowing that he had many sick missions planned. Baffin was his idea, and I was totally psyched when he called from Hawaii in late fall asking me to go.

We would not have the area entirely to ourselves. Daniel Ascaso, Javier Ballester, and Pepe Chaverri, all from Spain, arrived in Clyde River the same day we did, May 14th, and they, too, were intent on climbing big walls in the Sam Ford Fjord. We were relieved that our objectives did not conflict. The Spaniards had come for Kiguti, fabled to resemble El Cap, and, they hoped, some ice climbing. We had come for the Polar Sun Spire.

Information about climbing activity on Baffin Island's east coast is meager. From conversations and reading we thought that only two or three groups had ever climbed in Sam Ford Fjord, and no one had climbed anywhere else. Some time around 1978, an English group explored the fjord, but it is not clear what they accomplished. One Inuit man, who was living in the fjord at the time, recalled hearing voices on the formation Nuvualik (aka the Turret). Another source mentions two young Swiss men in the area around 1985. The only concrete information we had was from the summer of 1992, when Conrad Anker and Jon Turk successfully completed two Grade V climbs in the Sam Ford Fjord. As we would find out later, theirs were not the only ascents.

Timing our arrival had been the most complicated logistical element. Like the Spanish, we had opted for the cold alternative, approaching and climbing before the sea ice broke up. With the entire coast and fjords locked beneath a six-foot sheet of ice, we could travel by snowmobile, using huge sleds called komotiks to drag our 800-pound, six-week supply of food and equipment into the fjord.

The 12-hour ride from Clyde River into Sam Ford Fjord gave us a good taste of the cold feet that would be our companions for the rest of the trip. Iqaqrialuq, whom we had affectionately named "Gramps," because we couldn't pronounce his name, drove our sled, and we spent many hours marveling at his endurance. Gramps, 55, is an elder of the community, legendary for his skills as a hunter and survivalist. As he tooled us steadily along the coast we contemplated the huge expanse of frozen ocean extending unbroken, save for a few icebergs, to the shores of Greenland. The blinding whiteness of the ice and fog gave us a sense of vertigo and intensified our sense of isolation. The weather had been socked in since we arrived, with temperatures varying between zero and 20 degrees, so we were thoroughly stiff and frozen on our sled when we finally entered the inner sanctum of Sam Ford Fjord around 6 a.m. on May 16th.

Our first stop was below Kiguti, which was barely visible through the haze and fog. The Spaniards were still psyched, but it was hard to ignore the grim winter conditions. Their basecamp was more than two miles from the start of the climbing, but was definitely their best option, being one of the few place around where you could actually pitch a tent. The cliffs in Sam Ford Fjord generally rise directly from the ocean; considering that the fjord is said to be 2000 feet deep, you wonder how big they really are.

With the Spanish settled in their new home at "Windy Point," we continued towards the Walker Arm, a subsidiary fjord that branches to the west and south. Polar Sun Spire was now barely discernible through the low cloud cover. In a short period we witnessed several avalanches cut loose on its eastern slope. We could now see that the spire had an almost full northern exposure, and the face, with its miniature snowfields and black water streaks, looked more like the Eiger than the El Cap I'd expected. While we sat on the sled below Polar Sun Spire, in the entrance to the Walker Arm, considering our options, the fog that had been frustrating us since our arrival began to lift. In half an hour the skies were cobalt blue, and we were completely gaga: in every direction, huge granite cliffs rose directly form the ocean, most looking extremely steep. Warren and Jerry danced around the snowmobile, chanting like drugged-out hippies about the promised land.

Directly across the fjord, the Great Cross Pillar sported a 2700-foot southfacing wall, the sight of which inspired us to declare Polar Sun out of condition. Gramps took us on one sled to our basecamp below Great Cross Pillar while Jushua and Joannasie went hunting. They both killed seals, leaving a massive red stain on the ice just a few feet from our tent. Jerry voiced our concern that the blood might attract predators, but as usual, the Inuits just laughed at us. The hunting was good, and they stayed for two more days before leaving.

The Great Cross Pillar is named for a distinct cross that can be seen to the west of the main pillar. Formed by black water streaks, the cross was not obvious until pointed out to us by Gramps. Despite the cliff's huge dimensions, we found very few crack systems, as was typical for most of the rock in the area. The cracks we could see looked loose and chossy and it seemed that the best route lay in a direct line up the prow of the main pillar.

It took us two days to fix the first 700 feet to the start of a huge ledge that traversed the cliff for almost a mile. After the second day of fixing, Jerry and I rapped back to basecamp after 24 hours on the go. We found Warren, who had taken the day off to get organized, singing at the top of his lungs, and it didn't take long to realize he had been dipping into our secret stash. The party, unfortunately, soon came to an abrupt end when Warren's Walkman malfunctioned. He put the unit permanently out of commission with a 25-pound rock.

Basecamp was almost too luxurious, and we reluctantly pulled out on May 23rd, humping three haulbags and one expedition barrel the eighth of a mile to the cliff. We were equipped for 10 days that could be stretched to two weeks.

A long day's grunt of jugging and hauling deposited us at our first camp, on the big ledge, where we kicked back to chow and admire the scenery that had opened up dramatically. Polar Sun Spire dominated our perspective, but we could also clearly see the Second Turret and Broad Peak in the background. The latter, at 6500 feet, is the tallest summit in the area, and is still probably unclimbed; its east face rises straight from the ocean in Himalayan proportions, featuring two distinct walls, separated by loose gullies and snowfields. The upper headwall is a stunning overhanging prow for at least 1500 feet. The ice in the fjord below was uniform and perfect save for a small iceberg near the Walker Citadel, and the bloodstain near our camp. Above us, the cliff hung over our heads, more than vertical for 1500 of the 2000 feet that we had yet to climb.

Our most immediate problem was a large recessed alcove. Climbing through looked like mega-hard aid, and the risk for a ledge fall seemed unreasonable. Instead, we found a crack system on its left edge that led to a long, flaring chimney. It was my day to lead, and the first pitch rewarded me with solid rock and classic free climbing: splitter Yosemite-style hand and finger cracks. The chimney, however, was a different story. The flared sides were coated in potato chips, and I had to force a gripped, full-body stem to pass a loading chute of gravel and death blocks waiting for me at two-thirds height.

At the end of the day's climbing, as we would nearly each day, we huddled around the stove and drank hot chocolate from Pepe, the name we gave our flask, reliving the grim details of each pitch, swapping stories, and ragging on each other. We had spotted some movement on the ice that day, and speculated on what it might have been. Warren and I thought wolves, but oh, no, Jerry had it all figured out. "Those are Arctic condors," he said. "They have 15-foot wingspans, and fly just a few feet above the ice." The laugh we got out of that lasted for the whole trip.

The next day we awoke to high winds and a building storm front. Nasty-looking black and blue lenticulars were stacking up ridiculously high in a foreboding but spectacular backdrop to the walls and glaciers lining the fjord.

It was now my turn to rest, and I relished the chance to sleep in a bit late in the double portaledge. While Jerry and Warren began jugging our free-hanging ropes, I lounged by the stove, sipping my soup and wondering about the weather and Warren's pitch. Less than an hour into his 10-hour lead, which turned out to be the crux of our route, the weather broke and I was forced to seek shelter back in the ledge. Jerry swung his arms and legs around, singing obnoxious British army songs.

Warren had his mind on other things. From the belay he had pendulumed to a sideways hook move. It took him two rivets and several more hooks to cross 30 feet of blank rock to the start of a shallow blind corner. For the next six hours Warren used small heads and hooks to climb 75 feet without another hole. As he passed a small roof at the top of the corner, the Birdbeak he was on shifted badly. "Time bomb," he screamed, and the next thing I knew he had launched out of his aiders to go free. Double boots skating on the vertical granite, he manteled onto a small ledge. His last descent piece was a rivet level with the belay, and an evil-looking razor flake appeared to be in his flight path, about 40 feet below that. Hanging from one arm, Warren pulled off a loose flake of rock to create a foothold, then squeezed one butt cheek onto the ledge.

It was after this day, with his 10-hour ride in the belay seat, that Jerry decided to descend. There were several contributing factors, and it was a tough decision for everybody. At the simplest level, we were beginning to worry about supplies. We had already eaten four of our 10 days' ration, and it was obvious that we had more than a week to go. More important, Jerry was having a hard time with his psyche. Although he had been on many expeditions before, this was the first time that he had left a wife and newborn at home. His commitment to them was overwhelming him now, and he was having trouble focusing on the difficulties ahead. We gave him one haulbag filled with a portaledge and all of his personal kit, tied four ropes together, and away he went. We would not see him for another eight days.

That same day we fixed one more pitch to the start of "The Circle," the most obvious feature on our route; a beautiful 300-foot arching corner system. Our next camp would be at its base.

Belaying was turning out to be the great demoralizer of the climb, and portaledge life was the luxury that kept us going during the long cold days in the belay seat. Climbing capsule-style, we usually had camp completely set up at the end of each day's climbing. The hanging stove had the pleasant side effect of turning our little portaledge tent into a sauna. Unfortunately, the sauna also had a predictably unpleasant side effect. The steam from our hot drinks and noodle dinners coated the inside of the fly with condensation. Once the stove was turned off, the incessant wind turned the inside of the ledge into one of those snowy Christmas scenes. The wind gusted up to 50 miles an hour, which kept the ledge flapping and shaking so much that it was practically impossible to sleep. Thankfully, the 24-hour daylight allowed us to put away our watches and calendars, so we basically climbed whenever we felt like it. Most days were overcast, so we wouldn't miss out on any sun by climbing at night.

For the next several days we laboriously aided our way through a maze of overhanging, incipient cracks. The quality of the rock varied so dramatically that sometimes cracks would be bordered by entirely different rock: one side ballistic hard crystalline gneiss, and the other a pile of stacked flakes and rotten, pumice-like choss. The pick on my alpine hammer and the nut tool were invaluable for excavating placements. Sore eyes from rock dust became a problem, so we often led with goggles.

On May 31st, I led the hardest pitch of my life, a nine-hour effort with lots of hooking and copperheading. I drilled a bomber three-bolt station at its end to serve as our third and final camp. After fixing two more long pitches up an amazing overhanging knifeblade and Birdbeak splitter seam, we blasted free from our servitude of jugging and hauling, committing ourselves to reaching the summit. Two more pitches led to an incredible alcove whose roof succumbed to a slew of bomber A1 placements. Some scrappy pitches of 5.9 left only a mile of 3rd and 4th class between us and the real summit.

We built a small cairn, snapped a photo and headed down into a whiteout, reaching our hanging camp after 26 hours. It was our 11th day on the wall and we yearned for our basecamp, wondering if Jerry was OK.

Because our route was overhanging and traversing, we had left slings attached to certain stations and fixed pieces. The plan was to pendulum and hook fixed gear by tossing fifi hooks into the slings.

We rappelled to our fixed camp and rested for 18 hours, which would have been nice except for the waterfall around the corner kept dousing us. On the next day's first rappel Warren spent two hours trying to pendulum to a fixed Birdbeak. I strongly voiced my opinion that we should abandon it and find a new way down. Warren finally snapped. "Why the hell can't you just support me on this," he wailed, banging his head against the cliff. Finally, he gave up, rapped to the end of the rope and then swung onto a hook from which to drill a new station.

I could tell that Warren was really pissed off at me, but it wasn't until we hit the security of the big ledge that he really let me have it. "I hate you," he said with perfect honesty, and I truly believed that our friendship had permanently ended.

We were both pretty burned up, but after an hour or so I knew we had to reconcile. In the past, with other partners, Warren had always been the leader, the one calling the shots, and it was an intense strain on him to have me constantly challenging his judgments. By the time we reached basecamp and reunited with Jerry, we had more than 24 hours of rappelling behind us, and the whole thing had blown over.

Jerry had not had a good time while we were away. The stress of worrying about his family had driven him to the verge of a nervous fit, and he was soon hearing polar bears sniffing outside the tent. During one particularly bad spell of weather, the tent blew down, and in the 40-mph winds he was unable to reconstruct it. In desperation, Jerry called the outfitters on the radio and arranged to get picked up. A day later he was back at the Illauqs' in Clyde River. After a nice talk with his wife and some home-cooked food, he had returned to the fjord with his psyche back in shape to tackle the Polar Sun Spire.

After we changed and chowed in basecamp, it didn't take long for Warren to find the bottle, and tie on a good buzz when he did. We had talked about this bottle for a long time, and Warren was very disappointed that I would not join him in more than a few toasts to our new route. For payback, he decided to torture me by refusing to let me sleep. As soon as I started to get comfortable, he'd pull back my sleeping bag, and slobber and babble in my face. There is nothing worse than being trapped in a small tent in the middle of nowhere with a drunken fool.

Still relishing our hard-won rest in basecamp the next day, we heard voices, and were soon swapping stories with the Spanish trio, who had hiked the three miles from their basecamp at Windy Point to see us. They, too, had been successful, completing a difficult 3000-foot climb up the "Nose" of Kiguti. Their route, *Nirvana* (VI 5.10 A3), had only taken them seven days, but they had been very cold on the wall and were disappointed by the lack of free climbing and the abundance of loose rock. Still, they planned an attempt on the Fin, a 2000-foot overhanging prow that forms an extension to the Chinese Wall directly north of Kiguti.

Warren had been nursing a bad hangover all day, and in addition appeared to have caught a cold. He would rest while Jerry and I began to fix ropes on Polar Sun Spire.

Sloshing through the water that now covered the ice, Jerry and I worried about the vulnerability of our position. The Spaniards had spotted polar bear tracks less than three miles away, and without a weapon, we would be dead meat in an encounter. Polar bears are one of the few animals known to routinely attack humans. Full-grown males can stand as tall as 15 feet, weigh 1000 pounds, run as fast as 30 mph, and bite your head off in about .02 seconds. They have been known to hunt killer whales.

In one long day, Jerry and I fixed 700 of the roughly 4000 feet of this north-facing wall. It was by far the scroungiest heap either of us had ever seen — wet, loose, and constantly bombarded by rockfall. After one particularly close call, we abandoned our efforts, leaving the ropes fixed until we could discuss the situation with Warren.

The next day the Inuits showed up with two new recruits, Paul Gagner and Rick Lovelace. We spoke with them briefly, but they had been on the go for a long time and were anxious to set up their basecamp at the Walker Citadel. They planned to hike out on the ice, a committing prospect since breakup could begin at any time. It broke up, in fact, while they were on Walker Citadel, and they ended up getting stranded, and nearly starved before a group of Inuit hunters happened by.

After getting them situated, Jushua and Joannasie returned to help us move our camp across the fjord.

Jettisoning our hopes for Polar Sun Spire, we decided to attempt a route on the 2000-foot west face of the second Turret, but bad weather kept us holed in the tent for the next three days. Bored out of our minds, we finally shouldered our loads and headed up the glacier for the three-mile hike to the base. We got lucky and a 15-minute clearing allowed us to pick out a line. Warren and Jerry immediately set to work on the first pitch, leaving me to deal with establishing our camp. Not surprisingly, the weather was stubborn and decided to stay grim.

On June 20th we awoke to the first clear skies in two weeks. With a bullet bag full of our rack and a pack of extra clothing, food, and water, we blasted up our five fixed lines intent on reaching the summit. Two pitches of aid brought us to the base of a long chimney system that appeared to offer access to the summit ridge. The crux we called the "Tunnel of Hoar," a tight, iced-up slot. I threaded a huge chockstone, and, in bizarre, insecure positions, wiggled into the black depths of the five-foot verglas-coated bottleneck. Five grungy, wet, and icy pitches later, we gained the summit ridge, and also a spectacular vantage on the Tugalik formation, a huge, multifaceted wall offering several different climbing options, some as long as 4000 feet.

Several easy pitches later, after about 28 hours of continuous climbing, I was bouldering out the last few moves to the summit. Manteling onto a small ledge, I was blown away to find an ancient-looking 3/8-inch bolt with a heavy steel hanger. The Turret would clearly not be a first ascent (though our west-face route was definitely new), and we scrambled onto the summit a bit disappointed, but more curious than anything else. Who had climbed this mountain before us?

70

Warren and Jerry fell asleep almost instantly on the summit, and I was tempted to do the same myself. They weren't too psyched to get moving until I mentioned the possibility of waking up to an electrical storm. I hit a raw nerve, and within a few minutes they were getting organized for the 2000-foot rappel. By the time we finally arrived back at the base of the route we had been going for nearly 40 hours, and Warren had been routinely falling asleep in his harness.

After a day's rest, we were obliged to return to basecamp for our pickup by the Inuits the next day. It was raining and our loads were ridiculously heavy, but we were psyched to have the climbing completely behind us.

When Gramps and John arrived the next day, we quickly broke down camp and loaded the komotik for the return journey. Arriving at Windy Point, we found the Spanish not entirely happy. Their attempt on the Fin had been turned back after only five pitches by loose rock and poor weather. As a result, they had spent the last three weeks in their tent. They had no desire to return to this place and were quite surprised when we mentioned our plans for next year.

The ride out turned into the most grueling epic of the entire trip. The breakup of the sea ice was now in its early stages, and the surface was covered by pools of water and slush, some as deep as three feet. In addition, numerous cracks spanned the entire length of the fjord. Approaching a crack, Joannasie guided us carefully along its edge, scoping for floating chunks of ice we could use to form a bridge. Pulling a few of these together with a long hooked pole, Joannasie created a questionable passage. Unhooking the sled from the snowmobile, we pushed it towards the edge as fast as we could, jumping on at the last second for the wobbly ride across the 25-foot fissure. Joannasie then simply gunned the snowmobile and hydroplaned across.

Soon afterward the ice became a bog of slush and the sled refused to budge. Up to our knees in ice water, we tried to push it, our visibility limited to a few feet. The weather had deteriorated into driving sleet. Nobody was happy. I asked Joannasie, who was submerged in slush trying to reattach the track on the snowmobile, if we were going to die. He just looked at us and laughed, "Maybe yes, maybe no. I don't know." Our flight left in less than 30 hours. Joannasie announced that we were not going to make it. Just then a team of Inuit hunters emerged from the gloom. In a matter of seconds we went from seriously questioning our life expectancy to joking with a group of Inuits about the weather. We were amazed to see young boys wearing only nylon windbreakers and baseball hats, with no gloves. The entire return journey lasted more than 36 hours, much of it spent pushing through the deep pools of slush. We arrived in Clyde River with two hours to spare before our return flight to Montreal.

Stepping off the plane in Montreal, we had been awake for almost three days, and it was hard to believe that less than 12 hours before, we had been looking at polar bear tracks by the side of the floe edge. Warren and I had left a large stash of gear at the Illuaqs'; returning was only a matter of time.

First published in Climbing *No. 158, 1996.*

The Silver Chalice
A Himalayan odyssey

By Jeff Long

It was in the jails of Kathmandu that ghosts gave shape to me. It has been almost 20 years now, but I still see that rangy long-haired boy stumbling into the labyrinth. Half a lifetime later, I still accompany him following the dead back into the light of day. For the two men who helped guide me into manhood had already been killed as high within the Himalaya as they could get.

One of them climbed, the other killed. One was a pacifist, the other a medieval warrior. It was the gentle spirit — Fritz Stammberger — who carried his silver chalice from camp to camp and drank raw chang and rakshee from it like some Iron Age chieftain. And it was the warrior — Wongdu — who wore around his neck a silver prayer box containing a photo of the ultimate pacifist, the Dalai Lama. To this day, Fritz's widow claims her husband worked for the KGB or CIA, when in fact he was just a giant wearing crampons. It was Wongdu who fought the CIA's war. Both of them were exiles, condemned to circle the flame. No wonder I chased after them. Searching was everything.

I first entered Nepal in 1971 at the age of 19, alone, abandoning college, risking the draft and Vietnam for a dream of Everest. I wanted it to be the great mountains that shaped my soul. In those days Kathmandu was still a city of magic, not yet self conscious or jaded, and only pilgrims ventured there. Each tribe had its look: the hard-core heads their heroin eyes and loincloths, the dharma bums their red puja threads and aloofness, the world travelers their Balti vests and visa scams, the looming mountaineers their health, cameras, and eagerness to get out of the city.

The Cold War was raging, though at the street level in Kathmandu it only showed up as sideshow curios. For a few rupees you bought your Dostoevesky and Marx from the Soviet bookstore near a government hash shop, and your copies of Mao's Red Book from the People's Republic of China stall. Besides Peace Corps workers and embassy photos of astronauts on the moon, America's bid for the Third World mostly showed in the vestiges, in the whispers and shadows. Here and there, bits of jungle cammies from Vietnam flashed in the alleys. No worthwhile pie-shop gossip failed to mention the CIA. One evening I shared a meal of dahlboht with a paranoid Army deserter from Kansas City who carried a slingshot in his back pocket. We were the same age. Like me, he had always wanted to see the Himalaya.

Every traveler navigates with an interior map. Drawn part with prayer, part with the whispers of those who have gone before us, they chart a geography of expectations and fears and peculiar landmarks. For me, guidance always seemed to come in the form of eccentrics and radicals. Later on I would take my bearings from men like Fritz and Wongdu.

But in the beginning, it was two other characters who shaped my destinations and style. Ten years earlier, Woodrow Wilson Sayre had attempted a deliriously illegal ascent of Everest from the Tibetan side, creating an international scandal that almost wrecked the first "official" American expedition in 1963. During the same period, an equally maverick French scholar named Michel Peissel had infiltrated an ancient kingdom called Mustang, a tongue of the Tibetan plateau that extends into Nepal at an average elevation of 15,000 feet. Armed with accounts written by those men, I set off to conquer Everest and Mustang both.

I arrived to find Nepal a place of absolute freedom, and yet absolute limits. Nowhere was this more certain than along the border with Tibet, which was treated like a war zone. When I tried to travel north of the Annapurna Range into Mustang, a consular officer lectured me to the point of threat. No one went up there unless he wanted to disappear. Mustang had Khampas, I was told, whatever those were. They sounded more dangerous than yeti.

Turning to Everest, I landed one of the first permits to walk in along the northern route through Rolwaling Valley. I got to the top of Tesi Lapche pass, blew out my bum knee, retreated to a monastery for two weeks, and contracted worms. Fifty pounds thinner and limping ferociously, I returned to the University of Colorado looking like an opium addict.

My next foray to the Himalaya came in 1974. Through sheer luck I had landed a spot on an international expedition to Makalu put together by Fritz Stammberger. I'd never met Fritz, but in no time found myself under his spell. Big dreams, big heart, big calves. Fritz lived life the way I thought I wanted to. He was a German expatriate ski instructor who lived in Aspen, published *Climbing* magazine, and spent his free time climbing in remote ranges. Built like Conan, married to a Playmate of the Year, multi-lingual, brimming with charisma and a worldful of stories, he seemed to represent a giant step beyond my mousey university existence. Where I was shy, he was flamboyant and reckless and conspicuous.

Later I would learn that Fritz had been 22, also, on his first expedition to the Himalaya. On the eve of summiting on Cho Oyu, his two companions had developed pulmonary edema, and Fritz should have descended for help. Instead he chose to solo to the top. By the time he returned to the tent, one climber was dead. The other died on the descent. A German climbing magazine damned Fritz. He fled, first to Asia, eventually to Aspen. There he plotted his return to the 8000-meter peaks, specifically Makalu in 1974.

Three days after graduating with a devoutly useless degree in philosophy, I joined a half dozen climbers from as many countries in Kathmandu. Between repackaging food and raiding the bazaar for last-minute gear, I made a point of collecting more stories about mysterious Mustang. There were rumors on the street about a crude bridge that crossed a gorge. In the middle of the bridge was a wooden door which the Khampas locked each night. Beyond that point Nepal belonged to them. A group of Japanese climbers had tried to enter the region, only to be robbed and turned back in their underwear.

The Khampas were the front line of a Tibetan resistance movement and had been occupying Mustang since the Chinese invasion in the late 1950s. Under the leadership of a legendary general named Wongdu, these guerrillas would slip across the Himalayan chain into their occupied homeland, hunt down Chinese soldiers, ambush truck convoys, and mine the tortuous "highway" to Pakistan. Rumor insisted that the CIA was somehow involved. A Peace Corps worker swore the guerrillas had been trained in my home state, at the 10th Mountain Division's old Camp Hale above Leadville, Colorado. None of it made much sense to me. Certainly it made no difference.

It took three weeks to approach Makalu through the leeches and monsoon rains, and another two months to spin our web to 8000 meters on the unclimbed south face. For the first month I climbed and humped loads with Fritz, who anointed me Little Fritz even though I was two inches taller. During a storm, he shared his silver chalice with me.

At the end of two months, we placed our highest camp, poised for a summit strike, and then suffered a collective surge of weather, personality conflicts, and injuries. We missed the first ascent by a thousand vertical feet. I was awestruck as grown men wept and cursed and drank themselves into Shakespearean unconsciousness. Being young, I couldn't yet distinguish between tragedy and farce. Happily, by the time we got back to Kathmandu, Fritz's spirit was fully revived. The first thing he did was obtain the next available permit for Makalu. Several of us vowed to return with Fritz in 1977. The first crack in my immortality appeared a year later when Fritz's father, Wolfgang, called to say that his son had vanished in Pakistan. I was in Austria helping one of my Makalu comrades rebuild his burned home. It was here, in Arnold's bakery, that I read the German magazines about Fritz and the Cho Oyu tragedy.

When the news of Fritz's disappearance reached us, Arnold and I winked. Staging his own death would be vintage Fritz. Sooner or later he would show up, we knew, lofting some great story. But as the months passed and Arnold's Tyrollean chalet gained walls and a roof and it came time for me to return to the States, Fritz was still missing.

Fritz had gone alone, bent on soloing Tirich Mir. We debated the possibilities. Perhaps, seeing his silver chalice, some thief had waylaid him on the trail. His wife consulted mediums who believed Fritz was injured, but still alive, imprisoned in some Asian jail cell. None of us could fathom a mere mountain taking him down. Certainly I never thought it would be me who ended up in the Asian jail. As 1977 approached, I decided to carry on with Fritz's Makalu permit. By assuming the leadership, of course, I was making myself into Fritz, or trying to. At the time it seemed a duty. The expedition was mostly composed of friends, though I did allow on one stranger. He presented himself as a black-belt Born Again 5.10 bodybuilding bicycle-racing ex-football player with serious roots in Yosemite's Camp 4. His narcissism was staggering. No one could stand the sight, much less the sound of him, but his $8000 in Alaska pipeline cash was impossible to refuse. We called him the Silver Surfer.

In February, I flew back to Kathmandu. Like an old friend, the Mustang rumors were still crawling around the temples and alleyways. The rest of the crew wasn't arriving for another two weeks, which gave me time to chase after what remains to this day a classified U.S. government secret. The Khampa-resistance-movement story had grown on me, or me on it. A budding journalist, I fancied a scoop.

Anxious whispers kept warning me away from the story, but nearly everyone wanted to talk, too. Darting after slim leads — a crippled monk, alleged gunrunner, an American "wife" of Wongdu, anthropologists, exiles, quasi-diplomats — I came to understand that each new source considered himself the final authority. The Mustang program had apparently been terminated. "Dixie Cups," a Christian missionary explained. That was the CIA's in-house slang for its various indigenous guerrilla operations. "Use once, throw away."

Nevertheless, some said, the guerrillas were still fighting farther west of Mustang or deep inside Tibet. Or they were counting their gold in Kathmandu or dying of fever in the jungles of southern Nepal. Wongdu had been betrayed and shot to death, according to one source. Another argued that it was a twin brother who'd been killed. Wongdu still rode the range. Tibet would rise again

76

— whatever Tibet was. I still had barely an inkling of its history or people.

The Makalu 1977 gang arrived and it was back to the business of fun. In the two and a half years since Fritz's 1974 expedition, a team of Yugoslavs had polished off the south face. But the west face direct had never been touched. Indeed, like the backside of the moon, there were virtually no photos of this hidden face. We could still be pioneers. Our 1977 wild bunch took two weeks to march in to the radiant pyramid of Makalu. Right away things started to run amok. The day after reaching the mountain, our English poet-climber decided he's rather go whoring in Bangkok and promptly departed. Next day, the Silver Surfer took ill and it surfaced that, because his body was temple of the Lord, he had declined to be vaccinated. Before the whole group got infected with what appeared to be typhus, I had him evacuated and he never returned.

Over the next eight weeks, we laid seige, failed low, and trickled back to Kathmandu. It was a mean and trivial defeat made all the more so by our feuds and cowardice. I took the failure personally. The expedition had been mounted in a certain spirit, and I had failed that spirit. I had failed my dead.

The rest of the expedition went home, or so I thought. I stayed in Kathmandu, bent on salvaging something — my honor or romance, or narrative strand. Borrowing from Fritz's legend, I banished myself from home. With his panache as my example, I approached the Nepalese Army and offered to teach mountaineering to the King's soldiers. To my astonishment, they accepted. The colonel promised me a salary and a year-long visa. My bad fortune had reversed itself. Immediately I began plotting to work Everest into the military curriculum. Maybe I could even schedule a training session in Mustang and finish tracking down the CIA's Colorado connection.

Tales of the guerrilla movement were accumulating. I literally slept with them, notes and tapes piled on the bed in my room at the Kathmandu Guesthouse. Wongdu was becoming my jewel in the lotus.

Like Fritz, he had provoked realities so exotic they were almost fictional. Each man had placed himself in exile and then used it as a form of authorship, actively fashioning his own story. As a mountaineer, I was already keenly aware of the autobiographical possibilities on the edge of wilderness. Fritz and Wongdu were not the first to use the Himalaya as their own blank page. We all try to write ourselves upon our landscape. Fritz and I had tried it with Makalu. What made Wongdu so compelling was that he transcended his landscape and time. His tragedy spoke a strange resonance to the American experience.

In attempting to reconquer his country, Wongdu had faced the same odds as Geronimo once did in our own deserts and mountains. Indeed, he confronted essentially the same genocide that played out on the American frontier a hundred years ago. Tibet, like Texas or Wyoming, appealed to a population of "settlers" who poured into it in search of a fresh start and an abundance of natural resources.

Deng Xiaoping — the architect of Tibet's conquest — simply voiced a Han echo of old-fashioned Manifest Destiny. He had only two serious opponents: the Dalai Lama in exile and Wongdu in Mustang.

As I assembled Wongdu's portrait — there in Kathmandu, later in the exile-Tibetan community in Dharamsala and in a newspaper morgue in Delhi and in government archives in the U.S. — it was clear that he had been at least as creative and daring as Fritz. Stealth, horses, and a cache of guns made up his resistance to a realpolitik anchored by the People's Liberation Army, tanks, and Ilyushin jets. Wongdu's hazards dwarfed mine on the west face of Makalu. They undermined my playground attitude toward ascent. Here was risk in the service of history.

Wongdu had been among the first six Tibetan guerrilla leaders to be trained by the United States. He and five other volunteers were flown to a Pacific island, perhaps Guam or Saipan, where they spent four months learning how to read a map and work a radio. In the fall of 1957 they boarded a small black airplane piloted by an American. Individually equipped with a pistol, a machine gun, an old Japanese radio, $132 in Tibetan currency, and a bracelet containing poison to be swallowed upon capture, the guerrillas parachuted back into their homeland. Four of the six were destined for Lithang in southeastern Tibet. Of the four, only one was ever seen again — Wongdu.

Successive groups of guerrilla leaders were trained at Camp Hale in Colorado between 1959 and 1962. In an effort to cloak its covert training program in the heart of the Rockies, the CIA orchestrated a marvelous fiction, that an atomic "unit" was being tested near Leadville. Elk hunters, miners and the general citizenry of Colorado avoided Camp Hale.

My research continued to suffer one gaping hole. I had yet to locate a single guerrilla. Just the same, as I galloped around Kathmandu with a tape recorder and notepad in my jhola, it seemed only a matter of time. I was beginning to feel downright masterful in my self-made exile. On the Makalu climb, my judgements had crashed head-on against the huge west face. The Khampa story was like a balm, restoring my place in the world, however alternate that world was. Once again I had a purpose. Once again I had someone else's story to live.

Maybe I couldn't command an expedition, but through the authority of facts I could command an audience. In exile — even my artificial exile — I could belong somewhere. Mine was the sort of hubris Rudyard Kipling liked to inflict on his colonial dreamers and fools. Just when they think they've carved a foothold for themselves, the mountain vanishes.

My fall from grace arrived from out of nowhere. I was arrested for smuggling 7000 watches from Hong Kong, charged with ringleading an international racket, and drop-kicked into my first of three jails in Kathmandu. As it developed, upon returning from Makalu, the Silver Surfer had not gone home. He'd fallen in with the Indian Mafia and become a mule. Sensing danger on his last run, he asked me to take delivery of his "trekking gear" waiting at the airport customs office. Since I had to return the expedition's walkie-talkies through the customs office anyway, I agreed. It was not the last time my trust in the brotherhood of fellow climbers backfired, just the worst. I later learned he watched me get busted at the airport, then took a taxi all the way to Delhi, hopped on a plane to the United States, and put himself beyond extradition.

Every day, I was certain the mistake would be resolved and the jail doors would swing open. Nepalese officials candidly admitted my innocence to the American embassy. But unless the Silver Surfer returned to face the charges, they said there was little that could be done. The Nepalese have a phrase: Ke garne? What to do? Shit happens.

Through a friend, my anguished family hired a lawyer. After a month, Nepal's Supreme Court took my case as a test piece of law versus the monarchy's corruption, and promptly freed me. The ministry responsible for my arrest was rebuked. Unfortunately for me, the monarchy was not about to take the affront sitting down. In a bald expression of power, the King's customs men re-arrested me on the same charge, imposed a fine of $100,000, tacked on a five-year sentence for embarrassing them, and hauled me off to another jail.

Except for a raving tattooed Dutch schizophrenic who tore this clothes into one-inch shreds, talked to his anus, and ritually moussed his hair with and ate his own diarrhea, I was the sole Westerner in the Kingdom's prison system. Night and day I listened to men scream and moan, watched some die, witnessed cruelties large and small, sank into disgrace. I did push-ups and practiced my martial arts while guards spit on me from above. As the monsoon deepened and the rain turned dark green, I woke from dreams of Makalu to what seemed like some deep circle of hell.

Perhaps inevitably, it was the first prisoner on my first night who made the greatest impression on me. After 10 solid hours of interrogation, I got my handcuffs removed and was locked into a cell: bare concrete, bare light bulb, my own swarm of mosquitoes. There was no food or water, no bed, no blanket. Pooled in a dozen open rooms on the ground floor just below, several decades of raw sewage poisoned the night.

Part of me — the Huck Finn, the voluble Fritz — began to mentally catalogue my surroundings. In the morning, surely, they would release me and apologize and I could go on with my Nepalese lessons and my job with the army and my Everest and Mustang ambitions. What a war story this was going to make! My momentary enthusiasm flattened at a scream pitched so high it could have been the whine of mosquitoes. The scream quit. In its aftermath, all was silence and waiting. I stood stock-still.

Someone grunted at me, once, guttural. I peered through my bars across the hallway to the facing cell. The prisoner was a cheerful soul in his mid-50s or so. Tall and burly, he had wide Sioux cheekbones and a gold tooth that gleamed in the ebb and surge of Kathmandu's primitive electrical supply. A Tibetan, of course, much larger than any Sherpa. The greasy red prayer beads wrapped around his left wrist reached through my disbelief. I felt hope.

America? he asked. I said yes. He tossed across a blanket. Next came a straw mat and two small bananas. Too late, I saw that these were all he had. I said thanks in Nepali. If the man spoke Nepali, he didn't show it. He retreated to his far wall and sat down on the bare floor and closed his eyes.

In the morning I woke to his prayers. He made sure I received a cup of tea and an omelet made by one of the stick-thin guards, and paid for it out of his own pocket. When I had to go the bathroom, he instructed the guard to be quick about it. Downstairs I made the mistake of actually entering one of the dark rooms, not realizing the prisoners and guards simply perched on the door sill for their business. One step and I went skating through the inside of the human intestine, years of it. I fell and rolled and bellowed in the foul liquid. A half hour later, soaking wet from the faucet, I was returned to my cell, exhausted by the guard's insults. The Tibetan prisoner looked at me. Ke garne? Truly. We laughed.

My samaritan was an elderly Khampa. He drew a map to show where his home province of Kham lay in eastern Tibet. His geography — plus his age and his size and bravado — inspired me to take a not-so-wild guess. I said the word Mustang and named some of its towns. Teh, Tsarang, Kagbeni, Jomosom, Surkhang. My pronunciation earned a grin. I tried the title of the Khampa resistance movement. Chushi Gangdruk, which referred to the "Four Rivers, Six Ranges" of the ancient Tibetan province of Kham. The grin faded. I said the name Wongdu. He grew solemn and jutted his chin at me. My first Tibetan guerrilla.

On the third day, a Sherpa who spoke English landed in a nearby cell. Through him, I harvested more of the Khampa's story. The guerrilla's name was Lokpa. Around 1960, he had fled to Ladakh in northern India with his family. Eventually, refugees like him had numbered 85,000. The Indian government had funneled this diaspora far from the border into sparsely populated jungles, where many of the refugees died of disease. The casualties included Lokpa's wife and all of his children. He was matter of fact about the loss.

For the next year, Lokpa worked on a road gang. Then word came that the Chusi Gangdruk was reorganizing in Mustang. On foot with a few others, Lokpa made his way along the Kali Gandaki between the Annapurnas and Dhaulagiri. He took up arms and stayed for over a decade.

Later I would learn that some 2000 men like Lokpa had flocked to Mustang, drawn by the promise of American aid. They had waited for a year in caves and nomad tents. As time passed, the Red Cross reported starvation in the area.

Many of the guerrillas practiced shooting with sticks for rifles. Some survived by eating boiled yak leather from their boots. Some died for lack of food and shelter. Finally, in late 1961, two aircraft dropped enough guns for 475 men, medicine, food, and $1252 in local currency. Twenty-six Camp Hale-trained Tibetans parachuted in with the supplies, and 12 more Camp Hale graduates walked in from India.

Initially the guerrillas had every confidence that the reconquest of Tibet was at the tips of their trigger fingers. Until the Chinese fortified defenses along the Mustang border, guerrillas would ride horseback hundred of miles into Tibet, wreaking havoc on isolated garrisons and supply lines. At 35 cents per pound, the cost of trucking supplies thousands of miles into Tibet was an economic burden for China, and that was before the guerrilla sabotage. The raids were planned by CIA operatives who sometimes posed as Christian missionaries. Occasionally missions were led by agency contract mercenaries.

Then the operation was shut down. Ironically, the guerrillas provided information that helped doom their cause. Several mailbags of documents they had captured in Tibet were analyzed by China experts at the CIA's headquarters in Langley, Virginia. The documents clearly expressed China's determination to hang onto Tibet. The Chushi Gangdruk wasn't having the desired effect. The CIA began to lose interest in the Khampas, though it did continue to supply them into the late 1960s and to channel funds to them until 1971. But after Henry Kissinger's trip to Beijing in July of that year to explore detente with China, all American aid to the guerrillas ceased. The end was not far away.

I asked Lokpa about the CIA. He said firmly that he'd taken an oath not to talk about the Americans. Watching him, I could understand why some of the CIA's "special ops" officers involved in training the Khampas had become so attached to them. Instructed to encourage Tibetans' hope for reconquest, a number of the agents — some of whom were still chanting the Diamond Sutra and other Buddhist prayers years later — came to believe in the liberation of Tibet themselves. When the CIA pulled the plug on the operation, a number of agents furiously denounced Washington bureaucrats for selling them out.

I asked Lokpa about the final days in Mustang. I was thinking of what that British expatriate had told me: Dixie Cups. There was not a trace of bitterness as Lokpa supposed that the guerrillas had gotten too old. He had been on his way back to Tibet when Nepalese border guards apprehended him at the border and sent him here. What he had hoped to accomplish, I will never know. Possibly he was just closing a circle of his own. Born in Tibet, he may simply have wanted to die there. Lokpa's arrest held no great mystery. The key to understanding Nepalese justice is extortion. Lokpa was never booked or charged with any crime. He never broke any laws. Finally, after no eager relatives stepped forward to buy him out of our jail, the Nepalese shipped Lokpa away. He was sent north again and handed over to the Chinese themselves. (To this day, Nepalese soldiers and police regularly capture refugees coming out of Tibet, plunder them, rape the women, and often hand them back to the Chinese.)

I missed Lokpa's calm. It was hard to see men and women abused like wild animals from day to day. The torture victims lay piled in their cells like road kill. Every now and then the dead would be carried out through the blue mist at dawn. As the weeks stretched on, I found myself recalling the way Lokpa made himself a pivot in the center of the world. It helped tame the chaos.

With time I learned how to tell the criminals from the political prisoners. The political prisoners were the ones who got tortured the longest. My education to the world of man, as opposed to the world of mountains, had begun. The King's jails were filled with the people who would, 13 years later, lead the revolution that overthrew the monarchy in 1990. Shackled together, Naxalites — radical Maoists — hobbled about in pairs, some sporting ball-and-chain rigs riveted on by a blacksmith.

Besides the garden-variety thieves, whores, and murderers, there were a baker's dozen of lepers who had put one of their own out of his misery at the colony outside Kathmandu. As their faces froze into lions' masks and their toes and fingers eroded to nubbins, all 13 of them were serving the 20-year sentence that passes for a death penalty in Nepal. They were shy and utterly impoverished and kept to their own enclosure. I always recycled my Hindi cinema magazines to them.

A sense of vertigo took over. In my third jail, one Tibetan guerrilla became seven. In hunting for the story of the guerrilla movement, I had come to have its very leaders for my neighbors. Their melancholy attendant was a Tibetan disfigured by what looked like scars of severe smallpox. Like me, he slept on the clay floor by the cook fire. Unlike the others, he never smiled and never said a word.

Three years earlier, during the spring and early summer of 1974, the Nepalese government had promised the aging guerrillas that if they put down their weapons they could keep all the land they had settled and their homes in Mustang. Also their group would be provided $150,000 annually for three years for rehabilitation. The guerrillas hadn't budged. Why surrender? They had guns and high ground, and the Indian and Taiwanese governments were now feeding and supplying them. And Tibet remained occupied. The Chinese helpfully offered to cross Nepal's border and round up the Khampas for "development projects" in Tibet. It became a matter of national sovereignty for Nepal to take care of the problem.

In July 1974, as 10,000 Nepalese troops sealed off the southern approaches to Mustang, the Dalai Lama sent a 20-minute tape recording to Wongdu. Huddling with leaders of his scattered camps, Wongdu listened as the Dalai Lama greeted his Tibetan patriots. It was going to be difficult to put their

82

weapons down, the Dalai Lama said. But the guerrillas had to remember that the material world, apparently including the world of Tibet, is an illusion. Material possessions are secondary to determination. He asked his faithful to surrender their weapons. Dixie Cups. The CIA's term sobered me the first time I ever heard it, clean as a Zen koan. Sometimes I wonder if the Dalai Lama didn't use and throw away the Khampas, too.

The tape was played over loudspeakers at various camps up and down Mustang, and the leaders finally admitted that the end was at hand. There was deep sorrow and bitterness. One of the leaders killed himself. Several guerrillas slit their throats, jumped off cliffs, or drowned in the river. The Nepalese army entered the valley. Working north, camp by camp, they began disarming the warriors. Just as methodically they reneged on their bargain and began herding the guerrillas southward at gun point.

Outraged, the guerrillas spat on their leaders as they filed by. Lhoma Tsering, who had delivered the Dalai Lama's tape, and Wongdu's other lieutenants — Rara, Jurme, Tashi, Dhondup, Ngadrug, and Palga — were stripped of their guns and knives and either helicoptered or marched to captivity. These were the men I met in jail.

For three years the six leaders and their mute comrade had been imprisoned without trial by the Nepalese authorities. If and when they were brought to court, the charges would be "raising arms against the kingdom." Without these very men, however, the guerrillas would never have laid their guns down, and many Nepalese soldiers would probably have died. They would remain imprisoned for another three years when a letter-writing campaign in America helped force the issue.

The Khampas were purposeful, patient, vital. Before dawn they were always the first up and about, striding vigorously through the cool fog. Whenever one borrowed a book from me, even a dog-eared paperback it was always returned neatly clothed in a homemade dust jacket, the title in English and Tibetan. They gave me a 1957 Tibetan-English dictionary to help with the basics they were trying to teach me. It ignored Tibetan art, culture, and religion, focusing instead on such useful entries as the Tibetan for mortar, bazooka, drop zone, and parachute.

On hot, tedious September afternoons, Tashi would send his fighting kite up from the prison yard into the sky to challenge kiters from elsewhere in the city. He was a squat, powerful Khampa who sported a sky-blue Maryland Yachting Club cap given him, he claimed, by a CIA operative. He made his own kites by hand. Once a week, he lovingly braided the upper 50 feet of his string with powdered glass and glue. "Sharpening the knife," he called it. One tug of wind and the warrior turned deadly, ready to saw his opponents' kites free with an exuberant "la." It was Tashi's way of transcending jail.

One afternoon a fellow prisoner — a Hindi entrepreneur from Patan — invited me to tea. This particular jail occupied an ancient Rana palace made of mud bricks. What was left of the window sills bore beautiful wooden carvings. Their paint had long ago peeled away and the gods and goddesses were melting away, season by season. Time was king in here. Seated on a carpet while Mr. Patan's boy servant cooked ginger-and-milk chai over a fire on the floor, it was almost possible to envision myself transported to a medieval court — Marco Polo enjoying a brief detour.

We played a game of chess. Finally Mr. Patan got around to his proposition. Through the various connections he had come to understand that I might know a certain mountaineer who had stored some belongings at a friend's house. For a price, I could inherit those belongings. Which mountaineer, I asked. Mr. Patan didn't know the man's name, but he had arranged to have a piece of the cache brought for my inspection. My curiosity grew. We walked to the front gate where Mr. Patan's friend was waiting. He opened a burlap sack. There stood Fritz's silver chalice.

It was like a hand reaching out from the grave. Arnold and I had decided the silver chalice was long gone in Pakistan. Now it faced me through a net of chains and bars, a glittering, slightly dented holy grail. The man arranged a few other items on the ground: Fritz's orange helmet, a blue ski sweater, a single jumar. There was even more in storage, Mr. Patan assured me. He was encouraged by my shock. Two thousand dollars, he told me, a bargain.

Shaken, I retreated to my cell. This was a haunting, plain and simple. For months, even while sensing the fit was all wrong, I'd been trying to imagine what Fritz would do in my shoes. In trying to emulate Fritz, I allowed him to inhabit me. Increasingly, the possession had become apparent and costly. More and more lately I had wanted myself back again, even if it meant discarding his memory. Now suddenly, Fritz had found me. How the prisoners had connected him with me, I didn't know. But here it was again, the demand to carry forward another man's legend.

The resurrection could not have come at a worse time. For weeks my despair had been deepening. With each new jail, it seemed as if another sheath of Asian quicksand were closing overhead. I was losing all sense of purpose, all hope. The five-year sentence was coming true. Thoughts of suicide crept in, but not just any suicide. Not with Fritz in mind.

I began studying the west wall with an eye to escape. Under the nonchalant pretext of my morning and evening piss in the sewage trough running through the compound, I would stand facing the wall and analyze its parts. Twenty feet high, it crested, unfortunately, directly in front of the machine-gun post. It was the only wall on which the wild monkeys appeared every morning, however, I reasoned that the monkeys were proof of vegetation on the far side, something dense enough to cover my footrace into freedom.

I envisioned a moonless night with Kathmandu's electricity on the blink and a grappling hook made of bamboo. Never mind that disease and the food had whittled me down to bone and that I couldn't have done a single pull-up. In my dreams, I saw myself gaining the wall's crest with Ninja stealth. From there my fantasies got even wilder. In a moment of true inspiration, I decided to dodge all expectations and run north. I would escape via Makalu into Tibet. If Heinrich Harrer could do it, why not me? I asked a friend to buy some 8mm perlon rope from the trekking stores and smuggle it in to me in short pieces wrapped around the flask inside a thermos.

I wanted out or I wanted to die. Like Fritz's final escapade on Tirisch Mir, this was going to be a solo. I carefully kept my plans secret from the other prisoners. Even so I emitted clues. My new cellmates asked if I always wept in my sleep. By the end of the week, I no longer saw the machine gun nest and sentinels, only the wall. I was beginning to believe the rope was unnecessary. I was a climber, after all. It was only a wall. Before my strength degraded any more, it was crystal clear that I had to go for it. Despite the moon. Despite the guns.

My foolishness peaked one day at dawn. The fog was thick. I was alone. From atop the wall, a pair of monkeys were casing the joint. The machine-gun barrel was a vaporous twig, barely visible. As per my daily subterfuge, I hauled out the penis and started to piss. The wall was mesmerizing. There was a thin crack system in its cheap cement facade. Ten feet up the cement gave way to raw brick and an abundance of finger holds.

Suddenly there seemed no reason to wait. My decision had the feel of genius. No one would expect an escape during the day. For all I could tell, the machine-gun post was empty.

Still pissing, I edged closer to the forbidden zone. The gun barrel didn't move. I was fixed on the crack, in my mind already halfway to the summit. When suddenly, from behind, I was lofted into the air. Two big arms wrapped around me and squeezed hard. My feet sailed high.

Whoever the villain was shook me like a rag doll. Urine flew right and left, soaking us both. I fought. He shook me some more. Then I got my feet under me again and twisted loose and whirled around.

Two-hundred and twenty pounds of Khampa stood there roaring with laughter. It was Rara. The bastard. He had purposely spoiled my moment. Overhead the gun barrel had shifted from a line to a point. It was pointed directly at me. The guard had been tracking me all along.

I wanted to hit Rara. Instead, dripping urine, I began to laugh. I cried. I surrendered.

The Khampas had been watching over me. They had diagnosed my self-absorption. Rara had just rescued me from melodrama. Possibly to distract me, possibly to complete a different legend, they told me the rest of the story of Wongdu's death.

During the surrender in July 1974, Wongdu had waited at the northernmost tip of the Mustang valley. Possibly he anticipated the treachery. By the time word arrived of the betrayal, Wongdu knew it was too late to fight back. Instead, he and 35 men immediately mounted horses and climbed out of the stark valley, making their way into Tibet over two high passes. For several years, India had been recruiting Tibetan guerrillas for their Border Security Forces, and Wongdu knew that if he could reach India, his little band would be safe. For the next four weeks, India was his goal.

Back and forth over the high rugged watershed that forms the Tibet-Nepal border, Wongdu and followers rode and walked their horses. Twice the guerrillas had to retreat into Nepal to escape Chinese soldiers who were dogging their flight, but because the Nepalese terrain was too rough for their horses, they crossed back into Tibet each time. At one point, the Nepalese air-dropped soldiers to ambush Wongdu, but the guerrillas simply vanished. Traveling day and night, the group of Tibetans sped for the Indian border. Half a day short of the mountainous juncture of Tibet, Nepal, and India, looms Tinker, a 17,800-foot pass. In 1968 nearly 500 bedraggled refugees froze to death on this pass during a catastrophic mass escape from Tibet. It was in this haunted region that Wongdu sought to slip through the gauntlet of Chinese and Nepalese troops.

In the early afternoon of August 12, the party found itself hemmed in from the north by Chinese troops. Six men were selected to escort Wongdu over Tinker to the Nepal side while the rest stayed behind to fight the Chinese. Scant kilometers short of India, Wongdu and his tiny escort galloped straight into what was, this time, a well-prepared and massive ambush. Of his escort, four were killed on the spot, one escaped to warn his comrades, and was badly wounded and captured. He watched as Wongdu was riddled with bullets.

They pointed at the man with smallpox scars. Ask him, they said. That was the first I realized this was the survivor who watched Wongdu die. His scars were shrapnel wounds. He and I were the same thing, witnesses to men who had died in service to their own legends. The mute and I had survived more than their company. We had survived their obsessions, too. I put away my escape plans. The theater of suicide, the romance of soloing, were no longer options.

My release came abruptly. At the end of three months, having let Nepal's law — and lawlessness — play out, the American Embassy finally stepped in on my behalf. I was given barely one minute to collect my possessions, then ejected from the prison. Next morning I was to be deported from the kingdom, declared persona non grata. In a sense it was the exile I'd pretended in the first place. It was 3:55 p.m. That gave me only a few hours to finish what needed doing.

86

Against all advice, I returned to the jail and summoned Mr. Patan. Fifty dollars, I told him, take it or leave it. We settled on sixty-seven. He gave me his friend's address and I took a taxi out into the countryside. Fritz's effects lay piled in a mud-brick hut, rotting away.

Ravaged by the climate, it was a typical mountaineer's cache. Mildewed tents, soggy ropes, rusted pitons. In the corner stood a locked duffel stenciled with "Makalu International — 74." The sun was sinking fast. I slit the red cordura open with a knife.

Inside was a blue ski sweater and an orange climbing helmet. No journal, no maps, no clues. I rooted among worthless clothing and torn paperbacks. By handing the silver chalice to Fritz's widow, I was still hoping with one glorious relic to confirm the poetics of obsession. But the thieves had tricked me. The grail was gone, of course.

A year later, a Canadian expedition found a crumpled mummy on Tirisch Mir. An avalanche had rendered it to rags and bone. Another year passed before I saw a photo. It could have been anybody. A physician suggested that if I could find the body and bring back the jawbone or some fingers, simple forensics could determine if this was Fritz.

In all likelihood it was, though I never went. Also, I had learned everything I needed to from Fritz, dead or alive. Time passed. Apparently the glacier dragged its escapee back into the depths. The body has never been seen since. Ke garne?

The mountains are our underworld. If you doubt that, try the top of a Tibetan pass sometime. Lung ta — wind horses printed on slips of paper or cotton flags — gallop their prayers into eternity. Animal skulls, carved and painted, whistle into the void. Up there, every one of us is an exile only partway to somewhere, but with this difference between us: the living may not stay; the dead may not pass. The summits are our abyss.

Up there, one bears witness to the other, the summit to the abyss, what is half empty to what is half full. Just so we bear witness to our ghosts and they to us. In the end we are the measure of our desire. How full we fill the emptiness, that is our legend. How empty the legends are, that is the wind.

First published in Climbing *No. 153, 1995.*

The Lotus Eaters
Bittersweet adventures in the promised land

By Jeff Jackson

On the tenth day they made the land of the Lotus Eaters and put in there. The inhabitants met them with kindness and gave them their flower food to eat, but those who tasted it lost their longing for home. They wanted to dwell in the Lotus Land, and let the memory of all that had been fade from their minds. They wept, so great was their desire to stay, tasting forever the honey sweet flowers.

— Adventures of Odysseus,
by Edith Hamilton

The perfectly vertical cracks that swept up the buttress of Lotus Flower Tower in *Fifty Classic Climbs* inflamed my adolescent imagination, and inspired more fantasy than any Victoria's Secret catalog. The Cirque of the Unclimbables — the name alone issued a challenge.

As I grew older my infatuation with the region continued to grow. I discovered that the Unclimbables weren't really unclimbable, only unreachable in Canada's distant Northwest Territories — the cost in travel and gear far outstripped my paltry income. Nevertheless, the Unclimbables lingered in the backwaters of my consciousness. I read with great interest every story written about climbing in the region, from Layton Kor's description of the first ascent (with Royal Robbins, Jim McCarthy, and Dick McCracken) of the southeast face of Mount Proboscis in 1963, to Paul Piana's article on the second, and first free ascent, of the same face in 1992.

The authors used more superlatives than a new-age doctor describing a client's aura. Pristine fairy meadows. Clean, knob-covered rock. An unspoiled, alpine Yosemite. Was the Cirque the climbers' Lotus Land and the perfect granite the meat of the Lotus?

On June 13, 1994, Kurt Smith, Scott Cosgrove, and Greg Epperson were arrested on top of El Capitan in Yosemite Valley for using a power drill to place bolts. A couple weeks later, Kurt, with whom I had free climbed a new route on El Toro, a 2000-foot spire in Potrero Chico, Mexico, the previous winter, called — Epperson had decided to skip their planned expedition to free climb a new route on Mount Proboscis.

"Why's Eppi skipping out on the trip?" I asked.

"Personality conflict," Kurt said. "I have a ticket waiting for a taker. You in?"

"Are you kidding?"

On July 11, after a frenzy of borrowing money and packing gear, I boarded a plane in Austin and flew to Denver to meet Kurt. From Denver we flew to Seattle. From Seattle to Vancouver. In Vancouver I met Scott Cosgrove, the third member of our team.

From Vancouver, we flew north, jouncing over jagged black mountaintops and into the Yukon. We hopped from Prince George, to Dease Lake, to Terrace, to Smithers, to Watson Lake, where we provisioned ourselves with fresh fruit and vegetables. We also met our driver for the next leg, a blond kid built for hockey. A fresh scar traced a crescent around his right eye.

"Everybody calls me Stitch," he explained. "My 30.06 bucked and the scope tried to spoon out my eyeball."

We loaded the double-cab Chevy pickup and Stitch drove a dirt road for three hours to Finlayson Lake, where we were met by Warren LaFave, the owner/operator of the Inconnu Lodge and Kluane Airways. Warren, cheery, short, a little bald, threw our monstrous haulbags into the floatplane like he was hefting bags of leaves.

Soon we were flying over woodlands spotted with round, green ponds and lakes. One lake held a moose.

"Once a guest shot a moose in a bog like that," Stitch's voice crackled over my headset and made me jump. "We had to dress him out in the mud. That was a real bitch of a job, ay Warren?"

"It was a real bitcher," Warren agreed, "but we brought home 1100 pounds of meat."

"Eleven-hundred pounds?" Kurt asked.

"About the same as your gear weighs, boys. One dressed out moose."

The area's notoriously bad weather, combined with the slow pace of a huge free-climbing project, prompted us to plan for a five-week trip into the bush. Our extravagant comforts included two and a half cases of malt liquor and Outback Oven scones and pizzas. As we poached ourselves in the Inconnu's hot tub, Kurt and Cos filled me in on the particulars of the trip.

"The southeast face of Mount Proboscis," Kurt intoned. "That's the deal, man."

"Never come this far and spend this much money to repeat a route," Cos declared. "That's what Bridwell told me."

"We're looking for the killer crack line," Kurt said.

"Crack line?" I asked with building dread.

"No bolting," Cos said.

"High adventures," Kurt said, his hat pulled low over his eyes. "Free climbing in the middle of Out There, Canada, man."

"Sketchy pro."

"Bad weather."

"No radio contact."

"No way out," Kurt glanced at me from under the rim of his cap.

My spine jellied. "I can't wait."

Our remaining luggage was delayed in Vancouver. We missed the helicopter out to the Cirque, and, back in the lodge's bar, Kurt was hopping mad.

"We're screwed!" he screamed. He looked like he was going to kick a hole in the wall.

I glanced at Warren. He stood beside the billiard table, bemused, watching Kurt's tantrum.

"We'll be happy to do some work around the lodge in the meantime," I said.

"Oh, don't worry," Warren said. "I'll work you."

The next day, we dug a ditch. The day after, Cos and I built a dock on Finlayson Lake with Stitch, while Kurt drove to Watson Lake to fetch our luggage. Warren fogged the whole work area with a mosquito-repelling smoke.

"That ought to hold 'em," he said. Stitch looked skeptical and, sure enough, minutes after Warren lifted off the lake, I felt the first bloodsucker settle onto my forehead.

The next day, we loaded dirt onto a flatbed cart and transported it from the airstrip to the pasture beside the lodge. On one trip down from the airstrip, as I practiced surfing the wobbly rail of the cart, Cos described his recent injury: Salt Lake City. Four spotters. A dislocated ankle. But that's not all.

Cal, Cos's girlfriend, had volunteered to drive him home to Joshua Tree while he rode in the back of the truck and elevated his injured foot.

A wet road. A sharp curve. The truck spins, then tumbles. Cos regains consciousness 400 feet from the demolished truck and realizes that Cal must be dead. The pain in the casted leg creeps over his brain like red ants. His spine's a fiery coil.

Amazingly, Cal is all right, but Cos has shattered his heel and broken his back. He waits three and a half hours for painkillers. The doctors decide to amputate the hideously swollen foot, but Cos pleads for another day and the swelling subsides. A famous Bay area surgeon tells Cos to forget about climbing again.

Now, two years later, Cos has authored a 5.14a sport climb in Joshua Tree. This spring he and Kurt freed most of the *Muir Wall* on El Cap.

At six o'clock the next morning, under the perpetual thin sun of the Arctic summer, we climbed into the rented chopper and took off for Lotus Land. The blades whirred overhead like giant beaters and we rose straight over the Inconnu's freshly trimmed lawns. I could see Warren in the Beaver taxiing to the middle of McEvoy Lake with our moose-load of gear. Quite suddenly, we burst over the foothills surrounding the lodge and swooped into a precipitous valley bordered by black cliffs. The walls were cut by thin couloirs packed with ice. A buckled glacier tumbled down the flank of a mountain to the west like a river gone inert.

Seventy-five miles of wild country later, we stood on the only flat boulder in miles of choppy talus, surrounded by our baggage. We watched the helicopter duck around the corner of Eschelon Spire, and it was gone.

A noisy melt-water stream zagged through the boulders to the east. To the south, looking out of the Proboscis cirque, we were greeted by another range of granite spires and walls. A pyramid peak dominated the western skyline. Red scree spilled down Proboscis' west buttress like iron tailings spit from a mine. The scree made up the west bank of a small lake about a mile below our camp. Thick green moss covered the tops of the boulders pitched pell-mell around us. There was not a tree in sight.

A spit of snow extended from our camp boulder to a cook cave. Inside we found a two-burner Coleman stove and 600 feet of static cord left by the Skinner expedition. Someone else had drilled holes into the right wall of the cave and hammered tent stakes into them. On the left wall, under the overhanging eave, we noticed two bolts with gold hangers.

"Spaniards," Cos said, shaking his head like a judge.

To the south, the 2000-foot face of Mount Proboscis jumped out of the talus and dominated the view. The sun was out, shining off the gold and white granite. Flakes and knobs revealed themselves as a zillion shadows dappling the rock.

"There it is!" Cos yelled. He was studying the wall through the binoculars. "There's the line!" He reminded me of a sailor sighting a whale.

Just right of *The Great Canadian Knife* (Todd Skinner, Paul Piana, and Galen Rowell's route), a dihedral system ran for 300 feet and ended at a small, frowning ledge. From there, a blank pitch led to a system of hanging flakes, which terminated at another crack. Thin and exposed, situated on an overhanging shield of rock, this crack appeared to run continuously up the length of the wall.

The sky started sputtering rain at 6 a.m. We shouldered our packs and headed up the talus to the base of the wall. As usual, Kurt tied in first and shouldered the rack. I kicked up the 30-foot snow tongue that licked up the wall, and cleared a little ledge for the belay.

Kurt climbed fast, plucking tufts of moss from the dihedral and plugging Friends into knobby pods. Two hours later, he was close to the top of the first pitch. But the faster he climbed, the harder it rained, and soon the dihedral was running water like a sluice. Kurt stood up on his last placement and reached high to drill the anchor. Suddenly he was bouncing down the wall, gear jangling. The force of the rushing water had nudged his last two placements out of the crack.

It rained off and on for the next 10 days. We waited each morning for a break, then charged the crag to advance our lines. Kurt freed the first pitch the second day and Cos took the rack and aided the second pitch. I aided the third on day three, climbing out of the dihedral and onto the smooth, steep slab above. The fourth day, Cos and I traded pitches and free-climbed them, clipping the pre-placed gear. We then pulled the hardware and fixed Skinner's old static cord at our high point.

Back at camp, things were not going well. Despite our careful planning, supplies ran short. Rain mucked the beautiful gear. The Arctic temperature discouraged bathing, and soon the inside of my sleeping bag was glazed with a queer, invisible funk. Wet socks and boots played havoc with our feet and Kurt developed a mysterious blue hole in the webbing between his fourth and little toe. The anemic sun burned 24 hours a day and disrupted our sleep cycle. Rain beat our tent flies like tom-toms. Cos and I took pain pills recreationally.

A haze of ill will hovered over the camp like a cloud of mosquitoes. Beer was bug juice and the beer ran out quick. Kurt retired to a corner of the cook cave and turned up his Walkman. Cos assumed a sullen and preoccupied distance, burying himself in critical assessments of the sad state of American rock climbing. Despite a vow at the beginning of the trip not to discuss the El Cap bust, the topic surfaced repeatedly, and visibly drained both Kurt and Cos.

"We just wanted to climb the thing in the best style possible," Cos said again and again.

As much as we talked about it, I never did understand Cos' definition of style. To me, climbing was a spiritual pursuit. Rules were only applicable when they enhanced the experience.

Cos had learned to climb in Yosemite and Joshua Tree, bastions of traditional climbing. His stories of fistfights and chopped routes and broken friendships left me speechless.

"Why don't you leave the area?" I asked him.

"Because I still value the old style," he said. "I'm old school to the bone."

We played hundreds of dice games and argued for hours about nothing.

Cos shakes the dice and rolls them across the pan.

Kurt whispers, "Brick."

"Stop hexing me," Cos says.

"I'm not hexing you."

"What goes around, comes around," I say.

"Are you threatening me?" Kurt asks.

"I'm just saying that you better watch your back if you're going to start hexing this early in the game."

"Screw you both, then," Kurt says.

"Easy there, big fella," Cos says.

Kurt throws the dice and they rattle around. Cos whispers, "Brick." The dice comes up craps.

"See," I said. "That's exactly what I'm talking about — Karma."

Kurt reaches out with his foot and knocks over my tea. Cos cackles like a hyena, holding his balaclava over his mouth. I scoop up a handful of wet snow and throw it in his face.

"Go ahead, Peanut" I say. "Laugh it up."

The mood turns sullen.

"Anybody want to go bouldering?" I ask.

Cos looks at me like I've suddenly changed shapes. Surprise and fear register on his face. "Bouldering?" he asks.

"Yes," I say, "It's a type of climbing you can do without ropes."

"We're in the middle of nowhere," Cos says. "Rescue is impossible. What happens if you break an ankle?"

"How about you?" I ask Kurt.

"I'd rather pack my butthole with snow and stand on my head."

"I'll take that as a no."

The fourth pitch was a doozy. The cracks ran out and a smooth face swept up the wall for a hundred feet before any features reappeared. The rain turned to pelting snow as Kurt tied in and began the slow process of stancing and hooking to get the free-climbing bolts in.

"This is fun," he shouted.

Cos and I huddled on the portaledge, trying to keep the blowing snow out of our hoods.

"I can see the hook placements by watching where the snow builds," Kurt said. The next day he redpointed the pitch at .12c.

We continued our arguments in camp. I wanted to climb the .12c pitch before moving on. In fact, I wanted to climb every pitch on the wall, even if I had to toprope them. To me, each person not freeing every pitch was dissatisfying. Cos and Kurt, however, were convinced that we had to move quickly, and, watching the rain pouring off the lip of the cook cave, I finally conceded.

Back on the wall, I belayed Cos in pitch five, the Hanging Corners. He diced up the slick granite grooves on thin hooks and copperheads, reaching high to drill bolts above the underclings. The rain stopped and the wind picked up, blowing the clouds ragged. Cos whistled Zipadee Doo Da as he tested the sketchy aid gear. His rain jacket billowed up behind him like a superhero's cape and I thought, look, it's Doc Copperhead, master of aid.

In the cook cave, Cos tried to prep me for the next pitch, a slick, black waterstreak that gushed out of a groove at the base of the 700-foot crack. We'd nicknamed the pitch Extra Old Jingus, to honor the mink-bait stench that seeped from the Malt Liquor empties strewn around camp.

"It looks bad," he said. "Rotten as a tooth soaked in Coca Cola. Lots of heads. Lots of loose nailing. Maybe I should take it for you?"

"I'll give her a go," I said weakly.

Pitch six, the Extra Old Jingus, went free at a wet but moderate 5.11c. The black rock yielded knobs and incuts. I splashed my way to the small roof, stuck my feet in the veritable brook and clipped the anchors. Above, the crack sliced straight up through sunny granite.

Once we gained the crack the weather cleared and we continued marching toward the ledge; aid, free climbing the aid pitches, and fixing lines. Kurt's foot was ailing him, so Doc Copperhead valiantly took the sharp end and aided the next pitch, cocking units between knobs for protection.

That night at dinner, Kurt again showed off the blue sump between his toes. The right side of his foot looked like a bruised banana. When he squeezed it, pus flowed like lava from a volcano.

"Please," I said, trying not to gag, "save some for our oatmeal tomorrow."

Kurt freed his pitch the next day, moaning about blocked jams and looking atypically shaky on 5.12b.

Cracks have never been my forte. My memories of Yosemite are replete with pain. The fist cracks and offwidth on the Stovelegs left me feeling wormy and soft in the middle. The Valley finger cracks torqued and bruised my every digit. The protection always seemed shaky. I am a sport climber, a limestone guy, a chicken.

Cos and Kurt, on the other hand, had lived in Yosemite for years, repeating all the hard cracks and honing their technique. They recalled my nightmare climbs wistfully, as if a rope's length of 5.11 fist was a cucumber sandwich party. I knew better. That's why I ignored Cos when he pronounced pitch eight a "hike."

I pulled on my shoes and surveyed the line. Twenty feet up, a five-foot roof split the wall. Ten feet higher, another roof cut off my view. I belched loudly. "Oh, boy," I thought.

"I don't see a no-hands stance up there," said Cos, who hung beside me from jumars to photograph my attempt.

"So what?"

"It's not a free climb unless every belay is at a no-hands."

I let it slide, preferring to concentrate on the immediate thrashing.

"Did you marry Cristina because she was young," Cos asked, "or because you really loved her?"

"What?" I asked, but Cos just giggled wildly.

Like an undisciplined sailor about to be keelhauled, I stepped off the ledge and locked my fingers in the first jams. Using a combination of tips jamming and foot scums, I lurched up to the wide section below the roof and rested off a fist jam. A tentative stab at the lip landed a tips jam. My fingers scurried around, raking out pebbles and dirt. Although we aided every pitch and clipped in-situ protection for our free-climbing attempts, speed was the important consideration, and so I had neglected to brush this pitch. Ring, middle, and pointer fingers all had to go at the sharp lock but nobody liked it. Fading. The brain impelling the workhorse pointer finger to grip the sharpie, and my feet scrambled up to the lip of the roof. They stuck on two white knobs, the size and shape of egg ends.

I established a rhythm, wriggling my tips into dusty slots and paddling my feet up on sloping knobs. Soon, however, the sloppy footwork began to tax my forearms like a democratic congress.

Cos leaned over, clicking pictures.

"Any good edges up there?" I asked, red-faced but nonchalant.

"Not anything I'd call good," he answered, "but when you look up, it makes a really nice picture."

On a sudden wild hair, I struck out left onto the featured face, leaving behind the hateful crack. Ten, then 20 feet later, I arrived at a stance but couldn't reach the fixed wire Stopper to my right. Well below, the last brass nut glinted, daring me to fall. A thin, balancey shuffle got me the nut and a newly confirmed belief that one should never leave the crack.

A few easy moves. An off-balance stance. A request for Beta.

"Nothing at all to recommend," Cos said, disgusted and glaring at me with those cold, blue eyes. "Thin jamming," he said.

One tip buried in the flare, laying off my heel, I high-stepped and stabbed my ring finger into the final, too-small slot. The hopeless feet held. I grabbed a thin black layback and rocked onto the stance. "You're in," Cos said. "Good job. Clip the anchor."

I leaned in and touched my face to the rock and dropped both hands.

Dinner time, Cos tended the stove. Kurt soaked his toe in a Betadine solution. I sat on a moss hummock just outside the cave, scanning the endless mountains to the south.

"I wonder what Robbins thought of this place?" Cos said.

"Who cares?"

"I do," Cos said. "Those guys are my heroes."

"Those guys," I said, "and the armchair mountaineers that get pumped lifting a tallboy, are the ones that think you and Kurt raped El Cap."

"They just don't understand what we were doing," Cos said.

"Of course they don't," I said. "But 30 years ago, they were banging holes all over the same rock, leaving those scars that you and Kurt used for fingerlocks."

"They were pushing the edge," Cos said. "I respect that."

"Screw 'em," Kurt said, breaking a day-long silence.

The next pitches went without a hitch at 5.12, 5.11, 5.12- and 5.10. We rapped to the ground, fixing the 13 pitches to the ledge.

A light mist moved in and glazed the wall as we rappelled, and I remarked again on the stone's shiny, riverbed quality. Polished by thousands of rainy seasons, the rock glistened like two acres of jewels. I paused at the top of pitch 11 and looked down the singular crack, watching the water collect in the trough and run white, like a rapids, down the length of the headwall. It gushed out over old Jingus pitch in a fan.

I looked at the black sky to the south, and a clap of thunder boomed. Directly over the lake, a mile away, a thick shaft of green light rose straight into the clouds. It was rainbow light — transparent and glowing, beautiful but eerie. It cut across my vision like an apparition. The geometry shifted slightly, rippling like a sheet in the wind. The thunder boomed again, and I scooted down the lines.

"Aurora borealis," Cos pronounced later. "Northern lights."

We rested for three days, bouldering in the talus and following the progress of a family of mountain goats as they climbed Eschelon Spire. The baby goat had clip-clopped right through our camp one night at dinner, followed closely by his shaggy mom. He climbed the first hump wildly, jumping and kicking on the flat spots. When he tired 10 minutes into the climb, he dropped onto a moss patch and fell asleep. Mom clomped up a few minutes later and lay down, her flanks touching his. They slept for 10 minutes, then the baby woke and suckled. He leapt up and took off like a shot, uphill, taking a circuitous route toward the summit.

On August 5, 1994, 19 days after we started, Cos, Kurt and I blitzed the last seven pitches and became the fourth party to climb the southeast face of Mount Proboscis. Our route, *Yukon Tears,* established the third independent line and the second free climb. Four pitches of roped climbing had taken us from the ledge to the summit ridge, a razor-sharp tightrope walk interrupted periodically with fifth-class boulder problems. The southern exposure consisted of a 2000-foot drop to the talus. The northern exposure presented us with another sobering drop to a lake-sized glacier. Hundreds of spires and walls stuck up from the ice and once again I felt privileged to be there.

On the summit we found a small pile of stacked stones. In the middle of the pile Kurt uncovered an Ilex film cannister, circa 1960. Inside the canister, perfectly preserved in the refrigerated Arctic environment, we found Kor, Robbins, McCracken, and McCarthy's summit register. "FA Southeast Face Mount Proboscis," it said. "1963." It listed their names and the grade of the route, 5.8 A4. Under "Gear" it said, "Hundreds of pins."

We descended and began the long wait for the helicopter to arrive. For the next two weeks I felt like an exile. The Cirque was no Lotus Land; the climbs here no flower food. No land, however majestic and unspoiled, can replace good fellowship or provide internal harmony. After two giant free-climbing projects, my companions were sour and moody. They were bitter and introspective after the arrest on El Capitan. Climbing, for them, had changed forever. We avoided each other, and I suffered from the intense solitude.

The day before the chopper arrived, we all decided to head to the lower lake and go bouldering. We encouraged Kurt as he flashed Cos' V7, an overhanging crimp problem on golden granite.

Kurt stepped onto the grassy landing. He turned to look at the Southeast Face, rearing up like a great gate of stone. "I love this place," he said, and Cos and I nodded. The melt-water coursed along to our right, hurrying toward the unseen river. My mind stilled. For one moment the little worm that drove me to strive and argue, to travel and explore and bolt and rant and rave, to climb new routes, that little worm lay quiet, and once again, like Odysseus in the land of the Lotus Eaters, my thoughts turned toward home.

First published in Climbing *No. 157, 1995.*

Fast Train

Alison Hargreaves climbed Everest, unsupported and without oxygen. Two months later, she summitted on K2, but died with six others in a fast-moving storm, leaving behind a family and many questions.

By Alison Osius

Alison Hargreaves was pressed for time. The weekend we spoke last fall, she was less than three weeks home from an Everest attempt. On Friday, her book had come out, and she, an English climber living in Scotland, signed copies and did interviews in Edinburgh. Saturday she spoke at a mountain-literature festival in Leeds, England. She granted me interviews on Sunday and Monday, and Monday evening sorted photos. Tuesday she had a lecture at the Alpine Club in London, and an interview with a big London newspaper. On Wednesday were a book signing, a TV show, a magazine interview, and three radio interviews. Thursday was a sponsor meeting at Sprayway, Friday a book signing in Manchester.

But after Hargreaves climbed Everest (29,028 feet) May 13, unsupported and without oxygen, she *really* took off.

I reached her via an overseas phone call in early June, having made an appointment through her p.r. team, headed by Cally Fleming and Hargreaves' husband, Jim Ballard. Hargreaves was ensconced at the Nevis Range ski-area compound, doing interviews. How many? "Hundreds," said Fleming.

I had five minutes with Alison, who was home for two weeks before leaving for K2. Except for a day trip to Italy to see a sponsor, and one "fantastic" day spent with her two children at the beach, every day had been "chock-a-block" with interviews, she said.

In mid-August, the climbing world was stunned by news of Hargreaves' death on K2 (28,251 feet), second-highest mountain in the world, which according to one summitter, Greg Child, has only been climbed 124 times and has taken 45 lives (it is attempted something like 100 times annually, Everest 1000).

At the news I thought again and again of a few images and exchanges. One was how Hargreaves had told me that K2 was to be "just" by the mountain's *Abruzzi Ridge,* and non-solo this time. "I'm going to enjoy myself," she said. She'd been invited to join an American team there.

Another was her explanation at the literature festival of how she dealt with the risk inherent in her endeavors. When she undertook a climb, she said, she was extremely well-prepared, physically as well as in her knowledge of things like weather and the descent route. "I'm not bloody foolhardy," she said firmly. "I've got a hell of a lot to live for. I don't think I'm reckless. I think I'm conservative."

The image that kept me awake was from her book, *A Hard Day's Summer,* and a May newspaper interview, of how Ballard never saw her off with the children prior to a climb. She would slip away because Kate, 4, would weep seeing her mother leave.

We'll never know all the factors that made up the layers of Hargreaves' decisions to continue on K2. A lot of very big and very mundane bits of information are gone forever when a person disappears.

Even *driven* alpinists said that Alison Hargreaves, who died at 34, was driven. She was meticulous and careful, but alpinism is dangerous. As she built achievement upon impressive achievement, she was cashing in a lot of chips.

But I have a certain vivid memory of the fresh joy in her voice as she described for the nth time what it was like for her on Everest. She laughed as she spoke. "It was *amazing,*" she said with fervor. "That's all I can say. I've never actually felt that emotional about anything ever before." At the summit, she wept. "So many tears, it was unbelievable. Yeah, it really was amazing ... just ludicrous." She didn't really know why she was so overcome. "It was a combination of relief and happiness all rolled up into one. It was really funny, really funny."

After coming off the mountain, she went with friends to the Rum Doodle restaurant in Kathmandu, where Everest summitters customarily sign in. Describing it, she again laughed a little. "I went with some guys to go and sign my name, the last evening in Kathmandu, and I just got so emotional, so overwhelmed, I just could not sign my name. It was really weird. It was such a powerful thing."

Hargreaves first came to the fore of climbers' consciousness with a string of solos in the Alps in the spring and summer of 1993, including the North Face of The Matterhorn and the Grande Jorasses via both *The Shroud* and, in November, the much harder *Croz Spur.* Before that she'd piqued interest with her five-and-a-half-months-pregnant ascent of the North Face of the Eiger in 1988. Later came her wonderfully in-control ascent of Everest. After K2, she hoped to do Kangchenjunga, climbing the world's three highest

100

mountains, without oxygen, in a calendar year — a momentous triad.

Then came the news of what had happened on K2 — the deaths on Sunday, August 13, of Hargreaves; Rob Slater, 35, of Boulder; Jeff Lakes, 33, of Calgary; Bruce Grant, 31, of New Zealand; and Javier Escartin, 46, Lorenzo Ortiz Monson, 24, and Javier Olivar, 39, of Spain. In America, the news was almost immediately on-line Wednesday morning and passing around a huge outdoor-industry trade show in Reno.

At the same time, in a disturbing irony, Jim Ballard was calling *Climbing* magazine's office. He'd heard rumors that Alison had been killed and was trying to find out if they were true. He spoke quietly so as not to be heard by the children, yahooing in the background.

The climbers were probably blasted off the mountain by the increasing winds that reached full intensity lower on the mountain by 7:30 p.m., possibly hitting the top by then or working upward to hit at about 8 p.m. Grant and Ortiz Monson radioed from the summit at 6:30 p.m., Hargreaves and Olivar at 6:45 p.m. Slater and Escartin were on their way up and should reach the top soon, but the first four planned to descend immediately before the bad weather hit them. They were told to call again when they reached the Traverse (where the ropes started) above the route's Bottleneck Gully, but that call never came. The next morning a body thought to be Alison's was seen at 7400 meters, having either fallen or, more likely, been blown off, some thousand meters. None of the climbers was using oxygen; on K2, almost no one does.

Jeff Lakes nearly survived. He had turned back from his summit bid five hours earlier at about 1:30 p.m. on Sunday and reached Camp IV, only to be avalanched there in his tent. He huddled there that night, and the next morning tried to dig his equipment out, staying — in weather that was clear and even hot — until about 11 a.m. He struggled on to Camp III but reported on the radio that it was destroyed by serac fall. Though he had no crampons, axe, harness, or descender, he used his penknife to cut a piece of fixed rope to tie from his waist to the line, then came 2000 feet down the Black Pyramid rock band to Camp II, taking until 1:30 a.m. Tuesday, 36 hours altogether. He was now in the hands of friends, dehydrated and exhausted, but not frostbitten. He died in the night.

Two Spaniards, Jose Pepe Garces, 39, and Lorenzo Ortas, 42, who had stopped at their Camp IV, 150 meters higher on the Shoulder, at 7950 meters, barely survived. According to Ed Douglas of *Climber* magazine (UK), Garces' tent blew off the mountain, with Ortas grasping at it as Garces cut his way out of the back. Both waited in Ortas' tent until that, too, blew away, then huddled in the snow until dawn.

This K2 tragedy was uncannily like that of 1986, when five climbers, including Julie Tullis, the first and only other British woman to summit on K2, died in storm on the descent. Three other women have reached the top of the mountain: Liliane

Barrard, who also died coming down, and Chantal Mauduit, both of France, and the Polish climber Wanda Rutkiewicz, who was later killed on Kangchenjunga. [Since publication of this article, Mauduit also died in the Himalaya.]

A few days before the recent calamity, the rest of Hargreaves and Slater's team had gone home, conceding to abysmal weather, and Alison had nearly gone with them, but at the last minute decided to give the mountain one more try. She and Slater joined with the New Zealand team on the mountain.

Peter Hillary (son of Sir Edmund), 40, was quoted in the London *Independent* saying that the summit party was "blinkered by the summit" and used poor judgment. He had turned back on K2 at noon because, he said, he saw storm fronts approaching from the north and south. The others strove upward for another six hours.

Said Hillary, who stopped at the Spanish team's Camp IV, "I saw Alison and she simply said, 'I'm going up.' Nothing was going to stop her. ... Alison was a brilliant climber, but she had tremendous commercial pressures on her and she became obsessed." He also suggested that climbers in groups feel a false sense of strength in numbers.

Another issue of the *Independent,* however, quoted the frostbitten Spanish survivors: "The conditions on the mountain were very, very good. It was cold, but that's normal ... that made the snow very firm and ideal for climbing. There was nothing wrong with Alison's judgment," said Garces. "When the others in our team reached the summit, there was no snow and no wind. That was between 6 p.m. and 7 p.m., and then within 15 minutes the wind came up incredibly strongly. One minute it was fine, the next it was incredibly dangerous."

Scott Johnston, 42, of Bend, Oregon, who spent some 60 days on K2 with the American team and Hargreaves, said, "They made some mistakes, but they weren't suicidal, careless people." He told a story that was sometimes unsettling and sometimes wrenching. It began with the weather, which was "jerking us around," Johnston said. "All of us were getting frustrated, about to go off the deep end." Hargreaves, who had arrived hoping to spend only two or three weeks on the mountain, was especially distraught. As time went by, Johnston said, she "pulled no punches in saying she really, really wanted to get back down to her kids: 'I want to go home, I hate this, I want to go home.' She said she'd *never* go on a long trip again without her kids. She was so torn, she was at her wit's end." Her moods swung back and forth, he said.

Once she got out of basecamp and back on the mountain, though, her purposefulness returned, he said. "She would take the bit and run with it," said Johnston. "[Then] there was never talk of leaving. All of us would feel better on the mountain. None of us liked sitting around, especially Alison."

Professional and commercial pressures played a role, too. Doors had been opening for Hargreaves. She had received an invitation to meet the queen, and had been the keynote speaker at a luncheon of "famous women;" there was talk of movie rights to the Everest story. There were major sponsorships. Britons love to make heroes: after her death, Hargreaves filled the British press for days and weeks straight. There would probably have been a media blitz if she'd returned successful.

The turning point for Johnston and Kevin Cooney, 39, of Boulder came when they made another trip up to Camp III, and discovered — for the second time — that it was buried. "Kevin and I said, 'We're outta here,'" said Johnston. "We felt the conditions just were not safe." Richard Celsi (pronounced Chelsea), 46, of Seal Beach, California, called it quits the next day. Hargreaves came down the mountain two days later intending to go home, too. She and the three American men spent a whole day in the rain packing, dividing loads, and taking down tents. The next morning, again in rain, Hargreaves told Johnston, "Well, I'm not going to go." For weeks she had been setting dates by which she'd leave if weather didn't improve, and then letting them pass. Sometimes she'd change her mind five or six times a day, others said.

The three others helped unload her gear, and gave the two freshly unburdened porters loads of trash to carry out instead. "Alison was crying off and on," said Johnston. She cried hard when they left. "She couldn't let herself go home and do what she wanted to do," he said.

No one else was torn. Said Celsi, "Other than at a personal level, this wasn't going to change our lives. But it's fine to have a [climbing] career, and think about what certain climbs will mean to your career."

Hargreaves once told Johnston that if she could even have one chance to try for the summit, she could leave feeling OK.

Alison Jane Hargreaves was born February 17, 1962, and raised in Derbyshire, England. She was 5'4" and 130 pounds; she shared her weight, unlike many women, with no embarrassment.

She wasn't really a prepossessing figure. At the International Mountain Literature Festival, on first glance she could have been mistaken for a pleasant-faced librarian. "I'm not at all what people expect from me," she said. "I'm a far more normal female human."

Then you noticed an intent stillness in her gaze. There was a great directness to Alison, the feeling of a fist-strong personality. She had warm coloring, wavy light brown hair, broad cheekbones, and a sturdy, power-pack physique.

She was a combination of determination, competitiveness, and downright sweetness. Her manner in conversation was generally unaffected, friendly, and humorous. She made thoughtful little gestures, such as sending the 10-year-old son of one of Celsi's friends a postcard from K2, signed, "Climb carefully." In her signature, she always signed the "A" as a smiley face.

Alison began her career in outdoor pursuits at age 13, at her school, where Hillary Collins (later the widow of Peter Boardman) was her role model. "That's what I wanted to be, an instructor like her, [to] take people canoeing every day, always look brown and very fit," she said.

Asked if they were close, she said with a laugh, "I think Hillary used to find me a bit obnoxious. I was quiet, but would weave my way through and get things." Collins organized various weekend trips; Alison *always* went.

Alison's parents, brother, and sister were hillwalkers. "I don't ever remember not enjoying the hillwalking," Hargreaves said. She later returned to it, spending the year after her first baby was born "Monro bagging" with a papoose.

At 14 she got "absolutely obsessed" with climbing. She and her young partner, Bev, used to go to a climbers' pub every week. "We'd go around there every Sunday, to be around climbers. We just liked to see them. They used to have their coffee there, so we did. I just wanted people to [someday] accept me as a climber, I suppose."

At 15, she was about to solo *Black Slab* (5.6) at Stanage when asked to take a rope up for someone else. As she climbed, trailing the rope, another person traversed across her path, fell, and grabbed it. "Down he went, down I went," she recalled with a laugh. She broke the tibia and fibula on one leg, and the other heel. She begged the medics not to cut her boots and harness off. "They were so precious, they were *mine*, I was so proud to have them."

Hargreaves seemed focused, disciplined, and positive, but the issue of confidence surfaced often as she spoke. She said of her book, "I hate it. I absolutely hate it. I'm a very unconfident writer. If I wrote it again I'd do it in a different style. I'd be more open.

"I'm not a very confident person," she added. That was hard to reconcile with her feats as a soloist, but she clearly found coping with people and mountains very different. She said of her soloing, "Presumably I must be very good at it because I haven't fallen off yet."

Asked further about her nature, Hargreaves said candidly, "I'm obsessive. If I want something, I go to any lengths to get it. I was like that with boyfriends in school. Scheming and devious. I sometimes hate it in me, getting so devious, but it gets you somewhere. Sometimes it makes me stand back, and think, should you be doing that? Sometimes I think the more successful you are, the more you upset people."

Since her achievements in the Alps, she had reached a new state of acceptance in what she did and sought. "I've always felt climbing was incredibly self-indulgent. At the end of the day, it's only me that gets pleasure out of it, not the kids, not the husband. I get the ego boost." But after her book came out, and people began approaching to say she inspired them, she relaxed. "Now I feel I'm helping people, now I feel I can justify it. It's made me feel morally much better. I am what I am."

Coming into her own as a climber, she was very much preoccupied with her world and her place in it. While explaining that her lectures were at the moment still mostly to outdoor groups, she said, "I've got a much broader appeal because I have got the children and I am a woman. The book is already going into paperback. Normally that takes a year. There's obviously been a big interest in the women's market and general public. I do actually have quite a wide appeal."

Hargreaves liked goals, targets, lists of things to do. "What if I get up Everest? What'll be my next project? It worries me," she said last fall. Later came the K2 and Kangchenjunga plans, and she didn't intend to relax if she achieved her trilogy. "No. I'm sure I'll be wanting more and more," she said in our phone conversation in June. She was, for example, "desperately keen" to go to Antarctica; she had always been drawn to snowy wild places.

As full as her life was, she was not overwhelmed. "I need to have more than one thing at a time," she said. "To me, climbing itself is not fulfilling — if I got an agent, if the children grew up and went away, if I had seven days a week to go climbing, climbing wouldn't be enough. I'd need more."

"Alison was not just a good female alpinist, she was among the strongest and best of either sex," said Jeff Lowe, who climbed with her on the Northwest Ridge of Kangtega in 1986. "I was truly impressed by her ability to carry all the weight necessary for a 10-day alpine-style traverse, and her finesse in leading the technically difficult mixed rock and ice pitches."

Hargreaves' book promo material lists her pre-Everest records: in 1985, the first British female ascent of the Grandes Jorasses via *Croz Spur;* in 1986, the first woman to reach 7000 meters on Lhotse Shar; in 1987, the first British woman to climb *The Shroud* on the Grandes Jorasses; in 1988, first British woman to climb the Eiger North Face (while she was five and a half months pregnant); in 1989, the first British woman to climb the North Face of Les Droites; in 1992, the first female winter solo of the Matterhorn; in 1993, the first woman to ascend the six classic alpine north faces in one season.

One thing that drew fire from other climbers, however, was the last claim (which she penned herself). The six classic alpine north faces are those of the Eiger, Matterhorn, Grandes Jorasses, Dru, Piz Badile, and Cima Grande. Though Hargreaves had climbed the North Face of the Eiger before, with a partner, in 1988 (and it was very impressive to do it while pregnant), in 1993 she actually climbed the easier northeast face, the Lauper snow route. An Eiger North Face solo is a great prize, done, for example, by only four Americans, Mark Wilford, Charlie Fowler, Alan Bradley, and Jeff Lowe; the only woman to solo it was Catherine Destivelle of France, in March 1993.

Hargreaves was almost amusingly shameless about her sponsorships. In her book, besides listing them in an appendix as is common in expedition tomes, she peppered the text with brand names, as in, "I refuelled with a litre of Isostar (never known anything like it for rehydration!) and Jordan's Frusli Bars." Asked about those citations, she explained without a trace of apology, "It should be blatantly obvious to people that I needed the money and I couldn't have done it without it. You have to give these people some kind of payback."

After her successes in the Alps, Hargreaves tried to get on an Everest expedition, and couldn't come up with the money; then she got on another, had to produce $10,000, and chased around until she landed the equipment manufacturer Farino of Italy as a sponsor. On that, a medical expedition to the South Col, she turned back at 8400 meters with cold toes. Finally, she climbed Everest, via its North Ridge, exactly as she'd resolved to do — without oxygen and unsupported, even declining cups of tea when offered.

Greg Miller, an American who was heading up the North Ridge the morning of May 14, told *Climbing,* "Her tent on the North Col was next to mine, and she was completely cheerful the whole time, while the rest of us found reasons to whine — food, wind, cold, etc. On her descent she was skipping with joy, having summitted the previous day. Without oxygen. We briefly chatted, she said she looked forward to seeing her children and eating a real meal, and had a couple of weeks before leaving for K2. ... She looked very fit, and did not seem to suffer — physically or emotionally — from the deterioration typically associated with living at altitude."

When I asked her how the Everest climb had compared with her other major climbing experiences, she said, "Obviously nowhere near as technical. For example the *Croz Spur* was *much* more technical, but [Everest] just demanded so much willpower. Even just getting up and getting out the tent and, you know, just carrying heavy rucksacks and things, it's just physically very hard work. ... And having to think, right, well, tomorrow I've got to carry a load up to so-and-so, if I don't do that, it might not be in the right place ... I was incredibly motivated on this trip. Obviously part of that was the fact I'd failed in the autumn, and I didn't really want another failure. The thought of having to go through it all again was all too much. "

As of June, 32 women and 576 men had topped out on Everest. The first men to climb Everest without oxygen were Reinhold Messner of Italy and Peter Habeler of Austria in May 1978. The first woman to climb it without oxygen was Lydia Bradey of New Zealand in October 1988, though her ascent was unofficial and disputed. Hargreaves was the first woman, and just the second person, to make an unsupported ascent, and the second woman to climb Everest without artificial oxygen. The only man to climb it unsupported, and the only person to make a genuine solo, was Messner, in August 1980. Elizabeth

Hawley, a Reuters correspondent and climbing writer, has termed Hargreaves' ascent a "culmination" of women's Himalayan efforts.

Though Hargreaves was self-contained, there were 215 climbers on her route and the adjoining one during her weeks on the mountain. She was behind two Italian climbers, Marco Bianchi and Christian Kuntner, who had broken trail, joining them on the summit at 12:08 p.m.

It's an open question how much physical and psychological help a lone climber gets from other parties on the mountain. The climber can't help it if other people are on the route, but that makes a big difference in psyche and difficulty. With many climbers on a route, a trail forms.

What emanated from wires worldwide was: "A Briton has become the first woman to reach the top of Mount Everest alone, her supporters reported yesterday." The statements were attributed to Hargreaves' "training camp in Scotland."

Her camp's news release simply credited Hargreaves for being alone, unsupported, and oxygenless. It did say, "This is the most important climb ever undertaken by a woman in the history of mountaineering."

When I asked Hargreaves' about hers vis-a-vis Bradey's ascent, she answered readily. "Well, the difference is that I was carrying my own tent, all my own kit, above basecamp. I was making my own tent platforms and putting my own tents up and carrying my own stuff. So it was unsupported, as opposed to actually sleeping in somebody else's tent and things." Bradey was with others until high on the mountain, and used mutually established camps.

Did Hargreaves personally believe that Bradey reached the summit? She said she couldn't know without ever having met or talked to Bradey. "But quite possibly."

How did she feel about the words, "most important climb ever undertaken by a woman"?

"I don't actually know where that came from." She gave a mirthless little laugh. "I don't know. I can't see that it is."

Did she feel such statements were necessary regarding sponsorship and so on? "No," she answered.

If you're discussing Alison Hargreaves, you have to click in to her having children, because children are so consuming, with women usually the primary caretakers.

"When the time came, I wanted to have children," she recalled. "When I'd actually had a baby, something inside of me had been fulfilled, almost like nature waiting to have this baby. Then my body settled down, and I settled down mentally, and my stamina got much better." She felt, she said, that motherhood had made her a much more stable person, less likely to panic.

Hargreaves' children were part of her climbing life. When she soloed her Alps routes or training routes in areas like the Calanques, her kids would often be playing at the base of a route, or around the corner so that their voices couldn't drift up to her. Ballard, 49, would care for them, and fix pasta dinners for all. The family lived out of tents and a car all summer. More recently, traveling to the South Col with the British Everest medical expedition, she was concerned about taking the kids to altitude, and ready to respond. On the walk in, at Gorak Shep at just over 5000 meters, Kate said she had a headache, then became violently ill. Hargreaves took off down the mountain in the rain with Kate on her back, her other child, Tom, now 6, descending, too, as did Jim Ballard; eventually one of the big Sherpas carried Tom. It was dark, rough, and boulder-strewn, but, coursing with adrenaline, Hargreaves "could have walked for days."

"All that mattered was to get Kate down safe," she said. She, Tom, and Kate took turns singing. "They thought it was great, it was dark, they were being carried, it was exciting." She blazed along for nearly five hours, arrived at Pheriche, found a tea house, and made someone open it. The next day the kids were fine. Celsi, who was on that approach with her, recalled the whole experience as fantastic for the children, full of adventure, scrambling, and such games as high-altitude cricket.

Hargreaves didn't take the children on her second Everest trip, but hoped to bring them to Kanchenjunga.

Years before, she had canceled a trip to Alaska when she first found out she was pregnant, because an altitude specialist advised her not to go over 4000 meters. Plenty of people criticized her for climbing the Eiger while pregnant, though none to her face. Would it have bothered her? "No, because people will always find fault with you, no matter what you do."

Much has been made of Hargreaves taking risks as a mother. But look at John Roskelley, George Lowe, Alex Lowe — all fathers and bold alpinists. Or the late David Cheesmond, a father of a daughter; the issues of fatherhood versus risk are absent in all these men's cases. While Hargreaves was alive, a columnist in *The Times* of London criticized her "reality-denying self-centredness." (Readers defended her in subsequent letters.) After her death, a debate raged on the Internet and in the press as to whether she had been too selfish. To be fair, part of the debate is due the fact that she had made having a family part of her public persona. But only part.

Hargreaves herself actually accepted a variable standard. "It *is* different. I think a mother is more important to the child than the father. It's a terrible thing to say, but you carried the child, you bore it. A father can make up for things, but can't bridge the gap."

To mesh the worlds of child-rearing and risk-taking, she would compartmentalize: "I can go climbing, and that's climbing, and go back to the valley and be with the kids." When actually on a a route, she didn't think about the risk, but simply concentrated and thought about route-finding. "It's usually afterwards if I've had any doubt.

"The *Croz* shook me a little bit," she conceded. "One bit was very scary. My feet actually came off at one point. For awhile that shook me up. I don't like to be too close to the edge."

This year was the most time she had ever spent away from the children — 150 days. "If I thought that I was going to have to do that forever, then I would be seriously thinking about [my climbing career] again. Because I know this is just for now, I can cope with it," she said.

She was at the beginning of a new life chapter, both in the climbs unfolding before her and in other life decisions. Last fall, after speaking at the Banff Film Festival, she took a ski trip during which she excitedly asked the names of many of the peaks she saw, planning to come back and climb them. Last fall, she offered, on the record, that she was seeking an amicable divorce: "We've just sort of grown apart. We have totally different opinions. There's no animosity at all. I want to change things. I've got an awful lot of years left."

Hargreaves faced an ideological conundrum in terms of wanting to be accepted as a climber, not a *woman* climber, yet using her gender to get sponsorship. "It's easier for a woman to get coverage. In some ways, though, you earn it," she said. A man did not have to strive to be accepted as a climber the way a woman does, she said. "You can also say it's harder because as soon as I leave the kids I feel I should be there." She also pointed out how much time it took to get fit again after childbearing.

"In some ways I'm as keen now as I was 10 or 15 years ago," said Hargreaves. "I feel I've got as much enthusiasm as before. I'm behind, really. I've got four years [two per baby] to catch up. I've got to make up for lost time."

Hargreaves and the other climbers often said they never wanted to get stuck in bad weather up high on K2. Hargreaves once abandoned Camp IV when the wind picked up, for that reason.

The expedition cook, Ghulam Rasool, told Scott Johnston that Hargreaves sobbed in her basecamp tent, emerging once or twice for a cup of tea, the night before moving upward for the summit bid. On the morning of Saturday, August 12, Grant, Lakes, Hillary, Hargreaves, Slater, and Matt Comesky, 31, and Kim Logan, 43, of New Zealand left the American Camp IV at 5 a.m. and moved up to the Spanish Camp IV. They arrived at 8 or 9 a.m., too late for a summit bid, and met with the Spaniards. The first group decided to descend to Camp IV, with the plan to set off at about midnight and meet the Spanish somewhere above. The morning was hot and sunny, early afternoon brought clouds, snow, and spindrift, and at 10 p.m. the clouds receded again, though a bank remained in the north.

That night, Lakes and Hillary again left at midnight, and Hargreaves and Slater at about 2 a.m. with Grant and Logan, though Logan turned back with altitude sickness. Comesky also decided to descend. Hillary and Lakes went on until 4 a.m., when they stopped between the Spanish Camp IV and the Bottleneck, disliking the extreme cold and the look of the weather to the north. A vast, dark bank of clouds stretched across the northern horizon, though it had not moved near yet. They retreated to the Spanish camp.

Hargreaves passed Hillary, as he was descending, at just above Spanish Camp IV. "I said what I was going to do, which was to try to warm up in a tent, and she said, 'I'm going on.'" Slater too passed him. At 7 a.m. Hillary spoke via radio to Bruce Grant above, at the bottom of the Bottleneck. Grant said that conditions were really good, which prompted Hillary and Lakes to resume the climb.

But at the bottom of the Bottleneck, Hillary stopped for good, eyeing the clouds. A layer of altostratus and cumulus cloud in the north-northeastern area of China was banked up behind the Karakoram; a pillar of cloud was building up above K2. "There just wasn't enough leeway in it for me," he said. Lakes thought he'd continue for a while, saying he'd never forgive himself if the others summitted and he didn't at least give it a try.

The climbers above caught up with the Spaniards just at the bottom of the Bottleneck. Ortas had stayed in camp, and Garces turned back at the Bottleneck with cold feet.

Hillary could see Ortiz, Olivar, and Grant moving fast, then waiting for the other climbers. The second trio started across the Traverse.

Clouds drifted across the mountain. "Periodically I'd see this little line of people moving across," Hillary said. He couldn't be sure he was making the right decision: "You do think these guys might get up and come down and say how great it was, and you'll think, blast it."

Conditions deteriorated, and as Hillary made his way down in a whiteout, he got lost on "elementary" terrain between the Bottleneck and Spanish Camp IV, and Camps IV and III. At V p.m., the storm "turned on like a tap and it just roared." He reached Camp II at 7:30 p.m. Told that the others had summitted, he said, "Oh, my god," thinking the worst.

The storm that killed the summitters was part of a pattern of progressive buildup to the north, but this one came in earlier than usual — in late morning rather than late afternoon. The climbers had hoped the wind would stay as mild as it had been in the previous few days, but it seemed to be 70 or 80 mph even at Camp II, and was likely 100 or more up high.

"I can imagine the closer Alison got to the summit, the more eager she became," said Johnston. "It made her more willing to take the risk, to try to dash up there." It's also easy to imagine how frustrated the climbers had been, being on the mountain, knowing they were good enough to climb it.

Hillary felt the lessons to be learned were not to trust in seemingly gentle northerlies, but to be alert for weather coming from anywhere. He also called K2 a "seductive mountain. When you get to the Shoulder the terrain is easy and you start to focus on the [exposed] route above to the summit, and feel very secure, but it's too high to be able to stay there for any length of time if you're caught out by conditions. It's an awfully long way down." Finally, he felt that except in the case of a few individuals, people should fix more rope on the mountain. A 5- or even 3-mil rope left for direction between Camps III and IV would have helped him, and might have helped Lakes and perhaps some climbers in 1986. (Fixing in the Bottleneck and on the Traverse has been common recently, after fatalities there.)

Alison Hargreaves died in a swirl of sorrow, loss, and controversy. There was testimony in the end that pointed to obsessiveness, which may or may not have influenced final events. Teammates say that she and Slater at one point said they thought Cooney and Johnston (a marathoner and a former U.S. team nordic skier), who'd done the most trailbreaking, intended a secret summit bid, which was not the case. Then there was an incident in Camp III, when Slater and Hargreaves arrived to find themselves unable to locate a buried tent. They had only one sleeping bag and down suit between them, and hoped to go for the top. When Richard Celsi arrived at 6 p.m. after a 10-hour trip from Camp II, he argued with the two over their taking a pad from a cache he'd left two weeks before. They asked for help digging; he said he wanted to catch his breath, but soon helped. He has said that he dug for some 20 minutes, that Hargreaves then said she thought the tent was gone, and that five minutes later the two told him he looked terrible and should descend. At the same time they asked for his sleeping bag and some other gear. Celsi has said he told the two he was not altitude sick, then, amazed at the conversation, decided to quit the mountain, and headed down, giving over his bag, down suit, and food. Hargreaves trailed him down to Hillary's tent, 15 meters below. He thought she was going to offer him her water bottle, which would have been in line with her normal helpfulness, but she asked to borrow the overboots he was wearing, and he declined. It was dark, and the descent involved 34 rappels down the Black Pyramid over some of the most technical terrain on the *Abruzzi,* with some ropes frozen in place. "From the standpoint of a person who's fatigued, [that section] is the worst place to be," Johnston said. Hillary said, "We were very unhappy about the rappel, and tried to talk [Celsi] out of it. It was an uncomfortable situation."

To Celsi, the real issue was not illness or danger — he feels the two weren't thinking of the danger — but equipment. "Without the equipment,

111

their summit bid was over," he said, explaining further, "These people were [my] friends. We shared a lot. I tend to believe they got completely focused in a very selfish way. There's a fine line, with the need on big mountains to succeed, between focused and selfish."

The weather turned the next day and Hargreaves, Slater, and several other climbers at Camp III again retreated.

We cannot hear Slater and Hargreaves' side of the story, but according to Johnston and Cooney, Hargreaves later told them she thought Celsi was ill and could have died in the night. Johnston and Cooney felt if that was the case, Celsi should have been accompanied or carried bivy gear.

Hargreaves, Slater, and the others who died on K2 this year took a big risk. Had they made it, they would have been lauded for their boldness; after all, climbing history is replete with tales of great successes by people who have hung it out in the big mountains. But in this case they rolled the dice and lost.

Alison Hargreaves was a complicated woman, with ambition and single-mindedness mixed with team spirit, courage, and maternal devotion. K2 was one mountain in a long career.

Hargreaves was public property; her death, news round the world. It was especially painful to women climbers, many of whom had been trying to sort out their own conflicting obligations to self and family. We felt for her, trying to pursue her dreams. Some thought of those kids and wondered, well, *had* she been selfish? But we cannot judge that, not unless we are prepared to judge the entire pantheon of lost climber fathers. We can only draw our own lines.

In the end, Hargreaves was a great climber managing a hard balancing act. Obsessive, yes; tenacious, too, and tenacity is something all the great climbers have had in common.

I like to remember something she once told me in a climbers' pub. "If you're given opportunities, and there are two options, always take the harder one," she said. "If I choose the harder one, and succeed, I'll be really happy. If I fail, at least it was trying the harder one."

First published in Climbing *No. 156, 1995.*

Up Against the Wall
Searching for purpose on El Cap

by Pete Takeda

Up and down, up and down. Violent rocking, savage ripping. Feet are tangled in unyielding straps. Teeth are clenched in pained focus. Bull riding? Motocross? Bondage? No. I've been thrown from my portaledge by a 70-mph wind gust. Snow and rain blow up, then sideways, then down. The ropes are tangled, writhing with a crazy arrhythmic passion. Sodden loops of nylon whack at my neighbor's portaledges. The four haulbags thrash about, possessed by some strange force. Below, Jeff occupies the only haven in this micro-hell. I must untie and unclip my anchor to start the perilous journey to my new home, a single Fish portaledge, currently inhabited and verging on ruin. The terrible void yawns below.

Tucker was drunk. It was late winter. Short days, wet weather, no current significant other. No visions, no revelations, no end in sight. No escape from a ghetto social scene, Bombay gin, and creeping despondency.

My lot was fairer. A recent trip to Hueco tanks under the tutelage of Russ "The Fish" Walling had left my life (and car) a wreck. I will only say that the diminutive Asian (myself) can be hard pressed to emulate the robust cornfed types. The fleshier ones seem to be able to drink in greater volume and duration. The net result of this winter bash at Hueco was an extended mandatory sojourn to the Valley, and a serious reconsideration of "what's it all about."

"Tucker, we gotta get to the big mountains," I said. "The big-ass granite walls." Switching to my most genteel voice, I paraphrase Yvon Chouinard: "We must venture forth to challenge the great granite faces of the world. We must train ourselves to endure the intense suffering that is the prerequisite to any great work of art."

My mouth was working overtime — the usual shit-talking poser stuff. Nothing new. But for once, Tucker actually concurred. Next, we agreed that to act as an effective team, we needed to climb difficult routes together. Jeff joined us for a beer, and we enlisted him in our fantasy expedition. The night dragged on. We drank with fervor to forget the dreary present. We ranted and raved and planned. We would do a training route in the spring, then El Cap's *Aurora* in late fall.

Aurora was a fine candidate for an adventure — overhang, sustained, and technically difficult, it had seen very few ascents. Taking a line on the monolith's southeast face, *Aurora* was first climbed in the fall of 1981 by Greg Child and Peter Mayfield. The rating is VI 5.10 A5, and even after four ascents the route has retained its reputation as a scary heads-up undertaking. Pitch seven (the crux) had scored two 100-foot falls. Pitch 12 ascends the "Gong Flake," a huge radically expanding feature hanging menacingly above the belay, poised to kill both the leader and belayer. At a holiday party in El Portal I quizzed Mayfield about the Gong Flake. "Oh, it's still there?" was his surprised response. Telescopic scrutiny, though, had provided us proof of the flake's tenuous existence. Added to the technical difficulty was the threat of late-season weather. Some practice walls would be crucial. Our November jump-off date would give me an entire Valley season to ditch my sport-climbing obsession and focus on Big Walls.

But 10 partners, eight walls, two serious storms, one Grade IV first ascent, and 30 wall bivys later, I was burned out and dreading *Aurora*. Enough was enough. I wanted to hangdog on trusty bolts. I wanted to wear sticky slippers and tight trousers. But my whining fell upon callous ears. The plan was the plan. No deviation.

Strategy, preparation, and logistical hassles are often more time-consuming than the actual climbing. The bigger the project, the bigger the workload. *Aurora* demanded coordinating four people's conflicting schedules and collecting a large amount of gear. The headaches of preparation could make a whole separate story. Short days, potentially serious weather, and the sheer size of "Team *Aurora*" doubled the normal wall loads. Our haulbags would eventually tip the scales at 300-plus pounds.

Tucker Tech was my wall-climbing teacher, and was often amused by my epic antics. Tucker's confidence in my ability was such that he once stated, "I would sooner beat you on the head, stuff you in a haulbag, and drag your sorry ass up as climb any wall route with you." Like many of his Search and Rescue teammates, Tucker can be brutally honest, raving drunk, and downright rude. His sympathy and benevolence can be startling during their rare appearances.

I have also seen Tucker silently endure pain and anguish. During the third ascent of El Cap's *Lost World,* Tucker and I encountered a freezing storm that lasted several days. Retreat was impossible and our bivy gear was less than adequate — homemade "K-mart" portaledges sans rainflys, no sleeping bags, and hand-me-down nylon parkas. During this sobering, trial in which we spent 36 hours shivering in pools of ice water, I came to admire Tucker's stoicism and tenacity.

Highlighting Tucker's career is a five-week-big-wall solo binge — triggered by a sour relationship — during which he knocked off four El Cap routes. "I wanted to destroy every last grain of emotion.," he said later. "I wanted nothing more than to feel nothing." Looking at his long list of achievements, which includes countless first ascents and perhaps 30 Grade VI wall climbs, one can only wonder how much pain Tucker has encountered.

Jeff Perrin is a fellow Curry Company employee. He is the most even-tempered guy I have ever know, and generous beyond all expectations. His relaxed attitude seems to verge on carelessness at times; sometimes I feel that he flat out doesn't give a shit. For example, Jeff dropped the entire food bucket during a late fall ascent of *Mescalito.* One PowerBar per day barely saw us through the remaining six days of our trip. His cavalier outlook propels him up hard aid pitches at breakneck speed, while his recent six-day solo of El Cap's *Zenyatta Mondatta* epitomizes his boldness.

Greg Epperson, Epi, Epps, or the Epps Machine. His name is synonymous with distinguished climbing photography, and he is a nice guy. Epi had never done a wall; however, his drive to pursue his craft manifests itself in joining crazy projects like *Aurora.* Epi's role was that of photographer/documenter. He was in for a nice ride.

The three of us now gaze slack-jawed at the 600-foot static rope hanging free from *Aurora's* sixth-pitch belay. We have set the stage with three days of climbing steep, streaked granite. "This shit is nuts," I say. "Only the biggest idiots would fix this high. There's no reason for it." Fear emerges in the form of complaint. The thought of free-air jumaring the line 60 feet out from the wall is more than slightly disconcerting.

The others pulled a neat stunt yesterday by counterweight hauling our four fat bags to the belay. They had jugged to the high point while I loafed at the base, "haulbag packing." When the pulley and backup were ready Tucker and Epi acted as a counterweight and slowly lowered to the ground, with Jeff serving as the anchorman and slowing their descent with leather-clad hands.

Today, the trip up the line takes each of us at least 30 minutes of gut-churning, puke-inducing toil. "This rope is safe, this rope won't cut, I will never exert enough strain to cut this rope," is my mantra.

Repetitions count off as feet creep by, converting themselves into yards, and

115

finally noticeable distances. Hoarse and sweat-soaked from the 80-degree November heat, I am relieved and quite pleased to clip the belay. My next challenge is to ready myself for the next lead. The wild jumar, the beating sun, and my parched mouth cause me to gag as I look up. While prepping the rack I light up a Camel to calm my nerves.

Pitch seven, the "American Zone," is 150 feet long, circuitous, overhanging, and rated 5.10 A5. Mike O'Donnell and Chuck Clance have both lobbed for 100 feet off the pitch. Through the telescope the stone had appeared blank. Up close the American Zone is a series of thin flakes and grooves separated by unlikely expanses of streaked granite. Under my breath, I mutter, "nuts, yeah, Friends, yeah, pins, yup, heads, yo, hooks? for sure."

I'm ready for action. No stalling. "Be careful. You can die up there," encourages Jeff. The madness begins. An arrow, a #2 Camalot, then the first in a series of fixed copperheads. I am a bit leery of the heads because they're six to 10 years old. Furious bounce testing for the next 30 feet insures that the gear can withstand a minimal shock load. The head wires poke out at crazy angles. Feet barely touch the wall as my weight pulls the wire almost perpendicular to the stone, twisting at the beaten copper. Chouinard hook next, OK. Two Leeper points in succession. What next? I hear something. I look down. Tucker has finally made it up after a leisurely breakfast at the Ahwahnee Hotel. We exchange unpleasantries. My own meltdown asserts itself.

Hooking has taken me 15 feet above the last of the copperheads. It is a fair certainty that the successive blobs of battered metal will not arrest a 30-foot fall. Consequently, a mistake could result in a 100-footer. It is in my best interest to treat the next placement with respect and care. I crank into the substeps of my aiders and strain to daisy in tight. The angle is so kooky that the base legs of the Leeper pointed hook do not touch the face while its tiny point creaks back and forth. I search vainly for the obvious, the inobvious, and finally, the non-existent.

Above is the ledge. It is perhaps a foot wide, promising, maybe even hookable. If I could but latch the ledge then maybe I could get something to stick. A tiny flake! It is miniscule, barely within straining reach, hollow to the tap. It might take a hook ...The Chouinard hook comes off the rack. I carefully clip it to my aiders which in turn are attached to one of my daisies. Gingerly, I set the hook edge on the meager flake, and pull down on the daisy. The flake creaks. The hook digs in and sinks. Gritting my teeth, I squint my eyes and slowly ease a foot into the etrier step. I delicately transfer pressure from the Leeper point onto the Chouinard hook.

"Cool! This piece of shit's gonna actually hold," I think. Just stay put for a few more sec ..."

CRACK. The flake snaps and I am falling.

Adrenalin jolts my body. The fall of a lifetime is cut short by the pointed Leeper hook lodged to stone by a few millimeters of chrome-moly steel. Good thing I'm light. Through the haze I can hear Tucker explaining some jive about the pitch. He seems to know more about what is happening than I do. "Typical Tucker Tech," I mutter.

I down aid to a lower hook and shorten the Leeper's sling to a minimum. Placing it again, I strain into the high steps, and, using a right-hand edge for balance, slip my feet out of the aiders. "Slack," I yell. "I'm free climbing."

My feet paw for purchase on the slick brown stone. Groping at full extension, my left hand catches a sloping hold. I smear a wrinkle with my right toe, then slide my left hand an inch higher. No longer weighted, the Leeper hook drops to the end of my daisy chain and swings to and fro. Now both feet bicycle as I mantel onto the ledge. The rope drag, haul line, and rack conspire to pull me back into the void. But a high-step and friction rock-over put me eye-to-eye with an A1 pin placement. I mutter thanks to God and my FiveTennies. A few more hours of heading lands me at a rivet. I lower to the belay, the pitch half completed.

The most severe artificial pitch of my life ends the next day after nine total hours.

The ensuing pitches vary in character, yet each ropelength merges with the next to shape the greater continuity. The features mingle, building a sheer mosaic, bold vertical black, red bursts, and white highlights on a golden backdrop. The canvas extends in all directions, a dramatic stage for an intense drama. At belays I am awed by *Aurora's* meandering path, a passage that links fragile features. It is a thin line, tenuous, vulnerable, and wildly beautiful.

Jeff and Tucker make short work of their leads. Greg plies his trade with impressive calm. He is neither gripped by the exposure nor alarmed by his teammates' emotional flares. Team *Aurora* plods along in harmony, sharing humor, happy to be at work.

We are closing in fast on the Gong Flake, which we have christened "Tucker's Last Pitch Ever." Day three starts with pitch 11, Jeff's lead. The topo indicates two A4 sections, thus Tucker and I allow for a day of rest and relaxation. However, in a frenzied display of speed and finesse, Jeff blitzes to the belay in little more than two hours. His rapid lead includes a stretch of 13 consecutive heads and sporty hooking. Tucker and I have been taken by surprise. We are in the midst of our rest-day party when the bad news dawns on us. Tucker will die when the colossal meat cleaver pulls and cuts the rope. I will be sliced off the wall. Perhaps Tucker could ride the plate like a granite surfer, arrive at the base unscathed, and be in the Mountain Room Bar tonight. Not. Resigned to certain doom, Tucker jugs the trail line while I sadly clean the pitch.

117

Tucker hooks off a rivet and raps the flake with his hammer. Gong … gong … gong. I cringe. He drives an arrow to the eye with three gentle taps. "Yep, it's expando all right," he says. I'm too drunk to be scared and so is he. Tucker continues, placing TCUs and pitons that expand the granite blade. Each placement widens the fissure, rendering the gear below useless. Tucker mounts a TCU. It slips, then barely catches. In desperation, he fumbles for a Friend. The wrong size. He fumbles and drops it. A hasty, Hail Mary hook on a crumbling outside edge temporarily defuses the bomb.

"Good thing that hook held because he was lookin' at a monster ripper, te he he," I think.

Tucker finishes the lead as the sun turns red in the west. By that time I am neither scared nor elated, just hung over.

When I start a wall climb, I address all fears. Like an army general studying the troops of his opponent, I scrutinize the enemy. I weigh technical aspects and approach objective hazards with great dread. I try to envision "worst possible scenarios," paying scrupulous attention to detail.

By the end of day five we have arrived at "the worst possible scenario." Having fixed to the end of pitch 13, we are three pitches from the summit, but the weather is going bad.

We have spent the morning hours holding our rainflys in a vain attempt to stay dry. We are reduced to a fragile nylon fortress, continually harassed by an invisible and persistent enemy. The rainflys billow like sails as the wind gusts, stretching the seams almost to the point of tearing. My hands are frozen and the stress exacts a free-climbing pump, relentless and punishing. As the rainflys billow our ledges rise turbulently and then hammer down as the wind ferociously reverses.

Jeff, occupying the lowest berth in our porta-city, is experiencing the worst of it. His free-hanging ledge lacks stability and kicks around in the wind, a testament to *Aurora's* steepness and a harbinger of impending calamity.

I pray, over and over, "Oh, God, just make it stop."

Hours go by. A brief lull permits conversation.

"What's the forecast?" I ask Jeff, who is fiddling with our radio (stolen from our manager at the Four Seasons Restaurant, Mike Gover).

"Forecast calls for pain," he yells back.

"More rain! More pain! ARRRRGGHH!" interjects Tucker, who has moved into Epi's double-wide ledge to take shelter under the rainfly. Epi quietly snaps off film. During a lull, I can hear the wind whistling off in the distance. Suddenly the silence is torn by a huge gust and my thin nylon shell billows, then rips with a scream. I see a nightmare of frozen ropes and wildly animated gear. Another gust tosses me up and sails me horizontal, like a human kite. Shocked, I manage to yell, "Check it out. It's rodeo time!"

I feel like I could untie and fly to the summit. The nylon straps are wrapped around my legs, literally holding me horizontal in the 70-mph blasts. The ledge flaps violently about, threatening to smash my neighbors' heads and destroy their shelters. With my knife I frantically cut the whole flying mess loose. Tucker's abandoned ledge is next to go. The cots streak off, eventually disappearing around The Nose. I swing to Jeff's portaledge feet first. He grabs my legs and hauls me into his sodden home.

Jeff writes in his journal:

"This is going to be a very long night. There is so much rattling and swinging. This is ghetto. Pete calls it burial at sea. This is way ghetto."

Jeff and I sit, clenching the rainfly on a portaledge built for one person. Juryrigging an elaborate system of cut slings and soggy knots allows us a free hand. We each fire a shot of tequila. The warming rush comforts our hearts and soothes our taut nerves. We shake hands across soaked bivy sacks.

"Here's to the business," Jeff toasts.

"Yeah, this sure sucks. What's the forecast?" I ask.

Jeff smiles. "Forecast calls for pain."

We lie side by side in a space designed for one. Any movement is painful and the extremities grow numb with cold. Icy tendrils of water and wind torture our contorted bodies. My mind wanders, a hand comes unclasped from the rainfly and the wind gusts it up, snapping my drowsy brain into panicked reaction. The fly presses into my face. The wind eases. Night falls.

I am talking to my friend, Karine Nissen, who is standing in an immaculate, modern kitchen. White tile and radiant light embrace me with heat and comfort. Karine hands me a Peets Coffee catalog. "Pick one out," she says. I wander to the table and ease into the chrome and wicker chair. "This is real living," I say. Karine smiles serenely at me. A spotless coffee machine rests on the glass table, awaiting my whim. The thought of coffee slides my brain into neutral. I know everything is going to be okay. I sigh with pleasure. Drip ... Drip ... Drip ... what's that. Drip ... Drip ... Drip ... My pile jacket is leaking onto the floor. I look at my hands. They are wrapped in wet tape and sodden leather gloves. I notice my smell — damp and sour, like mildew. I realize my folly.

"Sorry, Karine, I've gotta go."

"Why?" she asks, concerned.

"I am leaving because I'm somewhere else and you are a dream."

The vision of Karine's face fades and I am sent roaring back into freezing, suffocating reality. My bladder is screaming for relief. My mouth is parched from dehydration. Jeff's feet are denting my head.

Icy mist streams through our lonely piece of the world. The dense clouds form a wall of darkness and opaque haze. Everything is frozen solid.

A distant voice calls, "Climbers on El Capitan, can you respond?"

Tucker, in the ledge above, stirs to life. "We are OK," he yells.

"We are ok, aren't we?" he asks.

The voice in the meadow calls again, "Climbers on El Cap, do you need a rescue?"

At least someone cares. In union we yell that a rescue is not necessary. I wonder to myself, "How long can this go on before we do need one?" The night is endless. Once again, I find myself exhausted yet unable to sleep. Five-minute micro-dreams are interrupted by 10-minute nightmares of consciousness.

The next day the sun comes out and gives us a shot at the summit. It takes hours for the ropes to thaw. We hurriedly pack the gear and begin climbing through water streaks and falling ice. Time is of the essence. When night falls the ropes will refreeze. Another storm could be fatal. We must make the summit tonight.

Jeff leads a ladder and hook pitch into the last two ropelengths of *Tangerine Trip*. It is dark by the time Tucker finishes the next lead. The final lead is mine. At 11:30 p.m. I claw onto the frozen summit of El Capitan. My breath condenses, obscuring the frozen fairytale landscape dancing in the flickering light of my dying headlamp. I crunch through shin-deep snow and anchor the lead line to a guarded tree. My boots are frozen solid. The rope is like lead.

Tucker comes up next. He stumbles past without saying a word. He seems to be looking for something. I think we all are.

First published in Climbing *No. 132, June 1992.*

Dangerous Liaisons
To kill or be killed when a Pakistan expedition goes wrong

By John Climaco

The guns pointed at me were not toys and the soldiers holding them, despite their mismatched uniforms, were not clowns. I hadn't expected AK 47s to be the biggest danger on the Baltoro, but then nothing on this expedition had happened as I expected. When our liaison officer finished screaming at me and the soldiers finally left, I sat down and held my head in my hands. The expedition had gone down the drain, I was going to jail, and we hadn't even reached basecamp.

Suneeb, one of our porters, sat down next to me. "This liaison officer," he said, "is crazy man, very bad man." I nodded. "You," he continued in a different tone, "are good leader for us, care for Balti people. He has insulted you, so tonight, Inshallah, we shall kill him. We will slit his pig throat."

I can pinpoint exactly when the mess that became our expedition to Chogolisa began: October 24, 1993. I was sitting below the west face of Cholatse, having just made the second ascent of that peak's Southwest Ridge. I was feeling pretty good about myself, a little too good in fact. I wished in my journal for a bigger, harder version of what we'd just done, something like Chogolisa. My mother always said be careful of wishes; sometimes they come true.

Eighteen months later Andrew Brash and I were in Rawalpindi sitting face to face with the man who over the next two months would turn my wish into a nightmare: Captain Mohammed Ayub, our liaison officer. Ayub immediately informed me that in Pakistan his army rank meant great status, something I could not possibly have as a civilian. "You," he said with an extravagant wave of his hand, "are nothing here." Captain Ayub had just returned from six months

121

duty on the Siachen Glacier, the front line in the border war with India, the highest battleground in history. It is not what military men consider a choice posting, and I had to wonder privately about Ayub's real status. He made no secret of his displeasure about returning to the "God-forsaken hell of the North," as he called the Karakoram Range.

"Many peoples have died in these snows," he explained while Andrew and I unpacked the $2000 of kit the regulations required we buy for him. "They are having parts of their bodies chopped off due from cold. This, I think, should not be happening to me." Reasonable enough. "So these," he continued as he pushed away a pair of brand-new plastic boots, "are substandard. I will not go to the mountains in these. And this." He held aloft a new down jacket. "Have you not brought another color? I am captain in Pakistan Army. This is not smart looking." Brash rolled his eyes. Though we'd only known the captain for 10 minutes, things already looked bleak. Then, dismissing our carefully thought out schedule, Ayub announced, "We cannot possibly rush up into the mountains tomorrow. I must have perhaps one week to buy the proper equipment, which you will pay for. Then, perhaps, we shall move from this place."

As Ayub stood there with his scrawny arms akimbo, I felt the Italian temper that has caused so much trouble in the past welling up inside me. With a conscious effort of will I controlled a feeling I would come to know well in the weeks ahead: the desire to throttle Captain Ayub. Instead, I pleaded that the current good weather would enable us to fly to Skardu and thus avoid the death-trap Karakoram Highway. I suggested that the extra cost of the hotel, food, and, of course, the captain's salary during the delay was more than we could afford. "Rule and regulation clearly tell expedition to come prepared to stay in Rawalpindi for two weeks," barked Ayub. "Two weeks! If you have not brought sufficient funds, then the expedition must be canceled immediately." I shut up.

I for one was not spending even one week in the sweltering hell-hole of Rawalpindi and I had only to glance at Andrew's widening eyes to know how he felt about the matter. We mentioned to the captain that we wanted to go to Peshawar and play tourists. He replied that we could not leave the hotel without his permission, and that visiting Peshawar, about four hours west toward the Afghan border, was totally out of the question. Again came the urge to throttle. I said nothing until the next morning when I asked for permission to go shopping. After noting his benevolence, Captain Ayub gave his blessing; we promptly left the hotel and went shopping ... in Peshawar.

Andrew was nervous about Peshawar from the beginning. A worker at the U.S. consulate there had recently been held at gunpoint for an hour in broad daylight and was only saved when her captor, still holding the gun to her head, was shot by a USDEA sniper. In Peshawar, the conduit for weaponry heading to the Afghan freedom fighters, every type of artillery and ammunition known to man is freely available on the streets. I thought it would be exciting, although I had second thoughts as we passed signs at the entrance to the city announcing, "You are now leaving the area where the Government of Pakistan can guarantee your safety."

Smoggy, crowded, and even hotter than Rawalpindi, the city itself turned out to be dull. The taxi ride home was not. Our driver was fluent in English and we took the opportunity to gripe about the asshole ruining our trip. "I hate the army, the police, the ISI (Pakistan's KGB) — all of those hooligans," the driver announced. "They killed my brother because he refused to pay their bribes. Would you like to see a photo of him?"

As we pulled into a police checkpoint, and the machine-gun-toting officer approached the car to demand his bribe, the driver handed back a photo. His brother, lying on a steel table, was missing the back half of his head, his eyes, and much of his chest. We didn't leave Rawalpindi again.

About a week later Captain Ayub finally exhausted his last excuse to delay us. Of course, the stable high pressure that had been parked over Pakistan since our arrival was also exhausted. As the rain poured down in sheets, flights to Skardu were grounded, which meant only one thing: the Karakoram Highway.

Careening through the rain-slick turns 500 feet above the Indus River, I thought over all I'd read about the highway. Some have written it is the most beautiful road in the world, winding as it does past Nanga Parbat. Others have said it's the most exciting, entertaining part of an expedition to Pakistan. Those people are idiots. In many places the highway is nothing more than a shelf blasted into the sheer wall of the gorge. More than once a timely deceleration saved us from being crushed under a falling boulder. This I can only attribute to divine intervention, since in his hash-induced trance our driver seemed unable to locate the brake pedal. It appeared at times as though he was trying to physically outrun death up the highway.

On a bed at the K2 motel in Skardu we spread out what was left of the expedition finances. Thanks in large part to Captain Ayub and his at-our-expense-account, our once Himalayan pile of rupees was down to a molehill. We'd been informed that the road to Askole — dubious in the best conditions — had been wiped out in 14 landslides triggered by the continuing rain. With Jeeps trapped between some of the slides, it was conceivable that we could shuttle loads over the debris. We figured we could afford two extra porter stages and still get back from basecamp. The porters, now camped outside the gates of the motel, would be our responsibility as soon as we started walking and we had to pay them something every day whether we covered any ground or not.

When to leave Skardu thus became a critical decision. Captain Ayub, interested only in lounging about the motel as long as possible, was of no help. After conferring with Phil Powers, leader of an expedition to Hidden Peak, and Issaq, our cook, we agreed to caravan the two expeditions together and make a dash for Askole the moment the rain stopped.

The rain finally turned to a drizzle, and two hours later eight climbers, 90 porters, three cooks, two liaison officers, and 2250 kilos of stuff were on their way to Askole.

"Have you any dynamite?" Captain Butt, asked me during a fuel stop.

"Why," I asked.

"To blow up the road, of course," he laughed as he walked away to buy some. Captain Monte Butt, the Hidden Peak liaison officer, was the antithesis of Captain Ayub. Monte, who spoke flawless English, became our source for advice on everything from handling the porters to fixing the road. As the five Jeeps rumbled along, Monte kicked back on the roof of one, grooving to London techno on his Walkman, while Ayub sat in the cab barking orders at the driver.

Caravanning worked well. The extra manpower allowed us to quickly fix bits of the road and keep moving. Our only significant delay was at the final police checkpost at Dasso, a windblasted cluster of police barracks sitting next to the last road bridge over the Braldu. "This is bogus!" the officer yelled as he thrust my peak permit for Chogolisa back at me. "You have made this up on your typewriter in America. You must go back to Islamabad and get another." I thought I was about to have a seizure and Brash looked like he was ready to slit his wrists before following that order. It was, of course, a subtle way of requesting compensation for his plight, stuck guarding Dasso Bridge. Captain Ayub spotted this amateur quickly and stepped in to settle the matter. If any money was to be bled out of the Chogolisa expedition, it was going into his pocket, not some bridge guard's.

Shortly after Dasso we came to a landslide that no amount of effort was going to fix. Monte surveyed the scene and walked away in defeat, holding his dynamite like a child with a broken toy. We'd made excellent progress in the jeeps, but it was still three and a half extra porter stages to Askole, one and a half more than we could afford. That was a problem. Thankfully, it was one we wouldn't have to deal with until later. We started walking the next day in steady rain and pounded our way to Askole. Along the way we crossed paths with a soaking wet Alan Hinkes, just returning from the summit of K2. "You should bloody well turn around now, lads," he said bitterly. "There's nothing up there worth this fucking walk." It was the best advice anyone could have given us. Of course, we ignored it.

The first few days of the approach proper turned out to be beautiful. We'd split off from the Hidden Peak expedition at Korophon, wishing them well and promising to visit them at their basecamp. The rain had finally abated and as we followed the Braldu River toward its source at the Baltoro Glacier, we finally

124

began to feel as though our luck had changed. Even the small catastrophes — the bridge guard who ripped us off, and the fixing rope some soldiers relieved us of at the Drumordu River crossing — these seemed minor now.

Two days later we reached the campsite of rDukus, where the view across the Baltoro toward the Trango group is surely one of the most impressive in the mountain world. Unfortunately, we couldn't sit outside and enjoy it because of the unbearable flies attracted by the stinking heaps of shit and garbage dumped there. As we camped in what amounted to an open-air toilet, the phrase "Throne Room of the Mountain Gods" took on new meaning.

rDukus is important for another reason. When you step off the grassy moraine onto the ice and rock of the Baltoro, it is likely the last step you'll take on solid ground until you return. This is significant to the porters, who usually insist on a cash payment in lieu of foam pads, shoes, or other equipment. They march onto the glacier unequipped to live on the ice, though large numbers suffer hypothermia or trench foot. It is not surprising then that the porters prefer to spend as few nights camped on the Baltoro as possible, which was fine with us. We decided to follow their pace to basecamp, having no idea when we left rDukus how much this choice would affect us.

On the six-hour walk from rDukus to Gore II, an army camp on the glacier and our destination for day eight of the approach, we were awestruck. Masherbrum, Gasherbrum IV, Broad Peak, and Mustagh Tower all came into view. The weather was brilliant and Andrew and I lagged behind the porters and Captain Ayub, absorbed in a photographic orgy. After about four hours of the walk we met one of our porters coming down the glacier from Gore II. He proudly announced that all the loads had reached Gore II and, as it was still early in the day and they were running low on food, the porters requested permission to continue on to Concordia. We sent him back to deliver our permission; this would mean reaching basecamp a day early and that would save the porters an extra night on the ice and, we hoped, prevent them from going hungry. It seemed like a great idea, so we were surprised to find all the porters sitting next to their loads when we reached Gore II.

The mystery cleared itself up when I saw Captain Ayub's feet sticking out of his tent, the only one set up. Gore II is at roughly 14,000 feet and he was totally spent from the walk. Whatever bullshit he was about to offer, this was the real reason for not moving on. Captain Ayub rose from the tent and announced, "We will only be doing whatsoever-absolutely it states in Rule and Regulation. You have said we will be camping at this Gore II and this is where we will camp."

"Yes, but the porters have said they are running out of food and need to get back home quickly," I offered in response.

"This is not my fuck-up!" Ayub snarled. "This is your fuck-up. Who are you? I have told you, and told you that you are nothing." Of course the one English phrase we'd added to his lexicon was "fuck-up." How appropriate, I thought. I felt my violent urges returning. "These Johnnies" — he waved toward the porters — "they do not know what is good for themselves." Beating his chest, he said, "I know what is good for them … and if I have to beat them to make them do what is best then I will beat each and every one of them."

After an hour-long harangue, I finally managed to slip my copy of the dreaded Rule and Regulation book in front of the captain, wherein he read that if I, as leader, put my reasons for disagreeing with him in writing, my decision was final. We were going to Concordia.

Or so I thought. I walked back to the porters and announced my victory. "Now it is too late, John," Issaq told me. "It will be dark soon and there are crevasses. We will go tomorrow." I threw up my hands, and turned around to go tell the Captain. He was busy supervising the disassembly of his tent when I told him we'd be staying at Gore II.

For a moment, there was silence. He stood up, turned around, and stared hard at me. In that instant my whole world collapsed to the small space between us. Then he started to shake; they were small tremors at first, but soon his whole body vibrated. His eyes bulged, his teeth started to gnash, and he seemed to transform into pure hate. I was scared.

"You-are-*joking*-with-*me!*" he screamed. He was beating his chest. "I am captain in Pakistan Army. Government of Pakistan has given me three stars. You do not treat me like slave!"

Spit and foam flew from his mouth as he continued screaming and beating his chest. Captain Ayub had gone insane. I tried to explain that I was only doing what the porters wanted. "It does not matter what they want. Why have you not asked me?" he spat in response. "Always asking this cook or Butt, never me. I am Liaison Officer. I am in command!"

His screaming was so loud that soon our audience of porters was joined by a group of soldiers, with guns, from the nearby army camp. Ayub saw them before I did and after a quick order they surrounded us and those guns were leveled in my direction.

Suddenly I had no desire to argue. I felt sick. My mind was filled with images of a taxi driver with half his head blown off. Was Ayub angry enough to kill us? There was no one for a hundred miles in any direction to stop him. I apologized but it was too late. The soldiers stood by as he continued his tirade. "You will not be allowed to leave Pakistan until the ISI has interrogated you about your crimes."

"Crimes?" I asked.

"You have called Pakistan Army a disgrace at the Drumordu River. You have photographed army camps and this is a treason, a violation of Official Secrets Act. This is punishable by death."

It was Ayub who'd called the rope-theft incident at the Drumordu River disgraceful, and the photos I'd taken were of mountains near various army camps. That was the truth, but we stood in a world where truth didn't matter. "I will now write your confession and you will surrender all of your film to Pakistan Army," Ayub said.

While I waited for my "confession" to be drafted, I returned to my tent and spooled up some unexposed film. Somewhere in the 50 rolls I'd exposed there was sure to be something objectionable, and I couldn't take any chances. When I returned, the captain was still quivering with anger and he handed me the most bizarre document I had ever seen. Written in the first person in my name was a confession of several crimes against Pakistan. I was supposedly admitting to photographing military installations, bridges, and aircraft. I had repeatedly insulted the Pakistani Army, the Government of Pakistan, and Islam. I had disobeyed direct orders from a Pakistani Army officer and threatened the same officer. At the bottom was a space for my signature.

"I can't sign this," I said shakily. "It's not true."

"It is true," Ayub replied. "I have said it is true, so it is true. You will sign!"

"No, I will not!"

During the tense hour that followed we went back and forth repeatedly. Finally, when the soldier's guns began to droop and Captain Ayub felt he was losing face, he snatched the paper and announced he would sign it for me. I watched in stunned silence as he put my name to the paper, folded it up and walked away toward the army camp to have tea.

I sat down and tried to clear my spinning head. What had just happened? What was going to happen next? It wasn't long before Suneeb sat down to answer my last question. Murder was what was going to happen next, because the expedition was completely out of control.

Ayub was serious, and seriously deranged. If he chose to, he could have killed Andrew and me and the only thing our families would ever know was that we disappeared while attempting Chogolisa. People disappear every season in the Himalayas. It would have been easy for him to kill us.

Or, I began to think, for us to kill him. The thought scared me. I was seriously considering killing Captain Ayub. It was insane: the whole place, the whole situation, and I had absorbed some of it. Ayub must have sensed this. He came back over and tried to make me sign a contract taking full responsibility for anything that might happen to him, including accident or poisoning. He knew we couldn't stay camped next to his soldiers forever. I thought I recognized some of my fear in his eyes. Again I refused to sign.

The expedition, as far as I was concerned, was over. The only way to solve our problems was to return to Islamabad and get inside the U.S. Embassy as soon as possible.

127

"We're going back to Islamabad tomorrow," I announced.

Ayub looked surprised. "No, we must continue. Fuck-up is finished. ISI will deal with you when you return."

Why was he arguing to continue the same expedition he'd done so much to destroy? Andrew figured it out: Ayub was being paid by the day. Inadvertently, I'd called his bluff and now had a bargaining chip.

"Tear up the confession," I said, "and we continue."

"Not today," Ayub answered, "but if you behave on the climb I will return your film and rip up your confession." It was a bizarre blackmail deal, but it defused a situation where violence still hung in the air. It is disturbing to admit now, but I wasn't thinking of killing Ayub as right or wrong. It was a purely practical decision. With a truce possible, a dead liaison officer would cause more problems than it would solve, at least for the time being. "Please don't kill him tonight," I later told Suneeb. "Wait."

The next day we reached Concordia, where we ran into some trekkers on their way out of the mountains. I decided to dispatch a letter with them. I didn't want to alarm my family but at the same time I wanted them to take some precautions for me. If I was tossed in jail when we returned from the mountains, I didn't want to spend one extra minute there. Captain Ayub was suspicious of everything, so I waited until dark before quietly slipping the letter to a beautiful Swiss woman named Maria, and told her to mail it from Geneva. It was ridiculous; I felt like a B-movie James Bond.

The following morning the laziest of the porters started suggesting locations for basecamp only 30 minutes out of Concordia. Andrew and I used every bit of charm we had to coax six hours of walking out of them. When they finally refused to go any further without pay for a full extra stage, we established basecamp. Which meant it was time to face up to an old problem: money, or more specifically, the lack thereof. At Concordia we confirmed our earlier suspicions that after paying these porters we wouldn't have enough cash left to pay for the return trip to Skardu. The concept of credit does not exist on the Baltoro, and if even one of our porters found out how broke we were, no one in Baltistan would come to retrieve us and our gear.

The payoff went smoothly except for the moment when I saw Ayub stuff a wad of our rupees into his pocket. He just didn't quit. When questioned he insisted it was his money, but offered no explanation of how it came to be in our pile of porter wages. As soon as the porters were paid, they took off down the glacier, apparently unsuspecting that they had our last rupees.

I woke up early the next morning to have a look at the spot that would be home for the next month. Though I couldn't see the northeast face, our proposed route, Chogolisa's summit was clearly visible 9000 feet above. I started daydreaming about walking across that perfectly flat summit ridge at 25,000 feet.

Issaq was soon standing next to me and brought me back to reality by handing in his resignation. I had never heard of a cook quitting an expedition, throwing away what might be his only opportunity all year to earn hard currency. Issaq claimed he was ill but it was clear that he just couldn't take another minute of Captain Ayub. When Ayub heard of the resignation he realized that he would soon be in camp alone with Andrew and me, and immediately announced that it was his duty to leave and find another cook. An hour later, Andrew and I were alone.

That afternoon Andrew also decided to leave, but only to visit the Hidden Peak team for a couple of days. I stayed behind to start a recon, while carrying gear up to the base. When I reached the bottom of the face the next morning it looked huge, and totally different from the 10-year-old photos we had. It looked suicidal. Andrew came to the same conclusion at Hidden Peak basecamp, and both of us started looking at the Northeast Ridge, an elegant line that had only seen one ascent, a huge siege that used 10,000 feet of fixed rope. An alpine-style ascent would be incredible.

Andrew returned two days later, as did Captain Ayub with our new cook, Gulham. I was a bit suspicious of Gulham, whom Ayub had found just hanging around Concordia. When I went to shake Gulham's hand, he thrust out a page from Jim Curran's book *K2: Triumph and Tragedy* that had his picture on it. The caption read, "Gulham: film porter impossible, opportunist." I'd had Curran to my house for dinner years before and remembered a story of a porter in 1986 who'd tried to slip out of K2 basecamp with Kurt Diemberger's tent and personal belongings after it was assumed, wrongly of course, that Kurt was dead. It can't be the same guy, I thought.

A week later, I changed my thinking. Gulham's kitchen contained, among other things, one of my sleeping bags, a pack, my spare boots, and Andrew's ski poles, spare hat, socks, gloves, and down jacket. Of all the men in Baltistan, Captain Ayub could have possibly found to replace Issaq, he picked the only documented kleptomaniac in mountaineering literature.

Despite Gulham's best efforts, Andrew and I were able to scrape together enough of our equipment for our first attempt, on August 13. The unlucky date lived up to its reputation. At our bivy at the bottom of the route the stove refused to light. After four hours of effort Andrew booted it across the ice and we returned to fetch the spare. We spent the 14th in basecamp under crystal-blue skies. It was the best weather of the trip and, looking at the summit of K2, we were sure that people were going for it. What we didn't know was that seven people would die for it that day, among them one of Andrew's good friends, Jeff Lakes.

The spare stove also refused to work and so on the 16th we were back at the bottom of the route with a fire-spitting conglomeration of every working stove part we had. It was dangerous as hell but at least it burned. We'd planned to climb at night so just as the sun set we started through the icefall. It was such a chaotic mess that there was no way we could reach the clean northern branch of the ridge taken by the Spanish in 1986. We opted instead for the southern branch and its 6000 feet of virgin terrain.

The initial climbing was easy and straightforward. We found a great bivy on the ridge proper and spent the day looking up at what we figured would be the crux of the route. Three thousand feet above, at about 20,000 feet, the ridge rose dramatically in a vertical ice cliff.

The next night, as we set out, the moon was a little smaller, the air a little colder, and we found some of the scariest terrain either of us had ever encountered. Somehow the ridge itself was split by crevasses every hundred meters. We'd never seen anything like it. Climbing along a 60-degree arete of rotten snow we'd suddenly find our tools and feet popping through into space. The view through the holes to the glacier below was sickening. At one point I had to tunnel more than a body length into the slope to find ice for a screw.

It was 2 a.m. before we reached the bottom of the ice cliff. We reckoned it was near vertical for close to 400 feet without any appreciable breaks. Andrew leads Grade 6 water ice, so when he said forget it, I forgot it. The alternative didn't look much better. We headed for a slot we'd seen from below, a huge partly filled crevasse formed by a serac that had calved from the ice cliff. Andrew swung his way over stacked blocks and an overhanging snow mushroom to gain the slot, and I led across its floor, expecting every step in the deep snow to collapse. It was 3:45 a.m., we'd been climbing for 11 hours, and there wasn't time to reach the ridge. We would have to bivy on top of the serac. We climbed up, chopped out a platform, and crashed until 10 a.m. When we awoke we had a whole day ahead to sit on our little perch. Looking around, we realized we occupied the only island of safety on the entire slope below the ridge.

After eight steep pitches the next night, we regained the ridge — and the crevasses. Andrew stepped through the ridge crest into a gaping hole. We continued upward on the ridge for another three or four pitches of terrible snow to a small, filled-in crevasse where we bivied.

When we woke later in the morning it was snowing, and had been since we'd gone to bed. If there was one thing the Northeast Ridge of Chogolisa didn't need, it was more snow. The following morning, August 18th, it was still snowing and a thick fog had rolled in from Kondus Saddle. Was this the same fog that engulfed the Duke of Abruzzi in 1909, the same fog in which Herman Buhl disappeared in 1957? It sure was the same mountain in damn near the same spot. We were getting scared.

At 2 p.m., we tuned in our radio and caught Phil Powers' end of a call to

Broad Peak. I heard Phil's voice crackling, "... can you tell us about the accident?" We jumped into the conversation. Seven people were dead. Jeff Lakes was dead. It was the final blow.

Jeff had really wanted to go to the Karakoram that year and asked Andrew if he could join us. We'd politely turned him down; we wanted to try as a team of two. So Jeff found his way onto a K2 expedition.

It didn't take a lot of talking to decide our climb was over. Descending what we'd climbed was impossible with our three screws and three pickets, forcing us onto the concave face between our line and the Spanish route. It took two days to get down, and the day after we reached basecamp the entire face slid, scouring clean all of our tracks.

During the six days we were gone, Ayub and Ghulam had been falling over each other to see who could steal the most. The shortwave radio, a camera, medicines, boots — they'd grabbed it all. We had to politely ask for individual items back as we discovered them missing. The only thing we really wanted now was to get the hell out of the mountains, and we sent Ghulam to find some porters. Not wanting to be alone with us, Ayub also took off for Concordia, promising to return with porters.

Ten days later the porters arrived, and two days after that I was again walking past Gore II, absorbed in all the bad memories of that place. I couldn't wait to reach a shower and a bed, but I wondered if I'd be enjoying those amenities in a jail cell. As I passed by the last of the rag-tag army tents, a lone porter, coming up the valley, stopped me.

"Mr. John, from Chogolisa expedition?"

"Yes?"

"I have Federal Express for you." He pulled a large red, white, and blue box from his pack. It was probably the highest and most remote delivery in the company's history, and certainly the most important package I'd ever received. Beside *Playboy* and *Penthouse* magazines was a letter from my father. My letter had reached him from Geneva just the week before, and according to my instructions he'd contacted my friend Eshun Khan, son of retired Admiral Sahid Khan, former Chief of Staff of the Pakistan Navy and presently Pakistan's Ambassador to the Hague.

According to the letter, Admiral Khan was mad as hell that we'd been treated so disrespectfully. He expected a phone call as soon as possible. I was laughing like a lunatic before I'd finished reading.

We broke the news to Captain Ayub that evening by asking him if he could help us arrange a trip to Karachi, where the Admiral lived. "It is much too dangerous there," he told us. "You cannot go."

"I think my friend can ensure our safety," I responded handing him the letter. I watched the color drain from Ayub's face as he scanned the page.

"Admiral ... Sahid Khan?" His voice quivered.

"Yes," I explained, "his son and I were great friends at university."

Ayub looked ill. He retired to his tent and we didn't hear from him until the next morning when he woke us with breakfast in bed. It was pathetic. The entire journey back to Skardu became one attempt after another by Ayub to make up to us.

When we reached the road, we told the porters we were broke. They took it surprisingly well; Ayub appointed one porter as representative to go with us to the bank in Skardu for the porters' money. The day after we arrived in Skardu, one seat opened on a flight out. Andrew and I agreed that I should take it and call the ambassador. I walked out onto the tarmac, leaving Ayub screaming at airport security to stop the plane.

"What would you like me to do to this man?" These were the first words I heard through the phone receiver after I finished my story. The casual power in Ambassador Sahid's voice stopped me cold. As soon as he'd answered my phone call, I felt safe. The passion and urgency of the days on the Baltoro evaporated. On the verge of winning the game of Pakistani justice that I'd been preparing for two months to lose, I hestitated. Captain Ayub had stolen from me, threatened me, and in many ways ruined my expedition. But was that enough to do to him what I suspected the ambassador could do? The silence on the line began to be uncomfortable.

"I just don't think that he should be allowed to do this again." That was all I could say, and as the words came out of my mouth, I felt sorry for Captain Ayub.

Eleven months to the day after leaving Pakistan, I was tromping down from *Point Five Gully* on Ben Nevis, Scotland, and ran into an English climber I'd met at Concordia at the end of our expedition. He filled me in on what happened to Captain Ayub.

"It was in all the papers after you left. Dishonorable discharge, lost his pension, court marshall. Probably in jail by now."

I shook my head and kept walking. So that was it, the end of the story. It wasn't the way I would've chosen to win, but as Captain Mohammed Ayub had taught me, in Pakistan they play for keeps.

First published in Climbing *No. 167, 1997.*

How to Climb 5.14
A slacker's guide to big-number success

By Matt Samet

If your name is Elie Chevieux or Garth Miller, stop here. If you don't on-sight 5.14, but instead toil like the lowest of serfs on routes of lesser grades, read on. After 10 years in the trenches, I can give you the psychological edge to succeed.

Ever since I topped out on my first pitch I've wondered just how difficult a piece of rock I could climb. When I was 12, my one-time mentor, Bob, an alpinist more concerned with safe mountain travel and the splendor of an alpine vista than the numbers game, told me that rock-climbing standards were advancing each year. This was in the early 1980s, and Bob thought that 5.14 was probably as hard as people could climb.

"So what would a 5.14 be like?" I asked after paddling my way up a 5.7 toprope that he had patiently set up.

"I don't really know," he answered. "Probably like a smooth, overhanging wall of glass with little bullet holes for the hands and feet. And the holds would always be just out of reach."

I carried that picture with me for years, but even now that I know better, I still quake in my boots at the mention of that improbable number — 5.14. Bob's description of the ultimate grade had conjured up visions of crazily bearded mountain freaks grappling with the underbellies of huge, unprotected roofs thousands of feet off the deck, all the while plugging sloped-out shot holes as their feet dangled helter-skelter in the winds of an oncoming storm. So when I picked up my first climbing magazine, I was disappointed to see that, instead of the Grizzly Adams types, it was the cafe-haunting, parapente-flying Euro weenies

133

who were pushing the envelope. And all those shiny bolts so close together ... what was up with that? Oh, well, I still figured that 5.14 had to be hard since I could barely toprope 5.10.

In the ensuing years, which coincidentally saw the birth and boom of American sport climbing, I decided that I too wanted to climb 5.14. In the summer of 1997 I finally realized my dream, sending *Zulu* (5.14a/b) in Rifle, Colorado, after years of artless bodgery in the purgatories of 5.11, 5.12, and 5.13.

Has that climb changed my life? No. Have I changed the sport? No way. The 5.14 grade was established in this country over a decade ago by Jibé Tribout (*To Bolt or not To Be*, Smith Rock) and people have been ticking it ever since. I'm just another hack, a johnny-come-lately thrashing my way up some over-sprayed pile that Sharma did in a day or two and could barely be bothered to remember.

Nevertheless, it was immensely gratifying to top out on the thing, putting 10 years of experience to the test and finally pulling it off. But, really, the afterglow wasn't that much different from the times when I sent my first 5.13a, 5.13b, or 5.13c. A quick rush, maybe a celebratory beer or two, a smidgen of false modesty, and then it was off to the next route.

As any fool who has realized a long-held goal can tell you, the real reward is in the process — the means more than the end. Thus, I have gone to great pains to study what it takes to climb 5.14. Ignore all those training books and articles from here on out. Ignore all those campus boards and system boards and wango boards and flavor-of-the-month pull-up rungs. They will just give you elbow tendinitis or make you so strong that you'll forget to use your feet.

Climbing 5.14 is all about sacrifice and attitude. You must cultivate an aura of monastic narcissism, bestowing godliness upon yourself as you proclaim your membership of the 5.14 Club from the top of some sooty, anonymous roadside cave.

So, here are some tips that I've learned along my way to 5.14, gleaned from careful study of the sorry antics of myself and my peers both on and off the rock. Enjoy, and I'll see you at the top.

The job/education dilemma. As most sponges know, a job or the serious pursuit of an education can cut into hard-core selfishness (e.g. playing Doom all day or trying to climb 5.14). Here are some sure-fire ways to get around the obstacles imposed by modern life:

1. String out a namby-pamby college career as long as possible, making sure to take frequent semester-long breaks to climb in Europe. In the meantime continue to collect parental checks and/or student loans (neither of which need to be paid back).

2. Upon graduation, take that "much needed" pre-work road trip, extending it until your very last peso. Still pumping out on 5.13c?

Shit — it's time to get a job.

134

3. Don't worry about using your degree to get a real job (it only makes you look desperate and silly). To create the kind of time you need to spend all day pissing off at the crag, find yourself work that is eminently disposable. Try menial labor — the pay is bad, you'll feel like you are cheating yourself, but, hey, you can quit anytime and go climbing. I can personally recommend furniture moving, snow shovelling, and tomato farming.

Bonus tip: Ignore all those articles about people who still find the time to climb 5.14 despite having real jobs and happy families. It's intuitively obvious that the so-called "5.14s" these guys and girls scrape up are at most 5.13c.

The relationship dilemma. Sex and romance are a bit like trying to climb 5.14 — elusive, indefinable, frustrating. OK, maybe that's not entirely true, but anyone who has done the grade will probably tell you it was because he or she had a supportive partner. Then again, if your attempts to climb 5.14 are unsuccessful it's probably because your partner "just doesn't understand."

That being the case, drop your lover like so much ballast and put an end to all the nagging and wanting to do "something besides climb or talk about climbing." Any partner who can't come to terms with your mind-numbing egoism, single-mindedness, and narcissistic sense of purpose is probably too selfish to understand you.

Find and date another climber. Yes, this probably means a penniless psycho just like you, but he or she will make a good belayer. Be sure you and your partner time each other on redpoint attempts and hangdog sessions — each one of you gets 45 minutes, no more. If your partner begins to show signs of climbing better than you, let her know you feel threatened by dissing her footwork.

Coping with failure. Sadly, it usually takes a lot of falling to eventually redpoint a 5.14. This leaves plenty of opportunity to throw a "wobbler," or adult tantrum. Use the Wobbler Equation to determine how long you are entitled to scream and sulk upon failure:

$$\frac{\text{Grade of Route}}{\text{Years Climbing}} \times \frac{\text{Relative Humidity}}{\text{Number of Attempts}} = \text{Time Allowed}$$

Thus, if I fall on a 5.14b, I've been climbing for 10 years, I've tried to redpoint the route 40 times, and I estimate the relative humidity to be 90 percent (and remember, "it's so greasy, dude" cannot be expressed numerically), then I come up with the number 3.15. Therefore, I am allowed to kick the rock and scream expletives for 3.15 minutes, after which I must come back to the ground and sulk for 3.15 hours. Simple math.

Notice that as the number of years you have been climbing increases, the time allotted for wobbling decreases. And also notice that if your number of attempts exceeds the relative humidity, time again decreases. This means you need to give up and try something easier. Sorry, dude. In my next article I'll explain and describe the "rad-boy" attitude quotient (pi divided by number of times you say "dude" per sentence) and how it can spike your equation.

Here are some suggested phrases you can call up at will during a wobbler in order to let your belayer and bystanders know that falling off wasn't your fault:

"I wasn't even pumped."

"I'm sick of this route."

"I'm just sick."

"You hosed me on that clip."

"I'm more of an on-sight climber."

"I hate this sport."

"Just dirt me."

Success. In the rare event that this article actually helps you climb 5.14, please contact the author so we can swap war stories and route beta. It is amazing how much kudos you can score from an ascent of a few feet of crumbly roadside rock. Just look at this article.

Published in Climbing *No. 177, 1998.*

Jigsaw
Heinrich Harrer's Puzzling Life

By Audrey Salkeld

In 1952, *Heinrich Harrer* wrote a book that became an instant best-seller and has never been out of print since. *Seven Years in Tibet* tells the gripping story of his 1944 flight from a World War II prisoner-of-war camp in northern India across the Himalaya into Tibet. After two rough years on the trail, Harrer and his companion Peter Aufschnaiter reached the capital, Lhasa, where they were befriended by members of the Tibetan nobility. Harrer became the young Dalai Lama's tutor and confidant during the last years of Tibetan independence. His book brought the plight of Tibetans to world consciousness, and over the years has appeared in 40 languages, selling more than 3 million copies. It has now been made into a $60 million movie starring Brad Pitt.

In 1950, Mao's invading forces streamed across the Chinese border into Tibet, forcing the Dalai Lama to flee from Lhasa. Harrer remained with him in the Chumbi Valley until March of the following year before crossing back into India. His long and exciting sojourn in his "second fatherland" was over. The Dalai Lama returned to Lhasa before going into exile in 1959. Over the years Harrer, now 85, has assisted scores of Tibetan refugees, seeing his help as a way of repaying Tibetans for their generosity when he was a refugee. "Helping them is the last task in my life," he says, and until recently Harrer had hopes that the film's publicity would aid his friends in their struggle against Chinese domination. Indeed, Harrer was enjoying a taste of glamour as the film's premier approached, reliving the great defining experience of his life.

All that changed May 28 when the German magazine *Stern* published a scathing article. "A bespotted hero ... Idol of climbers, tutor of the Dalai Lama

— and avowed early Nazi," was its stinging headline. Stern confronted Harrer with documents furnishing evidence of his past as sergeant first class in Adolf Hitler's notorious *Schutzstafel,* or SS.

As climbers the name Heinrich Harrer reminds us of another of his great books. *The White Spider* chronicles man's fight for the Eigerwand, the grim Swiss north face that had claimed the lives of eight men before Harrer and three companions made the first ascent in 1938. Published in English in 1959, the book became required reading for all aspiring alpinists. More than any publication before or since, *The White Spider* helped to dispel a then widely held belief that the Eiger was climbed by political fanatics with close ties to the Nazis.

Harrer's book put faces on the "fanatics," flesh on the bones of myth. Without glorifying sacrifice, he showed the past Eiger tragedies for what they were, the regrettable loss of young life. Evoking acts of heroism and the transcendental joy of success, he painted a picture of mountaineering that we could recognize. These men were not activists of some vicious regime or ideology, but bold north-wallers pushing the limits of extreme alpinism, as men and women at critical moments of climbing history have always done.

Could this man — so instrumental in divesting 1930s Teutonic climbing of its Nazi slur — turn out to have, as *Stern* suggested, a Nazi past of his own? This living legend, who spent almost all the war years as a British prisoner, this lifelong friend of the Dalai Lama and tireless campaigner for human rights — could he have once held quite different and sinister beliefs? Moreover, can we trust him today?

After World War II, American occupiers in Germany gathered the captured Nazi files that featured prominent figures in the Third Reich and its known associates. Three years ago these files, which occupy nearly eight miles of shelving, were returned to the German Federal Archives in Berlin. At the same time copies were made for the National Archives in Washington, D.C.

One pink folder among the personnel records caught the attention of the *Stern* reporter, Gerald Lehner: "Harrer, Heinrich, born July 6, 1912 — SS Unit 38, Sippennummer [family number] 73896." The folder was among a batch of materials documenting members of the elite and dreaded SS.

The bulk of the papers referred to the application in 1938 of the *SS-Oberscharfuhrer* Heinrich Harrer to marry Lotte Wegener, 18-year-old daughter of the celebrated geophysicist and explorer Alfred Wegener, who disappeared in Greenland in 1930. Any SS man wanting to get married had to satisfy Hitler's right-hand man, Heinrich Himmler, not only of his own so-called racial purity, but that of his future bride. Harrer and Lotte Wegener submitted family trees going back to the 18th century, and both were examined and pronounced fit by SS doctors. They married on Christmas Eve 1938.

That the Eiger climbers had caught the attention of the Nazi regime is no news to anyone versed in alpine history. After the successful ascent in July of that year, the four men found themselves sucked into a vigorous publicity campaign, masterminded by Dr. Joseph Goebbels' Ministry of Public Enlightenment and Propaganda. For two Germans and two Austrians (Austria had just been annexed by Germany) to succeed on what was popularly believed to be the most dangerous climb in the world was a propaganda writer's gift, taken as proof of invincibility. Harrer and his companions were paraded around the Reich as Aryan superstars.

A few days after coming off the mountain, their frostbite still heroically bandaged, they were presented to Adolf Hitler at the Breslau Sports Festival. A ceremonial photograph was taken that appeared later in a book about the climb, put out by the Central Publishing House of the Nazi Party. Above the caption "The greatest reward of all," each climber can be seen clutching a ceremonial box containing a signed photograph of the Fuhrer.

The victors were sent on a recuperative cruise around the Norwegian fjords and then enrolled as mountain-sports instructors for one of the Ordensburgen Castle Academies, the rigorous finishing schools designed to train future leaders of the Reich.

One of the four Eiger climbers, Anderl Heckmair, has written about those times. "Now others took over and did our thinking for us," he said. "Many years later it is easy to see what we should have done, but at the time we were more or less stunned by the reaction to our success and submitted to the will of others." All along, the climbers' idea of the greatest reward was to go on an expedition to Nanga Parbat, a stipulation they required before they would join the Ordensburg staff. As events in 1939 escalated toward war, however, their expedition was dashed. Hitler told Heckmair, "I need you and your comrades for quite a different task." Harrer alone was permitted to go on a reconnaissance to the Diamir side of Nanga Parbat, a trip organized by the German Himalayan Foundation and led by Peter Aufschnaiter. It was a small four-man venture, which traveled to the mountain in May and climbed the Mummery Rib to above 19,600 feet.

As the climbers made their way back through British India, the political situation in Europe worsened, and the ship to take them home never arrived. Harrer, in *Seven Years in Tibet,* relates how three of them made a break for it, hoping to get out overland through Persia. As the war broke out, all were apprehended and interned. Harrer wound up in a prison camp in Dehra Dun, from where in April 1944, after several attempts, he escaped with Aufschnaiter and made his celebrated trek across the Himalayas into Tibet. They arrived in Lhasa in the early days of 1946, almost barefoot and with their sheepskin coats in tatters. The war was over.

That much was common knowledge. The bombshell that came out of the pink file, and what has prompted accusations that Harrer is suffering a bad case of selective memory, was the suggestion that his association with the Nazis went back way before the year of the Eiger. As part of his voluminous wedding paperwork he was required to provide an abbreviated autobiography. Handwritten and tucked innocently between details of his schooling and skiing and climbing activities were the words: "in the SA since 1933, in the SS since 1938." Other papers in the application are more specific: "SA from October 1933 to April 1938, SS since 1 April 1938."

The *Stern* writer, Gerald Lehner, pressed Harrer to confirm whether the writing was his. Taken off guard, the old man agreed it was. After an awkward pause, he proffered, by way of explanation, "I must have wanted to boast a little there."

Credibility is stretched. Harrer suggests that he backdated his résumé to hurry along his wedding application when in fact you cannot imagine its smooth passage being threatened in any way. He and his young bride-to-be were perfect "Aryan" types: he a blond, blue-eyed hero of the Reich; she the daughter of a martyr to science, who had served her time with girls' division of the Hitler Youth.

If Harrer had voluntarily joined the SA and SS, and particularly on the dates indicated, then his contemporary "Mr. Clean" image is badly tarnished. The SA *(Sturmabteilung)* were Hitler's "storm troopers," most frequently remembered as rampaging "Brownshirts" meting out rough justice — including torture and murder — to those who did not share their views. The SS were the protective echelons of the Nazis whose duties later on would include exterminating the Jewish people. In the early days, before Hitler's assumption of power, members of the SA were drawn largely from disaffected old soldiers and the unemployed. This remained the case until after the Rohm purge at the end of June 1934 when in "The Night of the Long Knives," Hitler, feeling that the leaders of the SA force were becoming unmanageable and posed a threat to his own position, had them slaughtered. Later, as the SA grew more middle class, its violent image in Germany lessened along with its power, but in Austria, Harrer's homeland, the SA was forbidden, and the terrorists who contributed to their country's overthrow were drawn from closet SA and SS divisions. Austria's Chancellor Dolfuss was assassinated by Austrian Nazis in Vienna in July 1934.

The year prior, in 1933, the Nazis had gained control of Germany, and an official *Gleichschaltung* process began whereby every aspect of life, work, or leisure, was coordinated by the state. It was held paramount to win over the hearts and minds of the young, and all youth organizations were subsumed into the Hitler Youth. Attempts were made to enroll all male students in the SA and to subject them to at least one year's compulsory residence in

140

special "comradeship" barracks. SA membership rose from about half a million at the time of Hitler's appointment as Chancellor to some three million in 12 months. At that time, becoming an SA man was seen as a path to employment and special favors, and did not at that time carry an obligation to join the Nazi party.

Harrer, joining in October 1933, would have been one of this 3 million. Although the SA was then illegal in Austria, it flourished underground in some cities, and within some activities, like sports and mountaineering, whose clubs were already prohibiting Jewish climbers from joining, and went so far as to expunge Jewish names from guidebooks. It is worth noting here that Harrer's university town of Graz, in southeastern Austria, which had a long history of anti-Semitism, was later known to the Nazis as the "City of the Popular Uprising," the center of Nazi agitation within Austria with some 80 percent of the town's population professed Nazis at the time of the takeover.

The date when the documents show Harrer joined the SS is also significant. Not only does it predate the Eiger climb by more than two months, but other evidence shows that he applied to join the SS only one day before Austria was absorbed by the Nazis in 1934 — an uncanny coincidence that suggests Harrer had inside knowledge of the SA and SS's plans, contrary to his claim of having been a nonactive and apolitical Nazi.

Last June, just prior to his 85th birthday, Harrer paid a visit to Simon Wiesenthal at the Wiesenthal Center in Vienna, a human-rights organization for holocaust studies, to clear up the issue of his Nazi membership. Afterwards, visibly relieved at the cordial reception he said he had been given, Harrer issued a statement to the press. But, he failed to address critical questions raised first by Stern and then other publications. While conceding that the facts in many of the articles were true, though the implication put on them was frequently in error, he declared: "I was a member of the SS for a limited period in 1938 after I had gained national attention in Germany for my feat as one of four climbers of the Eiger North Face." *No mention here of "SA since 1933," nor of joining the SS before the Eiger climb.*

Harrer went on to say that, on agreeing to become an SS athletic instructor, he was issued with an SS uniform, but that he never taught a single lesson due to his participation in a 1939 Nanga Parbat expedition. And he only wore his uniform at the time of his December 1938 wedding, an occasion which was, he admitted, heavily publicized by the government.

Never, said Harrer, was he a dedicated Nazi, nor involved in any way with the heinous crimes of the period. Nonetheless, he regarded his involvement with the SS as "one of the aberrations in my life, maybe the biggest," and he deeply regretted it.

"My personal political philosophy grew out of my life in Tibet," Harrer continued. "It is a belief that reflects many tenets of Buddhism and places great emphasis on human life and human dignity. It is this philosophy which leads me to condemn as strongly as possible the horrible crimes of the Nazi period."

Harrer has published many books, each devoted to a specific facet of his life, a life which without doubt has been one of the most adventurous of the century, packed with opportunity and contrast. Strangely, none of his writings give a complete picture of himself, and his selective recollection leaves periods unaccounted for. Apart from any possible political activities when he was a student, some months remain where the record is unclear, months when he admits to being in the SS. So, did he have official duties? No one has said. In the weeks following the Eiger success, the climbers were obliged to fulfill publicity engagements, but — and on this Heckmair is adamant — only Heckmair and Ludwig Vörg (Heckmair's fellow countryman who participated in the Eiger first ascent) undertook the nationwide 80-venue lecture tour, not Harrer.

And what was Harrer doing during this time? By his own admission, he had dreamed of going to the Himalaya and Tibet long before he climbed the Eiger. At the 1938 Sports Festival in Breslau, Harrer was introduced to his SS boss, Heinrich Himmler, and he has related how Himmler confided, "I know of an expedition going to Tibet if you would like to go along."

Himmler's notions on ethnicity included a near-mystical conviction that the ancestral fathers of German "Aryans" were a race of Tibetan giants. Dr. Ernst Schafer from Hamburg was employed by Himmler in his Genealogical Research Center and by 1938 was making plans for an "ethnological" expedition to the roof of the world in search of this missing link. The Canadian historian Michael Kater, from York University, Ontario, has evidence to suggest the SS Expedition also wanted to persuade Tibetans to take up arms against the British. Himmler hoped a German-Tibetan alliance might conquer Asia, and that the empty spaces of Tibet would provide much-desired living space for cramped Germans.

The expedition arrived in Tibet, according to Kater's information, with 30 men and a large cache of weapons, and reached Lhasa early in 1939. The team was still in the field when war broke out. Could this expedition have accounted for some of Harrer's missing months? Harrer's lawyers deny he joined the Schafer party, and no one has identified Harrer on film of Schafer's expedition.

The American magazine *Summit* interviewed Harrer in the fall of 1991. He told them that when it looked as if the Nanga Parbat expedition wasn't going to materialize, he reluctantly agreed to appear in a romantic ski film being produced by Leni Riefenstahl. But in January 1939, the article said, "Harrer was called to the phone: If he still wanted to go to Nanga Parbat, he could join the

142

expedition, which was leaving in four days." He immediately broke his film contract, packed in a day, and headed for Antwerp to join his colleagues Aufschnaiter, Lutz Chicken, and Hans Lobenhoffer.

If that was Harrer's recollection, he has telescoped time. Chicken's account (*Himalayan Journal,* 1947) has the party leaving Rawalpindi on May 11 and, long as the sea journey was to India, it could hardly have taken three months. Another point of detail: Riefenstahl was in the United States publicizing her *Olympia* film until mid-January 1939. She was bored with mountain and ski films by this time and her plans for that year were to bring *Penthesilia,* an epic of classical times, to the screen. If Harrer had signed up to make a ski film — and it was still a popular form of entertainment — it's difficult to imagine Riefenstahl being involved personally.

The whole story concerning Harrer's Nazi past may well have died in press terms after the flurry of publicity following *Stern's* allegations were it not for the continued topicality of the *Seven Years in Tibet* film. Tri-Star, distributors of the movie, were at first wrong-footed by the unsought publicity, but remain fairly sanguine that it ought not to affect the film's chances at the box office. (Suggestions last year that Laszlo de Almasy, on whom the central character in *The English Patient* was based, might have been a Nazi collaborator failed to hinder that film from winning nine Oscars and earning millions.)

The director Jean-Jacques Annaud and scriptwriter Becky Johnson had always intended their film to be about a man's transformation and redemption. Brad Pitt's Harrer character was written to be unlikeable at the start of the movie: he is shown as an opportunist, a marketeer, and someone who abandons his pregnant young wife in search of personal glory. Only minor dialogue changes were deemed necessary in light of recent developments. Annaud has remarked that in any case he "suspected for a long time that one of the hidden scars Heinrich Harrer had to heal was left by a possible confrontation with the Nazis before he left Austria in 1939." But, Annaud added, "When he returned after the Second World War and seven years in Tibet, he devoted his life to nonviolence, human rights, and racial equality."

Harrer, the son of a postman, grew up in a simple wooden chalet on the mountain slopes above the village of Huttenberg, Austria. His mother and grandmother had been born in the same house. Harrer owns it still, and it is where he has established his Harrer Museum. The young Heini was a natural athlete, who scrambled over everything. He loved to escape into the local hills, the Karawanken, even though his parents felt he should be employing his time more profitably. "All our dreams begin in youth," Harrer wrote in the preface to *Seven Years in Tibet.* "As a child I found the achievements of the heroes of our day far more inspiring than book-learning." His heroes were men like the

143

Swedish explorer Sven Hedin and Professor Alfred Wegener.

Achievement was a strong motivating force, allied with dreams of travel and adventure. He yearned to be famous, and tried many sports before focusing single-mindedly on skiing and mountain climbing. Rigorous training won him a place on the Austrian Olympic ski team at the 1936 Winter Games in Garmisch Partenkirchen. A year later, he won the downhill race in the World Student Championships.

By this time Harrer was studying geography in Graz. The university's Department of Geophysics and Meteorology still bore the influence of its erstwhile head, the late popular explorer who developed the hypothesis of continental drift, Dr. Wegener. Harrer came to know the Wegener family socially, making a great hit with the widow, Frau Else Wegener, even before her daughter Lotte caught his eye.

To eke out his finances, the student Harrer worked as warden of the university-owned mountain hut, the Tauplitz Alm. He fetched stores, chopped wood, gave skiing lessons — and made friends in high places, for the Tauplitz Alm was a popular winter sports hideaway for many high-ranking Nazis. Above all, he maintained the pitch of his ski training, keeping himself supremely fit.

"But victory over human rivals and the public recognition of success did not satisfy me," he wrote of this period in the preface to *Seven Years in Tibet*. "I began to feel that the only worthwhile ambition was to measure my strength against the mountains."

We should remember what a firm place mountains occupied in the folklore of the day. Strong German and Austrian alpinists had not only been striving for the great north faces of the Alps, but unclimbed Nanga Parbat in the Punjab Himalaya had seen repeated Teutonic attempts throughout the decade. In 1934, 10 lives were lost there. In a spun-out epic the charismatic Willo Welzenbach, Uli Wieland, and expedition leader Willi Merkl died along with six Sherpas as they struggled to retreat in a storm. Three years later 16 more men died, buried by a massive ice avalanche as they slept in their tents. If the Eiger Nordwand had become the Mordwand (Killer Wall) in popular consciousness, so Nanga Parbat was seen as Germany's Mountain of Destiny. German effort and German dead identified it as a "German" peak, in the same way that the British had invested in Everest, and K2 would come to exemplify American aspirations.

In a society that held fallen heroes in high esteem, there was a strong feeling that Germans must avenge the Nanga Parbat deaths with ultimate success. An impressionable, hero-worshipping young man, Harrer was moved by the poignant examples of such national martyrs as Welzenbach on Nanga Parbat and Toni Kurz on the Eiger.

By 1938 Harrer was climbing some of the hardest rock routes in the Austrian

144

Kalkalpen and the Dolomites. Though his ultimate ambition was to climb in the Himalaya, it seemed to him an almost impossible dream for someone who was, as he said, neither British nor wealthy. "One had to make use of one of those rare opportunities open even to outsiders and do something which made it impossible for one's claims to be passed over," he later wrote. The only opportunity that seemed likely to deliver such a chance would be to succeed on the climb everyone was talking about: the 5000-foot north wall of the Eiger, which had claimed so many lives.

In July 1938 he completed the last paper for his final university examinations and the same day was speeding on his motorbike toward Switzerland. His partner, Fritz Kasparek, another Austrian ski champion, was already in Grindelwald, waiting and sizing up the scene. The only person Harrer shared his secret with was his future mother-in-law, Frau Wegener. She was under no illusions about the risks involved, but did nothing to dissuade the pair.

In later life Harrer would often say he believed in connections, the linking of events and opportunities. If he had not spent his boyhood in the mountains, he would never have become a ski champion. Without his more than 600 Alpine tours, he would never have had the audacity to attempt the Eigerwand.

The climb itself, the fortuitous joining forces with Bavarians Heckmair and Vörg, has passed into legend. As the four came down the West Flank after reaching the summit in a blinding snowstorm, the wet snow turned to rain. In the gloom below they could just make out the buildings of Kleine Scheidegg and what looked like a seething mass of dots. They could not know these were their last private moments.

On the ground the four climbers were surrounded by friends and well wishers, all wanting to thump them on the back. A flask of cognac was passed round. Representatives of the Sonthofen Ordensburg academy materialized to greet (and manage) them. Among the stack of congratulations waiting when they arrived back in Grindelwald were telegrams from the Fuhrer's representative, the Reich Director of Sports, Reich Director of Organization (Robert Ley, whose jurisdiction included the Ordensburgen), the Austrian Chancellor, the mayor of Vienna, various other Nazi notables, and the filmmaker Riefenstahl. Soon you could purchase postcards of the climbers and their route. Their Eiger gear, which had been stowed in a garage and included old socks, wet gloves, torn clothes, provisions, pegs, and rope, was rifled by souvenir hunters.

Later that year, when the book of the climb was compiled by Nazi publicists, each of the four was asked to contribute a section. Kasparek wrote on the history and victims of the Eigerwand, Vörg on the 1937 attempt, Heckmair on the climb itself — and Harrer drew what was in effect the short straw: it fell to him

145

to describe the aftermath. In his section Harrer says the sentences that have come back to haunt him over and again: "For us it is an inestimable reward to see the Fuhrer and be permitted to speak with him. ... we feel very proud. We climbed the Eiger's North Face over the summit to our Fuhrer!"

Many times Harrer must have rued the publication of this book, whose printing ran into thousands. There was no way afterwards of suppressing those extravagant and ultimately offensive words. Often, over the years, Harrer has been called to account for his "inestimable reward" remark and wearily reiterates that the phrase was not his, but that of a ghostwriter. "Some newspapers wrote that we all shouted Heil Hitler on top and did headstands for joy. Or, we stuck a flag up there. But it was blowing a blizzard, we were so muffled up, and our only thought was we don't have to go any further ..."

As for the war years, Harrer has said he received little or no news from home. The Red Cross tracked him down in the POW camp at Dehra Dun, but once he and Aufschnaiter escaped, he was out of contact again for another two years. It was only in 1947, in Lhasa, that he says he learned of Nazi wartime atrocities and saw the devastating pictures. "And you were photographed shoulder to shoulder with [Hitler]!" he berated himself in disgust. When he returned to Germany after his seven years in Tibet, he was formally deNazified in Graz. He professes surprise that the issue of his Nazi involvement should be raised again now, and asks, "Is someone trying to damage the film, and with it, Tibet?"

The international success of the book *Seven Years in Tibet* gave Harrer the means to continue an adventurous life. There were still mountains he wanted to climb. In 1954, he went to Alaska, and climbed Mount Drum with George Schaller and Keith Hart, and Deborah and Hunter with Fred Beckey and Henry Meybohm.

Then it was to the Ruwenzori in 1957, and in 1962 he did the first ascent of Carstensz Pyramid in what was then West New Guinea. As in Tibet, adventure alone was not enough; his fascination was with the people he met in out-of-the-way places. He likes to say he traveled with a mug and spoon — eating what the natives ate, living as they lived. Certainly he tried to learn and convey all he could of other cultures and promoted sensitivity in dealing with them. For his efforts he received the honorary title of Professor from the President of the Austrian Republic in 1964 and in 1992 the rarely awarded Medal of the American Explorer's Club. He continued to travel restlessly, sometimes with Leopold, King of the Belgians, as his companion. In 1975, he told *Alpinismus* magazine that he thought it a terrible thing for a mountaineer to remain just a mountaineer all his life and not to develop further in understanding. "I am against any kind of fanaticism, whether it's to do with religion, politics, or mountaineering."

146

Admirable sentiments, but the South Tyrolean climber, Reinhold Messner, for one, is skeptical. While seeing no reason why Harrer's Nazi past should be used to discredit him now, Messner says he feels "embarrassed" as a mountaineer that Harrer, like others, does not want to remember and accept responsibility for Germany and Austria's involvment in World War II. More than that, he feels that Harrer "still glorifies the ideals of that time," and describes how he has clashed with Harrer in front of television cameras: "Time and again he stressed how the 'bond of the rope' represented the great values of his life. Time and again he criticized us, the younger generation, who were unable to form rope-bonds for life, who lacked intensity, loyalty, endurance … It is those ideals of his youth — the same ideals as the Nazi propaganda — and also the lies of his life which leave me baffled. How can an old man live such a lie?"

It is easy to say now that Harrer should have come clean about his Nazi connections. Clearly, it is a source of deep shame to him that he was used by the Nazis, even at his wedding.

Still, Messner's doubt about "the man and political thinker" have led him to say: "Tibet could be a free country today if the young Dalai Lama could have had a wise teacher and adviser in 1949, 1950, 1951." Such an extreme view takes little account of historical realities, however. The Dalai Lama, still a minor at the time, was a nominal ruler only, dependent upon the advice of his regents and counselors. Harrer would have had no political influence, although as a Westerner fluent in English, he could prove a useful negotiator and translator when it came to foreign relations. Harrer's name is linked to several stories circulating of CIA plans to spring the Dalai Lama from Lhasa, both before and after the Chinese Communists marched in. An airstrip was stamped out behind the towering Potala palace to this end, and a documentary film of Harrer meeting with the CIA in Lhasa in 1948 is said to exist.

As it happened, such plans were thwarted. But as more Tibetans followed His Holiness into exile, Harrer helped them to sell the valuables and artifacts they'd brought with them. He became a dealer in antiquities, at the same time establishing his own museum. Its strong Tibetology department illustrates 2000 years of Tibetan culture — and Harrer clings to the vision that he and "Kundun" (as he addresses His Holiness) will live to see the day when they can return, with the collection, to the Potala in Lhasa in a free Tibet.

What are we to think of Harrer now, what to make of the incomplete jigsaw of facts, rumor, and ramifications? The pluses and the minuses? Nothing so far has come to light to indicate what he might have done (besides his sporting activities) in his Nazi role. Merely by embracing Nazism, he bears associated guilt for what came after, as do all former Nazis, but even Harrer's most vehement critics, like Rabbi Cooper of the Wiesenthal Center in Los

Angeles, point out there is nothing to link him to any atrocities. It is Harrer's silence they deplore.

It would seem that Harrer was duped and used by an unscrupulous regime, and for a proud man that is tough to swallow. There has been obfuscation on his part, too, though he may well now believe his own version of events. Meanwhile, Harrer has said he is producing an autobiography this year. He will call it *Meetings*. The opportunity is there for him to finally set the record straight about those pre-war years, write what he should have written decades ago. Whatever he writes, "Harrer liked to wear a white suit," says Trudl Heckmair, Anderl's wife. "Now the suit is not so white any more."

First published in Climbing *No. 172, 1997.*

Stasis
Change, loss, and survival
on the Moonflower Buttress

By Alan Kearney

It is a flawless November day in the mountains. The Pacific Northwest rarely gets a sunny day in November, let alone these past 10 of them. The snow crunches under my crampons and occasionally the crust collapses, dropping me half a foot. Frosted tree limbs sparkle as the sun reaches them and far to the west Mount Logan, Mount Buckner, and Forbidden Peak lie beneath a thin blanket of autumn snow. There is no wind, no one else on the mountain, and not a single thing to mar this otherwise perfect day, except that I have collapsed onto the snow and am sobbing.

Who knows what triggered these emotions: the crisp smell of mountain air, the sound of a far-off alpine bird, the whoosh of sun-warmed snow sliding off a slab, or just a suddenly consuming memory? I reel a bit and grip my ice axe, for below this gentle area of crusty snow the slope drops off steeply for hundreds of feet. I check my crampon bindings and slowly get to my feet.

The cause of these emotions is loss, too much in too short a time: a person I loved, my identity and confidence, and a good friend. Since I cannot go back in time, I can only remain where I am, emotionally stalled, or I can choose to go forward.

Two years earlier, my world had been shattered by a divorce, for the second time in my life. The first time it happened I was a lot younger and quickly substituted a climbing expedition for the loss. I could also rationalize it away because the person I loved fell in love with someone else. But when things fell apart a second time, climbing no longer healed the wounds. In fact I didn't want to go at all. Inwardly, I blamed climbing for destroying the marriage. In addition

I became acutely aware of all of my faults, boiling to the surface. For 18 months I asked a lot of questions, talked to a therapist, climbed sporadically and with limited enthusiasm. I seemed to be ambivalent at the center of a maelstrom.

And then something incredible happened: my good friend Steve Mascioli moved back to my town, Bellingham, Washington, with his wife and little boy after 13 years away. I had known Steve from the early 1980s when we guided together in the Cascades and Alaska. A graduate of Evergreen College, Steve came away with a degree in history but chose guiding and carpentry to pay the bills. He loved talking politics and philosophy while sipping a strong cup of coffee and smoking unfiltered Camels, although he later quit smoking. His favorite topics were the origins of climbing, significant climbs that changed the sport, and the heroes of old. He aspired to the great mixed routes, and climbed many in the Canadian Rockies — the North Face of Temple, the North Face of Mount Columbia, and the *Ramp Route* on Mount Kitchner — and eventually the Eiger North Face, with a Seattle partner, Bill Pilling.

Steve had been in town only two weeks when he called and came over to the house for a couple of beers. His huge smile and rasping laugh were the same as ever. Into the third beer he asked if I wanted to climb the *Moonflower Buttress* of Mount Hunter with him.

"Why me?" I asked. "I haven't climbed anything worthwhile in six years and I don't know if I can or want to do a climb that big and hard!"

Steve didn't look me in the eye. He twirled his beer bottle around and said, "You *have* done great climbs, and there isn't anyone better qualified to do this route."

"Ah, you must be referring to my alter ego, Hal," I said. "Well, Hal was suddenly disconnected 18 months ago." (Hal was an imaginary alter ego that I had used to get me up hard climbs, when my other half wanted to retreat.)

Steve, who had tried the climb three times with different partners, reiterated, "You have what it takes to get up a big route."

"It certainly is a worthy objective," I said slowly, "and it would give me something to focus on. We would have to put in some time on the waterfalls this winter. I could do that!" Steve's confidence in me worked and his faith was the cure I needed. Before we left to train in the Rockies I had practically agreed to go to Alaska and the 6000-foot mixed route. But I wasn't healed yet and I still had many scary days that reaffirmed my belief that ice climbing is a sport for lunatics.

Talkeetna was still a colorful Alaskan village. Although I hadn't been there in 14 years, the only changes seemed to be a few more buildings and higher prices. The essence of the place is its people. Alaska attracts eccentrics, including a huge bear of a guy with shaven head who called himself Trigger Twig. Trigger, part climber and part paramilitary fanatic, handed out business cards that claimed he would guide "very remote ice, very remote skiing, first ascents, [and] survival school, and perform alligator circumcisions."

150

Hudson Air Service had moved over to the airstrip with the other bush pilots, and although Cliff Hudson, a pioneer Alaskan bush pilot, doesn't fly anymore, we could still coax a story and a smile out of him. His son, Jay, had put on a few pounds and was constantly busy flying and running the business. During the trip up to Anchorage and our brief time in Talkeetna, I began to notice that Steve was subduing an urge to voice his determination for getting up the climb. He told me that during his three previous attempts on the route, he might not have completely committed himself to finishing it. I was still puzzled why he thought I'd make a difference, but after the physical conditioning and many pitches of frozen waterfalls Steve and I had managed the previous winter, I had to admit I was very excited about returning to the Alaska Range.

Beneath the Cessna, miles of snaking glaciers and a sea of peaks unfolded before our eyes. Since climbing in Alaska in the early 1980s I had been to the Nepal Himalaya, the Karakoram, and Patagonia. The length and breadth of Alaskan glaciers and the tremendous relief from tundra to summits puts Alaska in a class by itself, though. Besides, it lacked the hassles of permits, dysentery, theft, foreign language, and jet lag. Twenty years ago I first came to the range and climbed a diminutive 12,000-foot virgin peak between Hunter and Denali. I had made several more trips in the late 1970s and early 1980s, climbing Hunter, Foraker, Denali, and a couple of summits in the Kichatnas. I learned how to climb big mountains and wait out bad weather on these peaks. Like so many climbers before me, I fell under the spell of the granite buttresses, iron-hard couloirs, and delicately corniced ridges.

The plane bounced three times on the rutted snowfield airstrip of the Southeast Fork of the Kahiltna and came to a stop almost directly beneath Mount Hunter. In the crisp air of 7000 feet, we claimed an unoccupied tent site and unloaded three weeks of food and gear. With the tent up and a hot mug of cocoa in hand I settled back for my favorite part of expeditions: looking out the door at the mountains with nothing to do. Fog and clouds seeped into the Southeast Fork, delaying our start on the route. For several days a pattern developed of midday snowstorms and partial clearing. We waited, and inside Steve the tension began to build.

He was eager to get on the *Moonflower Buttress* and said that this was the last year he would be able to attempt it.

"Why?" I asked.

"Because by this time next year I will have two kids" — his wife, Lisa, was six months pregnant — "and won't be able to get away."

As climbers grow older and accumulate responsibilities they become increasingly concerned over the amount of time they have to get out and climb. I didn't believe what Steve said was true since I had met Lisa, and the two of them seemed to communicate well and respect each others' needs. But I could not argue.

151

As comfy as basecamp was, I also wanted to get on the route and see if I could still climb. I didn't want to let Steve down, or myself.

June 2 was clear and cold. Also in camp was a small group of friends — Steve House, Steve Swenson, and Eli Helmuth — who gathered around as we readied our packs and sleds for the two-mile ski to the route's base. They stood around with hot drinks as we made last-minute adjustments to our loads. Steve Swenson clipped my sled to the rear of my pack and said, "Don't have too much fun up there." As I glanced up at the huge dark wall I felt hollow, lacking in the exuberance of my partner or the excitement I had experienced before on other climbs. The big alpine game is risky and one or both of us might die.

I felt better once we reached the start of the climb and when Steve offered the first lead I said, "Yes, I'll take it." I could have memorized the topo, figured out which leads were easier, and then chosen odd or even. But at least there, on the first day, I plucked up a bit of courage and grabbed the initiative.

Soon my calves were aching on the moderate but steel-hard ice and the doubts came flooding back. Steve could have led the pitch so much faster and probably wouldn't have bothered placing the several screws that I did. At some point, however, you have to disregard what other people think about your abilities and concentrate: "This is what I can do today. I'll just keep plodding upward and try not to retreat for lame reasons."

Steve shot up his lead and suddenly it was my turn again. It was a drier year than usual and the Klewin Couloir — ice and mixed climbing at about 85 degrees — looked hard. The left wall was smooth bare rock, while in the right corner glistened a narrow ribbon of thin ice, barely wide enough for one crampon. I desperately wanted to relinquish the lead to Steve, but when I mumbled my apprehension, he said, "You can do it. I have complete confidence in you." This was not your ego partner who hogged leads whenever he could and chided you when you climbed too slowly. Here was a person who was strengthening a friendship with every word. I already hoped to climb more big mountains with him.

I took a long time on the tricky and strenuous pitch, but made it to the belay without mishap. So far, so good. When faced with staying put or moving forward, I managed to creep on and recapture lost confidence. Bit by bit I was reaching into the past and dusting off the joy-filled memories of alpine climbing. Above and below me were the clear cold expanse that has no smell, and the closeness of the giant peaks with their windswept summits. There was no where else I wanted be.

Two more days and as many bivouacs got us a third of the way up the route. On many pitches, the ice was thin and the climbing challenging. Hauling the packs was almost worse than leading, at least physically. I managed my share of the leads, except for the A3 up the Prow, a quarter of the way up the 4000-

152

foot-plus buttress, where I deferred to the faster Steve. Late on the third day we reached the First Ice Band, over a third of the way up the wall, where a long lead up moderate ice gained a bivy site.

After I took a long time leading the ice pitch and placing screws, Steve arrived at the belay annoyed, and said: "Why didn't you just climb the snow to the left? It would have been a lot faster."

I defended myself by saying that the snow was warm and unstable and offered no anchors, but felt chagrined. However, minutes later I recalled that Steve had always been bolder in style and I more conservative, and that some differences in opinion were to be expected.

That evening clouds and warmer air began to move our way. Thinking we might be stuck on the tiny ledge for awhile if the weather turned bad, I insisted we spend some extra time making it wider. It was always Steve's way on climbs to get by with less. To him the ledge looked more than adequate and he felt it a waste of time to do more chopping. We crawled inside the wall tent and got the stove roaring and hot drinks on their way. Partway through dinner the first snowflakes, big and soggy, began to fall.

All that night and the next day the spindrift dumped down. The dull roar of big sloughs coming from up high, occasional rockfall, and the eerie silence in between made me uneasy. I tried to discuss the changes in the weather and especially the change in temperature, but Steve seemed detached and turned the discussion to the climbing above.

Something was bothering me, a vague feeling with no concrete signs. It was as though an air-traffic controller sensed two planes were going to collide in mid-air, but everything looked normal on the radar. And, like the controller without anything to act on, I continued to go about my business normally, for the most part chalking the concerns up to my own unfamiliarity and fears. I thought once the storm subsided and the snow stopped sloughing we would be able to continue up. The wall was too damn steep for slab avalanches and as long as the ice was frozen to the wall the climbing would be fantastic.

By now, like many successful alpinists, Steve was totally consumed by the climb. "This is the coolest place anywhere," he said. "When I'm up here I don't think about anything else. Lisa got her doctorate in biology. Well, this climb is *my* doctorate."

On June 6, our fifth day on the mountain, the storm died. I wondered if it was too warm to climb but Steve seemed to think the route was safe and he had been up on it three times before. In fact his high point on the last attempt was here at our bivy, atop pitch 15. I sensed it was extremely important for him to break new ground. We fixed more hot drinks and delayed our departure until afternoon. In Alaska, one can climb well into the night — sometimes through the night, depending on your energy.

At about 2 p.m. we finally got packed with the hopes of climbing up through the Shaft, the technical crux of the route at 80 to 89 degrees, and past halfway. Steve led an easy traverse right and up to the base of a huge slot capped by a many-ton elongated snow mushroom stuck beneath a rock overhang. He eyed it warily and moved the belay to the right edge of the slot. From two good screws he hauled the gear up while I began traversing with jumars to the belay. I arrived at his stance and nervously sorted gear beneath the giant blob. If the entire thing fell we could both be killed, but mountain routes are constantly threatened by these types of hazards.

There was something peculiar about this snow mushroom, however. A sense of dread about the thing prickled the back of my neck. It was as though I was a tiny morsel of prey paralyzed by the gaze of a large predator. I was powerless to do anything but climb up and get past it. Running on instinct, I tried to climb the pitch quickly and get us both out of here. It was one of the few rock pitches on the route and at 5.8 seemed underrated. A final short bit of aid and a few offwidth moves ended at the base of an ice ramp leading up to the Shaft. I climbed up and left to a point just clear of the left edge of the mushroom and quickly twisted in a good screw at waist height.

Just as I leaned over to put my crampons back on I heard a dull whump and Steve yelled, "Alan, the cornice!" Six feet to my right the entire thing dropped away from the overhang, broke into several huge chunks the size of small cars, and scraped Steve off the belay. The weight of Steve and all our gear sucked me tight into the biner that was clipped to the single screw. Somehow it didn't break. Steve and the haulbags were hanging off the end of the 180-foot 11-mil rope some 20 feet below the destroyed belay station. I couldn't quite see him over a rock bulge, and screamed his name several times with no reply. He was surely dead, and I was absolutely alone more than 2000 feet up a big alpine wall.

If by some remote chance he was alive and badly injured, how in the hell would I get out of the tensioned rope and down to him? One of the many thoughts that raced through my brain was to just lean back gently, and cut the rope. What was the use of living? My life had been shit lately anyway. Even if I could get down to him what would I find? CPR and everything else I knew wouldn't be worth a thing here. Radios and cell phones? Steve and I believed in neither. My other thought was: "This really did happen and I'm still alive." While the shock did not wear off, a new and intensely powerful feeling took over and kept me in its grip for three more days. Terror.

For a while I did nothing but stare at the ice screw at my waist and the cable-tight bright green rope. I have no idea whether 10 minutes or an hour elapsed before I even thought about doing something. After the whump of the cornice and Steve's shout of warning it was eerily quiet. There was no breeze, just the faint sounds of melting ice and falling pebbles.

154

Again I seemed to be in a state of paralysis. I was loathe to do anything since any move I made could kill me. It is the nature of the human spirit to want to live. Perhaps the eternity of death scared me more than anything. And at that moment I felt I was being offered only seconds and minutes.

I deliberately valued the seconds and minutes I had, and then ran through possible scenarios. The 9-mil haul line seemed to be stuck on something and wouldn't budge. The third, tiny 6-mil line was with Steve and the gear. I had only a few screws, cams, Stoppers, and my wits. How could I get down the loaded rope and anchor it to the single ice screw? What would happen if I cut the rope?

I had, as usual, a couple of 6-mil prusiks on my harness. But a new thought suddenly terrorized me; did I put the pocket knife in the chest pocket of my suit that morning? It was not in the right pocket but hiding beneath a candy bar in the left pocket. For safety I secured the tool's lanyard to my suit zipper.

I sorted through the various actions and results, rejecting many and accepting only one: I must use one prusik to anchor the tensioned rope to the screw, anchor myself to the tensioned rope and the screw and then cut the welded knot attaching the rope to my harness. If the screw and prusik held I might be able to downclimb the tensioned rope with my remaining prusik as a self belay. I could not use any of my remaining two screws to backup the anchor since I might need them below to drill V-threads or for rappels.

If I was to survive I must repress for now the tragedy that had just occurred, and focus minutely on every action. The screw might or might not hold; but it was only one of a hundred steps leading to the glacier that could go haywire. I couldn't get too anxious about that one tenuous screw; there would be many more. I rechecked the prusik and started cutting. The last strands of the kernmantle parted and the knot oozed through the biner. Including our combined body weight and gear, my entire world was now suspended by a 6-mil prusik clipped to a single screw. I attached my last prusik to the anchored rope for a self belay and began downclimbing. After passing several loaded anchors I got to a small stance in 30 feet. Again I tugged on the haul line, which was buried under a pile of rubble from the cornice. It came free.

I could see Steve at last. He was slumped over in a pretzel position with the haulbags still below him. I yelled his name hopelessly. No response. Below him a long red stain streaked the granite where his life had drained away. Chunks of ice or rocks in the cornice had cut several bad gashes in our rope. I was extremely lucky to be alive. Had the rope cut, Steve and I would have both hurtled through space, since his belay station was wiped out (one screw ripped, the second held but the biner broke). It was not likely I would be granted any more "luck." What happened now would be a result of my actions ... unless the warm weather melted off more blobs.

After I retrieved the haul line the remainder of the day became tedious work. Getting to Steve's body, salvaging the haulbags (since I needed the food, stove, fuel, tent, and sleeping bag) and fixing a rope back to the previous bivy site took many hours. I could have used a couple more screws hanging from Steve's harness but could not force myself to touch him. Would he hang from this wall for months and years? I had no idea and didn't feel it was my place to cut him free.

By now I was becoming so focused on my own survival as to be functioning within an invisible sphere of my creation. The sphere was small — perhaps 10 feet in diameter — and somehow seemed to defend me from emotion, rockfall, or storms. I needed auxiliary power to maintain my sphere at full strength. Somehow I was going to get down the wall. I was going to survive.

I re-erected the tent at the bivy ledge and while the stove was melting snow I sorted through our gear trying to decide what to save and what to throw off. Into the save pile went Steve's camera, film, and his bandanna as a memento. The reject pile held most of his bulky personal gear, including his bright yellow foam pad. I considered the pad. If I stood on the ledge in the afternoon and waved it back and forth, any of the rangers at Kahiltna Base would see it in their spotting scope. Did they even know there was an accident? Hell, I could stand on the ledge for days and wave the stupid pad and no one might see it. The pad would be a micro speck against the enormous wall. I rejected the idea and vowed to get myself out of this predicament.

I woke up at an unknown hour still wearing my suit and boots, with my bag pulled over me like a blanket, and heard a chopper hovering right outside the ledge. I was thrilled to be rescued so soon after the accident and hurriedly undid the tunnel entrance to look outside and start waving and yelling. I got my head out the door but saw only murky fog. No sound, no ranger dangling from a cable and no chopper. I had been dreaming. My sphere was on the ice ledge and within it I could create rescues and transport myself somewhere else. The sphere had a dual ability; it could protect me, but it could also torment me.

Hours later I awoke again and contemplated the remaining descent. I had only come down 150 feet at this point. My complete aloneness terrified me all over again.

I also realized I was extremely short of sling material and began cutting the straps off Steve's pack and all of the tent cord that could be spared. The soupy fog that had moved in during the night persisted, cloaking key features. As I brewed up cocoa and filled my thermos with instant coffee I considered my three biggest fears: getting lost in the fog, running out of anchors, and a hung-up rappel rope.

It was time.

I tossed off Steve's pack and watched it bounce down the first ice field; like its owner just a lifeless form at the whim of the mountain. I belayed myself across the ledge to a fixed rappel that Steve had pointed out. He said the rap would lead straight down to McNerthney's Dagger, a narrow ice hose that we had climbed, and avoid the long and tedious Tamara's Traverse, below the First Ice Band. Pity I only had the one 9-mil rope and slender trailing line. Knowing the 6-mil's tendency to stick, I was reluctant to attempt full rappels. I devised a safeguarding system before casting off on each single-anchor rappel. At each station I got in several pieces of gear, threaded the 9-mil through the best anchor, got into my descender and loaded the rap rope while still clipped loosely to the extra pro. If all looked good, I removed the backups and gingerly started down the wall.

I did several 80-foot raps down steep rock to a point where I could see the top of McNerthney's Dagger. It was at least 160 feet of blank rock away, with no chance of finding anchors. The temperature seemed even warmer, and all around were dripping icicles and small snow blobs. It was a dreadful place and I really didn't want to use the spare small line. I threaded a long sling behind a jammed boulder and tried to extend the sling out over the rock edge a bit, but I didn't have any material to spare. Small pre-tied loops of tent cord dangled from my gear sling, but I'd need those down below. With no other options, I tied the 9- and the 6-mils together, performed my backup ceremony, and stepped over the lip.

A free-hanging rappel dropped me spiraling through the mist to land right on the ice hose just below a previous belay stance. I got in a screw and a couple of cams in the adjacent rock, and pulled. *Nothing happened.* I tried to stay calm. It wouldn't do any good to scream and yell up here. Were the ropes twisted? I couldn't tell because the fog had moved in thicker than ever. Should I prusik back up the ropes and try to reset them with longer slings? *Think, damnit, think.*

One more option. I attached my one remaining waist prusik to the 6-mil, gave myself some slack on the belay anchors, and hurled all my body weight onto the stuck lines. They moved a foot. I did it again and the ropes broke free. By the time I had pulled them down, I was shaking all over and dripping in sweat. That was the last time on the descent I used both ropes.

Above and to my left was another snow mushroom, smaller than the one that had killed Steve. With four rappels directly below it, I was gripped by paranoia. I skipped my backup procedures and slammed in single pitons for anchors. Finally the rap route took me out of the line of fire and beneath a small rock overhang where I caught my breath. Still trying to conserve sling material, I threaded three strands of tent cord through a wired Stopper for the next rap. For some reason I had not tied off the 9-mil after pulling it down from the last rappel. Holding it in my left hand while tying knots with my right, I brought my left hand up to fiddle with the knots — and dropped the rap line. With lightning reflexes fueled by terror-induced adrenaline I grabbed the rope out of midair.

I was consuming luck at a rapid rate and reassessed my mental condition and my goals for the day. Instead of attempting to reach the glacier, I decided to slow everything down and return to the systematic approach, reinstating all previous safety procedures. My goal became our first bivy site about 800 feet above the glacier.

The second night alone on the wall was a little better than the first. I had made it a long way down, was comfortably settled on an ice arete, and could see the glacier through patches of clearing fog. Thoughts of Steve darted in and out like random flashes of lightning in a storm.

I had at least eight more 80-foot raps to do, not much gear left, and a crevassed glacier to cross. Another storm was developing and spindrift was sloughing on both sides of the tent. One idea for crossing the glacier was to crawl on my hands and knees while dragging my pack in the hope that if I fell it would slice into a crevasse lip and brake me. The idea was a desperate one that came from remembering Douglas Mawson's epic survival in Antarctica after his two partners died. He towed a sledge, which nudged into the snow and stopped him each time he fell into a crevasse. My other thought was to use ice tools as buried snow anchors and self-belay across the glacier using prusiks and resetting anchors every 180 feet. Time-consuming but safe.

The pluses were that I was virtually unhurt, I still had both ropes despite nearly dropping one, I had at least four days of food and fuel, the tent was intact, I was warm, and my brain was functioning as best it could. I wished my robotic alter ego would reappear and take over for the rest of the descent. I hated the wimpy, frightened, indecisive jerk I had become.

Throughout the night, slides roared down on either side of my frail tent. Early in the morning the storm subsided. Occasionally the glacier appeared through shreds of clouds. There appeared to be a tent and two dots that were presumably climbers several hundred yards from the route's base. It might be my friends Majka and Eli, who had attempted the route earlier and were here to clean a fixed rope.

"Hello!" I shouted. A faint reply came wafting back up and I couldn't tell what the response was, English I hoped. "I'm coming down alone, don't leave without me, I want to rope back to the airstrip." Several tense seconds passed and then I heard an unmistakable "OK." Relief washed over me to actually hear living people since for two days I had been uncertain about my existence, not really even sure if I was alive, dead, or trapped in a nether world. Those dots below could establish my existence or evaporate when I reached them, as the rescue helicopter had. The sphere was tormenting me again. Somehow I must make it protect me for several more hours.

The last rappels were slow as I drilled one V-thread after another, taking my time to thread and tie knots neatly, tidy the ropes and set my feet with the care of a craftsman. I didn't attempt any further communication with my visitors, who turned out to be Majka and Eli, until 50 feet from the bottom, and then called, "Steve was killed. A cornice fell on him." In a few more minutes I was with them and related the story. I got a hug, sipped some hot coffee from my Thermos, and was amazed that I had survived. Eli had a radio and called Kahiltna Base: "Alan is down safely ... Steve didn't make it." Those people were real and after three days the protective sphere deactivated itself; I was in their protection.

Roped to my friends I started the long slog back to the airstrip. With few decisions to make my brain shifted into a pattern that would last for months, one of unanswered questions and a deep introspection of why we climb. Why was I alive and not Steve? Why did the cornice fall just then? Would Lisa hate me for being the person with him when he was killed? Why didn't I assert my feelings about the warm condition of the route?

Months later at Steve's memorial service, his brother Bill read a piece he had written about why he thought people climb: "It strikes me that when you're on a mountain, surrounded by nature at its most elemental with nothing but your skill and your love for what you're doing that, at those times everything gets stripped away, and what's left is just life, and death, and the raw beauty of the mountains." How concise! For all my years of attempting to express my love of the mountains and climbing, Steve's brother achieved what I had not.

And for nearly six months the questions came and went.

The bird has flown over a nearby ridge. The sliding snow has come to a stop far below and the memory of Steve lingers, as does the wisp of a cloud on a distant summit. Carefully I hike down snow slopes and through a hemlock forest, and make the long-sought decision. I have the first clear sense of my existence and purpose in three years. I want to move forward, where destiny will provide rich memories, both happy and sad, of climbing in the high places and the friends with whom I share this life.

First published in Climbing *No. 177, 1998.*

Dissent on Denali

Ninety-two years ago, the explorer Frederick Cook said he'd reached the summit. Was he telling the truth, or just the coolest lie ever? The battle still rages.

By Bill Donahue

"What is true in a man's life is not what he does, but the legend which grows up around him. ...You must never destroy legends."

— Oscar Wilde

By the time they reached that last windblown pitch, they were exhausted and chilled to the bone. "We breathed heavily," the explorer Frederick Cook wrote of his 1906 attempt to become the first person up Alaska's Denali, "and our hearts labored like gas engines in trouble. ...The mind was fixed on the glitter of the summit, but the motive force was not in harmony with this ambition."

And yet they toiled on, Frederick A. Cook, the Brooklyn physician who would later claim discovery of the North Pole, and his Tonto, a burly Montana blacksmith named Edward Barrill. Imagine them that September 16, their backs bent to the ardor of a pure, holy struggle, their mustaches frosted with ice. Cook and Barrill wore flimsy canvas rucksacks and camel-hair capes. They were climbing without crampons, and even their hike inland to the base of the 20,320-foot mountain had been, as Cook noted, a matter of "crossing life-sapping marshes and tundras ... always with the torment of death before us."

"One hundred steps," Cook wrote in recounting his summit surge for *Harper's* magazine, "and then a halt. ...Another hundred steps ... and so on in our weary efforts to rise. ...I shall never forget the notable moment when the rope became taut with a nervous pull, and we crept impatiently over the heaven-scraped granite toward the top." Cook and Barrill clasped hands on the summit; they gazed down at the "narrow, winding, pearly ribbons" of rivers below.

Or so the story goes.

Before Frederick Cook even got out of Alaska, a young climber, Belmore Browne, decided he was a liar. Browne, a junior member of Cook's expedition,

161

had stayed near the Alaskan coast, to collect plant specimens, and when Cook returned, boasting that he'd zipped up Denali and back in less than a month, Browne sniffed a hoax. "I knew it," he said, "in the same way any New Yorker would know that no man could walk from the Brooklyn Bridge to Grant's Tomb in 10 minutes."

A feud was born. In the nine decades since *Harper's* ran a photo of Edward Barrill clutching an American flag on the supposed pinnacle of North America, no question in mountaineering has caused more bickering and acid indigestion than Frederick Cook's claim to Denali. What began as a gentleman's disagreement, the no-nonsense Browne versus the dreamy-eyed Cook, blossomed into a war, a still-fulminating battle between reason and romance that has engaged a cast of thousands, including Cook's Polar rival, Robert Peary; the editors of *The New York Times* and the directors of the National Geographic Society; huge crowds cheering at train stations; President Franklin Roosevelt; and even the ghost of John F. Kennedy.

There are no neutral parties in this feud. In one corner, you have Browne and his heirs — skeptics who have systematically torn Cook to bits, discrediting his Denali photographs, unearthing geological errors in his field notes, and in general carrying on like beady-eyed scientists gone berserk. David Roberts, author of *Great Exploration Hoaxes,* notes that these critics have exposed Dr. Cook's fraud "more conclusively" than any other hoax in "the history of exploration." They have proven, even, that Cook never made it within two vertical miles of Denali's summit. But they have not prevailed. In the other corner, Frederick Cook, dead now for over half a century, still looms as a climber in whom we can believe very deeply.

We live in a prosaic era, a time in which almost any bozo with a checkbook can attempt Everest, and Dr. Cook shines to us as a paragon of a grander age. In his day, large chunks of terra incognita were still left. Explorers were romantic heroes, and Cook was the most romantic of all. He was a lifelong loner and a writer whose four books eloquently extolled the "mystery and promise" of the outdoors. He was soft-spoken and kind, and it's easy to regard him as a martyr. Both of Cook's great exploration claims — Denali in 1906 and the North Pole in 1908 — were ultimately trashed; the man was tossed into federal prison, on charges of mail fraud. And yet he died insisting that he was honest. Is it any wonder, then, that there is a fan club still loyal to the doctor and his great, good lost cause?

This club, the New York-based Frederick A. Cook Society, has 150 members. The most devoted are tweedy codgers who cling to that quaint notion of heroism, and to a conspiracy theory. According to the Cook Society's unofficial creed, Frederick Cook was savagely ruined by the "Peary cabal" — that is, the Philistine sponsors of Robert Peary's 1909 North Pole attempt. The National Geographic

162

Society, *The New York Times,* and a coalition of industrial titans known as the Peary Arctic Club had, the Creed posits, a vested interest in ensuring that their man was credited with the greatest exploration prize of his era. So, pulling strings (supposedly), they saw to it that Cook was kicked out of New York's prestigious Explorers Club in 1909 and ravaged by the press.

Fueled largely by a recent $500,000-plus bequest from Cook's late granddaughter, the Society uses a myriad of tactics to counteract the cabal. It publishes a slick quarterly newsletter; offers its historian $150 an hour to ponder, say, what Cook ate for breakfast on the flanks of Denali; and grants scholarships to teen researchers who toe the Cook line. The Cook Society's members have always clung most fiercely to the dubious claim that, in April 1908, their man became the world's first human to attain the North Pole. They have expended millions of calories refuting the testimony of Cook's two Eskimo aides, who said that Dr. Cook actually hung up his mukluks hundreds of miles from the Pole, just off the northern tip of Axel Heiberg Land. But on a recent dank day, Cook's fans shifted to their alternate passion: Thirty-five of the faithful convened in Seattle for a symposium on the peak they invariably call Mount McKinley.

The attendees wore ties, and were as grim as a clutch of professors contemplating the meaning of Melville. Ted Heckathorn, the conference coordinator, delivered the keynote address right after luncheon as one elderly spectator copped a few Z's. Heckathorn invoked the name of Scott Fischer, the Seattle guide who died on Everest, describing his and Fischer's 1994 trip to Denali. "During my last visit with Scott," Heckathorn intoned with the sort of gravity usually reserved for reading brass plaques, "he told me, 'I stood where Cook stood [on Denali's east ridge] and I matched him. I looked up the same ridge and saw the route to the top. It was doable.'"

Nobody said anything; a silent awe hung thick in the room. And the pessimist in me kept thinking that, at any moment, Bradford Washburn could burst through the door.

Eighty-seven years old, with a voice like rough sandpaper and a will of wrought iron, Bradford Washburn is the Cook Society's nightmare. He is the last remaining mountaineer who knew Belmore Browne, and a man who believes that Cook's summit stories are nothing more than "lies conjured up at Cook's desk in Brooklyn, New York." He is the director emeritus of the Boston Museum of Science, and he is obsessed. For over 40 years, Washburn has ground each and every one of Cook's romantical Denali assertions through the mill of scientific analysis. Cook's passage about scaling the "heaven-scraped granite" atop Denali? Washburn has climbed the mountain three times, and his summit photos reveal that the peak is buried in at least 60 feet of snow and

163

ice. Cook's claim that he could see "steaming volcanoes" from the top? Washburn points out that intervening mountains would forbid such a view. And the stunning black-and-white photos Cook published in his 1908 book, "To the Top of the Continent?" Oh, my.

To really understand Washburn's intricate relationship to those pictures, we need to go back to 1910, the year that Belmore Browne returned to Denali. Browne located, and then photographed, the very rock on which Barrill had stood with his flag. The rock, it turned out, was located 19 miles southeast of the summit, at an elevation of just 5260 feet. It is now called "Fake Peak."

Browne, a painter, died in 1954, but he bequeathed to Washburn a picture of Denali and how, really, could Washburn refuse the mantle of skepticism? In 1956, the geologist traveled to the mountain to finish his mentor's work. Washburn indicted six more of Cook's published photos.

For instance, he duplicated a picture captioned "In the Silent Glory and Snowy Wonder of the Upper World, 15,400 feet" at the rather inglorious altitude of 5240 feet on Denali.

For years afterward, Washburn merely trusted that his camera told the truth. In 1996, though, he took his incrimination of Dr. Cook to its logically final step. Washburn brought Cook's "summit" photo, along with H. Adams Carter and Browne's "Fake Peak" pictures (above), to the very lab that had analyzed the Zapruder film, the grainy home movie of the Kennedy assassination. Itek Optical Systems of Lexington, Massachusetts, pored over the photographed rocks, annotating every nubbin and crack and ultimately producing a lengthy report that concludes that Browne and Cook had photographed "the same peak."

But the photographic evidence isn't even the linchpin of Washburn's anti-Cook proof. There is the affidavit that Barrill, Cook's climbing partner, signed in 1909, confessing that the Denali claim was a hoax. And then there is the question of timing. The Cook party stood on the Alaskan coast in mid-August of 1906. A succession of early frosts hit them and Cook, suspecting an early winter, abandoned his summit dreams. He decided that he would merely do reconnaissance for future ascents. But then on the flanks of Denali, he glimpsed the dawn in "its fetching polar glory. There was a burst of fire," he wrote in *Harper's*, "and with it the great glittering spires above blazed with a glow of rose." He and Barrill decided to press on. Cook later claimed that, from basecamp, they climbed up the gently sloping Ruth Glacier and then up the treacherous East Buttress, a total of 44 miles, in eight days.

Of the thousands of people who have climbed Denali since the Alaska missionary Hudson Stuck notched the first undisputed ascent in 1913 (on the relatively gentle Muldrow route), only a handful have done it inside eight days. And the East Buttress, particularly, has taunted its suitors. When New Hampshire's Jed Williamson led the first modern party up it in 1963, it took

164

him 25 days and a wealth of fixed rope. Williamson never touched the terrifying double-fluted ridge Cook says he conquered. This hairy, approximately three-quarter-mile-long stretch of the Buttress has been attempted, but only once — by a party Walt Gonnason led in 1956. Gonnason failed.

"Look," Washburn says, "all I'm interested in are the facts, and the fact is that Frederick Cook just said he climbed Mount McKinley so he could drum up money for a trip to the North Pole. The fact is that that guy was such a con man he could have sold cracked ice at the North Pole. I have told this to those Cook people. I have challenged the Cook Society to a debate three times, but every time they've said they're too goddamned busy. They don't have the guts to face me, and they can't wait till I die; I know it. But before I get hit with a heart attack and get dragged out feet first, I'm going to put together a book telling the definitive story. I'm not going to leave those Cook people *one millimeter* of rope to work with."

Oh, the world is full of bullies, and Frederick Cook doesn't need their abuse; his life was too hard. Cook's father died when he was five and, as a shy, lisping teenager in Brooklyn, young Fred worked as a rent collector to support his family. He paid his tuition at Columbia University by running a milk-delivery business, then went to medical school. His wife and infant daughter soon died, after a complicated birth, and he turned to long books on exploration to escape grief. (He later remarried and had children.)

Eventually, Cook eyed a newspaper ad calling for an expedition surgeon. He applied and then sailed north with Peary, to begin an exploration career that, even his critics concede, was outstanding. In 1897, Cook traveled to the Antarctic with the Norwegian explorer Roald Amundsen and saved Amundsen's crew from death by delivering what was then novel advice: He told the explorers to eat penguin steaks to avoid scurvy as their boat sat locked in the ice for a year. In 1902, trying to reach the North Pole with Peary, he journeyed to 84 degrees north, and the next year he made an undisputed circumnavigation of Denali, a feat that was not duplicated for over 70 years.

No one will ever know exactly what Frederick Cook did when he was kicking around in the Arctic in 1908, but he was anointed a hero in April 1909 when he mushed into Annoatok, Greenland, claiming to have reached the North Pole the previous year. The Royal Danish Geographical Society awarded him a gold medal for discovery; a crowd of 15,000 greeted him in St. Louis, bellowing "The Star Spangled Banner." But by September, when Peary returned to the states from his own Arctic journey, dark clouds were forming.

The Peary Arctic Club began holding clandestine meetings aimed at destroying Cook's reputation. The Club's president quietly paid Edward Barrill $5000 to sign an affidavit, and on October 15, 1909, shocking news seeped into the headlines. In a page-one story, *The New York Times* quoted Barrill saying that Cook had never made it higher than 10,000 feet on Denali and had "doctored" Barrill's climbing diary, so as to conceal the lie. Barrill described a hike that included a four-mile detour to the top of Fake Peak and ended low on the Ruth Glacier, at 4900 feet. *The Times* rejoiced "Smashed is Dr. Cook," and two days later, Belmore Browne drove another nail into Cook's coffin. Before a committee of the Explorers Club, Browne asked Cook to defend his Denali claim; the doctor demurred. "Now, gentlemen," he told the Explorers, "I have been suddenly thrust into a controversy and I have not had time to breathe, have not had time to eat, and it doesn't seem to me that you should expect me to go into any details just at this moment."

Cook canceled his imminent lecture tour. He vanished from the public view but remained, his fans claim, the victim of a grisly conspiracy. In 1923, soon after he had launched a new career as an oil prospector, the doctor was charged with fleecing his company's stockholders — with circulating sales pitches that made great, gushingly fraudulent claims about his Texas oil fields. A federal judge dissolved Cook's oil business and sent the explorer to the federal pen in Leavenworth, Kansas.

Cook had hundreds of sympathizers at Leavenworth; indeed, on the night before he was sprung, in 1930, the prison's staff honored him with a rare farewell dinner. Still, he was filled with despair. "Few men in all history ..." he wrote, "have ever been made to suffer so bitterly and so inexpressibly as I." He spent much of his last decade writing a gloomy, unpublished memoir, "Hell is a Cold Place," and on his deathbed in 1940, he received at last one stroke of grace — a pardon from President Roosevelt.

The Associated Press reports that Cook greeted his pardon with a pained celebration, wheezing, "Happy. Thanks." It was a fine story, I thought, but I'd heard a more splendid version of Dr. Cook's exit, one that had him growing delirious in his last moments and whispering in an Eskimo tongue. Sheldon Shackleford Randolph Cook-Dorough, the Georgia lawyer who serves as the Cook Society's official historian, told me this tale, drawling reverently over the phone. He also told me, "I have made Dr. Cook my life's work." Indeed, Cook-Dorough (no relation to the august explorer) had read the entire 32-volume transcript of Cook's oil trial twice, studying 20 hours a day until, he claims, small flecks of tissue detached from his retina, causing him to see tiny black dots on the page. I was thrilled by the man's single-minded devotion, so I decided to fly into Atlanta to interview him in person. "Wonderful," Cook-Dorough exclaimed. "We shall talk all day and long and into the night, for Dr. Cook was truly a great man and ..."

On the evening I arrived, Cook-Dorough, 69, came out to the airport to meet me. Never mind that I'd never told him my flight number, or even what I looked like. He presumed, I imagine, that our mutual fondness for Dr. Cook would make everything right. We didn't connect but, as we later established, we actually did cross paths in the concourse, our eyes locking fatefully. Frederick Cook's most loyal apostle, Cook-Dorough is hale and ruddy-complected, with an unruly thatch of gray hair and a great urge to testify.

We met the next morning in the living room of Cook-Dorough's spare apartment. A portrait of his great-granddaddy, a Confederate general, hung on the wall and we discussed the sad case of Brad Washburn. "From the very beginning of his career," Cook-Dorough said, "Bradford Washburn was tainted. He was associated with the sponsors of Peary's trip to the North Pole, the National Geographic Society." The truth is that Washburn has created several National Geographic maps, but has received only one Denali-related paycheck from the Society — a $1000 research grant. Nevertheless, Cook-Dorough carried on. "And when any one of us is ushered into a field of study by people with fixed opinions, we absorb those opinions. It's very human, of course."

Cook-Dorough argued that he himself was guided into the Denali controversy by a level-headed soul. His grandfather, he said, talked "with great admiration about Dr. Cook, breakfast, lunch, and dinner" for eight straight years and, though the man died before Sheldon was born, his ardor flowed into his progeny's blood. As a law student in the late 1950s, Cook-Dorough read tomes like Cook's "My Attainment of the Pole." "I learned of all Dr. Cook had done," Cook-Dorough recalls, "and of how he had been relegated to the trash bin of history. And one day it hit me: 'This is a monstrous injustice!' I was overwhelmed by the personal tragedy of it. I abandoned my law books and rushed to the library."

For decades, Cook-Dorough focused his studies on the Polar expeditions. His interest in Denali wasn't piqued until 1977, when, at the funeral of Cook's youngest daughter, he glimpsed the diary Dr. Cook had kept on his climb. Another Cook descendent showed him the ancient document, briefly, before depositing it in a bank vault and Cook-Dorough was not able to give the diary the homage it merited until 1996. Then, he spent three months studying its 172 pages with a magnifying glass. He transcribed the tortuous cursive and gleaned cold proof of Cook's triumph — most notably, the gradual decay of the doctor's penmanship.

"As he ascends," Cook-Dorough explained from his perch on the gold velvet chair in his living room, "his legibility declines markedly until, at above 14,000 feet, he's just jotting things down. The phrasing is disjointed. The rarefied air of the higher elevations makes it difficult to collect one's thoughts, you know, and when Dr. Cook is hanging off cliffs or freezing at 16 below, the writing becomes even harder to read. You can almost see the pain he felt in grasping the pen."

Cook-Dorough has never personally experienced rarefied air. But of late he's been taking weekly strolls through Atlanta — hour-long walks he devotes exclusively to ruminations on Cook. He has also disconnected his phone, a distraction to study, and stopped going to the symphony or the opera. Dr. Cook is never far from his mind. "Sometimes," he said, "I just explode with joy. I remember Dr. Cook's achievements and I think, *That is magnificent!*"

Cook-Dorough kept talking. We talked on all morning — four hours without ceasing, even for a drink of water, and at last I asked him what his next project would be. Over the months that followed, Cook-Dorough would write me seven letters, as long as 11 pages, some rendered meticulous by a hired typist. The letters lauded Dr. Cook as "a hero, a very gifted man, a pioneer ethnologist;" they bespoke a tremendously restless passion. But now, in his living room, all Cook-Dorough could do was sit and grin beatifically. "The evidence for Dr. Cook is so monumental," he said, "I feel the major work has been done. I feel satisfied."

Satisfied? I didn't like that at all. What I loved most about Cook's fans was their dissatisfaction, their disdain for accepted truths and their unceasing pursuit of the Real Facts. I needed one more dose of quixotic fervor, so in the end I visited Ted Heckathorn. The host of the Seattle conference, Heckathorn also led a 1994 expedition to Denali. The $30,000 trip was funded by the Cook Society and it was clearly a seminal chapter in Ted Heckathorn's life. When I stepped into Heckathorn's home just north of Seattle, a photo from the trip, a huge shot of a sunlit glacier, hung over the shiny faux fireplace. "The Ruth Glacier," he pronounced with earnest pride. Heckathorn, 59, is a balding, sinewy retiree cum full-time freelance historian, and that afternoon he explained in intricate detail how his photo was connected to the vindication of Cook.

"You know," he began, "we really need to consider the drawing on page 52 of Cook's diary." Cook claimed that this squiggly sketch depicted a Denali neighbor, a spire he called "Pegasus Peak," as seen from far above the Ruth Glacier, at about 11,700 feet on the east ridge. Heckathorn aimed, in 1994, to prove that Cook's sketch was legit — that the doctor had indeed rendered it on the ridge.

The expedition started as almost a party, with suppertime sing-alongs and even a cameo appearance by Cook-Dorough, who hung out at the base of the Ruth, endeavoring hopelessly to learn the basics of alpine ropework. Eventually, though, Heckathorn left camp and climbed to 9000 feet on the glacier, a few miles past where he shot the huge photo. His guide, the late Scott Fischer, kept going; Fischer picked his way up to the spot where Cook had supposedly penned his sketch. Then he glimpsed the very view of Pegasus that the doctor had rendered and his certainty that Cook was a liar started to fade.

"We looked up at that double-fluted ridge," recalls Denali guide Vern Tejas, who was climbing with Fischer that day. "There were fingers of snow on it that extended 10 feet out over a sheer 1000-foot drop-off, but Scott was convinced it was doable — maybe even with the horsehair rope and the buckskin shoes of Cook's era. He wasn't exactly saying that Cook did it with that gear; he was saying that he, Scott, could do it. But we talked about getting someone to sponsor us to replicate Cook's climb. We kicked the idea around." When Fischer and Tejas descended, they shared their new open-mindedness with Heckathorn.

"It was awesome," the historian reminisces. "I could almost hear the Mormon Tabernacle Choir!

"Brad keeps pointing to the photographs," Heckathorn continued, "but they're just not material. I'm convinced now that Dr. Cook was carrying bad film packs. He'd bought his film early in the year and now it was September and they'd been going through streams and fog and heavy snow for months. His real summit film was probably water-damaged, so he used other photos to express what the summit looked like. Or maybe he just didn't bring his camera to the summit at all. Cook told one reporter that he left it in camp on the last day of the climb."

We were still standing in the living room, peering at the drizzle in the woods outside, and Heckathorn began to ravel off onto a new, utterly tangential topic — Robert Peary's shadowy ties to Kudlooktoo, an Eskimo who murdered one "Professor Marvin" in the Arctic in 1908. He drew me downstairs, into his basement study, to consult various documents on this conundrum and finally, after an hour, he segued back to Denali and its infamous "heaven-scraped granite."

"I know how Brad feels about the top," Heckathorn said with concern, "that there's a lot of ice, and no exposed rock up there. But the real question is whether there was exposed rock up there in 1906. There was a huge earthquake on McKinley in 1912, and the whole Muldrow route was turned into a jumble of ice. I'd like to know how the earthquake changed the configuration of the summit."

I pointed out that, according to Washburn, Denali wouldn't have a granite crown even if it were bare of snow. The uppermost rock on the mountain, Washburn says, is black argollite.

"No, no," Heckathorn said. "There are serious problems to Brad's thinking there." Last year, it seems, Heckathorn enlisted Vern Tejas to rappel down from Denali's summit and pluck the two highest rocks he could get. One rock, it turned out, was white, the other was black. Heckathorn sent the white rock to a geological lab, so that it could be professionally identified. "The report was faxed to me," he said with great satisfaction. "Granite."

I wanted to ask Heckathorn why on earth he was investing so much sweat into studying what one guy did in the bush of Alaska 90-odd years ago but he was still talking, with zeal. I couldn't cut in and finally I realized that, in truth, I didn't need to. We were surrounded by old books, and you could smell the mustiness of them and see the cracks and the dust in their brown leather spines. You could open them up, as Heckathorn had been doing all afternoon, and gaze at their fading black and white photograph plates. Here was a comely troupe of Eskimo maidens dancing near the North Pole; here was some long-dead explorer peering woefully at an endless snow-and-ice covered sea; and here was "Frederick A. Cook, MD" wearing a silk cravat and a round-collared shirt as his liquid blue eyes, noble and hurt, fixed on the camera. The past, it struck me, is enchanting — a million-branched river of stories. I could understand the urge to dive in and believe.

After a very long while, I made it out of Ted Heckathorn's basement. I climbed up the stairs and got in my car and drove off towards home, and when I got onto the highway I remembered the last page of Cook's book on Denali. The doctor wrote of taking Ed Barrill's flag and pressing it into a small metal tube. The tube was left, Cook said, "in a protected nook a short distance below the summit." Ted Heckathorn hopes to search for it some day. "I'd like to get up there with a metal detector," he said. "The tube could have been swept away in a storm or smashed to bits by tumbling rocks, but who knows? It's possible that if it was tucked away well, that tube could still be there."

I hope he finds it.

First published in Climbing *No. 176, 1998.*

Skyhooking
And how it was my first job

By Greg Child

Climbing is, more or less, my profession, but it got me fired from my first job. It happened in Sydney in 1973 when I was 16, working in a cockroach-infested furniture assembly plant in the suburb of Doll's Point. I had hired on as a "glue man," an unglamorous job that required a compressed-air-powered pistol to squirt glue onto the plywood skeletons of chairs and lounges. Another drone on the line then stuck on the comfy foam padding and colorful Naugahyde covers to make a luxurious lounge suite. The glue was a sickly pink color the consistency of bubble-gum, and it spat out of the pistol in an erratic, snotty stream. Within two days, my clothes were covered in the stuff. I signed on for the low-paying job for one reason only: to get enough cash to go on a climbing trip.

Most of the tools in this chemical-scented atmosphere were powered by compressed air, which produced a constant thump and hiss of electric generators and pumps that inhaled at one end and farted productively at the other to spit out glue, paint, staples, or nails. The noise was deafening, although to get the job I had had to take a hearing test.

While I sprayed glue I daydreamed of the climbing trip I had planned for the Blue Mountains. In particular I thought about an aid route I wanted to climb there on a chossy slice of sandstone named Dogface. Dogface had been formed just 40 years earlier by a massive landslide. The few parties to climb it compared its stone to that of a vertical beach. Nevertheless, it was the closest thing to Sydney resembling a big wall, and I spent my lunch half-hours eating Vegemite sandwiches, and scanning Royal Robbins' book *Advanced Rockcraft*

171

(although I spiritually identified more with Warren Harding). All summer I'd been accumulating big-wall paraphernalia for my adventure, and one day I brought to work my most recent acquisition — a skyhook — which I proudly displayed to my fellow workers.

The skyhook greatly amused the lads, partly because at the time in Australia there was a Top-40 band named the Skyhooks. They had a hit song with a line that went: "Whatever Happened to the Revolution? We all got stoned and it drifted away." My co-workers, oriented as they were to football, cars, and surfing, found my explanation of the purpose of the skyhook even sillier than my earlier revelations to them that people actually climbed cliffs for fun.

One fellow, a staunch trades-unionist known as Terry the Welder, was especially intrigued by my skyhook. His job, day in and day out, was to fabricate steel bar stools. Then, one day he showed me a huge three-pronged grappling hook that he'd welded up.

"What's this for?" I asked.

"It's a Cloud Claw," he said with a derisive cackle.

The lads called me Rocky Rock Climber, and they asked me to bring in other bits of climbing gear, as well as climbing magazines, for lunch-time show-and-tell sessions. Another bit of gear they fell in love with was the RURP.

"What does RURP mean?" asked Rick the Stapler as we punched out one day. Rick's job was to staple the Naugahyde covering onto lounges. He had a family of four and was barely paying the bills on his $4-an-hour job, yet drove a souped-up Holden Torana with mag wheels that he probably ended up paying off years after the car was rust.

"RURP stands for Realized Ultimate Reality Piton," I said.

"No shit? Well, Rocky, I'm off to the pub to have a Realized Ultimate Reality Beer, then I'm headed home to shag the trouble 'n strife," he shouted, gunning the engine of his Torana.

Being a union man, and the company shop steward, Terry the Welder advised me rather presciently one day that climbers should get themselves organized.

"I'll bet my last quid that the day will come, son, when you climbers will have some bloody-minded government factotum trying to stop you from climbing your cliffs. Remember, son, the only way for the working man to remain free is to form a union. You gotta stand up to the bastards or they'll grind you into the dirt! Am I right, Hedgehog, or am I wrong?"

He was asking for verification from the beady-eyed spray painter, Gary the Hedgehog, so named because of his resemblance to the furry burrowing creature.

"Yes, Terry," nodded the Hedgehog. This lad had spent every working day of the last six years in a booth spray-painting bar stools. He wore a respirator, but even so his teeth were rimed with black paint, as were his fingernails. He was nearsighted and wore Coke-bottle-thick glasses that were speckled with paint.

His confinement in the painting booth had dimmed his wits, and he rarely said anything beyond "yes" or "no."

Terry the Welder was also an inveterate gambler, always studying the racing form in the newspaper, and listening to horse and dog races on a little transistor radio he kept jammed to his ear. One day he bet me the price of lunch that he could beat me in a race up the factory wall. Terry would use his Cloud Claw; I would use my skyhook. The 18-foot wall was made of concrete cinderblock with big, flat edges between the mortar. I figured that I could fly up it using a skyhook and a Cliff Hanger, another hooking device of British manufacture. Utilizing the info I'd gleaned from Robbins' book, I would clip an aider to each hook and shuffle them from edge to edge up the wall. Just like in Yosemite.

On the appointed race day I brought my harness, aid slings, and some carabiners to work. While I set up my climbing system, Terry rigged a rope to the end of his Cloud Claw and swung it dangerously back and forth. His plan was to fling the claw into the rafters and batman up the wall. While the two of us readied ourselves for take-off, bets were collected by another staple-gun man, an ex-army veteran nick-named Gumjob, a toothless chap who had lost the bottom set of his dentures.

"Left 'em in Vietnam," Gumjob told me. "They were soaking in my cup while I was sleeping in a village one night. Then shooting sprang up all around us. I jumped up and started running and firing off rounds. Totally forgot about me fangs. Some VC papa-san is probably wearing them right now."

"Go!" The race began.

I stretched up and placed a hook on a cinderblock, stepped up the ladder on my aiders, then stretched up again and placed the other hook. Beside me, Terry swung his claw toward the ceiling. It missed the rafter and clanked onto the floor.

"Bugger!" he shouted, and gathered the rope for another swing.

"Come on, Rocky!" shouted my backers.

"Come on, Terry," yelled his.

I was halfway up the wall when Terry's claw found its mark and he started strong-arming up the rope. I slapped the top of the wall at the same moment as Terry. The race was a tie. No winner, no cash gains for the punters, and they showed their disapproval by letting fly a barrage of glue and staples that pummeled us as we hung from the rafter. Angered by the pink glue glomming onto his overalls and shouting that he'd feed a knuckle sandwich to the glue sprayers, Terry attempted a speed descent of the rope connected to his Cloud Claw. He slipped and fell into a pile of empty cardboard cartons, and his impact rousted a dozen-or-so fat cockroaches.

"Cocky alert, cocky alert," the crew shouted in unison. An even greater ruckus ensued as weapons were fired at the bugs. Hobbling the insects with glue then shooting them full of staples was standard operational procedure at the factory, and there were numerous old encrustations of roach guts, glue, and staples around the factory floor.

Our shouting and commotion roused the manager, who was sequestered away in his air-conditioned office. We called him "The Mirror," because his inevitable response to any request to fix a broken tool or adjust the short-changing of an employee's pay packet was, "I'll look into it." His face went red when he witnessed the chaotic scene.

"What the bloody hell are you lot playing at? Get back to work! And you," he roared, aiming his finger up at me, 18 feet above the cockroach battlefield, "consider yourself sacked, you clown."

I didn't really care that I'd been fired as I had already planned to quit at the end of the week to embark on my climbing holiday. Which brings me to my ascent of Dogface: I never climbed it. A week after my termination from the furniture factory I fell 80 feet to the ground from a climb at Mount Piddington in the Blue Mountains, and was hospitalized with a smashed tibia and fibula. My accident made the Sydney newspapers: "Youth Slips From Rope," ran one headline.

I never saw any of the crew from the furniture factory again, but while I languished in the hospital I received a get-well card signed by those salt-of-the-earth, cockroach-killing, blue-collar pranksters. If I recall correctly, the scrawled message read: "We always knew you were a bloody idiot. Next time take a Cloud Claw with you."

First published in Climbing *No. 177, 1998.*

Wall Rats
Yosemite's dream weavers

By John Long

I lived in Camp 4 for eight summers, and though during that time I climbed more than 20 walls, I never considered myself an authentic wall rat. I'd knock off two, perhaps three a year. A wall rat might do 10. And not the trade routes like El Capitan's *Nose,* where the going is straightforward and a fit free climber can really make time.

A wall rat thrives on routes where the cracks are like breaks in an old mirror, where nearly every piton hangs three-quarters of the way out of its slot, where there are no cracks at all and you must hook dimples and scallops and bash malleable copper and aluminum swages into seams and pin scars, where a single rope length might take eight hours to complete, and the whole climb, 12 days.

I didn't have the patience, or the mind, to do anything but dabble with these big-time "nail-ups." Although leading on them scared me, it was doable, lost as I was in the function. Belaying, however — tending the leader's rope, stranded in slings for days at a go — drove me crazy. The intensity of the belay is made more so by the long silences. Once the leader is 75 feet out, you have to scream to hear each other. You're essentially alone, too much alone. A couple of days of that and I had summit fever, the overwhelming desire to get off the climb — and that's just when a wall rat would hit his stride.

When wall climbing reached its peak during the mid-1970s, Camp 4 was divided between the wall rats and the free climbers. We free climbers outnumbered the rats 20 to one: proof, they reckoned, that they were the genuine article, since in any community it's always the few who do the crucial work. There were never many rats. Their craft was too dangerous and required too much suffering. Exposed as they were to sun and wind and long nights dangling in hammocks lashed high above the rest of us, they nonetheless lived in a somewhat sheltered world. Their crusade — if you could call it one — had slowly turned in on itself since Royal Robbins and the boys climbed the first wall, the Northwest Face of Half Dome, in 1957. In the ensuing 15 years, the rats had become increasingly detached and self-contained, finding security and even safety of a kind in the yawning void that the rest of us would pass through only at the fastest possible speed. In a very real way their game was drama in which they held fast to their outlandish roles, and seemed as bound by the fatalities of fortune as the protagonists in a classical play.

They called us free climbers "cuties" and "lightweights"; athletic enough, but lacking the essential steel to manage days, sometimes weeks, stapled to a big cliff. Yet they were always goading us to join them on some grim wall.

Many of us were wall climbers — on a limited scale, granted — but rarely did a season pass when a hard-core Yosemite climber didn't slug up a couple of walls. So the rats' needling — which for me started in late May and continued till the moment I left in August — had a grating, cumulative effect because it was not strictly true. If I said as much, the rats would jeer and taunt and berate me, then start waxing poetic about some giant new climb up some giant wall that I knew damn well would embrace great suffering and labor and terror — for me anyway.

I could almost always brush them off, but if I was reckless enough to let my pride get caught up in the whole affair, I'd call their bluff (in fact, they'd called mine), and find myself bashing up a wall with a couple of them. Twice I got suckered because I couldn't sufficiently recall the epic I'd had the first time around — when a projected four days turned into eight; when I took a 60-foot fall; when we ran out of food and water the last two days and our urine turned brown and my vitals ached for a month afterward; when I wished my parents had never met and I swore off climbing forever.

Many rats were extravagant characters like the wandering prospectors of the Old West: fiercely private and independent. They cared little for supposed glory and nothing at all for fame. Having their exploits publicized or praised was considered poor form because their game was like all obsessions: personal. However much they liked the hazards, toils, and long silences on the high crag, their climbing went beyond liking in almost all directions. What made them rats was who they became when they were pasted high above the world. A few were rich, rebelling against comfortable limits; most of them were poor. They all seemed to do just a little better on the walls than on the ground.

Most rats had their share of things going wrong, which all seemed to come from life on the ground. So they'd jump onto a wall and for a week or 10 days could get free of the ground, and the ground of them. Eventually, the walls

176

became their natural homes and their appointed refuge from a world that confused or annoyed them. But a few were different. They loved the ground, but the high crags even more. Zorba the Greek used to dance to forget the pain. Yet when he was happy, he danced just the same. I think if there had been a high crag in Greece, Zorba would have been a wall rat.

Necessity determined that they'd haul duct-taped water bottles, portaledges and hammocks, Gore-Tex rain-flys spangled with patches, ensolite pads and sleeping bags with names sewn into them (rarely their own). They'd also hauled boxes of Milky Ways they'd pinched from the lodge store, and cans of peaches in heavy syrup, tuna in spring water, greasy foot-long salamis and summer sausages, Pop Tarts, smoked oysters, Cracker Jacks, jelly beans, and Life Savers to slacken "Kalahari Throat." And sodas that would explode when opened but cut through the gunk that accumulated in your mouth after a day's climbing and so were treasured like diamonds. But it was the other things they hauled that said who they were.

Ron was an extraterrestrial buff, and he hauled pseudo-scientific texts about flying saucers and alien sex. He'd also haul a pair of "4-D" glasses, ludicrous red plastic jobs he had paid serious money for that any sane man could have bought at a joke store for a buck. Through these glasses he could "see" the gaseous trails of Venusian ships.

Hugh and Steve were two of the best rats in the business. One time they hauled (along with three cases of Moosehead beer) a bag of golf balls they'd filched off a driving range in Palm Springs. They teed up on El Cap Tower, a spacious, flat ledge about 2200 feet up the cliff. Along with 200 golf balls, they'd brought a three-iron, a driver, and a thatch of Astro-Turf, and they spent a June afternoon banging great drives into the meadow below. Several cars were struck, windshields shattered. The rangers closed the road down for three hours, and fanned out on horseback looking for a sniper. Cars backed up, overheated, rammed each other. Tourists fought. There were several arrests. The case was never solved.

Before he died soloing on Higher Cathedral, Joe hauled a hibachi up Half Dome and Mount Watkins. Russ hauled a small acetylene torch so he could barbecue franks. Along with half-gallons of Diet Coke, Charles hauled up a dozen Frisbees and hurled one off the wall every night. When he finally ran out, he grew bored, and led the last 900 feet of an extremely difficult new climb in half a day.

Jeff hauled a brass crucifix, a wallet photo of the Virgin, a fake Spanish doubloon, a slingshot and 50 marbles. I don't know why he hauled those things, or what he did with them. Bernie soloed the Leaning Tower and Half Dome wearing a yarmulke — partly from authentic devotion, partly because he was "so bald you could see his thoughts." Tom hauled a harmonica, a kazoo, and a

177

10-pound ghetto blaster on which he played the soundtrack from Doctor Zhivago till we were ready to murder him — and we would have if he hadn't been six-foot-three and 225 pounds.

They traded off hauling the bags, sharing the weight of strange lives, dragging up the wall what others did not want, including each other. They hauled the clouds and the rain and the sun pounding on their heads. They hauled thirst that would have killed a camel. Until an avalanche swept him off Mount Kenya, Dan hauled a medical degree up El Capitan. Others hauled scabies and the drip, smashed fingers and swollen feet, broken ribs and broken hearts. One rat hauled leukemia up El Capitan at least three times that I know of. They scattered his ashes over Washington Column from a Stearman biplane.

They hauled the very mountain, shards of it flaking off under 10,000 hammer blows, sticking to their faces and necks and hands, stinging their eyes, blinding them to everything below. They hauled the pull of the earth and they hauled the earth itself because they could never leave it completely behind.

Take Darrel, known affectionately as "Cro-Magnon," a Canadian woodcutter and the most stalwart bastard ever to swing a piton hammer. He had one bucktooth and a face like a cigar-store Indian. His fractured speech was the most conspicuous proof that he was self-educated. If he wasn't, his teachers should be flogged. He seemed to survive exclusively on malt whisky and "branch water," as he called it, and at the wee hours he could always be found stumbling back into Camp 4 with a load on. The next morning, it was straight back to the hair of the dog that bit him. Whenever he had a little more liquor on board than usual, some fellow rat would drag him off to El Cap, Half Dome, or Mount Watkins. It'd take him several days to dry out and hit his stride. The second he did, he wanted off the wall and he wanted liquor so he'd take over all the leading and climb furiously to get the business over with. By the time the team would top out, Cro-Magnon was in mint condition, while his partners looked like they'd just crossed Chihuahua on bare knees. Then it was straight to the liquor store for Cro-Magnon, then back onto a wall, then back into the bottle and it was just one crazy, endless go-around.

They hauled the stress of men engaged in dangerous work and they made jokes about it. They hauled their honor with them, for they were its only custodians. Some hauled loneliness so deep and so treasured they would share it with no one — like "Private Dave" from Montana, 30-something and heroically laconic, who always climbed his walls solo, which is twice as dangerous, three times the work and a hundred times more frightening. (If any climber should feel like the last soul on earth, he's the one hanging alone in a hammock in the dead of night, half a mile up a big wall.) After a long climb, Dave would join in at every campfire, laugh, and carouse with climbers he'd known for 10 years. Then, slowly, we'd see less and less of him, until finally he'd start laying out gear

178

on a tarp and borrowing water bottles. And where was Dave going? "Back to the high lonesome," he'd say, grim as a hangman, "where there ain't no people at all — yet." Private Dave preferred his own company, and up on the high lonesome, he and the work understood each other perfectly.

The sun and moon would come and go, but time was frozen for the rats. They climbed a foot a minute — maybe — working toward the sky, hammering, always hammering, beyond willpower and resolve because it was all instinct, an emptying of thought. They had no commission and no guarantees, no boss and no pay. They took insane risks. They'd wander over vast oceans of vertical rock, seemingly with no scheme or objective, because the yawning void was their overriding purpose. Their quest was their religion, and in religion seeking is finding. In other ventures, it's the object of the quest that often brings satisfaction, or something incidental picked up along the way. But in the rat's theology, desire was fulfillment, so to travel hopefully was better than to arrive. The summit meant nothing, the wall everything.

Eventually, some rats moved on to big mountains in Peru, Bolivia, Tibet, India, and China, and many of them never made it back. Over time, the others ran out of Frisbees and golf balls, tired of Cracker Jacks and Doctor Zhivago, could no longer see anything through their red plastic glasses, could no longer haul a world of their own making. By twos and threes, the rats left Yosemite and for many years, the walls were nearly silent.

They were the genuine article. They hauled life and death in the same bag. We called them wall rats and they hauled with them a dream now lost in time, like the slipstream of Venusian ships.

First published in Climbing *No. 143, March 1994.*

By the Book

Climbing the world's highest peak has become a routine if strenuous mountaineering exercise, a matter of tactics and logistics. Or has it? A look at what happened on Mount Everest in May 1996.

By Michael Kennedy

Summit day on Mount Everest is all about numbers. The South Col, the site of the highest camp on the Nepalese side of the mountain, is at 7906 meters. The summit is at 8848 meters. Climbing 90 meters per hour you should gain the difference of 942 meters in about 10 hours. Add a couple of rest stops and some time to enjoy the view on top, and you're looking at 12 hours up. Six hours for the descent makes it 18 hours round trip.

Then there's the oxygen. At an average flow rate of two liters per minute, a bottle will last six hours. You'll carry two — with regulator and mask, they'll total maybe 15 pounds — and your Sherpa support climbers will carry a third for you. That gives you 18 hours of climbing time.

You have to get to Camp IV first, of course, and that involves a dizzying amount of organization and hard work. Well before arriving in Nepal you have to negotiate an Everest permit with the byzantine bureaucracy of the Ministry of Tourism. You have to put a team together, and either raise the money you need or find experienced climbers to pay their own way. If you're running a guided expedition, you have to budget for guides' wages and expenses and find enough motivated and financially solvent clients to fill your trip.

You have to hire a crew of experienced Sherpas to cook, carry loads, fix ropes, establish camps, and break trail. You have to organize all the food, fuel, tents, ropes, oxygen, and sundry expedition supplies you'll need. You have to be sure your team stays healthy and acclimatizes well as you establish the route and stock the lower camps. Then you have to orchestrate these disparate elements so you end up at the South Col at the right time with sufficient ropes, tents, and oxygen for a reasonable chance at the summit.

It's all a matter of tactics and logistics, a routine if strenuous mountaineering exercise. The numbers add up. If you leave at midnight you can get to the summit by noon and be back in Camp IV just before dark. *If* the weather and snow conditions are good. *If* you are strong enough and determined enough. *If* nothing unforeseen happens.

One climber adept at making the Everest equation work was the New Zealand climber Rob Hall. Well-organized and vastly experienced — he'd climbed five 8000-meter peaks in the course of 30 Himalayan expeditions — Hall had made four ascents of Everest before 1996. He'd guided three of those trips, bringing a total of 39 people to the summit, including assistant guides and Sherpas. His company, Adventure Consultants, is widely regarded as one of the best in the business. In the spring of 1996 he was back with another group of clients, eager to make his fifth ascent, the most ever for a non-Sherpa climber.

A quiet and gentle man, Hall was renown for his caring relationships with clients. "Rob was so nurturing, so encouraging," says American climber Ed Viesturs, who summitted Lhotse in 1994 with Hall after the two had guided Everest together. "He had a genuine desire to get people to the summit."

Assisting him was Michael Groom, an Australian who had climbed five 8000-meters peaks and was intimately familiar with the South Col/Southeast Ridge route from three previous attempts, including a successful ascent in 1993. Hall's junior guide, a trainee of sorts, was Andy Harris, a strong and competent New Zealand guide who hadn't been higher than 7000 meters before.

Also on Everest last spring was a group led by Scott Fischer, a popular Seattle guide who had summitted Everest without oxygen in 1994. A committed environmentalist, Fischer had spearheaded the efforts of his team to remove 5200 pounds of trash from the South Col that year. Charismatic, outgoing, and well-known for his sometimes hair-raising exploits, Fischer was a larger-than-life strongman who'd climbed Lhotse, K2, Ama Dablam, and Broad Peak, descending the last with his clients in August 1995 just ahead of the storm that killed six climbers on nearby K2. Although this was his first visit to Everest as a guide, he'd been running his own company, Mountain Madness, and teaching and guiding all over the world since the early 1980s.

"Scott was a cowboy," says Neal Beidleman, one of Fischer's assistant guides on Everest this year. "He'd say, 'Hey, we're gonna climb this thing.' Then he'd look around and say, 'We need some food, we need some equipment. Grab some food, grab some equipment.' It was a different style, but it worked for Scott."

Beidleman, an engineer, ex-ski-racer, and mountain runner from Aspen, Colorado, had climbed in Alaska and South America. In 1992, on his first trip to the Himalaya, he reached 8000 meters on K2, and in 1994 made a rapid ascent of the normal route on Makalu with Anatoli Boukreev, the climbing leader for Fischer's Everest trip. An ex-cross-country ski coach and professional mountain guide from Kazakhstan in the former Soviet Union, the immensely strong Boukreev had more than 20 years of high-altitude experience, including two oxygenless ascents of Everest. In 1995 alone he had climbed Everest, Dhaulagiri, and Manaslu, the last in winter.

For most of its history Everest has been the almost exclusive domain of the world's best climbers, people like Hall, Groom, Harris, Fischer, Beidleman, and Boukreev. To be invited on an Everest expedition was an honor earned only after you served a long apprenticeship on lower peaks, and to actually reach the summit elevated a climber to the upper firmament of mountaineering stardom.

By the mid-1980s, however, the mountain's stature had diminished some-what. The main ridges and faces had all been climbed, and books like Tom Hornbein's *Everest: The West Ridge,* the story of Hornbein and Willi Unsoeld's remarkable first ascent and traverse during the 1963 American Everest expe-dition, had inspired generations of aspiring Himalayan climbers. Several oxy-genless ascents had been made since the first, in 1978, by Reinhold Messner of Italy and Peter Habeler of Austria. Messner, in one of the greatest moun-taineering achievements ever, had even soloed the peak, again sans oxygen, in August 1981. Two Poles, Leszek Cichy and Kryzysztof Wielicki, made a grueling winter ascent in February 1980. By the end of October 1985, 187 individuals had stood on the summit.

But a singular event that year would change forever the way people looked at Everest. Dick Bass was a brash Texas businessman with almost no moun-taineering experience before 1981 when he climbed Denali, the highest peak in North America. While descending to high camp, he came up with a unique idea: why not climb the highest point on each of the seven continents? Shortly after returning from Alaska, Bass got in touch with another hard-dri-ving executive, Warner Brothers president Frank Wells, and learned that Wells, too, had the same project in mind. Unabashedly amateurs, Bass and Wells were willing to spend whatever it took to complete what they aptly dubbed the Seven Summits.

Being the highest and hardest, Everest didn't fall easily to the pair. They helped bankroll four expeditions before Bass became the oldest person to summit Everest on April 30, 1985. Their 1986 book *Seven Summits* (written with another Everest veteran, Rick Ridgeway) reached a wider audience than the typical mountaineering title and awakened a previously untapped interest in high-altitude mountaineering. "People read the book, then decide they're going to climb Everest," says David Breashears, an American climber and film maker who accompanied Bass on his successful climb as well as two earlier attempts. "When you know that a 55-year-old Texan has gotten up Everest, you figure you can too."

What many people overlook, however, is the significant high-altitude experience Bass had gained from his multiple tries, and that underneath his "aw-shucks-I'm-just-an-amateur" bravado, Bass is a powerhouse, one of those unique individuals gifted with a special talent for altitude. He was assisted, moreover, by two guides: Breashears, who had four Everest attempts and one success under his belt prior to 1985, and Ang Phurba, a very experienced Sherpa who would summit again in 1988 and 1993.

On their summit day, the three were alone on the mountain, and from Camp IV to the top they used just 10 meters of fixed rope, on the Hillary Step, the most exposed part of the entire route. At Breashears' insistence, Bass used oxygen on the way to Camp IV, but they didn't sleep on oxygen the three nights they spent there. For summit day, Breashears and Ang Phurba had only a single bottle each, Bass two.

Bass's 1985 ascent signaled the dawn of the age of guiding on the highest mountain in the world — you could now, at least in theory, "buy" your way up Everest. Over the next several years, executives, doctors, and other well-heeled mountaineering aficionados flocked in increasing numbers to companies like Adventure Consultants and Mountain Madness, intent on conquering Everest or even the Seven Summits. It was a lucrative and expanding market, and one that Hall, Fischer, and a growing number of other professional climbers were eager to tap into.

People willing to spend up to $65,000 to climb a mountain are a unique breed. "There are three types of guided clients on Everest," says Breashears. "Trophy hunters, dreamers, or a mix of both." In Hall's group were Yasuko Namba, a Japanese businesswoman who had climbed six of the seven summits; at 47, she would become the oldest woman to climb Everest. Doug Hansen, from Renton, Washington, had turned back from the South Summit with Hall in 1995, and then worked at two jobs, building houses during the day and sorting mail at night, to pay for his 1996 trip. Frank Fishbeck, a Hong Kong publisher, had made four previous attempts on Everest, all guided. Three doctors, Seaborn Beck Weathers, from Dallas, John Taske, an Australian, and Stuart Hutchison, a Canadian, and an executive, Lou Kasischke, from Bloomfield Hills, Michigan, had each been on several previous guided trips to Denali, Aconcagua, and the like.

Jon Krakauer, a journalist from Seattle, Washington, was something of an anomaly among Hall's clients in that none of his previous climbs were guided. He also had no experience above 17,000 feet. Even so, he was a seasoned climber who had soloed a new route on the Alaska's Devil's Thumb and climbed the remote West Face of Cerro Torre. Krakauer was not just a paying

184

customer, either. He'd been sent on Hall's expedition to report on the boom-
ing business of guiding Everest, his trip paid for by *Outside* magazine. (His article appears in the September issue of that magazine.)

Fischer's people, too, were a varied bunch. Charlotte Fox, a ski patroller from
Aspen, had a wealth of experience both on her own and with guides, including successful trips to Gasherbrum II in 1994 and Cho Oyu in 1995. Her
boyfriend Tim Madsen, an Aspen native, hadn't been above 14,000 feet, but his
natural athleticism and background as a ski racer and ski patroller would serve
him well in the Himalaya. Seattle contractor Klev Schoening, an ex-ski-racer
who had spent his whole life climbing in the Cascades, had summitted
Aconcagua and Kilimanjaro; Everest would be his first guided climb. Lene
Gammelgaard hoped to become the first Danish woman to summit Everest,
and Martin Adams, a Texas businessman, had summitted Denali and been to
Broad Peak and Makalu, all on guided trips.

New York socialite and *Vogue* contributing editor Sandy Hill Pittman had
attempted Everest in 1993 and 1994. She had also climbed six of the seven
summits. Although described by *Vogue* as a "world-class mountaineer,"
Pittman's high-mountain experience has been largely limited to guided trips.
And like Krakauer, she was more than just another client. As the self-described
"communications director, writer, and climber for Sagarmatha '96," Pittman had
arranged, at a price, to file daily reports about the Fischer expedition's progress
on her NBC-sponsored website, "Everest Assault '96." (She also wrote a story on
her Everest experiences for the August issue of *Vogue*.)

By the evening of May 9, it looked as if all the numbers were going to add
up for Hall and Fischer. The last of their 14 clients had arrived at Camp IV on
the South Col late that afternoon. That didn't leave much time to recuperate,
but besides the headaches, lassitude, and fatigue most people experience at
8000 meters, everyone felt reasonably good. Accompanying them was a con-
tingent of experienced Sherpas, several of whom would assist with the summit bid. Others would wait in Camp IV, ready to help or rescue the returning
climbers. An afternoon storm, common on the upper reaches of Everest in the
pre-monsoon season, had blown itself out by 7:30 p.m. as the climbers settled
into their tents for a few hours of fitful rest.

The Everest game has always been an expensive one to play, and it's become
increasingly so in recent years. Take the peak fee. In 1991 it was $2300 for a team
of any size. In 1992 the fee rose to $10,000 for a team of nine climbers, plus
$1200 for each additional member. Then in 1993 it went to $50,000 for five
climbers plus $10,000 each for up to two more. Early in 1996, the Nepalese
Ministry of Tourism upped the ante once again, this time to $70,000 for a team
of seven, plus $10,000 for each additional climber up to a total of 12.

The costs of food, fuel, equipment, fixed ropes, and Sherpa staff haven't risen as dramatically, but they figure prominently in the final cost. Oxygen, too, is a major expense, and you need to provide it not just for your climbers, or guides and clients, but for the high-altitude Sherpas as well.

The result is that in Nepal, even the barest-bones private Everest trip costs around $25,000 per person. (Tibet is cheaper, mainly due to significantly lower peak fees.) For a guided trip you'll need to budget that much in expenses for each guide, plus their wages (at an average of $20,000 each), and amortize the total among the clients. Say you've got six clients and three guides. You'll have $135,000 in expenses and wages for the guides, giving you a total cost per client of roughly $47,500. If you get $65,000 from each, and keep your costs in line, you're making a profit (out of which you'll have to pay your office and staff expenses, advertising, and other overhead).

So whether you're spending it or receiving it, there's a lot of cash on the table on Everest these days. In peak fees alone, the Nepalese raked in over $800,000 last spring. One result is the increasing commercialization of the mountain — of the record 30 expeditions there in May 1996, at least seven were guided — but taking paying clients along is just the most obvious way to make money on Everest.

Direct media involvement is another. Krakauer and Pittman's writing assignments have already been mentioned. Breashears, who before 1996 had been on Everest nine times, most of them as either a guide, cameraman, or producer, led a well-funded team making a large-format film for the IMAX theater chain. Individual climbers, too, frequently profit from an Everest connection, often in less obvious ways.

One is simply getting someone else to pay for your trip. Raising money for Everest may be difficult, but it's much easier than funding a climb on Uli Biaho or Gasherbrum IV or some other obscure peak. Free gear and other perks are also easier to weasel out of companies when the world's highest is your goal, even more so when you've gotten up it. Professional climbers and adventurers, like Italy's Hans Kammerlander and Sweden's Goran Kropp and Americans Ed Viesturs, Alex Lowe, and Greg Child, are more likely to land lucrative endorsement contracts and prestigious guiding assignments once Everest is on their résumé. Even run-of-the-mill summitteers can parlay their success into slide shows, magazine articles, free gear, and invitations on future Himalayan trips.

Totem and commodity, an object of intense and at times morbid fascination, Everest also represents the essence of mountains and mountaineering for a public with no direct experience — and little interest — in any other form of vertical endeavor. Although over 600 people have climbed it since 1953, in many countries an Everest ascent still makes you a national hero. (In the United States, Aunt Millie at least knows what you're talking about when you mention the peak.) "People are humbled by the notion of Everest, its enduring myth of invincibility," says Breashears. It possesses an undeniable cachet, a sense of prestige and distinction that no other mountain comes close to matching.

With oxygen or without, guided on the "Yak Route" on the South Col or alone on the North Face, an Everest ascent is a great personal achievement. You have to put one foot in front of the other yourself. No matter how you do it, Everest counts.

Hall's group left Camp IV first at about 11:30 p.m. May 9, and Fischer's group, with Boukreev and Beidleman in the lead, moved out a half hour later. Fischer brought up the rear, as the three had agreed, to catch up with any stragglers. As leader of the expedition and the one who had taken their money in the first place, he would make the tough decisions about who should go on to the summit and who should return to camp. Another team, Taiwanese climber Makalu Gau and his two Sherpas, Nima Gombu and Mingma Tshering, left around midnight as well.

As was his wont, Hall kept a tight rein on his people. "Rob made it clear that we were all to stay together," says Krakauer, who along with Groom and Ang Dorje, Hall's head climbing Sherpa, broke trail for several hours. The three reached the Southeast Ridge at about 5:30 a.m. as the sun rose, and waited at a level spot on the ridge known as the Balcony for the rest of their team to catch up. By now the New Zealand, American, and Taiwanese groups were thoroughly intermingled, and people straggled up to the Balcony in twos and threes over the next 90 minutes. True to their word, Krakauer, Groom, and Ang Dorje waited as members of Fischer's team and Gau's group passed.

Before leaving basecamp for their summit bid, Hall and Fischer had talked about how they could avoid any bottlenecks as they tackled the upper part of the mountain. They agreed that Sherpas from each team would go ahead on summit day and fix additional ropes as needed above the South Col. Ang Dorje and Lobsang Jangbu, Fischer's head climbing Sherpa, were assigned to this task, but they didn't get the planned head start.

Lobsang, who was climbing without oxygen, was preoccupied with another task that morning. He'd been "hauling the assertive New Yorker [Pittman] up the steep slope like a horse pulling a plow," according to Krakauer in his *Outside* article. Asked about this later, Pittman said that Lobsang had girth-hitched a sling around her harness first thing in the morning and started "dragging" her up the mountain. She felt "uncomfortable and awkward," but hoarse with laryngitis she couldn't protest. In response to allegations that she'd made special financial arrangements with the Sherpa, Pittman said she didn't know why Lobsang had singled her out for special attention, and wondered if Scott told him to do so.

Whatever the reason, Lobsang wasn't out front as originally intended. Perhaps miffed that Lobsang was still below with Pittman, Ang Dorje, who had arrived at the Balcony early enough to fix the ropes himself, was apparently unwilling to do the work on his own. Now, partway up the Southeast Ridge above the Balcony, a series of rock steps stymied upward progress. Without fixed ropes in place, no one was moving.

After an agonizing delay, Beidleman grabbed the ropes and went ahead, fixing the rocky sections of the ridge with Ang Dorje's help. They reached the South Summit, just 100 vertical meters below the top, at about 10 a.m.

Meanwhile, several of Hall's clients had experienced problems. Frank Fishbeck had turned back shortly after leaving the South Col. Beck Weathers, virtually blinded at altitude as a side effect of an earlier eye operation, had implored Hall to allow him to stay at the Balcony in hopes that his vision would clear. Hall, who initially offered to send a Sherpa down with him, relented after extracting a promise from Weathers that he'd wait at the Balcony for him to return.

John Taske, Stuart Hutchison, and Lou Kasischke got stuck in the bottleneck that developed in the rock steps and at 11:30 a.m., feeling that they had little chance of reaching the summit before 1 p.m., elected to descend with two of Hall's Sherpas, Kami and Lhakpa Chhiri. When they passed Weathers on the way down he reaffirmed his intention to await Hall.

Traffic jammed up again at the South Summit, and exactly who would fix ropes on the Hillary Step, the final difficult section before the summit ridge, again became an issue. There was another long delay before Boukreev led off. The wind had risen and the mountain's characteristic snow plume began to arc out over the Tibetan side of Everest. Above the Hillary Step, Beidleman fixed the last of the ropes to a point just 150 meters from the summit. Boukreev, the only one other than Lobsang climbing without oxygen, arrived first at 1:07 p.m., followed by Krakauer at 1:17 p.m. Harris and Beidleman joined them a few minutes later. After that, "The floodgates opened," says Krakauer.

No one gets up any high peak without possessing a tremendous amount of ego and drive, the ability to justify the hazards involved, and a penchant for discomfort and hard work. When it comes to a prize like Everest, people tend to push even harder, to stray that much closer to the fine line between success and disaster.

Sheer numbers, too, breed a false but comforting sense of security. It took 26 years for the first 90 ascents of Everest, yet in the spring of 1993 alone 90 people reached the summit, the greatest number ever in a single season. Everest permits last May listed a total of 398 foreign climbers and high-altitude Sherpas, and that doesn't include cooks, liaison officers, and other expedition staff at basecamp.

188

Small wonder, then, that so many come down with Everest Fever, a peculiar resolve characterized by self-absorption and a certainty bordering on hubris. The malady stuck with particular force this year. "People were very, very confident," says Breashears. "They seemed to have forgotten that they were on the highest mountain in the world."

Decisions that would be inconsequential on a lower peak can have a profound affect above 8000 meters. Take turnaround time. "You have a limited amount of time with oxygen," says Viesturs, who has now climbed Everest four times, twice without oxygen. "You can't keep pushing it. At some point you have to be really, really strict."

If his team wasn't on the summit by 1 p.m., Hall had insisted throughout the expedition, they would go down. "Rob had lectured us repeatedly on this point," says Krakauer in his *Outside* article. Fischer had talked about summitting by 2 p.m., but he never pronounced a fixed time. Sometime on May 10, however, both leaders made the decision, consciously or not, to ignore their own rules. In doing so, they had to realize that they were straying into a gray zone where the likelihood of running out of oxygen, getting back to Camp IV after dark, or some combination of the two would become a real possibility. It's likely, too, that Hall and Fischer, the other guides, and the clients didn't give adequate weight to the insidious compounding effect of the delays at the Southeast Ridge and the Hillary Step, the steady accumulation of 10 minutes lost here, 20 minutes there, a half-hour somewhere else.

It's easy to imagine how you would feel standing below the Hillary Step at turnaround time, knowing that the summit was less than an hour away. If you had 20 years of expedition climbing to draw on, and your brain wasn't too addled by exhaustion and lack of oxygen, you might be able to evaluate whether or not you had sufficient reserves to keep going. You might even chance the summit, gambling with the near certainty that you'd run out of oxygen and get into camp well after dark. You'd hope to make the right decision, the prudent one, but it would be very hard to turn back, especially in good weather.

Consider, then, how a less-experienced client might feel. You've labored long and hard to get in shape. You've traveled halfway around the world, far from family and friends, and endured for weeks the privations of Third World travel, sudden storms, and high altitude. You probably haven't slept or eaten much since Camp II. You've put yourself in the hands of an expert, someone who will give you the best possible chance of getting to the summit, and you've paid a lot of money for the privilege. If you still feel the summit is within your grasp, when the guide tells you to go down it's going to seem arbitrary, even cruel, no matter how late the hour.

The bottom line? "We think that people pay us to make good decisions," says veteran Teton guide Peter Lev, "but what people really pay for is to get to the top." That's something that Hall and Fischer, with all their savvy and experience, would have undoubtedly known.

Other less obvious pressures may have affected their judgment on summit day, if not before. Guiding is a business, and the point of business is to make a profit. Marshaling their resources for a second attempt would have cost Hall and Fischer a significant sum, especially for oxygen, which runs about $500 per bottle delivered to the South Col. A second attempt would also take more time, and probably eliminate at least a few clients too tired to trudge all the way back up the mountain again. Satisfied customers, flush with success, and the favorable media attention likely to be garnered from such heavy hitters as Krakauer and Pittman would reflect well on Hall and Fischer's professional abilities and help secure a steady stream of future business.

In spite of their friendship, Hall and Fischer were competitors. Hall commanded immense respect among other expedition leaders and potential clients. "In terms of guiding on Everest," says Beidleman, "he was the man." The easy-going Fischer wanted a piece of the action and was starting to get it. Perhaps, as Krakauer suggests in *Outside,* they were "... playing chicken up there, each guide plowing ahead with one eye on the clock, waiting to see who was going to blink first and turn around."

Not that any of this was obvious or stated. In all probability no one on Everest even thought of it other than on a subliminal level. Big money, big media, and big status, however, are a powerful mix, and they exert an insidious and potentially dangerous influence. High-altitude mountaineering is an extremely risky game for even the best climbers, and doubly so for guides. Intuition, a gut feeling for subtle signs of trouble, is a critical component in the internal system climbers use to evaluate what's going on around them in the mountains. It's also a faculty that's easily obscured by ambition, pride, conviction, and all the myriad other emotions that help drive people engaged in difficult endeavors.

Krakauer tagged the top and headed down almost immediately, concerned with his dwindling oxygen supply and anxious to get to the South Summit to pick up his third bottle. Harris left a few minutes later. Soon others started to arrive, first Adams, then Schoening.

The weather held, with deep blue sky above and scattered clouds below. "There was no sense of alarm on the way up," says Schoening, who spent 15 or 20 minutes on top before heading down on his own. "I felt we were within the window." Beidleman, too, says he thought they were fine in reaching the summit when they did. He figured that Fischer was down below urging their clients on, and took comfort from the fact that more experienced guides like Hall and Groom were still on their way up as well.

Unknown to anyone, the normally strong Fischer had struggled all day to catch up and thus never got into a position where he could turn back the slower members of his group. He and Lobsang carried radios, but there was apparently little communication between the two that day. Fischer got bogged down near the end of the conga line of climbers weaving their way up the narrow ridge between the Southeast Ridge and the South Summit, and when he reached the Hillary Step, he was too far behind his group, and too late, to do anything.

There was a long wait before Groom summitted at about 2:10 p.m., followed a few minutes later by Namba. After spending about an hour on the summit, Boukreev decided to head down, and he and Adams left within a few minutes of each other. Beidleman had become increasingly anxious about the time. "I was getting super antsy," he says. "When Martin and Anatoli left it set off a signal."

Hall, Hansen, Ang Dorje and Norbu were partway down the summit ridge. Fox, Madsen, Pittman, and Gammelgaard, along with four of their team's Sherpas, Lobsang Jangbu, Nawang Dorje, Tenzing, and Tashi Tshering, were not far behind them. Gau and his Sherpas were also on the summit ridge, although it's unclear exactly where they were in relation to the others.

Boukreev waited above the Hillary Step for Fischer, the last in line, to come up the fixed ropes. After consulting briefly with the American leader and getting his OK, Boukreev decided to go down to Camp IV as quickly as possible. "I was worried mostly about people running out of oxygen," he says. "I thought it best if I am able to bring back more oxygen from the South Col." Boukreev quickly outpaced the other descending climbers, passing Krakauer, Harris, Adams, and Schoening in the vicinity of the South Summit.

Krakauer, like the others, had gotten caught up in the bottleneck at the Hillary Step. He had also run out of oxygen, and when he reached a gap in the fixed lines above the South Summit he was reluctant to go on, fearful he'd black out and fall off the ridge. Groom, who was now descending, gave Krakauer his own bottle, and the two climbed the remaining distance to the South Summit.

Revived by a fresh bottle of oxygen from the cache there, Krakauer headed down into the clouds, reaching the Balcony at about 4 p.m. The weather steadily worsened as he descended. Weathers, who had been at the Balcony for nearly 10 hours, was shivering violently. Krakauer offered to take him down, but with Groom and Namba close behind, Weathers decided to wait. Krakauer kept going, digging the intermittent fixed ropes out of the fresh snow. Adams, meanwhile, had gotten disoriented and wandered east onto the upper Kangshung Face. Groom helped get him back on the right path, and Adams followed Krakauer down the snow gullies and tricky powder-covered shale leading toward the South Col, and safety, 500 meters below. By dusk, each had reached Camp IV separately.

When he left the summit with Fox, Madsen, Pittman, and Gammelgaard at about 3 p.m., Beidleman knew they would probably get back to camp a little after dark.

191

The weather, still clear on the summit, was becoming worrisome. "The storm was visible below us," he later reported in an on-line dispatch. "It was snowing, but we didn't know that. I was just feeling incredible nervous energy to get the hell down." He passed Fischer between the summit and the Hillary Step.

It was the last time the pair would meet. "He said he was having trouble, but he was *Scott,*" Beidleman says. "I wish now I'd been paying closer attention." Assuming Fischer would tag the summit and quickly catch up on the descent, Beidleman continued down. Lobsang, who had climbed Everest in 1994 and Broad Peak in 1995 with his friend and mentor, was waiting on top. Fischer reached the summit at about 3:30 p.m., shortly after Makalu Gau, Nima Gombu, and Mingma Tsering.

By about 4 p.m., when Beidleman and his group arrived at the South Summit, things were beginning to get serious. They were running on empty, having already put in 16 strenuous hours of climbing with little or nothing to eat and drink. It was now a near certainty that they'd run out of oxygen before reaching Camp IV. Pittman had been faltering for several hours, and she crumpled face down in the snow and asked for a shot of dexamethasone, a powerful steroid that temporarily relieves altitude sickness. Fox gave her the intramuscular injection right through several layers of clothes.

The clouds lowered and visibility shrank to a few yards as the five resumed the descent. Snow began to fall and the wind became ever more fearsome as they struggled down through the gloom, past the Southeast Ridge and the Balcony. Halfway down the fixed ropes, Schoening stopped to wait for Gammelgaard, who had shouted for assistance. Sharing Schoening's remaining oxygen after Gammelgaard's had run out, the two encountered a struggling Namba farther down. After assisting her for a while, Schoening and Gammelgaard pulled ahead. They were starting to lose sight of Camp IV in the growing storm and darkness, and by the time they got to the bottom of the fixed ropes, their oxygen was finished.

Namba, who had also run out of oxygen, collapsed on the last stretch of fixed ropes. Beidleman got her down and started dragging her toward Camp IV, only a half mile away and 200 vertical meters below. The group now numbered eleven: Beidleman, Namba, Fox, Madsen, Pittman, Schoening, Gammelgaard, Groom, Weathers, and two Sherpas from Fischer's team, Nawang Dorje and Tashi Tshering.

Darkness had overtaken them, and as the storm intensified so did the seriousness of the situation. The featureless snow of the South Col offered few landmarks to guide them back to the tents. Earlier, on the way to the summit they'd dropped down a few meters from Camp IV into an indistinct bowl, then climbed a steep ice bulge to the broad, low-angle snow slopes leading toward the first fixed ropes. Now, given the wind and whiteout, and the exhaustion of so many of the group, Beidleman reasoned that it would be best to contour left, around the bowl, and head for the eastern edge of the wind-blown scree slope on which Camp IV lay. That way they could bypass the ice bulge and avoid a potentially exhausting climb back up to the tents, however small the distance, and use the scree as a landmark. The bowl poised yet another hazard: it dropped off gradually to the west, and Beidleman worried that people might inadvertently wander too far in that direction and fall down the Lhotse Face.

They contoured left as planned, but soon became disoriented in the raging blizzard. Communication was almost impossible and it became increasingly difficult to hold the group together. Beidleman remembers walking over a slight rise, then sensing an abyss. He was lost in the storm. "I knew that if we kept wandering around," says Beidleman, "pretty soon we were going to lose someone." It would turn out that they were near the edge of the Kangshung Face, very close to the tongue of scree leading back to Camp IV.

Screaming into the wind, he did his best to round up the 11. Everyone was suffering various degrees of exhaustion, hypothermia, and hypoxia, and their oxygen had long ago run out. "The only obvious option was to huddle up," says Schoening, who up until this point had held out the hope that they'd make it back to camp. The night before, the storm had cleared fairly early. "Now we latched onto the hope that it was going to clear at 10:30 p.m." They beat each other on the back, rubbed their arms and legs, yelled encouragement, anything to keep awake and stave off the brutal cold.

Boukreev had reached the South Col at about 5 p.m. Concerned with the time and the advancing storm, he headed out an hour later with oxygen and supplies and searched fruitlessly until 8:30 or 9 p.m. By this time, Adams, Krakauer, and some of the Sherpas had returned, but at least 18 people, including all three leaders and the 11 climbers huddled at the edge of the Kangshung Face, were still unaccounted for.

Stuart Hutchison, one of the three in Hall's group who had turned back early in the day, ventured out several times to look for the missing climbers, never going more than a few meters from the tents because of the fierce blizzard. Independently, he and Boukreev each tried to rally help, but no one at Camp IV was willing or able to go out.

At about midnight, a brief clearing allowed Beidleman and Schoening to orient themselves. Figuring that their only hope was to get to Camp IV, where they could hopefully send out a rescue party — "The grim reaper was one step behind us," says Beidleman — they set off with Gammelgaard, Groom, and the two Sherpas. "I was at the absolute limit of my endurance," says Schoening. "It was all I could do to keep Lene on her feet." Weathers, Namba, Fox, and Pittman were too debilitated to move. "I just wanted it to be over," says Fox.

Two months after the ordeal, Pittman says she wasn't terribly cold at the huddle and just needed oxygen and something to drink. In her feature article in *Vogue,* she writes, "I was afraid I might die out there, not from hypothermia but from dehydration." She also says that she didn't know what Beidleman and Schoening's intentions were when they left.

"After midnight, the clouds parted," she writes in *Vogue,* "and the stronger ones among us took the opportunity to run for Camp IV. I could not keep up. 'Don't leave me out here! Please, Neal, help me run,' I begged, but the young triathlete kept going.

"'If you can't run, then fucking crawl!' he commanded over his shoulder as I watched his headlamp fade."

Beidleman rejects the suggestion that he deserted Pittman and the others. According to Schoening, Pittman was "totally incoherent and hysterical" at the huddle. "I can't swallow Sandy's implication that we abandoned her," he says. "It was clearly our intention to get help. There was no other option." Madsen is more circumspect. Both Fox and Pittman were very weak, he says, and with communication almost impossible in the wind, no real discussion occurred between him, Beidleman, and Schoening. Madsen assumed that they would send help. Even though he was functioning reasonably well and was almost certainly capable of getting back to the tents unaided, Madsen selflessly decided to stay to assist the other four.

Buffeted by the wind and still not certain that they'd even make it, Beidleman, Schoening, Groom, and the two Sherpas staggered the remaining 400 meters to Camp IV and collapsed into the tents. Boukreev got directions to the others still out in the storm, but on his first attempt he couldn't find anyone. Sometime during the night, Weathers got up, and according to Madsen, mumbled something to the effect of, "I've got this all figured out," then stood up on a nearby rock. The wind knocked him over, and after that he didn't move. Namba, too, was unresponsive.

After returning to Camp IV for more information, Boukreev went back out again. This time he located Fox, Pittman, and Madsen. Namba was still with them, lying comatose and near death in the snow, and although his pack was nearby, Boukreev didn't see Weathers.

Leaving a bottle of oxygen for Pittman and Madsen to share, Boukreev half-carried Fox back to Camp IV, then returned to the others. The oxygen had helped revive the two Americans, but they were certain that the Japanese woman was dead. Weathers was nowhere to be seen. With Pittman over his shoulder and Madsen following under his own power, Boukreev dragged into Camp IV at 4:30 a.m.

Sixty of the 660 people who have climbed Everest since 1953 have done so without supplementary oxygen, several of them multiple times. Messner,

194

Viesturs, Marc Batard (France), Tim McCartney-Snape (Australia), and Lhakpa Dorje have each done it twice, Boukreev and Lobsang Jangbu three times. Another Sherpa, Ang Rita, holds the record: he's made it to the summit an astounding 10 times, all without oxygen.

Sucking on bottled Os may be anathema to purists, but climbers who use this aid are by all accounts stronger, more alert, and warmer than those who don't. Not that oxygen is a panacea. It reduces the effective elevation the climber is operating at by maybe a thousand meters, and even then you're functioning at a third-grade level. If you run out, you're in for a rough ride. "It's like you hit a brick wall," says Beidleman. "You're used to having the extra oxygen, and when it's finished your body and brain both slow down incredibly. It's worse than if you just climbed to that elevation without oxygen."

That's exactly the point, says Boukreev, who has been widely criticized for guiding without oxygen on Everest. "I like to depend on myself, not oxygen." Oxygen, he says, is like a drug that temporarily masks the symptoms of altitude. "You are totally dependent on it, and withdrawal is very dangerous." Boukreev maintains that he didn't use oxygen this year precisely so he could perform *better* than those who did. "My particular physiology, my years of high-altitude climbing, my discipline, the commitment I make to proper acclimatization, and the knowledge I have of my own capacities, have always made me comfortable with this choice." Nevertheless, he did carry one bottle of oxygen, a regulator, and a mask for emergencies as far as 8500 meters.

Given his climbing record, experience at high altitude, and almost superhuman strength, Boukreev may well be right to forgo the use of oxygen for his own climbs. He also says he had Fischer's explicit permission to do so on Everest. For an individual, going with or without the bottle is a personal choice. When it comes to guiding on Everest, however, few agree with Boukreev's conclusions.

The consensus is clear and unequivocal. "You have to use oxygen," says Viesturs, who typifies the response of every guide I spoke with (Viesturs himself has guided with oxygen on three Everest trips). "Anyone, no matter who they are," says Breashears, "is stronger and more able to help others with oxygen." Alex Lowe, a two-time Everest guide and a climber widely recognized for both his strength and technical skill, says he thinks it is "completely irresponsible" to guide on Everest without oxygen.

Beidleman, who toyed with the idea himself, says he asked Hall for his advice. Hall was emphatic in his response. "You've got a climber's hat and a guide's hat," he admonished. "Don't get them confused." Perhaps that, too, is one of the unspoken problems of Himalayan mountaineering in the 1990s. The increasing demand for high-altitude guides means that some climbers regard guiding less as a profession than as a way of fulfilling their personal ambitions. Beidleman, for one, admits that a large part of his initial motivation in guiding for Fischer was that he "really wanted to climb Everest." To his credit, in the end Beidleman more than lived up to the traditional guide's maxim: "You're here for the clients," as Viesturs puts it, "not for yourself."

In many people's eyes Boukreev violated this crucial tenet by descending on his own. All the guides I spoke with, including several Everest veterans, say they are puzzled by Boukreev's outwardly selfish actions. Breashears, despite his admiration for the Russian's mountaineering achievements and his efforts in the early hours of May 11, is severe in his appraisal. "Anatoli comes off as a hero for rescuing his clients, when he should have been with them in the first place so perhaps they wouldn't have to be rescued."

Boukreev bristles at the suggestion that he had anything but the best interests of his clients and fellow guides at heart. When he started out from the summit, he hadn't yet decided to go all the way down to the South Col. "I needed to see the situation with our group," he says, pointing out that he and Beidleman were not in radio contact with Fischer. "I was worried about the long time between Klev and the rest of our clients." After passing Hall and his clients and the rest of Fischer's group, Boukreev consulted with Fischer at the top of the Hillary Step. The clients and Sherpas were nearing the summit, apparently in good shape, and there was no clear indication that the weather would deteriorate later that day. He felt confident that Beidleman, Fischer, and the Sherpas would be able to handle the descent.

"I said to Scott that the ascent seemed to be going slowly and that I was concerned descending climbers could possibly run out of oxygen before their return to Camp IV," Boukreev says. "I explained I wanted to descend as quickly as possible to Camp IV in order to warm myself and gather a supply of hot drink and oxygen in the event I might need to go back up the mountain to assist." He had outlined the plan and gotten Hall's approval several minutes before, and after getting Fischer's OK he headed down.

At the time, Beidleman says he assumed that Boukreev intended to escort Adams and Schoening down the route, a fair division of labor given that they had three guides for six clients. Neither could anticipate, of course, that Fischer would soon be incapacitated. Regarding the oxygen supply, Beidleman points out that Fischer's party already had at least three or four extra bottles of oxygen on the mountain, in addition to the three bottles already allotted to each client and the two for each Sherpa. Fischer had also stationed a Sherpa at the South Col to help the descending climbers.

In *Outside,* Krakauer suggests another line of reasoning, writing that "… Boukreev's impatience on the descent more plausibly resulted from the fact that he wasn't using bottled oxygen and was relatively lightly dressed and therefore *had* to get down quickly." For all the reasons cited above, Boukreev is quick to point out he feels it's safer for him to climb without oxygen. He was

196

dressed in comparable, if not better high-altitude gear than others on summit day. Further, he had been told by Fischer to use his experience and judgment to ensure the safety of the clients. "I was authorized to climb without oxygen, because Scott Fischer was comfortable with my climbing history and capacities," he says. "I think my work and efforts on May 10 and 11 are an endorsement of Scott's confidence."

The fact that Boukreev probably has more experience with high-altitude climbing than almost anyone lends notable credence to his actions. He helped fix ropes on May 10 and was first to summit, ahead of his oxygen-using companions. His last-ditch effort to rescue Fischer on May 11, and his subsequent solo speed ascent of Lhotse (in a stunning 21-hour, 16-minute dash from basecamp on May 17) are ample testament to his incredible strength, skill, and drive. And the reality that Boukreev alone — of all the people who had made it back to Camp IV — was able to go out repeatedly into the storm and bring back all of Fischer's clients alive, is a powerful argument in favor of the decisions he made.

Whatever one may think of Boukreev's actions, they have brought to the surface a question that has been long debated. Since climbing on Everest and other 8000-meter peaks is such a serious and demanding task, is guiding on these mountains even reasonable? If so, what are a sensible, sound set of assumptions for guides and clients to operate under?

Viesturs is one who clearly believes in the future of high-altitude guiding — he's on Cho Oyu with a group as you read this — but last May's tragedy has sharpened his thinking. Perhaps because of the money, egos, and ambitions at stake, he says, guides have been more flexible on Everest than on other mountains, more willing to bend the rules. He thinks they should, if anything, be more strict, more by the book. No matter how much guides and clients might want it, both groups should recognize that not everyone is capable of climbing Everest. "Some people should be left out," agrees Breashears. "This year, no one was willing to say, 'You're just not fast enough to get up Everest.'"

Viesturs is unsure about whether he'll guide on Everest in the future, but if he does it will be on his terms. He would like to take smaller, more carefully screened teams. Even before getting to the mountain he would set up specific and clearly communicated goals — for example, going from Camp I to Camp III in six hours — that clients would need to achieve in order to have a chance at the summit. "I have too much respect for Everest to take just anyone up there," Viesturs says. "They have to earn it."

Boukreev echoes this idea, but thinks that guides should be even more demanding in terms of client preparation. Before you go to a high 8000-meter peak like Everest, he says, you should climb one or two lower ones; before that, you should do some 7000-meter peaks; and before that, you should have go to

6000 meters. "It is impossible to obtain and to master all of this experience in one expedition," he says. "Every step demands a separate expedition, and time after it to recover, to recollect, and to think through the experience." In Boukreev's view, guides should go through a similar progression, not just for their personal climbs but as a working guide.

Lowe, however, is one Everest veteran who won't be going back again as a guide. He says taking clients up Everest goes "beyond the line where you are in control," and that it was pure luck that nothing bad happened on his two previous trips. "I'm happy to tell my clients in the Tetons that I can take care of them," he concludes, "but I can't guarantee that on an 8000-meter peak."

Climbers on the South Col awoke on the morning of May 11 to learn that seven people were missing. Namba was apparently dead, and no one had seen Weathers since the previous night. Fischer, Gau, and Hall, the leaders of the three expeditions, were all missing, as was Hall's client, Doug Hansen. Andy Harris, who Krakauer had seen within 30 meters of Camp IV the evening before, was nowhere to be found.

Hutchison and a team of four Sherpas set out early on May 11 to look for Namba and Weathers. With Boukreev's directions, they soon found the bodies and discovered, to their horror, that the two were still barely alive and severely frostbitten. "[Weathers] was as close to death as a person can be and still be breathing," says Hutchison in *Outside*. He and the Sherpas decided that the all-out effort that would be needed to even try to save Namba and Weathers was too risky given the dire circumstances elsewhere on the mountain. Later that day, however, Weathers amazingly roused himself and stumbled into camp. Severely frostbitten — his nose and right hand were eventually amputated — Weathers was evacuated from Camp I at about 6100 meters on May 13 in a daring helicopter rescue by Lt. Col. Madan K.C. of the Nepalese army.

Fischer, it turned out, had been suffering from more than just the occasional slow day in the mountains. He started his descent sometime after 3:30 p.m. Lobsang stayed behind to recover his ice axe from the top of the last fixed rope. By the time Fischer and Lobsang were reunited a little above the Balcony at 6 p.m., Fischer had begun to show signs of cerebral edema and severe hypothermia. Short-roping him through the growing storm, Lobsang got Fischer as far as 8300 meters, about halfway down the fixed ropes. Here, unable to drag him any farther, Lobsang made Fischer as comfortable as possible. As he was about to head down for help, three Sherpas arrived with Makalu Gau, the Taiwanese leader. Gau, who was as incapacitated as Fischer, was also unable to continue, so the Sherpas left the two and descended to Camp IV.

The morning of May 11, four Sherpas set out to rescue the pair. They tried to revive Fischer with oxygen and hot tea, but although still breathing he was totally unresponsive to their efforts. They had better luck with Gau, and after a great deal of effort the Sherpas got him back to Camp IV, leaving Fischer for dead. Boukreev, hopeful that Fischer was somehow still alive, went up later that day. After confirming Fischer's death and recovering his camera and other personal effects, the Russian dragged Fischer's body away from the fixed ropes and covered his friend's face. Gau was helicoptered out two days later with Weathers, and is now recovering from his frostbite and other injuries in Taiwan.

In all previously-published accounts (including a story in the June 15 issue of *Climbing* and his *Outside* article), Krakauer had reported with absolute certainty that he'd encountered Harris at the top of the ice bulge on the evening of May 10 and watched him walk toward the tents at Camp IV. The assumption was that he'd become disoriented in the whiteout and fallen down the Lhotse Face.

A conversation in mid-July between Krakauer and Martin Adams triggered something. Was it possible, Krakauer asked, that it was Adams, not Harris, who he'd seen? Adams was skeptical at first, but soon became convinced this was the case. The two had been leapfrogging each other through most of the descent, and were likely to have ended up near the ice bulge at the same time. Clad in bulky clothes and oxygen masks, they were both out of it enough by then that neither could be sure of who they'd seen. No one besides Krakauer recalled seeing Harris anywhere below the South Summit.

A few weeks later, after a lengthy conversation with Lobsang and a close look at Ed Viesturs' photos of Hall's remains near the South Summit, Krakauer realized he *had* made a mistake.

The saga of Hall, Hansen, and Harris is a convoluted one, and given that all three are dead it's certain that some details will always be murky. What we do know is this. Hall waited on the summit for the ailing Hansen to arrive, and, according to Lobsang (who was heading down the summit ridge at the time) the New Zealander even went partway down the ridge to help his friend and client up the final few meters. The two were last to leave the summit, and Hansen, who had run out of oxygen, collapsed above the Hillary Step on the way down.

Harris had remained at the South Summit, presumably to help Hall and Hansen, and Lobsang last saw him heading up toward them sometime after 5:00 p.m. What happened after this is a mix of fact and conjecture.

When Viesturs, Breashears, and their film team went to the summit on May 23, they found Hall's body in a depression near the South Summit, his head toward the Kangshung Face and the upper part of his body buried in snow. Nearby were two ice axes, which Krakauer recognized in Viesturs' photos as belonging to Hall and Harris. "There is no question, one is Rob's and one is

Andy's." Partway along the ridge leading toward the Hillary Step was another ice axe which, without a photo, no one can positively identify, but it seems plausible that it belonged to Hansen.

It's possible, then, that Harris reached Hall and Hansen on the evening of May 10 somewhere in the vicinity of the Hillary Step. He may have been able to bring them some oxygen from the cache. A garbled radio transmission intercepted at basecamp at 2:46 a.m. suggests that the three were still struggling towards the South Summit at that time. Perhaps Hansen slipped and fell off the ridge, as the third ice axe implies. In a radio call at 4:46 a.m., Hall reported that "Harold [Harris's nickname] was with me last night, but he doesn't seem to be with me now. He was very weak." No sign of Harris has been found aside from his ice axe, so perhaps he, too, slipped off the mountain near the South Summit, or during an attempt to descend during the night.

Hall kept in sporadic radio contact with his compatriots at basecamp and Camp IV throughout the day on May 11. Enfeebled by the bitter cold and howling wind, frostbitten and hypoxic from nearly two days above 8500 meters, much of that time without oxygen, he was unable to move from his perch near the South Summit. He was patched through twice on a satellite telephone to his wife, Jan Arnold, in New Zealand. The couple had summitted Everest together in 1993, and Arnold was now seven months pregnant with their first child. She knew exactly how dire the circumstances were, but Hall stayed cheerful to the end. "Sleep well, my sweetheart," he told her at 6:20 p.m. May 11, in the last anyone would hear from him. "Please don't worry too much."

In the months since May 10, a relatively clear picture of the tragedy has emerged. On one level the facts are stark and unforgiving. Twenty-four people went to the summit from the South Col that day. Five of them died, and two of the survivors suffered horrible injuries. The rest have all returned home to families and jobs, friends and lovers and children, and endless questions.

It is easy to analyze after the fact, to pass judgment, especially from the comfort of a desk at 6000 feet in Colorado. What we have to remember is the human side of the events described here. Everything that transpired during those storm-filled days on Everest was the result of a series of superficially innocuous miscalculations and seemingly harmless decisions, all made by people with the best of intentions. We judge people by the mistakes they've made, but forget that we are all frail, imperfect, prone to the same errors ourselves. As one client put it, "It's hard to find a villain or a hero in this situation."

There is a sad inevitability, too, in the unfolding of this story. People have died in the mountains as long as they've been going there, and as much as we like to think we can control the hazards inherent in climbing all we can really do is accept them. "Commercial or private, it had to happen one day," says Mike

Groom. Or maybe it comes down to luck. You roll the dice and see what comes up. After all, the summit of Everest is as close to space as you can get on foot, and the margin for error in reaching it is as thin as the air at 8848 meters.

First published in Climbing *No. 163, 1996.*

Tales from the Gripped

Spooky stories from the desert,
in which the author suffers at
the hands of his partners, the
rock, and Utah's 3.2 beer laws.

By John Sherman

"This is not negotiable."

Tom Cosgriff was on the line, feeding me some bull.

"Listen, we had a deal," I said. "Remember? We were going to climb illegal desert spires until we got caught or you had to go back to Norway."

"No. We gotta climb A5 in the Fisher Towers." Cosgriff was adamant.

"Tom, you aren't getting me anywhere near those petrified turds. Besides, they're legal. What fun will that be?"

"This is not negotiable. We're going to the Fishers."

Damn him. How could I say no? He never does. Like the first climb we did together — *Gorilla's Delight,* a classic 5.9 in Boulder Canyon — me with a knee that bent only 60 degrees, Cosgriff with a cast on his wrist. No problem. Now the poor bastard spends most of the year stuck behind a desk in Norway, eyeing some plump blond secretary gobbed in makeup. I relented. Nevertheless, deep down I knew this was his way of getting even for that time I visited him in the Yosemite jail, the time I asked if I could borrow his haulbag, since he wouldn't need it for awhile.

He did bend an iota, though, and I got my sentence reduced. We'd climb the 350-foot Gothic Nightmare, hidden far behind the Titan in the Mystery Towers group of the Fishers. Endwise, it looks like one of the Coneheads wearing a jester's cap, dangling bells sprouting out of the top. From the side it resembles a sailfish fin. The Gothic was still unrepeated after two decades, a fact that appealed to Cosgriff. It was rated only A3, a fact that appealed to me.

There was one hitch: we needed gear, lots of it. Hence my descent into the abode of the Evil Doctor, Tom's pal, *Climbing* magazine's gear editor Duane Raleigh.

Had I not been with Tom, Raleigh would surely have never let an arch-traditionalist like me in his house. As it was, Duane was nervously trying to keep an eye on me, his gear, and his wife, all at the same time. In the gear room, my comments on some non-standard items were not well taken. When we left, Duane pulled Tom aside and whispered the doctor's orders: "Make him suffer."

At first, the suffering was limited to humping gear up the long approach, dumping it at the base, and hiking out. Then it intensified when we went for beer and pizza at Moab's famous Poplar Place. The jalapeno, garlic, and green pepper combo was, said Tom, "the most evil pizza I've ever had." Tougher to swallow was the wimpy 3.2 stout. The waitress assured us, "A lot of people are really happy to find beer like this in Utah." Yeah, that's like the happiness one feels when he's in jail, and only getting "befriended" by the little guy.

The next day we both felt like we'd passed a hibachi's worth of glowing briquettes. We tried a new, uglier approach through several inches of snow. Conditions on the Gothic were wretched. All around, the snow was melting, loosening stones, which hit others, until thunderous rock slides would rip down the walls of the Mystery Towers amphitheater.

We had reached the base, and were now committed to bucking out double loads in defeat. We hadn't climbed an inch. There was no sense in lugging out the beer, so we sat in the saddle between the Citadel and the Gothic Nightmare, and swilled. By the time we had split a six of King Cobra tallboys, tons of debris had worked its way down, and our psyche had worked its way up. Tom started leading.

Only the thought that Tom was suffering more than I was made the shady north-face belay stance bearable. He stepped on a drilled pin and blew the hole apart. He nailed knifeblades into millimeter-thick calcite seams. With enough pounding they'd go to the hilt and hold body weight. This was Tom's idea of a great vacation.

A few hours later he was at the belay, and I was following. I could've cleaned the pitch with a Fisher-Price hammer. Now it was my lead.

"Damn it. This isn't funny." My yelps only made Cosgriff laugh harder. "Shit shit shit shit shit." My voice was getting higher. "Watch me." It was 20 degrees Fahrenheit, I was in tennis shoes and thin wool gloves, and I was free climbing vertical mud. Not out of my own free will. The perfect #3 Friend placement I had excavated from the mud, jump tested, and moved up on had just exploded, leaving a depression the size and shape of a chili bowl. The only reason I hadn't fallen was that one foot was stemmed onto a knob. Now I was stuck: one foot on the knob and my shoulder pressed against the opposite wall of the dihedral. All the nearby holds were covered in dirt from my attempts to excavate the next placement. The pump flooded in.

Every piece was a time bomb, and if I fell, it would be onto the anchor. The day before, Tom had stopped me climbing so he could tie off the belay line. He hastily put another bolt in the anchor because the old ones were pulling out under this weight.

"If I get down to that last piece, I will lower off, let Tom finish this, and retire from aid climbing forever." Such were my thoughts, and "What if I don't?"

I reached down below my feet to the last piece, my balance big-rack, clothes-bundled, tilt-out awkward. My hands and feet were slipping on the dirt. I could grab the stem of the Friend, but knew that it would rotate out if I tried to lower onto it. My only hope was to clip on some aiders and step in.

I had one lousy inch of nylon to step through but it was lying flat against the wall like it was glued there. I tried to flick the aider away from the wall and kick my foot through, usually an easy trick, but not with the top step. The curses spilled out of my mouth in angry tones, plaintive tones, and tearful pleas.

One lousy inch of nylon.

The pump clock was ticking down. Then, like in some McGyver script, when he defuses a nuclear device with a pocketknife, as the timer reads one second left, my foot slid through. I eased my way down, clipped into the piece, and rested my helmet against the wall.

The panic vanished, replaced by a nervousness about the piece I was resting on. Then came a bigger fear. Not the threat of imminent injury, but the fear that if I didn't go back up, I would be a chickenshit forever.

I can't remember how long I hung there, regrouping mentally, forcing the decision, willing courage. Finally, I stood up, grabbed my hammer, and started gouging at the crack through the mud, waiting to hear that scraping sound when I reached real rock, my mind focused on one thing: making that next piece stick.

The summit ridge offered sunshine and snow and no evidence of how Bill Forrest and Don Briggs traversed it to its far-away highpoint. All we found was a hawser-laid rap sling encircling a pile of rubble; 20 years ago it was a sturdy pinnacle. We sat on the ridge, with nothing to do but listen to the intermittent rumble of the towers and walls eroding around us. Four trips in and out, a 200-mile beer run to Grand Junction, and two short, frigid pitches on the north face were all for naught — we bailed.

What possessed me to go back? Or should I say, Who? Not Cosgriff. He was pecking his keyboard, sneaking peaks at chunky hips and painted lips, and suffering through economically induced sobriety (seven bucks a beer in Norway). No, only one other person could drag me back to the fudge-brownie and stale-bread summits of the Mystery Towers. My partner of countless Eldo epics; the man who sent me on my first heading and hooking lead on El Cap, without telling me that the first ascensionist had decked on the same pitch; The Provider who lent me his portaledge, which ripped, sending me for a headfirst, 4 a.m. wakeup call; Mr. Confidence, Mr. Cockiness, and lover of all that is ovine — Robbie Slater. The Team was back together.

This time it was June. The beauty of the maroon-walled, Roadrunner/Coyote approach canyon was lost in the heat, loose sand, and shoe-sucking quicksand.

Our objective was all three Mystery Towers: the Doric Column, the Citadel, and the Gothic Nightmare.

First was the Doric. Say it fast and it sounds like Dork, which is just what it looks like.

Kor was first to try it, but backed off when he saw how much drilling would be required. Forrest and George Hurley then bagged the first ascent in 1969, sneaking onto the summit while their British partner Rod Chuck, tired of being bombarded at the belays, rested on the ground. The Yanks pulled their ropes on the way down. Chuck was not amused. Twenty-three years later, in 1992, a fellow Brit, Steve "Crusher" Bartlett, revenged the injustice, making the second ascent with George "Chip" Wilson.

The first pitch was mostly free climbing. A 5.7 dirt mantel gave me brief pause, half an hour or so, for reflection. It wouldn't have taken so long if I didn't keep glancing down to see our half-naked companion sunbathing at the base. Knowing Rob's penchant for flat-chested blondes, I had no worries about him being distracted from his belay duties.

Soon, the anchor was cause for thought. Crusher's bolts, now two months old, were already coming loose in the soft rock. I drilled another, feeling the vibrations through my feet. Later, I could feel Rob clean pins 40 feet below.

The next three pitches climbed a mud-encrusted chimney/groove that resembled the inside of a giant gutted fish. Here, the second-ascent crew had freshly riveted Forrest's bolt and bathook ladder for us, so progress was quick and easy for the leader. For the belayer, it could never be quick enough. Mud clods bombarded the belayer's helmet every few minutes, and goggles, bandannas, and long-sleeved shirts couldn't keep the dirt from grinding against the teeth, plugging the ears, and invading every pore. Days after the ascent my nose continued to produce twin strands of red-brown mucus.

On top we basked in the late afternoon sun, strolling about the spacious summit, clambering up the boulder marking the high point. Forrest and Hurley, not having known they'd bag it the day they did, had not left a register. Crusher had, however, with a note that said, "The Citadel is next."

The Citadel and the Gothic — both unrepeated, both prizes, both tottering piles of choss you could piss a bolt hole into. Crusher might come back any day, so the Citadel was next.

The Citadel looks like an Olympic medals stand viewed in a funhouse mirror, the kind that stretches you out so you look like Manute Bol. The first pitch appeared to be a casual dirt scramble, so I volunteered for the lead.

Off-route from the start, I had soon paddled across a dirt slab I dared not reverse. I had no gear in, and below was series of 35-degree dirt shelves with six-foot drops between them. It would be an ugly fall, like rolling a 165-pound baseball down 10 flights of stairs.

As the dirt under my feet continuously gave way, I slowly walked in place. I desperately needed pro, but the only weakness in the rock slab at my chest was a seam thinner than a pencil line. I had no RURPs, so I pounded two knifeblades in. One actually went in half an inch, before it busted off the side of the seam. I tied off and equalized the pins, then agonized over the flexing 5.5 mantelshelf in front of me for another 15 minutes.

I figured I'd rather fall going up than going down, and figured I had little choice. What I didn't figure was that the dirt above was dark brown, facing south, and now heated to over 100 degrees. When I got there it was too hot to hang onto. Fortunately, the angle was low enough that I could chop steps with my hammer, like ice climbing in the Sahara.

A hundred feet of zigzag climbing had netted me only 40 feet in elevation. The next anchor was half a rope away so it was decided — I don't remember by whom — that I should lead up to it and get us a full rope off the ground. Had I read Hurley's 1970 article on the Mystery Towers in *Climbing* prior to our ascent, this would surely have been Rob's lead. In it, Forrest recounts the fall he took on this pitch when a bolt broke under his weight. He had removed the bathooks below, and the only pro left between him and a lengthy fall was a fold he tied off in the mud curtain. Miraculously, the thread held.

I had read about the Mystery Towers in the guidebook, however, and was aware of certain tricks used to ascend them: the curtain tie-offs for one, pins forced in calcite veins for another, and angles driven into mud tent-stake style. Within 30 feet I had employed techniques two and three, as well as some steps carved in the mud. I reached a bolt and promptly backed it up with the worst bolt I ever placed.

Next came a blank section. The only hint of passage was a couple of millimeter-deep dimples, the remnants of bathook holes. Given that most of the old bolts were now hanging about an inch out from the rock due to erosion, I figured that Forrest drilled bathook holes roughly an inch deep. At first I tried to preserve Forrest's pattern: two to three holes, then a bolt. In the last two decades, however, not only had the rock changed, but so had the technology. Bathooks were no longer in vogue, so as Crusher had done on the Doric, I put rivets in my freshly drilled inch-deep holes. An ethical quandary ensued. Forrest had taken more risk — his hook holes were empty after he passed them. He had nothing to stop a fall except a bolt every 15 feet or so

— small consolation in this rock. At least I had eight cents worth of soft steel carriage bolt plugging every hole, plus thicker bolts backing up his coffin nails. It didn't seem sporting, even if my rivets were the weakest money could buy.

I stopped backing up Forrest's bolts, and began tying off their exposed shanks and using them as rivets — the ones that didn't pull out in my fingers, that is. I nailed whenever possible. Fifty feet above my last bolt, I shuddered, looking down at the string of bent rivets and shaky pins beneath me. A long stretch and I hooked the pick end of my hammer through the rotting slings and gingerly pulled upon the anchor.

Slater chuckled up the next pitch, in the process performing the impossible — he fixed a pin in the Fisher Towers. Half an hour of pounding wouldn't get it out. Half a year of erosion probably will.

We were keeping the same pace as the first ascent — 100 feet per day. In the guidebook, the Citadel is listed as Grade V, even though it is only 400 feet tall. At the rate we were going, it would be a Grade VI. Every bit of work done by the first-ascent party had to be redone. The old pin scars and bathook holes had long since eroded away, and only a handful of original bolts still supported body weight.

Day three on the Citadel. We started up the fixed lines early — the thermometer read a mere 95 degrees. The long summit pitch was mine, the endless belay session Rob's. The first 80 feet was mostly putting in rivets, the only fun coming when I plucked out the old bolts — some in only a quarter inch — with my fingers.

I reached a shoulder on the arete and balanced across a doormat-width of mud gangplank to the final headwall. Sheer walls dropped away on either side. If the ridge should crumble, I thought, I have to fling myself over the opposite side, so the rope would catch me. At the base of the headwall, I clipped the old bolt anchor, gratefully. I had plenty of rope left so, after hauling up some water, kept going.

Above, the rock was so decomposed that it was turning into mud in situ. I went to work on a crack. A few taps sent in a one-inch angle. Fingers pulled it out. Ditto for the inch-and-a-half. Ditto for the two-inch. Ditto for the three-inch bong. Now I had a fist-sized hole in the crack pouring sand. I might as well have been nailing a giant sugar cube.

Twenty-five feet up was a three-bolt ladder to the solid capstone summit crack. The only way up would be to nail the mud curtain. I grabbed the three-inch Longware bong, a historic borrowed piece of iron, angled it down slightly, and pounded it in until only the sling on the eye poked out through the mud. It went in like a dull knife punched into a jack-o-lantern.

Pounding in the next bong, I could feel the whole curtain shake. I returned to the ridge to test it, a pattern I would keep up as along as my chain of aiders would reach.

The line went straight up, and a fall would certainly intercept the ridge; I would end up either draped and broken over it, or pound into it then fly down the exposed face on the right or ricochet down the steep flute on the left.

The last 12 feet had taken four hours. I had drained the water bottle at the ridge. We had enough light to make the summit, but I didn't have enough nerves left. In my exhausted and dehydrated state, it would be easy to make a mistake. Day three ended 20 feet shy of the top.

The next day I went back up, shoving a few of the placements back in with my hands. Soon I was grabbing the rappel slings snaking through the crack at the summit. They came free in my hands, rotted through by 23 years of sunshine and wind.

As Rob pulled over the lip, he declared it the coolest summit in the desert. Just like he had with the Doric Column. Just like he had on every spire he'd climbed. We sent the temptingest trundle in celebration.

We had run out of time. The Gothic Nightmare would have to wait for another trip.

Eleven months later it was a race. With the exception of the Titan, the Fisher Towers had been virtually ignored for two decades. Now they had become trendy among some of the Boulder crowd. Rob had ticked nearly every Fisher Tower in the guide, and in his outspoken way, had declared his intention to be first to top them all. Others soon declared their intention to beat Rob, then begged him for Beta and pin lists. "The race will be over when I finish," was all Rob would tell them, "no sooner."

I just wanted to do the three Mystery Towers and in the process settle my score with the Gothic, preferably with the second ascent.

Rob had been in the Fishers every weekend for four months. Loyal to The Team, he had been saving the Gothic to do with me. Our experience on the Citadel convinced us this would be more than a weekend project, and Rob had a Monday-through-Friday job. Hence we extended honorary Team membership to Mike O'Donnell, Rob's *Sea of Dreams* partner: a soft-spoken, red-haired brute from Boulder with a list of wild escapades rivaled by few, including a failed attempt at the Gothic in which an expanding flake both he and I had nailed came loose on its own, fell 25 feet, clocked the retreating Mike in the head, and split his helmet from one end to the other. Mike and I would fix up to the summit ridge, then Rob would meet us and triumphantly lead to the top.

The changes a year makes. The popularity of the Moab area had spread like a cancer, and Onion Creek had been "discovered" by the hoi polloi. Tents and campers filled every turnout. Mountain bikes jammed the road. Little TP flags fluttered in the bushes — signs of the reverence Joe Sixpack pays the wilderness.

When Cosgriff and I had approached the Mystery Towers two years before, we saw not a single footprint. The canyon was wild, the approach inobvious, the directions in the guidebook poor, the towers hidden from sight until halfway in. It felt as if nobody had walked this wash since Forrest and crew had rolled in the wheelbarrows supporting their ballsacks.

Now Mike and I followed numerous foot and paw prints up the approach. Mike explained that this had become a popular day hike for the Kumbaya-ers, as he refers to the crowd of hippie mountain bikers who now call Moab their own. He started mimicking their behavior, whistling as if calling a dog, and saying, "Dark Star, come here, boy."

We turned the corner where you get the first view of the Doric, and saw a party rapping down — the fifth ascent in less than a year. The Mystery Towers were a mystery no more.

The rock on the Gothic makes the Titan look like granite. Once again I drew the first pitch, which entailed tied-off knifeblades, expanding blocks, and dirt-dagger free climbing. I hadn't nailed for a year and was pretty spooked. In the South, they'd say I was shaking like a dog shitting peach pits, but this was more like a dog passing sea urchins. Fortunately, it was a short pitch.

Mike methodically worked out the next pitch, knocking off loads of mud and rotten rock. Most fell to the side of me, but one chunk exploded on my belay plate, making me happy I hadn't opted for a hip belay.

After nailing the expanding mud-block traverse the first-ascent party had bathooked, Mike started chain-smoking. Belaying me on the next lead didn't help matters, though I did my best to help him quit; from 20 feet up I dislodged a chunk of rock that whistled down to knock Mike's "twitch stick" from his lips.

I wriggled into a short chimney between slightly open scissor blades, and I could easily peer down both the north and south faces. O'Donnell was belaying on the north side. The chimney expanded on the south side. I said, "Listen to this," planted my left foot on the north face and shoved lightly with my right. A portion of the wall the size of my body slowly tipped off like a tree being felled, then traveled 300 feet before creating a thunder that echoed through the valley for minute after satisfying minute. A fine trundle is a rare and beautiful thing. I was reminded of Kor's words when asked why he climbed the desert towers: "Not so much because they're there, but rather because they may not be there much longer."

Even more of the Gothic disappeared when I groveled on top of the knife-edge ridge the next day. I punched and shoved until the ridge was a foot lower, and the medium I would mantel onto resembled rock. A short stroll along the dirt ridge, similar, but wider than the citadel's gangplank, got me to the anchor and the end of my leading commitment.

Now Rob had joined us, and went to work. After 60 feet, he stopped at a saddle between two gargoyles, midway along what the first ascent team dubbed "The Traverse of the Goblins." The saddle was composed entirely of cobbles, a three-foot-thick layer, every one of which you could pull out with your fingers. No way to nail it or drill it, and free climbing would be nuts. Luckily for Rob, a storm was moving in, and his partners called for a retreat.

The weekend was over. We sat in a Mexican restaurant discussing our plight. I wasn't about to leave. O'Donnell felt likewise. Outside, the streets of Moab were flooding. This, and a job commitment, convinced Rob to flee. He drove us out to the Onion Creek road, where my van was parked. It was a moonless night and still raining. He dropped us at the first stream crossing, then left us to die.

The first crossing turned out to be an insignificant tributary we had never seen water in. We didn't know this until we reached the real Onion Creek. We stood on the bank — what was left of the road — and listened to boulders rolling down the torrent. I half-expected to see my van float by. We stood in T-shirts, shorts, and flip-flops, me with a bag of provisions, Mike with a borrowed tent, and Rob long gone with the tent poles.

I wrapped myself in the tent, Mike wrapped himself in the fly, and we hiked back to the highway. No cars. Was it flooded now, too? Closed for the night? The Rob-left-us-to-die jokes turned into serious talk about what to do next.

I'm not one to throw away beers, even if they are Utah 3.2 road-pops, but I ditched the sixer, something I would do only in the most dire circumstances. The nearest ranch house was seven miles distant. We started hiking.

Finally, a caravan of rafters drove by and took pity on us, two drowned rats wrapped up like nuns with tents over our heads.

"What are you doing out here?" they asked.

"Rock climbing," we replied.

"Climbers? That explains it."

They dropped us off in Moab, where, once again, we knocked on the door of the patron saint of Moab mud-nailers, Kyle Copeland. If it weren't for his hospitality and gear, we would have never gotten into this mess.

Betrayal. The Team ripped asunder by filthy lucre. Rob knew that next Friday was the only day I could go back. O'Donnell was going to be there. I told Rob he must call in sick, especially since he'd already told his competitors that the second ascent was a done deal.

"You've got to wait until Saturday," Rob pleaded. "I'll lose 6000 dollars if I don't go to work on Friday."

"Don't give me this bullshit about chicken feed. This is the second ascent of the Gothic we're talking about."

O'Donnell and I went back alone. Forrest had told Slater that from the summit ridge up it was all drilling. Indeed, the only pins he placed were Lost Arrows pounded into bolt holes; the rock was so bad in places that inch-and-a-half long bolts wouldn't cut it. I finished Slater's lead. Mike led to the glorious summit.

The very top is the size of a park bench, and perfect to sit on. It was time to lift a Mount Everest malt liquor, toast the first ascensionists Forrest and Briggs, toast ourselves, toast Rob who would jug up the next day, and toast all those who have sought adventure in these most stupendous of choss heaps.

"Here's mud in your eye."

First published in Climbing *No. 140, 1993.*

No Epics,
No Suffering,
No Mixed Climbing
Breaking promises on the Frendo Spur in winter

By Andrew Kirkpatrick

With the last of our energy, we forced open the frozen door to the Aguille du Midi téléphérique and crawled inside. The door blew shut, sealing out the storm that raged outside, putting a full stop to the strain of the last three days. Both of us lay there for a long time, staring at the icy ceiling, neither of us wanting to speak and spoil the overwhelming return of peace and safety. My hands were frozen and blood covered my face. The rope lay at our feet; new a week ago it was now a frozen, torn mess. Our rack was gone, left strung along the final pitches high on that 3600-foot face, left without a second thought as we battled to reach the top in a violent winter storm.

There would be no handshakes of success — people seldom celebrate survival. All I could do was lie there feeling guilty for dragging my partner through a near-fatal obsession with an obscure, seemingly third-rate winter route.

After two failures, the *Frendo Spur* had become my Moby Dick, and it had gone down with a hell of a fight. Unlike the unfortunate Captain Ahab, I would live to "hunt" again, but I knew my partner, Aaron Foreshaw, wanted to stay firmly on dry land after this voyage — we untied from each other for the last time.

Our partnership was looking a bit shaky long before we even arrived in Chamonix that winter. Aaron had always been a quietly driven climber, having climbed in the Alps and Norway in summer and winter. He was never afraid to stick his neck out, whether it was balancing up an unprotected gritstone 5.11 or carefully frontpointing up some Scottish ice horror. But for some reason, this year he didn't have the same psyche. Maybe it was because he was coming to the end of his Ph.D. in physics, and his "real" life was about to begin. He'd also just settled down with his girlfriend and bought a house. It had taken a lot of persuading to get him to come on this trip.

It was my third winter season, and I had big plans. The weather was good and, despite Aaron's cautious approach, I intended to make the most of the excellent conditions. He told me he wanted to avoid epics and suffering — any routes involving any "full-on" mixed climbing — which I found puzzling since these things were always the bread and butter of any great winter climb. In the end I suggested the *Frendo Spur* on the Aguille du Midi, which I was hoped would look like an easy option to Aaron.

"Look, Aaron, it'll be a path. First winter ascent in '64, hardest pitches only 5.6, tops out at the Midi téléphérique," I reasoned. "We'll take one day's food, probably blast up it in a day. What do you think?"

"OK, but I'm here on holiday. Got that? I've had enough suffering and epics, I just want to go climbing, that's all, just climbing, right!"

"Trust me."

I'd failed on the *Frendo Spur* the winter before with one of Britain's best alpinists, Dick Turnbull, mainly due to a British approach to winter alpinism — too heavy, too slow, and too cautious — coupled with poor conditions. Although both of us should have known better, we got on it expecting an "easy winter tick," forgetting that if you came across a 3600-foot 5.6 in Scotland in winter you'd approach it with a little more respect. The route also has a reputation for epics: Nearly every climber I've ever talked to has wild stories of big lobs and desperate climbing on the "easy 5.6 pitches." A real alpine, slap-in-the-face route it seemed.

Later, I learned that the original, and most of the few subsequent winter ascents had avoided the main buttress, the meat of the route, by climbing a snow couloir to the right, which has had the indignity of being skied and boarded the last few years. Still these climbers had claimed success on the *Frendo Spur.* Pouring over photos of the face, I'd spotted a new variation, a direct start, up the left-hand side of the buttress that promised plenty of Scottish action. I assumed that once on the route Aaron would get into it; if not I was prepared to push our partnership a little.

Aaron planted his axes and looked up from the bergschrund.

"Mixed climbing, I knew it," he spat out. "The normal route goes up the snow ramps 'round the corner. There's no direct start in the guide."

"It looks fun," I ventured.

"It's too bloody cold for fun. I'll warn you now — I don't want to have an epic, scratching around on icy rock for two weeks, OK? By the way, why have we got only one rope?"

214

"So you can't wimp out and abseil off, that's why."

Several hours later we joined the normal route after some difficult climbing up icy granite grooves. Aaron arrived at the belay grumbling and looking a bit perturbed. So far the climbing had proved harder, slower, and more insecure than expected, and we were still only on the lower unrated section of the route.

The next pitch split out left from the summer route, and began with a wall of stacked flakes leading to a steep slab with an icy fist crack. Aaron eyed the difficulties for longer than was necessary, so I offered to carry on leading before he had the chance to persuade me to retreat. He accepted. My parting words were designed to cheer him up a bit, as the sound of grating steel and smell of scratched granite drifted down from my tools. "Ah, don't you just love the smell of sulphur in the morning."

Looking down the spur, Aaron measured our height by the lengthening shadows moving across our tracks down on the glacier. "Afternoon actually," he said wryly. Hammering a Spectre into a crack, I pretended not to hear.

We squandered the rest of the afternoon wrestling with a fantastic icy offwidth, then danced away the evening in a mixed couloir. Then, the cold alpine night arrived unannounced.

"Aaron! I'm coming off!" I yelled. "Back up the belay quick! No, watch me. Try and shine your head torch on my front points. No, stop, you're blinding me!".

It was incredibly cold, I was freaked, and Aaron was pissed off. He had a front-row seat beside a large spiky flake as I fought my way up a three-inch-wide strip of plastic ice in the back of an 85-degree groove. The higher I climbed, the heavier the rope felt. It hung unhindered by protection down to Aaron, who shivered silently as the temperature dropped off the scale of our cheap thermometer. Trying hard to keep his frozen hands paying out rope, Aaron did a fine job of tracing my flight path onto his spike belay.

"One more meter," I thought, "one more meter and I'll find some gear and lower off."

But there was none. Stupidly I tried to gain more purchase by swinging my adze at the next section of thin ice. The ice shattered, leaving only a crackless groove. Trying to stay calm, I carefully stepped back down into my last crampon placement, but as I weighted it, the ice buckled and fell away, sending my crampon screeching and sparking down the granite until it miraculously caught a stubborn piece lower down. Pressing my head into the groove, I thought I would puke up the fear, but managed only a pathetic dry heave.

"Andy, what's going on up there? Hurry up, I'm freezing to death!"

A desperate lasso maneuver followed by a Tarzan swing saw me screech and spark into another corner, which accepted a one-inch angle to the hilt.

"Aaron, take! Lower me. I've had it."

Back at the belay I collapsed with fatigue from 14 hours of leading. Hanging pathetically off the flake, hands frozen into bloody claws, contact lenses deforming with the cold, all I wanted was a drink of water and for Aaron to take charge.

He looked at me with disdain. "I thought we were supposed to be avoiding epics."

Turning, he focused his headtorch beam on a steep patch of snow on a hanging slab 30 feet below us.

"We'll bivy there," he commanded. "I'll lower you down, and we'll use the peg up there as the main belay, OK?"

I didn't have the energy to answer.

During God-awful bivies, I often pass the time reminiscing about worse nights I've endured — freezing at minus-30 on the Jorasses or being buried alive by spindrift below the Dru. I find that this puts my present discomfort into perspective. Yet at that moment, hanging from a Tri-Cam, on a one-bum-cheek, sloping snow ledge, I found little comfort.

Squirming and grunting, I struggled to get my extremely large sleeping bag out of my extremely small rucksack without dropping anything, or sliding off my narrow perch. Aaron was in his bag, boots off and stove on, before I'd even found my headtorch.

He chose that moment to make the point that technically I'd lied to him because he was now "suffering." Below shone the lights of Chamonix. I imagined the friendly laughing groups huddled around warm creperies, wandering from bar to bar then returning to beds warmed by blond Norwegian goddesses.

"Andy!" Aaron woke me up from my daydream. "Are you OK? Get in your bag before you freeze."

With great difficulty I removed my right boot shell, tied it into the belay, and wrestled with the other. For some reason my mind wandered to the implications of dropping a boot so high on a winter route. The next thing I knew my boot was slipping off the end of my foot. I watched it fall, then amazingly drop into the snow inches from my feet. Letting out a nervous laugh, I bent down to pick it up. Aaron, seeing what was about to happen, gasped, as the boot slowly slid away from my fingertips and toppled into the darkness. For a few seconds there was a plasticy echo as it rattled down the face, then silence.

I put my head in my hands. For a second I was more upset about having to retreat again, losing all that hard-fought ground. Then reality set in. How was I going to get down without getting frostbite on my left foot, and how were we going to retreat with only one 50-meter rope and a minimal rack?

Aaron tried to comfort me, "Never mind, It could happen to anyone ... I suppose we'll be going down tomorrow then?"

216

I sat there for a long time, shaking my head, vowing to give up climbing for good, sell all my gear, maybe even spend the rest of my holiday with my wife, somewhere sunny. Suddenly, a huge spotlight came on, shining up from the Midi Plan, illuminating the whole of the spur for the tourists.

Aaron shifted in his sleeping bag. "Bloody great, how am I going to sleep with that shining in my eyes all night!"

"Oh, God, what am I going to do," I said.

Then all hell broke loose.

A serac weighing thousands of tons split from the face, and exploded into a barrage of whirring debris. The rumbling grew into a sphincter-tightening thunder as house-size blocks rained down around us. I buried my head and waited for the impact.

Coughing up ice crystals we opened our eyes and found to our surprise that we were still alive. A great cloud of ice particles and debris rolled out across the glacier below, spectacularly illuminated by the spotlight. I felt humbled, stunned, and more alive than ever.

Aaron was right — winter alpinism is madness. Why risk all the good things in life — love, friendship, food, and gritstone — to suffer for days on end, kidding yourself that you're really in control? And for what? To climb classic summer rock routes that are out of condition?

The rope slithered down from our final abseil, off our last piece of gear sometime the following afternoon. With all my socks, a mountain mitt, and a strapped-on Rambo on my bootless foot, I tried to run across the glacier, praying we'd be spared any more trundling seracs. Six hundred feet from the face I stopped dead and rubbed my eyes.

There before me, standing upright on a pile of ice debris, was my boot.

As I picked it up I instantly forgot last night's vows of giving up climbing. I'd got myself down in one piece. Hey, it wasn't that bad. Turning to face the mountain, I held my boot aloft and vowed I'd come back.

Once at the téléphérique station, we collapsed in front of assorted, bemused Japanese and Italian tourists, "Alpinists!" they cooed, and snapped away.

"Aaron, get two returns. We'll come up tomorrow and finish the route."

Shaking his head Aaron pushed his credit card under the glass.

A few days and two bivies later, we were 2100 feet up the spur, sitting below the final crux. I woke early and fired up the stove. Aaron forced open his frozen sleeping bag and shifted painfully as he tried to come to terms with another day.

"My arse will never be the same. I don't think I can last another bivy like that. I just hope you can get up this pitch today or we're really fucked."

I looked down at Aaron. His face was cut, bruised, and frostnipped, and I wondered how on earth I'd persuaded him to come back on this bloody route.

"We'll be in Chamonix by tonight, don't worry," I said, pulling on my plastics (now complete with tie-in loops).

Two long, scary hours later I was still leading. Sky-hooking, pegging, and dry-tooling I found myself committed to a desperate sequence of footless torques protected by a stacked Hex 7 and Rock 10. If I fell, and they pulled … I had no illusions about the outcome.

The mountain allowed me to live, although not without payback. Just below a thank-God ledge, my tool popped and smashed me in the face, breaking my glasses and narrowly missing my eye. A deep scar would remind me for a long time never to underestimate an "easy 5.6." Aaron jumared the pitch, swearing at the stupidity of mixed climbing, until he saw the stacked gear and the blood. He was silent after that. Pulling onto the belay, he looked tired and strung out. I was lucky; I'd led most of the route and had little down time to think about the seriousness of our position. I was actually beginning to like it here.

"Sorry, Aaron, I shouldn't have persuaded you to come back."

Looking up the next chimney pitch, he slowly removed the gear from his harness. "It doesn't matter. We're nearly there now. Here, take the gear."

It was then that I realized that this route was changing us both. After every pitch I felt stronger, more confident, more and more in my element, whereas Aaron seemed increasingly convinced that this kind of climbing wasn't for him.

An hour later, the oppressive blackness and complexity of the upper rock spur finally gave way to the simple white landscape of the final icefield. We stood together, and for the first time in two days, relaxed a little. I wondered for a moment whether I'd shake Aaron's hand or hug him when we reached the Midi station, imagining it would make everything all right. All the pushing, anxiety, and resentment of being dragged onto such a route would have been worth it, wouldn't it? Anyway it hadn't been all that bad.

"Your lead, Aaron, a nice bit of ice to see us home."

"Maybe this isn't such a bad route after all," he said, giving a labored smile.

Aaron led off up the ice arete as the first flecks of snow fell, as a massive storm moved in, unseen, from the east.

I still see Aaron from time to time. He works in London now. I know he doesn't climb any more because I've still got his gear. We try to avoid the subject of the Frendo when we meet, although his girlfriend once told me he'd realized mountaineering wasn't for him on that climb. He'd grown up, she said.

And me? Sitting on some God-awful ledge, hungry, cold, and nervous, I often think about Aaron — spending his holidays in Spain, Jordan, or the States, happy, relaxing in the sun and sleeping with the woman he loves, while I cud-

218

dle up to some other poor lost soul. I also wonder what life would be like for me now if, below the Frendo, I'd failed to find my boot, and just walked away from it all.

First published in Climbing *No. 174, 1998.*

Ten Years After
Seeking desert solitude at Red Rocks

By Michael Benge

"The publication of a guidebook for a developing climbing area often creates controversy. Some people feel that such a book will bring more climbers to the area, leading to a deterioration of the wilderness climbing experience."

— Joanne Urioste in the Red Rocks of Southern Nevada, her guidebook to the area.

I first visited Red Rocks shortly after that guide came out. The memory of that trip is still fresh as the dry canyon air. A friend, Steve, at Camp Four in Yosemite had sketched a couple of topos, exhorting us not to miss the place. Why not? Yosemite was so urban, so hassle-ridden. On the tail end of a 10-week road trip, I was ready for a change.

Red Rocks was vast, a sandstone escarpment extending for some 13 jumbled miles, yet a mere 30 minutes from Las Vegas. On the drive in to Black Velvet Canyon, we repeatedly scraped the VW bug's bottom in the washes, and wondered whether we were on the right road. Once we found the place, we pitched camp and stuffed our packs with gear. We hiked across rolling desert toward the canyon, brushing past Joshua Trees, cholla with their mean yellow tines, dagger-pointed yuccas, and a number of other prickly flora. Dropping into a dry wash, we crunched along on gravel and sand, and scrambled over big, smooth, swirly boulders of red, pink, yellow, and grey. The redbuds boasted full lavender bloom. Croaking frogs signaled the clear, spring-fed pool ahead. In the sand were big round tracks — a lion had drunk here, maybe that morning, judging by the prints' crisp edges.

Soon, the walls closed in. Huge, black walls. That couldn't be the route ... could it? Where was the trail? Everything shot up so steep and sheer. At the cliff, more magic revealed itself — holds, everywhere holds, made-for-climbing holds. *A Dream of Wild Turkeys* (5.10-) presented perfect little incuts every time we reached up. Solid rock, too. Pitch after pitch, bolt after bolt. How long could this go on? Finally, we unroped. A thousand feet of scrambling led to the top. Which gully down?

Had to move, getting dark. Scraped raw by stout manzanita, pierced by another cactus. Aaagh! Full moonrise, thank God. Endless dead-ends. At last, a smooth slope. The car, camp, to ourselves. Beer. Burritos. Vegas a faraway glow. Thank you, Steve.

Ten years later, I pick up Michael Dorsey at Vegas' McCarran Airport — buzzing, ninth craziest in the country, I've heard. One-armed bandits hit you up as soon as you step off the plane. Michael looks the same as he did when we climbed here in the mid-'80s: ponytail, youthful face, but more weathered when he squints. He's still living the simple life: rents a house in Boulder with his girlfriend, teaches English at CU, writes short stories that go over my head. Climbs a lot. Likes offwidths.

No 10-week road trip this time for me — mortgage, marriage, progeny. Can't complain now, I'm here. But Vegas energy is creepy. Prolific cranes compete for the skyline, theme casinos for your wallet. What a deal: bet-loosening free drinks. 90,000 rooms. Eleven of the world's 12 biggest hotels. Everybody smokes.

We turn onto West Charleston. Its strip-mall line-up has stretched halfway to Red Rocks. Big-city traffic. For three or four years running, Vegas has been the fastest-growing metropolis in the country, chewing up the desert. A climber and lifetime resident here, Randall Grandstaff, said the population has doubled in five years. Gated "communities" keep the riffraff out. Green lawns butt against desert hard pan, draining the Colorado River, which is dry before it reaches the ocean.

Mike Ward remembers when Charleston was a gravel road. He's riding the wave. His Desert Rock Sports, once a little hole-in-the-wall on Charleston, now looks like the Boulder Mountaineer. Enough climbers live and visit here now to support Powerhouse, Ward's new crag-like gym.

Finally, we pass the last bulldozer churning up earth and dust. The scenic loop, already? A fleet of tour buses unloads at the visitor center. The tourists line up for the outhouse, interact with the indoor exhibits, then pile back in. Just the way the BLM likes it.

Let's keep going to Black Velvet. The washes that thrashed the VW are smoother now — you could get a rental car in here. About a dozen of them inhabit the parking/camping area, in fact. A couple dozen vehicles total. Grandstaff says there might be 40 or 50 on a busy day. We find a spot, semi-level. No privacy but who cares. We're among climbers, and we're in the desert. Even the dust blowing in my eyes feels good. It's hot.

But not up the shady canyon. I wrap up in the rope bag to stay warm belaying. Whiskey Peak's *Triassic Sands* (5.10) isn't quite the right geologic era, but the climbing is just fine, on fine-grained Aztec sandstone. Like Canyonlands'

Supercrack, with varnished face holds. Five other parties have been on the route today, say the bong-packing pair at the base. A southerner, Chad, is above us soloing it, having an epic: stuck ropes, getting dark. Never heard so much cussing. We wait for him at the bottom, just in case, listening to the frogs. "You don't wanna know what I was doing up there," he says.

A silvery full moon overwhelms the horizon as we hike out. So still, quiet. A braying burro interrupts our thoughts. Burros are as common here as deer in Yosemite. Don't feed the burros, say the signs. People do anyway.

We rise to clanking pots. The day is clear and windy. A few smart climbers sneak out early to be first on their routes. A steady stream of pile jackets stride off with fistfuls of TP. Watch where you step. Why isn't there a latrine here?

The BLM manages Red Rock Canyon National Conservation Area. Some locals say the agency takes a head-in-the-sand approach to climbers. Are climbers too much trouble? In a way. "In terms of care and feeding, climbers have needs disproportionate to their total numbers," says Park Manager Dave Wolf. What he means is that climbers don't just pass through, they camp.

As of January 1997, the BLM closed Black Velvet to camping, primarily because of overuse, according to Wolf. "We were seeing a significant amount of new area disturbed and human sanitation problems were increasing. The area is not appropriate for permanent facilities."

Strange rhythms. Today, *Triassic Sands* is deserted, the Velvet Wall crawling. Some kind of herd mentality. This is the land of extremes.

Everybody knows that about the desert, but look at the Velvet Wall. From the mid-'70s through the mid-'80s, the Uriostes happily bolted multi-pitch sport climbs before we called them that. Their *Dream of Wild Turkeys, Yellow Brick Road,* and *Prince of Darkness,* all 5.10s, are sandwiched between the trad routes of the same grade: *Fiddler on the Roof* and *Rock Warrior.* Members of the '80s trad brigade — Jay Smith, Richard Harrison, Nick Nordblom, Sal Mamusia, and Paul Van Betten — engineered *Rock Warrior,* dinking bomber nuts in seams and banging in the occasional quarter-incher. A statement. An experience. Guess which routes are most popular today?

We connected the chalk dots on *Prince of Darkness.* A vertical edgemill, as one jaded climber said. Nobody bothers to scramble the easy 1000 feet of 4th class to the top now.

Excuse me, sorry, mind if we rap by you?

Sure, no problem.

Rope!

Sir, would you make sure I'm tied in right, says the young climber.

Better to tie in directly with the rope than clip in with slings; I'd equalize the tension, too.

I've been climbing mostly at the Gallery, he says. 5.12s and 5.13s, but my friend dragged me over here.

Good luck.

Next day, we dance to the tune of the *Fiddler on the Roof,* a steep, mocha-brown slab, so smooth it looks unclimbable. Just the sight of the notorious traverse above the lip of the huge roof bunches up my belly. My lead. I'm immediately lost, too high, 20 feet out. Wake up, reverse, breathe. OK, start over. This must be the crux. Up, down, up, down. Where have all the bolts gone? Commit, you chicken. Finally, the belay.

It's Michael's turn. That bolt's a long way up, he says. Blank, too. And no chalk. Holds materialize out of the veneer, and he finds the route. He gets gear when he can, the way we did on *Rock Warrior* a decade ago. Only two bolts. A masterpiece pitch. Good job — he's come a long way. I remember catching him on a 30-foot near-grounder on his first 5.8 lead.

Four more pitches almost as brilliant. *The Fiddler* is the best route I've done here.

The dreaded resupply trip. Easter Sunday in Vegas: little girls in yellow bonnets in line at the drugstore with brown-bag derelicts. A brown cloud, traffic, manic energy. I lost my wallet, says Michael. Pick-pocket?

We visit the local climber Dan McQuade. Three pit bulls, five climbers, one woodie. Do your dogs bite? Bob Marley is on the posters and the stereo. The scene takes me back. The wild seed is still there, hibernating but stirring. I could handle a couple of months of this.

Dan suggests we do *Cloud Tower* (5.11d) on the formation of the same name in Juniper Canyon. Kinda early in the season for something that hard, we protest. Too much time in ski gloves. Not as hard as the guide makes it out, he says.

It's getting dark, and the Oak Creek Campground is full when we head back out. The Ghetto it is, then. Off Charleston, Dan had said: just head into the desert on one of the dirt roads. We weave around trying to get our bearings in the twilight, and finally settle on the first level spot we find. Weird vibes. Shell casings everywhere. Discarded appliances. Our "site" comes complete with spring-loaded couch and bashed-in TV. People have told us of bullets whizzing overhead on the weekends. Yahoo city. This place sucks, but it's free. (Not anymore, though. The Howard Hughes Corporation owns this chunk of desert, and has recently shut it down. It plans to develop the area, including two hotel/casinos.)

Vegas shimmers.

Orange-tainted sunrise. Other campers dot the area. Coffee up, rack up. We'd been climbing in Black Velvet until now, so we hit the scenic loop for the first time this trip. It's early, and only one car occupies the parking lot that is the trailhead for our route and the over-popular *Crimson Chrysalis,* also on Cloud Tower. We thought there'd be more climbers because of the legendary queues for that route, at 5.8, one of the area's best. Under a cobalt-blue sky, we cross Pine Creek; at only 4000 feet, we find ponderosa pines. The remnants of a larger forest? We suck in the earthy, fresh smells. Just getting to the climbs is half the fun here.

A friend, Peter, and his teenage client, Chandler, hike with us, their target *Crimson Chrysalis.* We all grunt up the final steep hill to its base. Where did all these people come from? Three parties linger at the base, and two more are well up the route. People hike in from the highway to get here first. They must have started in at 4 a.m.

Peter and Chandler opt to follow us up *Cloud Tower.* The guide says this is the *Astroman* of Red Rocks. Moderate and fun crack climbing for a few pitches leads to the crux. Looks like the chocolate dihedral of *C'est la Vie* in Eldo. Yellow and green lichens spatter the wall. The thin corner eats up small nuts but spits out fat fingers.

We turn a corner to the last pitch, right out of Canyonlands: a laser-cut dihedral crack, Santa Fe pink. Michael conserves the gear for the crux he's expecting, but reaches the anchor first.

Rappelling, we descend into the bristly netherlands. One more rap from the ground, I wander across a brushy ledge, searching for the final ratty sling. What's that rumbling? Oh, Jesus. A refrigerator-sized block breaks into coolers, showering down around where Michael is. Was? Silence, then the sickening smell of rock dust.

I'm OK, he says.

Chandler, rappelling above, couldn't have been expected to know the *entire ledge would blow.* What can you say now anyway? Don't do that again?

Back to McCarran, where I trade in Michael for my friend Jim Cardamone from back home in Carbondale. Another working, family type.

We punch it to the refuge of Black Velvet.

"Hi, Michele."

Goddamnit. He's got that friggin' cell phone out, calling his wife.

(Hey, can I borrow that thing?)

Pumped for a dose of *Epinephrine,* we're up with the sun. Hiking in, we're smug that we'll have first dibs today, but another party is already roped up on the approach pitches. Scramble like mad. I'm being an asshole, but don't want to be under anyone. Claw up just on their left. They sense my frenzy, and let us pass. Thanks. Chimneys. Most people hate them, but not these. We relax and enjoy them. Clean rock, varied moves, classic technique. Push with the hands, knees, and heels. We find face holds, a hand crack.

Out of the chimneys and onto the face, we clip plenty of bolts, though still toss in the occasional nut or Friend. Great face holds — varnished plates surrounded by yellow sandstone — but be careful which ones you grab. Only one dicey section: up high, with creaking flakes, way out from gear.

We're over 1000 feet up now, feeling free as the swooping swallows. The main Velvet Wall is below. The guide says 18 pitches, but using long slings and a 60-meter rope, we cut it to a dozen.

With only 700 feet of scrambling to the summit, we unrope and slow down. The moves are easy 5th-class, but in many spots the exposure is such that you must not fall.

Black Velvet Peak. A real summit. It's a lonely place, a rocky, inhospitable wasteland. Gaping canyons to the west and south. An inkling of geologic time sinks in. Things are so simple, unfettered, up here. That overwhelmed feeling I get in civilization floats away on the wind. Shared feelings, mostly unspoken, make it hard to head back down. We savor this wild spot a moment more. My friend Bob Sloezen soloed the route, and said a desert bighorn showed him the descent.

OK, let's bushwhack. We weave and bob down the sandstone ridge, keeping a vigilant eye for that next cairn. Not a bad descent, if you don't get lost.

Next day, at *Dark Shadows* in Pine Creek Canyon, we're the first ones there, but soon four or five more parties trickle in, guidebook in hand. Look at the guidebook, look at the cliff.

I can see why they came. *Dark Shadows* (5.8) is a tremendous route. Short approach, four fun pitches. Perfect rock, in places jet black, varnished to a sheen. Steep, with jams that swallow your hand, jugs you can't let go of. A creek runs by the base — it's hard to pull your ropes without getting them wet.

The day before leaving, we hump in to Oak Creek's *Eagle Dance,* expecting company. It is high season, with spring vacations in full swing. Not a soul is there, and we see barely a sign of passage. The same bolts are here as 10 years ago, too.

Sun-baked rock, utter quiet.

Red Rocks. Still the same but different.

First published in Climbing *No. 168, 1997.*

Rewriting Annapurana
Was the cornerstone of 8000-meter history really a myth?

By David Roberts

June 3, 1950. From their wind-lashed tent at Camp V on Annapurna, Maurice Herzog and Louis Lachenal set out at dawn for the summit. For two months Herzog, Lachenal, and the cream of the French alpine elite had struggled just to get in position for such an assault. Now, with the monsoon season nearly on them, they must either press to the top, or turn around and accept that they would not be the first to break mountaineering's coveted 8000-meter barrier.

Hoping originally to climb Dhaulagiri, the team had spent weeks getting lost on the approach, thanks to old and grossly inaccurate maps. Deciding at the last moment that Dhaulagiri looked too formidable, they chose to attack Annapurna instead. Pushing through into the deep chasm of the Miristi Khola, they discovered a possible route on Annapurna's north side. Doggedly the team broke trail in the deep snow and placed a string of camps up the face.

All through the day of June 3, Herzog and Lachenal trudged in fearsome cold toward the summit. They reached it dangerously late, only hours before sunset. Herzog, in a euphoric trance, loitered and stared at the universe while Lachenal frantically urged descent. Herzog then dropped his gloves and watched, stunned, as they slid out of sight. In the dusk, the two victors almost missed Camp V, where Lionel Terray and Gaston Rébuffat stayed up all night brewing them drinks and whipping their frozen feet and Herzog's hands with rope-ends in an effort to restore circulation.

The inevitable storm hit as the crippled quartet staggered down, losing the route, and bivouacking in a crevasse into which Lachenal had providentially plunged. Emerging from the crevasse the following morning, Terray and

Rébuffat discovered they were snowblind. All four had reached their limits and stumbled lost, calling pitifully for help. Lower on the mountain, the third pair of climbers, Marcel Schatz and Jean Couzy, setting out from Camp IV, heard the cries, and climbed up to their teammates. Schatz approached Herzog, embraced his friend, and murmured, "It is wonderful — what you have done!"

Thus began the terrible retreat, with Lachenal and Herzog carried groaning on the backs of Sherpas and porters; the painful but futile abdominal injections supposed to alleviate the effects of frostbite; the first amputations, performed by the expedition doctor in the field; the return to France, as conquering heroes in the eyes not only of their countrymen, but of a public the world over.

In the hospital at Neuilly, Herzog dictated *Annapurna*. But the trance that had seized him on the summit persisted beyond the expedition. Despite losing all his fingers and toes, Herzog rapturously claimed, "I was saved and had won my freedom. This freedom, which I shall never lose, has given me the assurance and serenity of a man who has fulfilled himself." The book closes with a line as resounding and memorable as any in literature: "There are other Annapurnas in the lives of men."

Today, Annapurna is the best-selling mountaineering book of all time. It has sold over 10 million copies and been translated into 40 languages. Despite (or because of) its gruesome tale of frostbite and amputation and near-death, Annapurna motivated a generation of aspiring adventurers, myself included, to become mountaineers.

In recent months, however, a controversy over Annapurna has erupted in France, threatening to tarnish the legend. The occasion is the publication of two books: the first biography of Rébuffat, written by Yves Ballu *(Gaston Rébuffat: Une Vie pour la Montagne),* and the first faithful, unexpurgated version of Lachenal's posthumous diaries *(Carnets du Vertige).* The revelations of these two iconoclastic accounts have intersected with dark rumors long suppressed beneath the surface of what has become the Annapurna myth — a tale of valor and perseverance that bolstered post-war France in the aftermath of the country's humiliation by the Nazis and rescue by the Allies.

The controversy undermines Herzog's portrait of a harmonious, self-sacrificing team devoted to a common goal. Annapurna, according to Rébuffat and Lachenal, was a rancorously divided expedition; Herzog's leadership was inept and capricious; and the truth of what happened on the summit day has yet to emerge. These gloomy inklings have fanned to life old demurrals among other Himalayan mountaineers, who wondered out loud — but until now, only within earshot of fellow mountaineers — whether Herzog and Lachenal actually reached the summit. Could Annapurna have been a hoax?

Though the controversy has not caused a splash in the United States or

Britain, the furor is the stuff of headlines in France, where mainstream publications such as *Le Monde* and *Libération* have given it feature play. At age 78, Herzog himself is the only climber still alive from the 1950 expedition. A figure no less revered in France than Sir Edmund Hillary in New Zealand, Herzog has greeted the charges with apoplexy and outrage, firing off letters of rebuttal. According to close sources, the peace and fulfillment of Herzog's life have been shattered by the dispute.

The controversy has an importance far beyond the airing of decades-old dirty laundry. What really happened on Annapurna in 1950 goes to the heart of the cherished tenets that drive mountaineers to pursue our glorious but — in Terray's memorable epithet — "useless" passion. And the critical examination of any national myth has a significance that transcends mountaineering.

Thanks to his amputations Herzog was unable to climb seriously after Annapurna. Meanwhile, he was showered with laurels. As leader of the expedition and author of the landmark book, Herzog's eclipsed Lachenal in stardome by early 1951, *Paris-Match,* which had broken all its sales records the previous August with a special on Annapurna (the cover photo showing Herzog hoisting the Tricolor on the summit), ran a six-page feature lionizing Herzog but hardly mentioning Lachenal. Herzog's only partner, according to the article, was one "Foca who accompanied him to the summit" — Foca being the brand name of Herzog's camera. The expedition leader went on to be mayor of Chamonix, and Minister of Youth and Sport under Charles de Gaulle.

Of the euphoria that bathed Herzog, Lachenal tasted not a drop. Honors meant little to him, while the loss of his toes was an irreparable blow. In Terray's autobiography *Conquistadors of the Useless,* Lachenal's best friend and climbing partner movingly recalls: "In the end he recovered sufficiently to work as a mountaineering instructor, but he could never recover his genius. This curtailment profoundly changed his character. Once he had seemed magically immune from the ordinary clumsiness and weight of humankind, and the contrast was like wearing a ball and chain."

Seeking a desperate compensation, Lachenal turned his intensity toward wild driving at top speed and reckless solo skiing. He suffered a number of auto accidents, and died on the glacier called the Vallée Blanche above Chamonix in 1955 when he skied unroped into a hidden crevasse.

This dark side of the Annapurna legacy was long known only to the cognoscenti, and for one reason. Before setting out for Nepal, the team members had met in Paris to pledge unquestioning obedience to Herzog, and to sign a contract agreeing to publish nothing about the expedition. Herzog's book would be the official and only account of the climb.

In 1955, as the contract's moratorium expired, Lachenal had been preparing to publish his diaries. When he died, Herzog arranged for his brother Gérard to edit the material that would become the book *Carnets du Vertige.* Herzog also became the *tuteur* of Lachenal's widow and children, providing financial and moral support for Madame Lachenal, and taking walks in the woods and providing ski outings with Lachenal's sons.

Carnets was published in 1956. A modest success in France, it has never been translated into English. Lachenal thought himself a clumsy writer, but his unvarnished prose has considerable force. His account of summitting Annapurna, however, was curiously flat:

"Finally we are there. An arête of snow hemmed with cornices and three summits, one higher than the others. It is the summit of Annapurna ... I do not even take out my camera, but use the Foca of Momo [Herzog].

"Without waiting any longer, we descend."

Over the years, however, Lachenal's son Jean-Claude, who inherited his father's diaries, guarded a bitter secret. The published *Carnets* was a far cry from what Lachenal had actually written. Gérard Herzog, in collaboration with his brother and Lucien Devies, father figure of French mountaineering, president of the Himalayan Committee, and sponsor of the expedition, had censored out virtually every passage that struck a less than honorific note, gossiped about comrades' foibles, or even reported Lachenal's dissatisfactions.

Enter Michel Guérin, a keen climber who had become a specialist publisher of mountaineering classics. Living in Chamonix, Guérin befriended Jean-Claude, gained access to the original manuscript, and offered to realize the son's dream of publishing an unexpurgated version. The decision was not an easy one for Jean-Claude, knowing the furor a new edition would create and the pain it would cause the *tuteur* who had guided him through his own bereft childhood. Ultimately, however, he decided his father's truth was more important.

Comparing the 1956 and the new editions of *Carnets,* one is shocked by how radically Gérard Herzog altered Lachenal's text. The original is full of bickerings and disagreements, and with the blunt candor of a montagnard, Lachenal casts a cold eye on the official hoopla that Launches the expedition: "Reception at the ambassador's house. High society dinner in a high-society apartment. Bored me to tears."

Rébuffat, too, was disenchanted by the nationalistic baggage the expedition carried and, as the trip progressed, he found himself miserably at odds with his teammates. In the letters wrote home to his wife, extracted for the first time in Yves Ballu's biography, Rébuffat described a collection of prima donnas: "I don't even have a friend. I've sacrificed a lot for friendship, and today, in this adventure, in The Adventure, I am alone ... [The others] have the air of being completely at ease in their egotism. Among us there is no team spirit, only a necessary politeness. What hypocrisy!"

The question of what happened on June 3 is the critical issue for Annapurna. In Herzog's stirring account, he himself is the "motor," the confident leader who carries the pair to the summit. Obsessed with the fear of frostbite, Lachenal seizes Herzog two hours below the top and demands, "If I go back, what will you do?"

"I should go on by myself," answers Herzog.

"Then I'll follow you," pledges Lachenal.

In the original *Carnets,* in a section suppressed in its entirety by Gérard Herzog, Lachenal writes that he was indeed afraid of losing his feet to frostbite and urged turning around short of the summit. He continued not because of a strong sense of nationalism — "I didn't owe my feet to the Youth of France" — but because, "I thought that if he [Herzog] continued alone, he would never return. It was for him and for him alone that I did not turn back."

Interviewing Maurice Herzog last December, *Montagnes* magazine asked him why the negative passages in Lachenal's *Carnets* had been excised. Herzog answered, "If none of that was published, it's because it didn't interest the editors." Defending the contract guaranteeing that his narrative would be the only one to emerge from Annapurna, Herzog bristled: "It's not necessary to write several books about one adventure. This kind of proceeding is never good. There was no censorship, no secret jealously guarded. My book was read by all the members of the expedition before it was published. All of them told me they agreed with what I wrote."

Aside from Lachenal's writings we have the version of the summit day Rébuffat heard from Lachenal. Yves Ballu goes even further than Lachenal himself in reinterpreting the events of June 3. For the biographer, Lachenal's loyalty to a spaced-out Herzog sprang from a venerable alpine distinction: Lachenal, Terray, and Rébuffat were professional guides; Herzog, Schatz, and Couzy "amateurs." A guide never abandons his client, and Lachenal, with such routes as the second ascents of the Eiger Nordwand and the Walker Spur on the Grandes Jorasses to his credit, was far more experienced in the mountains than Herzog.

Cast in this light, viewed more than four decades hence, Lachenal's behavior on June 3, 1950, looks not only more sensible than Herzog's but more heroic, while Herzog's summit euphoria looks more and more like the delusions of hypoxia.

The doubts over the years in certain quarters as to whether Lachenal and Herzog actually reached the top spring in part from the celebrated summit photo. Beyond the triumphant Herzog raising the French flag tied to his ice axe, a snow ridge seems to angle toward higher ground. In his recent rebuttals, Herzog has emphasized that a cornice prevented the pair from standing on the very top, and that the illusion of a ridge leading to higher ground was a trick of camera perspective. Last December *Montagnes* published for the first time all five photos actually taken on the "summit." By themselves, they are inconclusive and the only picture of Lachenal, a blurry portrait, shows him slumped on "the highest rocks" in a decidedly unvictorious posture.

It is possible that Herzog and Lachenal, hypoxic and exhausted, could have confused a bump on the ridge for the summit. But for all the damning details their books have brought to light concerning the Annapurna expedition, both Yves Ballu and Michel Guérin cast their votes in favor of Lachenal and Herzog having actually reached the top. For Guérin, the bottom line is Lachenal's bedrock integrity: "If Lachenal had wanted to avoid writing that he was on the summit, he would not have worded it otherwise." In Lachenal's diary for June 3 there remains that plain statement: "It is the summit of Annapurna."

At Harvard in the early 1960s, I became a serious mountaineer. With a classmate named Don Jensen, I formed a special bond that led us for three successive summers to Alaska, where we attempted new routes on Denali, Deborah, and Huntington. Like kids of my generation in the vacant lot pretending to be Mickey Mantle or Willie Mays, Don and I nursed a shared fantasy that we *were* Terray and Lachenal. With his stocky build, his strength and fitness, his deliberate manner, Don was Terray; thinner, more impatient, hotter tempered, I played Lachenal.

We went so far as to address each other as "Lionel" and "Louis." Passages from the lore of our heroes' conquests became canonic mottos on our lips: On the crux move of a route on Cannon Cliff, for example, Don might shout out, "Guido, the sardine tin!" (On the first ascent of Fitzroy in 1952, Terray and Guido Magnone were stumped by a short blank wall just below the summit. Out of pitons, they thrashed around, until Terray cried, "Guido, the sardine tin!" Earlier that day, the pair had used a knifeblade to pry open their sardine can. Terray dug the piton out of his rucksack, pounded it into a thin crack, aided the move, and sprinted to the summit.)

In 1965, Don and I, with Matt Hale and Ed Bernd, climbed the West Face of Mount Huntington. The year before, Terray, lured to Alaska by the celebrated mountaineer and photographer Brad Washburn, had led a strong eight-man team on the peak's first ascent, by the Northwest Ridge — not without an epic struggle that included Terray severely spraining his elbow in a fall. All through July on the Tokositna Glacier, Don would quote over and over again his favorite line from Terray's Huntington article in the *American Alpine Journal:* "It is not the goal of *grand alpinisme* to face peril, but it is one of the tests one must undergo to deserve the joy of rising for an instant above the state of crawling grubs."

Back in Chamonix, Terray learned of our climb. Having never heard of these four young Americans, incredulous that they might have succeeded on a harder route than his, Terray wrote Washburn inquiring whether we might have lied about the climb. Washburn wrote back vouching for our ascent, but before Terray could read the letter, he was killed in a thousand-foot fall off a rock climb in the Vercors of France. Roped to him in death was his Huntington teammate Marc Martinetti. Friends who found the bodies at the base of the cliff speculated that the pair had finished the hard pitches of the climb and were traveling, roped together, when one of them slipped.

Terray was only 44 when he died. In France, the mourning was a national event. I bought the issue of *Paris-Match* with his rugged face on the cover; the blurb, as I recall, read "Mort pour la Montagne." For selfish reasons, I mourned the near miss of our intersection in life. Every young climber's dream is to win the notice of his heroes. I had done that, only to have Terray die wondering if some college kids had faked the second ascent of Mount Huntington.

Intrigued and disturbed by the new controversy swirling around Annapurna, I traveled last May to France to investigate. The weather on my arrival was splendid. Chamonix, that village plunged at the bottom of a claustrophobic alpine valley, seemed a sunny place, open to the sharp aiguilles and gleaming glaciers to the south.

My first walk took me to the Chamonix cemetery. Just inside the gates, I found Terray's tombstone, an unshaped slab of brownish granite with a wooden plaque bolted to the stone, declaring only:

LIONEL TERRAY

1921 + 1965

Above this laconic inscription dangled a tiny bronze Christ. The earth covering Terray's coffin ran riot with pansies and forget-me-nots.

A few rows away I found Lachenal's tomb. On a larger slab than Terray's, of grayish granite, I read:

LOUIS LACHENAL

GUIDE

1921-1955

VALLEE BLANCHE

25-11-1955

From the ground before the stone sprouted lilies and the gray-green plants the French call *corbeille d'argent*. Within the flower bed reposed a small statue of Christ crucified; like his friend Terray, Lachenal was Catholic.

Through Michel Guérin, whom I had befriended, I was invited to dinner at the house of Jean-Claude Lachenal. A shy, portly man of 54, a former ski instructor who never climbed seriously, Jean-Claude fiercely guards his father's legacy.

With Guérin and other friends of Jean-Claude, I sat at the dinner table as his wife, Arlette, laid out a hearty spread of sausage from the Grisons, ham, cheese, goose pâté, bread, and homemade cornichons. As the champagne and red wine flowed, the group waxed reminiscent.

I asked Jean-Claude why he thought Herzog had received such disproportionate credit for Annapurna, at the expense of his father. "It was easier to find Maurice Herzog in the salons of Paris," he said, cocking a jaundiced eye, "than Louis Lachenal in the mountains of Chamonix.

"Five years after Annapurna," Jean-Claude went on, "Herzog and my father climbed Monte Rosa together. Herzog wanted the press along. My father said, 'No, not with any publicity.'"

Did he, who had been seven, remember his father's return from Annapurna? "He was very low when he arrived," said Jean-Claude. "The great Swiss climber Raymond Lambert, who had also lost his toes, came to the head of my father's bed in the Chamonix hospital, to show how he could still climb without toes. Lambert joked, danced, played soccer."

I toured the comfortable chalet, which Louis Lachenal had built with his own hands, employing a beautiful dark varnished wood, on a sunny hillside directly opposite the great North Face of the Dru. Every detail bespoke loving craft, from the central roof beam inscribed in Latin, "EDIFICATA ANNO DOMINI 1949," to the cunning attic door disguised as a fold-up staircase. "We slept up there when we were little kids," said Jean-Claude.

As we grew tipsy, Jean-Claude brought out some remarkable keepsakes. I held a long, rusty soft-iron spike. "This was a piton Anderl Heckmair drove into the Eiger on the first ascent in 1938. My father brought it back from the second ascent, with Terray, in 1947." Next Jean-Claude handed me the head of an antique ice axe. It had been left in the Ruwenzori Mountains of Africa by none other than the Duke of the Abruzzi, then retrieved by Lachenal in 1952.

Awed by these talismans from the immortals, I was unprepared to hold the next relic thrust into my hands. It was a sort of homemade book, bound between heavy pieces of cardboard. I opened the cover, and stared in shock at what I realized was Lachenal's Annapurna diary. In a tiny hand, in spidery blue ink, Lachenal had covered every square inch of paper with meticulous jottings. Entranced, I turned to June 3 and read the passage I already knew by heart.

Thanks to Michel Guérin, the next day I had the privilege of meeting Marianne Terray, Lionel's widow, in the chalet he built in 1947. Like Lachenal's house, Terray's stands proud on a south-facing hillside. His looks out at the Aiguille du Midi.

At 85, Madame Terray is active but hard of hearing. "Maurice Herzog was not a very well-organized leader," she recalled. "He was full of disorder. But physically and morally he was full of courage. And after the death of Lionel, he did everything he could for me and the children."

"Marianne goes three times a week to Lionel's tomb," Michel had told me before our visit. "She talks to him, asks his advice. If she finds her lost eyeglasses, it's thanks to Lionel."

Now Madame Terray concurred. "He is always present. For me, he isn't dead. For the children also. I don't believe in death. He's somewhere else. I don't know where. He's just gone somewhere."

The cozy chalet had the feeling of being still inhabited by Terray. The study was like an accidental museum. Madame Terray invited Michel to look inside a high cupboard. On tiptoe, he pulled open the door, reached inside, and retrieved an old, scarred rope, and a beat-up rucksack. "I've never seen this before," Michel mused. The pack had holes torn in it. Michel opened it. Inside, we saw a smashed headlamp, stirrups, broken carabiners.

It hit us both at the same moment. This was the rope and pack and hardware Terray had been carrying on his fatal climb in the Vercors in 1965.

I looked at my friend. Stricken — for Terray had been his paragon, too — he turned away. Tears choked the back of my throat.

In the silence, I took a single broken carabiner and turned it this way and that. It was the closest I would ever come to meeting the hero of my boyhood, to sharing with him the mountains for which he had lived and died.

After all these years, how much does what really happened on Annapurna in 1950 matter?

It would be wrong, in this revisionist climate, to paint Herzog as a villain, a control freak and expedition dictator of the Karl Herligkoffer stripe. On Annapurna Herzog never led from the rear; he did his share of load-hauling, took his share of the hard leads. Always he put himself on the line with his teammates. And in later life, he proved a loyal and compassionate friend. Nor would it be right to see *Annapurna* as a cover-up, a piece of fiction. For a person of Herzog's mystical and romantic bent, the book reflects an internal reality.

For me, the recent controversy has diminished Herzog's *Annapurna*. I no longer regard that book as a plain tale of what happened on the mountain in 1950. It is, instead, one man's idealized dream of the perfect ascent.

But the controversy in no way dims my admiration for the Annapurna climbers — in particular, for Rébuffat, Lachenal, and Terray. Tempted by fame and glory on a scale no French mountaineers had ever attained, they turned their backs and plunged once more into *grand alpinisme.* On Annapurna, for them, in the end, it was the climb that mattered.

First published in Climbing *No. 173, 1997.*

The Bird

Worshipped, loved, loathed, and emulated, Jim Bridwell defined climbing's outer limits for two generations.

By Geoffrey Childs

Everybody has a Jim Bridwell story. My favorite takes place sometime in the 1960s. Bridwell and fellow Yosemite lifer Jim Madsen have driven up to Glacier Point and are engaged in a bit of pharmaceutically enhanced eco-tourism when a tourist approaches with his poodle. The dog snaps at Madsen's ankles and Bridwell remarks to the owner that he should put his pet on a leash. Disgusted at having to share the view with two such obvious degenerates, the owner refuses. The dog snarls again. Madsen boots it over the edge.

"OK," Bridwell tells the dog's horror-struck owner, "you don't have to."

Whether your sensitivities let you laugh at that story, or whether the story is even true — and Bridwell insists that it is not — is immaterial. What is important is the tale. The strongest ties we have in climbing are our myths: the fables spun from parking lot to bar, from one crag to another, from climber to climber until the details are so convoluted and confused that all that remains is the telling. The written word can't capture what it really means to climb. The things that happen on rock are simply too visceral, too complex and personal to lay down on a page. The best climbing stories are the ones told out loud. And no one has had more stories told about him than Jim Bridwell.

The Bridwell legend is, of course, a caricature. Only slowly does the iconoclast whose dry wit, supreme talent, and incurbable wild streak that forever changed North American climbing come into view. Part genius, part rowdy, the real Jim Bridwell is a pastiche of contradictions, both more and less than the sum of his tales. At 54 he is soft-spoken and reflective, still fit, and percolating with plans. He is wary of interviews. Celebrity, he knows, is a double-edged sword: an opportunity wrapped in the heavy strands of both adoration and vilification. Getting to know him, like climbing a wall, is a long and complicated process.

I first ran into Jim Bridwell in 1975. It was a heady time for both of us. I had just climbed the *Regular Northwest* Face on Half Dome in a methodical two and one-half days. Bridwell, partnered with John Long and Billy Westbay, had made the first one-day ascent of El Cap's *Nose,* and was preparing to tackle the vast and uncharted real estate to the left of the *North America Wall,* a stretch that under Bridwell's tutledge would usher in modern-day big-wall climbing and be known as the *Pacific Ocean Wall.* I was quietly stealing a shower at the Curry employees compound when the front door exploded open. "Bridwell's here!" someone shouted. Naked and soap-covered, I stepped out to have a look. On either side of the door stood a small group of sun-buffed minions. In the middle was Bridwell. He was leaning over the sink washing his face. He looked gigantic. Dusty blond hair hung to his shoulders. The muscles on his back looked as if they were cut from stone. He was dirty enough to merit a shower, and perhaps just a little uncomfortable with all the fuss.

He is still uncomfortable with all the fuss. Reputation, he will tell you is more important than recognition, and despite having one of the best-known names in American mountaineering, he is happy to move through crowds unacknowledged. Called a visionary by climbers as diverse as Royal Robbins and Jared Ogden, he is perhaps more gamesman than shaman. Like all great athletes, Bridwell's contributions to mountaineering have stemmed from a profound understanding of the game. He feels its currents and flow almost intuitively.

Midway through his fourth decade of hard climbing, Bridwell is still focused on the next step, which he says is "technical climbing at altitude." He will produce a photo of some Himalayan or Patagonian or Alaskan wall and trace a line where his route will go. He knows every challenge by heart. "We will climb this in the dark," he says pointing to a couloir. "This is where the big-wall section begins." At an age when most of his peers have settled down to career paths and pension plans Bridwell is still hungry, still driven to make a statement.

He is probably the only one who thinks he has to. For most of us, Bridwell has already done enough. From the mid-1960s until the late-1970s when the best climbers in the world were American, Bridwell was the best climber in America. And whether it pleases you or not, Bridwell is about as quintessentially American as it gets. Obsessive and distracted, heralded and hated, he is what attitude looks like harnessed to the business end of a climbing rope.

"To put Bridwell into context," explains his long-time friend John Long, "you have to understand that the accomplishments of the generation that preceded us were mythical. We thought of guys like Robbins and Chouinard as icons. But Bridwell told us there were no myths — there were just rock climbs. And Bridwell was no icon."

Indeed, as the heroic figures of Yosemite's Golden Age were abandoning the stage, it was Bridwell wearing purple bell-bottoms, a paisley vest, and a tatty bandanna who stepped up and showed the world that anything was possible, if you had enough courage. Bridwell widened the definition of "Yosemite style" to encompass everything that went into building a life around climbing. In his glory days you could feel his presence in Camp 4 like a jolt of electricity.

Jim Bridwell may not have invented the low-ride but anybody who has been in Yosemite and pushed their personal limits, stolen food off a tourist's tray, offended public decency, got drunk at their picnic table, played out their stay on crackers and relish, or slithered onto a half-driven RURP 2000 feet above the barbecued air of El Cap Meadow has stood along the banks of the river Bridwell and wondered at his beauty.

Not that the waters have always run sweet and clear. Away from the cliffs and mountains, Bridwell has backwashed into eddies of failed schemes and indifferences. The stubbornness and why-not attitude that have served him so well on walls have hobbled him on the horizontal. Yet, as the current crop of young climbers goes out into the world to put up their own masterpieces, they do so in a landscape shaped by Bridwell's imagination. The *Nose* in a day, the *Pacific Ocean Wall* and *Sea of Dreams,* his ascents of Cerro Torre, Pumori, and Moose's Tooth were more than just routes, they were strides into the unknown that have inspired the brightest stars of a generation and left in their wake an unrivaled legacy of brilliant style.

To Bridwell, adventure *is* style. His obsession with minimizing bolts, for example, is less about ethics than playing dice with the limits of possibility. He can be a stern task-master, but, says Billy Westbay, "He was always pushing us to be our best."

But as with all great achievements, there has been a cost attached.

"People don't look at me and say, 'my how normal you look,'" Bridwell has said. "You know why? Too many lines on my face! From too many days looking up into the sun, or over my shoulder at the storm clouds — of being terrified. But you have to deprive yourself to learn, to move ahead."

The deprivation is, at times, much more apparent than the learning. Strands of grey infiltrate his still dusty-blond hair. His gaze is less penetrating, wearier than it once was. The line of his shoulders has been stooped by years of carrying heavy packs and hauling loads. Shaking hands with Bridwell is like picking up the roots of an old tree. His skin is hard and taut. His expression is frequently that of vague distraction, a look that turns easily to anger. He is not glib. He does not hold disparate thoughts in mind easily and the halting, off-track associations that spike his conversation, like the weathered texture of his face, are legendary. As with so many of the myths and rumors that surround him, the description "head of a 70-year-old, body of a 25-year-old, and attitude of an 11-year-old," captures his appearance at the cost of understanding the content of his soul.

Impatient and demanding, a man of towering ambition, Bridwell has never let hubris rob him of his ability to view mountaineering within the greater context of life. A father, a husband, a pirate, and a pioneer — he has dreamed big dreams and made them happen. He has rolled the dice and had them come up sevens. The stories, as rich as they are, only tell half the truth.

When in the 1970s every other climber in the world looked up at El Cap's terrifying geography and sought out its avenues of escape, Bridwell reveled in its mysteries. "I always tried to be open to things," he says. "A new route, a new piece of gear, different ways of doing things — I always liked the idea of trying to see things from a different perspective." What the rest of us thought to be questions of gear and logistics he understood as a test of faith — that if you believed it could be done, then you could do it. When we looked up we saw granite. Bridwell looked up and saw the future. Then he went out, threw himself headlong at the impossible, and in so doing rewrote the history of climbing.

James Dennis Bridwell was born July 29, 1944 in San Antonio, Texas. His father, Donald, was a war hero and an officer in the Army Air Corps. Like all military families, the Bridwells moved often. So often, in fact, that by the time Jim entered middle school he could more easily list the states he had not lived in than the ones he had.

Reclusive by nature, Jim spent much of his childhood alone, working on projects, playing with his toys, or exploring the woods. Later, as sports began to occupy a greater percentage of his time, he seemed to grow out of himself a little. A natural athlete, he excelled at everything and had it not been for yet another family move, Jim might have spent the 1970s dishing up split-finger fastballs for some triple-A farm team instead of putting up hard aid routes in the Valley. But arriving as a freshman at San Mateo High School in California, he discovered that the teams had already been chosen. Once again on the outside, he drifted away from sports and into falconry.

"I must have been a pretty strange kid," Bridwell laughs, thinking back to those days. "I was always hanging out in the woods, hiding in blinds and reading books."

One of those books was a guide to the national parks. Under the title "Yosemite National Park" Bridwell found a two-page photograph of El Capitan. Even at age 17 he was tantalized by its oceanic scale. A few weeks later he came across another article — this one of an ascent of the Fisher Tower's Titan featuring photographs of Layton Kor. "That was it, man!" Bridwell remembers thinking. "I was already climbing cliffs to capture birds. I figured, hell, I can do that, too."

The next day Bridwell and his buddies were rappelling dirt mounds on a manila rope stolen from a transmission tower. Recognizing the limitations of this set-up, Bridwell soon enrolled in a Sierra Club basic climbing course. "I was pretty good at it right away," he concedes. "But what I liked best about climbing was that I was accepted as myself." As his skills grew, however, he realized that his instructors, "were not the serious guys I had read about in *Freedom of the Hills.*" The real climbers, he knew, were in Yosemite.

A superb middle-distance runner, Bridwell was offered a track scholarship to Purdue University. He turned it down in order to follow his high school-track coach to San Jose State. He enrolled intending to graduate, but climbing was already exerting an increasingly powerful attraction over him. During the summer of his freshman year he made his first trip to Yosemite Valley. By the time he returned his interest in formal education was at an end. Bridwell lasted just four semesters. In the spring of 1964 he quit school and left for the Valley. "Hell," he explains, "I had important climbs to do."

Pitching his tent beneath the pines — not far from the location he would later make famous as the "rescue site" — the 19-year-old Bridwell looked around and took his bearings. Everything seemed inordinately rich and infinitely better than he ever could have imagined.

With Royal Robbins in Europe and Yvon Chouinard in the army, the reigning god of Camp 4 in the early 1960s was Frank Sacherer. "When I first arrived in Yosemite," Bridwell says, "there was no guidebook and no information. The only protection was pitons. Climbing was dangerous and people played it cautiously." Everyone, that is, except for Sacherer, who was insanely bold and emphasized a minimum of gear and a maximum of commitment.

Bridwell's natural athleticism and youthful boldness brought him immediate attention, and it took Bridwell just two weeks to elbow his way into the inner circle's pecking order. Jim Baldwin, a well-liked Canadian, was the first to call him by name, but it was Sacherer who saw his potential. When they finally climbed together the impression Sacherer left on his young protégé was to last a lifetime.

In Sacherer, Bridwell found someone for whom climbing was not just a pastime but the definition of who and what he was. The abandon with which Sacherer threw himself at routes opened Bridwell's eyes to the fact that pushing the limits meant stepping over the line, holding nothing in reserve. Tormented and intense, Sacherer asked just as much from his partners as he did himself. He pushed and bullied, turning free time into work-out sessions and meals into rewards. By the end of his second season Bridwell had accompanied Sacherer on the first ascents of *Ahab* (5.10a) and the *Crack of Doom* (5.10d) as well as the first free ascent of a Yosemite grade V — the *North Buttress* of Middle Cathedral (5.10a).

According to Bridwell, when Frank Sacherer left Yosemite in 1966 to take a job in Europe as a physicist, "He had free climbed routes that the best climbers of the day said couldn't be done free. He had climbed routes in a day they said could not be climbed in a day. In the 1960s, Sacherer did more to advance free climbing as we know it today than any other single person."

Partnered by period luminaries such as Mark Clemens, Peter Haan, Jim Pettigrew, Kim Schmitz, Madsen, and others, Bridwell now set about putting Sacherer's philosophy into practice. Relying on pitons hand-forged by Yvon Chouinard in the Camp 4 parking lot and Austrian kletterschues, Bridwell and his cohorts practiced a ground-up ethic that outlawed previewing, hangdogging, or resting on gear. Even short routes were ventures into the unknown. Of that period, Bridwell's ascents of *Outer Limits* (5.10c), *Catchy* (5.10d), *Wheat Thin* (5.10c), *New Dimensions* (5.11a), *Butterfingers* (5.11a), and the *Nabisco Wall* (5.11a) remain his greatest works.

By the summer of 1967 Bridwell had become one of the Valley's best known habitues. Spending his winters in Tahoe where he worked as a ski instructor, he was invariably among the first climbers to return to the Valley in spring and among the last to leave in fall. It is an indication of the high regard in which his climbing ability was held that the park service placed him in charge of organizing and managing their high-angle rescue team. It was a move that would change the Valley's social structure forever.

Described by Doug Robinson as "the most trampled and dusty, probably the noisiest, and certainly the least habitable of all Yosemite campgrounds," the Sunnyside walk-in site — known to climbers as Camp 4 — was the home of every climber who entered the park. Figures as diverse as John Salathé and Don Whillans had rolled out their sleeping bags on its hallowed ground. Fetid and loud, Camp 4 probably generated more stories per square foot than any of the vertical real estate surrounding it. Handing control of its choicest sites over to Bridwell, a future park superintendent would later confess, was "not the wisest policy decision we ever made."

Neither was it the worst. Lost amid the skewed tales of wild times and "living as one with the dirt" is the fact that Bridwell and his hand-picked gang of rescue technicians actually took their duties seriously. Rappelling off the summit of El Cap to pluck an injured climber off a ledge and deposit him safely on the ground posed technical and logistical problems no one had ever grappled with before. Over the next 10 years the confederation of park personnel and climbers that formed Yosemite Search and Rescue (YOSAR) laid the foundation for today's high-angle, search-and-rescue techniques.

On the domestic front, it is probably not too big a stretch of the imagination to suggest that Bridwell also found in Camp 4 the neighborhood he had never known as a child. Like him, its eccentric retinue of loners and misfits had escaped the suburbanized wasteland and aching loneliness of middle-class

America to throw up their sun-faded tents and live, as Doug Robinson so perfectly phrased it, "like hobos in a paradise of stone." Now, with the keys to the asylum in hand, Bridwell moved quickly to create the city of his dreams.

Peopling the rescue site with the cream of Yosemite climbers, Bridwell and his chosen few lived as beggar kings beneath the great sweep of the Sierra in a New Jerusalem of golden light and endless days. Secure from site fees and visitor permits, Bridwell, Schmitz, Madsen, Phil Bircheff, and a changing cast of others built a peasant meritocracy where the only things that mattered were how hard you climbed and the quality of your vibe; where anything was possible and the worst disappointments were quickly healed by the gentle hiss of an evening breeze and the deep relief of a morning cigarette.

Then, as now, days began with the dregs of any available liquid left over from the night before and a spoonful of whatever remained in the pot. By 8:30 a.m. the more industrious residents of Camp 4 would walk across the street to the cafeteria. Half coherent and with sticks and leaves clinging to their hair, they would then forage the abandoned food stuffs of horrified tourists until security, satiation, or disappointment sent them home to engage in the perpetual discussion of routes, partners, gear, and weather. Optimists worked on their dilapidated cars, the intellectuals read Ginsberg and Ferlingetti, folk music drifted in the breeze, and by 5 p.m. the secret expeditions to new routes were old news. It was the perfect idyll.

Outside the Valley, however, another revolution was taking place. The values that had stood one generation through depression and war were being tossed away. Riots, assassinations, and the insanity of Vietnam were rattling the streets. Everything was upside down. Authority was in retreat while psychedelics, free love, and social agitation were everywhere. Everywhere, that is, but Camp 4. The gap was to be short-lived. Since the climbers of Camp 4 were already leading an alternative lifestyle, it only led to reason that the drugs and women could not be far behind. And when they arrived, "The Bird," as he was now called, was ready.

"Almost every climber I knew used drugs," says Bridwell of those days. "We didn't use them on routes. It wasn't like that. We were using hallucinogens to help us understand what we were experiencing from a point of view seldom visited by the western mind. We were trying to make sense of this new awareness. To unfold the mysteries. Drugs were equipment."

It was a difficult adjustment for the old guard. Their crew-cut and orderly world was gone. The momentum was changing. In Camp 4 the beat poetry, mountain chablis, and bongos of the 1950s had been replaced by Mararishi Yoga, blotter acid, and fuzzy riffs on cheap guitars. Yvon Chouinard, Royal Robbins, Warren Harding, and their cohorts had set a high standard. But although their final statements — the *Muir Wall, North American Wall,* and

243

the *Wall of Early Morning Light* — were grand gestures, when the end of the Golden Age came it was marked by petty disputes, chopped bolts, and personal vendettas. A gilded era was gone and, as Bridwell puts it, "The Gods were bitter in their demise."

By the time the 1970s dawned Camp 4 was a changed place. The dulcet good-life was gone. Now it was louder, funkier, and much more crowded. Though the summers were still reasonably peaceful, spring and fall brought hordes of long-haired outsiders seeking to imprint themselves on the walls. The scent of Camp 4's wood smoke mingled with that of pot. The midnight scuffings of bears foraging for leftovers were drowned out by arguments over chalk and passive protection. Coming to the Valley in those days was like going to church in a bad part of town. Climbers went there knowing about the gods and of their patron saints — Herbert, Frost, Roper, Pratt, and Kor — but it was the renegade that everyone wanted to emulate. Bridwell. Outsiders were happy to engage in the rumor-mongering and self-justification of life on the lower rungs of the social ladder. Tales of Bridwellian misconduct, arrogance, and daring were favorite topics around dinner. Deprecated and envied, Bridwell was dean of Camp 4, and lord of all he surveyed.

John Long arrived in Yosemite in 1971 with Bridwell in mind. Brash and muscular, toting an impressive résumé and carrying a chip on his shoulder the size of the Columbia boulder, Long pulled in and headed straight for the rescue site.

"I went to Yosemite dead-set on proving something," says Long. "I wanted to be part of the cutting-edge group. I wanted to climb with the best climbers in the world, to push the world standard. That meant climbing with Bridwell." Two hours after arriving he got his wish. "Bridwell took me up the left side of Rixon's and that was kind of an eye-opener. But I felt like he was totally open to me," says Long. "I felt extremely comfortable with him immediately."

The relationship was to be a profitable one. With the changing of the guard, many of Bridwell's old partners had either left the Valley or scaled back their climbing. With Long and a number of others in tow, Bridwell again picked up the pace, training and climbing harder than ever. Soon the rescue site and its environs teemed with talented young climbers — John Bachar, Ron Kauk, Werner Braun, Mike Graham, John Yablonski, and many others. Wild and unfettered, they took to the rock like iguanas during the day and happily indulged themselves in the raucous parties and loose living of Camp 4 by night. There was no longer any philosophical agenda to getting stoned. It was recreation, pure and simple. One more way of expanding the high that was life in Yosemite.

"There were neighbors, love affairs, slums, parties, gymnasiums, loonies, territorial disputes, degeneration, and inspiration," Kevin Worral, a frequent partner of Bridwell's, says of those days. There was the Mountain Bar for scrounging drinks, the fireplace lounge for sitting out storms, and, if you were quick enough, free showers or a plate of purloined leftovers at Curry Village. "There was just nothing like it," says Billy Westbay. "There was this incredible energy. Everybody feeding off each other. It was an untouchable growth period."

As the energy increased so did the output. Bridwell's 1973 article for *Mountain* magazine entitled "Brave New World" stoked the fires even higher. Extolling the techniques and standards of Valley climbing, Bridwell's words excited climbers from around the world to come to Yosemite and test themselves in its granite crucible. With visitors from Japan, Italy, France, Korea, England, and Spain all elbowing their way onto the walls, a hybrid of new ideas and bold one-upmanship infused the Valley.

"Everything in the 1970s was open-ended," says John Long. "All of us believed Bridwell's credo that 'anything was possible.'"

EB's, tape, chalk, tincture of Benzoin, and nuts accelerated the pace of change. It was as if a veil had fallen. As if everything was up for grabs. The possibilities were mind-boggling and nobody understood them better than "the man." Playing minister and mayor, new-age Sacherer and old-age Ahab to this motley parliament of Ishmaelites, Bridwell set out to push the envelope. Where walls were concerned, the more he climbed the more he saw what was out there. And how vulnerable it was. Like the generation before him, Bridwell understood that any place on Yosemite's undulant granite was reachable if one was willing to spend enough time with drill in hand. An example needed to be set of what could be achieved by minimizing bolts and maximizing the adventure. Finding the line to best express that credo was the challenge.

Likewise, 5.11s were now routine. As harder and harder climbs went up, they were almost immediately surpassed. Conversations focused only on pushing into the next realm of possibility. Dale Bard, Mark Chapman, Kevin Worrall, George Myers, Westbay, Ray Jardine, Rick Reider, and Bev Johnson joined the chase along with the likes of Jim Erikson, Art Higbee, Henry Barber, and Jim Donini. Close behind was an even bigger rogue's gallery of misfits and mutants, all of them pushing and probing at the next inconceivable first.

"We just fed off each other, and that allowed us to achieve more than if we were on our own," says Billy Westbay. "We were able to discover more of what we could really do ... because we could dream big dreams."

No one dreamed bigger than Bridwell. Always stirred to his best performances by competition, Bridwell now set out to set the highest possible standard. Over a two-week period in the summer of 1975 he climbed the *Nose* in a day (VI 5.10 A2) and put up the *Pacific Ocean Wall* (VI 5.9 A5) — routes that placed him alone atop the world of technical rock climbing.

"The *Nose* was great," says Westbay, his partner on both routes. "Our goal was to get back to the Lodge for last call. And when we walked in everybody was so stoked. We couldn't buy a beer."

245

The *P.O. Wall* was another matter. "It was really intimidating up there," Westbay laughs. "We were pretty freaked." And with good reason, for Bridwell and company were nailing into a realm of technicality and commitment that had never before been explored. Coaching and prodding his team through pitch after pitch of desperately hard nailing, Bridwell seemed to know just how hard to push. At mid-height on the seemingly blank wall, when one member of the team insisted on going down, the Bird gave in. "Go ahead," he said, nodding toward the gaping void below them. "You can take two ropes and go." He didn't, of course, and four days later the team completed the hardest big-wall route on the planet and put high-end Yosemite wall climbing out of the reach of mortals.

"[The *Pacific Ocean Wall*] probably changed me more than any other route," Bridwell would say later. "After that, I knew that no matter how bad things looked I could still do it." Bridwell's skill on hard aid has left a lasting impression on everybody who has climbed with him. Nobody has ever mastered great difficulty with less showmanship. "You could never tell where the hard bit was [by watching Bridwell]," says Westbay. "He just kept at it, never seeming to push it but never seeming to slow down, either. Just really clean and steady."

Now into his mid-30s and with 15 years of hard climbing behind him, Bridwell could have walked away after the *P.O. Wall* and still have been remembered as one of the great rock climbers of his era. Nothing could have been further from his mind. Routes in the mid- to late 1970s like El Cap's *Mirage* (VI 5.11 A4), Half Dome's *Bushido* (VI 5.10 A5) and *Zenith* (VI 5.10 A5), and Mount Watkin's *Bob Locke Memorial Buttress* (VI 5.11 A4) upped the ante even further.

The *Sea of Dreams* (VI 5.9 A5), completed in 1978 with Dale Bard and Dave Dingleman, was perhaps the touchstone of the period. This seemingly featureless line linked an intricate network of shallow seams, expanding flakes, and hookable edges. Equipped with multi-RURP belays and including an if-you-fall-you-die pitch, the *Sea of Dreams* remains a highly respected undertaking and presaged the extreme seriousness of today's hardest aid lines.

Clearly, Bridwell was at the top of his form. No one before or since has owned a place and time in quite the same fashion as he ruled the granite walls of Yosemite National Park. Nobody expected that he was already in the process of transforming himself into one of the world's foremost alpinists.

"I thought you could make money with a slide show of big walls," Bridwell explains, "but the real market seemed to be for alpine climbs. I'd always harbored an alpine desire but California climbers were considered rock jocks. Guys from Colorado and Washington were the ones that went on expeditions."

Recognizing his lack of mountaineering skills, Bridwell had quietly set out to fill the holes in his résumé. He dove in at the deep end. In the summer of 1974 he drove to Canada to attempt the then unclimbed Emperor Face on Mount

Robson. Turned back by a recalcitrant car, he instead soloed Washington's Mount Shuksan before returning to the Valley. After the fabulous summer of 1975, he headed for Patagonia.

To anyone else, the unclimbed east face of Cerro Torre might have seemed something of a stretch for a Valley boy who barely knew how to strap on his crampons. In Bridwell's mind, it was the next logical step. The majority of the route was a rock climb and he was the fastest big-wall rock climber on the planet. The ice at the top he would figure out. Unfortunately, his attempt with Kim Carrigan was cut short when the Australian was deported from Bolivia with visa problems. Bridwell didn't get back until the winter of 1979, when he again arrived with the east face of Cerro Torre in mind, but switched his attentions to that tower's *Compressor Route* after a Christmas Eve encounter with a young American named Steve Brewer. Using borrowed equipment and climbing alpine-style, the two notched the route in just under two days — a shockingly fast time on a route that many believed could only be climbed siege style. Their ascent sent ripples of shock throughout the international climbing community.

Like the *P.O. Wall,* Cerro Torre also held revelations. Exhausted and pressing their descent into a storm, Bridwell fell from a rappel stance and plummeted through space. "It took a long, long time," he says of his 150-foot tumble. "I was waiting, wondering why nothing was happening, watching the rock go by. It was very quiet. I was very clear. You have this capacity to separate your physical body from consciousness, and while I was aware that I was falling I was also very, very calm."

Regrets, secrets, judgements, and the certainty that there was still "plenty of time" passed through his mind. With only three turns of one-inch webbing around his waist for a harness, the impact Bridwell experienced upon hitting the end of the 9mm haul line snapped his ribs like carrot sticks but saved his life.

It was not to be his last brush with the macabre. Over the next several years each big climb seemed to come equipped with its own unique horrors. A winter ascent of the Moose's Tooth in Alaska with Mugs Stump resulted in a do-or-die rappel from high on the route. He climbed the *Shroud* on the Grand Jorasse outside Chamonix, France, only to find out that his early mentor Frank Sacherer had been killed by lightning on the same route a year earlier. Returning to Patagonia he dodged storms and falling rock to put up several new routes. He climbed Pumori in winter, traveled to China, Nepal, and nearly died from an intestinal worm contracted during the first coast-to-coast traverse of Borneo with Rick Ridgeway and John Long.

While sponsorships occasionally helped support Bridwell's climbing habit, the majority of his financing came from hard work. In addition to ski patrolling and YOSAR, he toiled on oil rigs, guided, and took whatever odd jobs he could string together. Having married him in 1976, Bridwell's wife, Peggy, presented the Bird with a son, Layton, in 1979. Bridwell was a proud and doting father. This "magical child" provided new incentive for generating income. Leveraging his climbing skill, Bridwell found work in Hollywood as a rigger and technical advisor, wrote books, and published articles. He also made frequent trips back to the Valley. In the early 1980s he established a string of noteworthy routes including Half Dome's *The Big Chill* (VI 5.10 A4), *Shadows* (VI 5.9 A4+) on El Cap, and, one of his all time favorites, *Zenyatta Mondatta* (VI 5.7 A5), an El Cap horror show that he describes as a mini *Sea of Dreams* and "no place for those with a faint heart."

"When I arrived on the scene in the mid-'80s [Bridwell] was pretty much considered the father of modern aid climbing," confirms Pete Takeda. "Bridwell is in a class alone. A lot of other people have done more routes, but Bridwell was the one who crossed the line. He went after these rotten, expanding features by using heads and hooks and riveting and stuff like that. The things that everybody else was trying to stay away from."

But despite his high profile and sterling résumé, the Bird's stubborn unwillingness to accept limitations gnawed at him. As a second generation of friends drifted away into marriages and careers, he kept at it, constantly searching for new climbs, new partners, new directions.

"We climb onward," Royal Robbins once wrote, reflecting on his ascent of El Cap's *North American Wall.* "Searching for adventure, searching for ourselves, searching for situations which would call forth our total resources." Climbing has always held those overtones for Bridwell, too. Every summit for him was laced with a sense of incompleteness; every insight braided with a mixture of doubt and desire; every dream a path stretching out through the graveyards of lost friends and forfeited ambitions.

By the late 1980s Bridwell was beginning to feel the toll of time. Though he was climbing as well as ever, he was a father and for the first time in his life had to scramble for income. He rigged for commercials and a series of made-for-television movies. He did more guiding and became a special trainer for the U.S. Navy Seals. He gave lectures and designed equipment. As always, though, he climbed. In 1992, at age 50, he climbed the Eiger's North Face and was cranking solid 5.12.

I can see Bridwell right now — sitting at the table of his modest home in Palm Desert, California. The window open, a cigarette hanging between his lips. There is a cup of black coffee in his hand. A steno pad covered with notes lays by his right elbow. A breeze sweeps down off the San Jacintos and rattles the paper like bones.

To say Jim Bridwell's life experience has been rich is one thing. To say it has been charmed is another. Despite a career that has been blessedly free of personal injury, Bridwell has seen his share of death. Stump, Madsen, and Baldwin all died in climbing accidents. Bridwell's mother died while he was in Patagonia. Guiding in the Tetons, he watched a client fall to his death. The murmur over that one was particularly ugly. Accusations were made; lawsuits filed. The Bird's self-promulgated reputation as a wild man hurt him. "We are," as he has said, "our own creations."

Such self-absorption extracts a price. Bridwell has been called the Chuck Yaeger of serious climbing — someone who was prominent in his time, who gave more than he took, who was peerless as a performer. Americans, however, are prone to taking pleasure in the demise of their idols. "It takes a lot of 'atta boys' to overcome one fuck-up," Bridwell sighs. And the likelihood is that he will be as well remembered for his wild bouts of drinking as for the days and nights he spent chasing the wildest dreams of a generation across the vertical landscape of El Capitan.

No one is more to blame for the misunderstanding than Bridwell. In these days of media intrusiveness and voyeurism he has never made a point of tending very carefully to his image. "Climbing is not that important," he says in his own defense. "It's the camaraderie, it's overcoming elements in myself that matters. The thing that I have enjoyed about it most is that there is no superficiality. The idea is to set a goal and do the best job you can. What are [the] seven to 10 days you spend on a wall compared to life? The values people talk about are imaginary. It's all an illusion. You make yourself up as you go along. You are a viewpoint, a set of beliefs, that's all. People take themselves seriously because they want to be separate. But if you are still conscious when all is said and done, you'll be laughing.

"People trash each other," he sighs. "My gut feeling is that you should judge others the way you judge yourself. I've set high goals for myself and I've always been willing to suffer the consequences if I didn't get there. It's not how good you are, it's your vision, what you contributed. I gave what I had."

You may be surprised to learn that Jim Bridwell believes in God. He thinks the shit is about to hit the fan. "[The world] can't go on this way very much longer," he says. "What will happen, I don't know, but it won't be good." He believes that psychedelic drugs were an absolutely positive force in his life, but he doesn't do them anymore. ("They don't make good drugs [these days]," he complains.)

Bridwell regrets never having had any money. He is sorry that he hasn't spent more time at home. He would very much like to find the funding for another trip to the Himalayas. So it goes.

"To really understand Jim Bridwell," says John Long, "you'd have to go back and climb what he did, when he did it." Both tasks have merit; neither is likely. "I guess," Bridwell replies, "that makes me an enigma."

Not really. Like all of us, Jim Bridwell wants it both ways. He wants people to see him for who he is in the full light of everything he has accomplished. He wants to be respected. He wants to do more big climbs. He wants the past to be seen for what it was and not for the myths and misinformation that cloy at him. He wants to be half as much appreciated in his own country as he has been abroad. He wants most to be remembered for the good he has done, and that might be an impossible request from someone who has lived his life like a climb — minimal gear, maximum commitment — throwing everything he had at every moment. "Americans are tough on their heroes," says John Long. "The things that made him so good as a climber make him a pretty easy target for people who don't really know him. I know it bothers him, but his answer has always been to go put up another route. To let his climbing speak for him."

First published in Climbing *No. 179, 1998.*

The Gift (That Keeps on Giving)

Dealing with partner loss, posers, and a hard new route in Alaska's Ruth Gorge

By Mark Twight

When you're looking at life through a strange new
room maybe drowning soon, is this the start of it all
... the lights look bright when you reach outside time
for one last ride before the end of it all.

— *Ian Curtis*

We were late and that made us lame. Scott Backes and I had just climbed a new route on the south face of Pico del Norte in Bolivia. From our bivy at 17,000 feet we'd climbed the 2800-foot line in just over four hours — eight minutes longer than we had intended. We had agreed to turn back at 3 p.m., but having hung it out on the thin ice and mixed climbing we figured the summit was worth a visit.

We did it "naked," without ropes or packs. We carried water and Gu in our pockets, stashed our ice tools in the waistbelts of our harnesses when they weren't in our hands, and brought one collapsible ski pole each for low-angle snow sections. Our light clothes kept us warm while moving but didn't allow us to stop on top for long. We hugged. I cried, because this was our last alpine route together. Scott was retiring from the game. The route and the style we did it in were a testament to our closeness and the total trust of our partnership.

After a few minutes on top we downclimbed to the east. We had taken our ethic — the biggest objective with the least amount of gear — another step, for us. We might have gone further ... It was going to be a long, thoughtful road back.

In La Paz, after a day of psychedelic visions, celebration, and other third-world absurdities the route named itself in our hotel room — *Fuck 'em, They're All Posers Anyway.* Which is how we both felt about most of the alpine pretenders who were popping up on the scene — those who wrote "*Sea of Vapors*, Grade 7," on their résumés after they'd done it in Grade 5 conditions.

Scott turned away from hard and dangerous routes to father a family. I watched, disappointed and jealous, angry, and full of love. At first I thought it wouldn't matter. But the more I considered sharing those routes with another person, the less they appealed to me. Who, for example, shared what Scott and I shared? Our tastes in music, art, trash, talk, training, and mountains, our bullshit macho fronts and compassionate insides? Where were my peers? Some dead, some retired, most living elsewhere, a few I had never met. Without the sacredness of the partnership, without its intimacy and trust, climbing lost its attraction. My spirit for it withered and died. I quit and spent myself elsewhere, shooting pistols and pictures, and digging into my psyche. I felt a twinge of envy when I heard about guys getting up things, or even failing marvelously. But mostly I took my blinders off, stepped outside of climbing and had a good look around. Life outside of climbing isn't bad. I discovered that people who perform at the highest levels of their disciplines share emotional characteristics with top climbers. It opened my eyes. It didn't change my elitist attitude, of course, but the flavors were novel.

From my new, non-climbing perspective, the state of the sport looked bleak. Explosive popularity leading to overcrowding and resource closures, money-hungry manufacturers cutting corners to address the new breed of casual user, leaving the hardcore hanging by the threads of gear that didn't live up to its advertising, and sponsor-hungry FNGs spraying half-truths and hype in hopes of attracting benefactors.

I revel in foul words and confrontation, but only if they're honest words that stand tall on the strong back of actual achievement. Instead, what I heard was baseless sputtering by climbers who hadn't put their time in yet loudly shouted that the existing grades weren't hard, and asked, "What have these old guys been doing, anyway"? I asked how anyone could possibly be "redefining the whole sport of ice climbing" on one-pitch routes in Colorado? Man tends to strip great disciplines into their component parts for easier practice and comprehension. I wondered how this reductionism became the driving force in ice and mixed climbing. My disgust kept me at arm's length from climbing.

I was living in Boulder, Colorado, and hadn't climbed for a year when John Bouchard, one of my early mentors, came to town. He told me over breakfast that it had taken him two full years to become a climber again after taking seven years off to fly paragliders. I realized I didn't want to lose that kind of time or get left behind, so I started training. The first few weeks in the weight room hurt; coming back from zero was demoralizing, especially when I knew exactly what lay ahead. Alpine climbing is suffering and weakness and maybe, when you're lucky, fulfillment. I remember good days when the strength of the gods flowed through me, but mostly I look back and see failure and ass-kickings stitched together by occasional success and slowly emerging self-confidence. Knowing that the mountains could swat me dead from one second to

the next taught me humility. Something a roadside route, no matter how difficult, will never teach a man.

Steve House had been calling off and on for a couple of years, looking for a
like-minded soul to go alpine climbing. I'd been hearing about him. His 36-hour
first ascent of the *Fathers and Sons Wall* on Denali — a route that had rejected a number of previous attempts — put him on the pages of the magazines.
After he soloed a new route on the 6000-foot West Face of the West Buttress of
Denali, my peers and I started wondering where he came from. He certainly
wasn't doing these routes in a style he learned in this country.

I asked around. It turned out that he had learned how to alpine climb while
visiting Slovenia in the same environment that produced the likes of Silvo Karo
and Janez Jeglic. My old partner Barry Blanchard had climbed with him and
confirmed his talent. Bill Belcourt, a fellow "no-future cynic," assured me that
House "climbed like an old guy," meaning that he put in gear like someone who
had been, and wanted to be, around for awhile. I liked his style; he'd named his
Canadian Rockies testpiece *Two-Piece Yanks* as a retort to the condescension
and provincialism he experienced while climbing up there; all hot Canadian
climbers, it seems, wear stylish one-piece suits. He intentionally undergraded
the route, calling it "M6+, let them choke on that." But the ultimate recom-
mendation came from Scott, who christened him the "Great White Hope of
American alpinism." Steve and I began entertaining ideas of going north in the
spring, which was far enough off that it was just talk. I maintained my distance
from actual climbing.

The more I watched and read about climbing, the more disgusted I became.
Man was bringing his emotional sloth and self-aggrandizing exaggeration into
ice and mixed climbing, something that could only happen when the disciplines were undertaken away from the risks imposed by the mountain environment. Activities that used to be called "training" quite unexpectedly became
a sport in and of themselves. The "new" protagonists turned ice climbing into
sport climbing, with roadside Hot Flashes and grading arguments, overhangs,
chipped holds, pre-protected and rehearsed routes, exhibitions, and competitions. While the climbing was powerful, a trifle dangerous at times, too, the
engagement was small and the intellectual commitment and knowledge
required to succeed relatively low.

The polarization between alpinists and sport ice/mixed climbers was instan-
taneous, based on the young guns' posturing and lack of humility. The poor bastards either didn't understand or refused to acknowledge the difference
between what they were doing and the real thing. Physical proficiency is easy
to come by. But there are no shortcuts to the psychological strength that has
kept guys like Scott Backes, Jay Smith, Steve Swenson, Jack Tackle, and John

Bouchard alive in the mountains for many years. Because of this conflict none of these "old" guys is going to mentor the young guns in the mountains, which means a precious few of the revolution's participants are applying their new-found skills on hard alpine routes. No one is waiting in line for the alpine hor-rorshows but plenty of people wake up early to take their shot at an early repeat of *Amphibian*.

The hype pretended that M7 or 8, or 12 for that matter, had never before been climbed until the current practitioners rap bolted some overhanging choss heap, rehearsed it, climbed it, did photo shoots on it, and treated it as commerce. The reality is that hard mixed climbing was going on in the moun-tains long before the "M" grades were created. Most of this climbing was referred to on route topos as "hard mixed," an ambiguous description for an equally ambiguous form of climbing on a medium that changes from day to day and year to year. For example, on my route *Beyond Good and Evil* in the French Alps, the aid was eliminated on the "second ascent," not by talent but by ice plastered eight inches thick and six feet wide over what had been a thin crack in a corner. Worse, on this and other claimed "ascents," no one has climbed the last four pitches — which are the most complex and dangerous ones on this route. This kind of misrepresentation made me sick.

Mere words can not fight a disease. Talk minus Action equals Zilch. I had to go climbing. A man can only lead by example.

News filtered south that the winter had been unusually mild in Alaska. I remembered the grin on Mugs Stump's face when he talked about the Alaska Range in March. He said dozens of lines were frozen onto absurdly steep faces, climbable if you had the vision and the skills and were willing to take the sometimes frigid temperatures. Alaska is a cheap date where it doesn't cost much to get hammered by big mountains. It's the perfect place to bite off more than you can chew.

Steve was game. I invited a third because, although three might be slower, it is safer, and I wasn't willing to go north with a guy I'd never met. I convinced "Jonny Blitz" to get off the couch. Jonny hadn't been alpine climbing in nine years, but he'd been training so I knew he'd be strong enough. We had been friends for 15 years, and I thought that Jonny's presence might offer the same psychic closeness I felt when I climbed with Scott. I had several agendas to ful-fill, which was unfair to Steve, as he'd never met either of us. Still, I figured if he couldn't take it, and flourish, we probably wouldn't make a good team in the future.

Everything froze. Olive oil, canned meat, cheese, nothing escaped — except the sweetened, condensed milk and that's weird science. The thermometer read minus 30 until we broke it. It's probably better not to know. But three days of normal March temperatures in Alaska gave way to warmer conditions and we wrapped our minds around the idea of climbing. Our reconnaissance ski tours hadn't yielded the endless supply of ice we expected. Very few lines looked like more than powder snow over granite, or they were in the shade 24 hours a day. One south-facing gully on Mount Bradley stood out, though. It looked discontinuous, but we thought we could piece together thin ice smears to bypass each chockstone or dry chimney. We packed three days of food and skied toward the gully, which threaded up between granite pillars, passing beneath Yosemite-steep walls taller than El Cap.

Five pitches up, the gully split. The branch we were in closed off, and the ice around the dead end overwhelmed our collective psyche. We searched for a way to aid past it, but without hooks the compact rock and the weight in our packs shut us down. There were two hours of light left. We were failing. Steve took it harder than Blitz. No big deal for me, though. I've failed a lot. It was just the Alaska Factor kicking in.

We skied and ate for a few days. Our glacier pilot, Paul Roderick, even flew in a pizza. With no other lines begging to be done we decided to return to the gully on Mount Bradley. At this level it's rare to "on-sight" a route; research and failure are the name of the game. Or maybe we were just too stupid to get it right the first time. We'd have to settle for the "redpoint."

We traded away food for more hardware and headed back. The first five pitches passed easily. I drew the sixth pitch out of the dead end. The psychological crux involved pulling off 90-degree ice onto a 70-degree snow ramp with nothing but my axes buried in snow between me and a certain 50-foot ledge-dive. I named the pitch "The Super Third Eye Opener," because Blitz and I were sick of climbers naming pitches of alpine routes after happy little experiences, or to express their hippie love of the beautiful environment. Proper alpinism is not beautiful — it's war, a struggle that is glorious in its own way. Beauty is for the ground, postcards and glowing prose written long after the fact.

While we climbed we laughed and joked, tentatively giving a little bit of ourselves and then pulling back to see the reaction. No one admitted to fear or misgiving. But the climbing was harder than I'd imagined, and I was still uncertain whether the route would go. We'd dropped some crucial nuts when a carabiner gate froze open and flipped off the rack. As a team we weren't climbing fast, although sometimes Steve was rushing. Speed is safety but when the speed is out of sync with the environment, movement is choppy and inefficient, and details slip away.

Higher, Blitz scrapped with a foot-wide, 70-degree ice runnel while I belayed and Steve dug out a bivy ledge. Dusk was on us. I followed quickly, wanting to wring one more pitch from the day. Things always go bad at once, never by degrees. Darkness, thin ice, then no ice and no gear, no way to back down, the right-size cam in Jon's belay anchor, diminishing ball size, an embarrassingly unstylish squirm upwards, and finally many pitons at the belay.

When people ask what it was like, I try to explain without resorting to blow-by-blow descriptions. Prose cannot communicate each nano-second of the moment your tools rip and you know the entire reality of the fall you will take, from the little flake hitting you in the teeth to how small you are in relation to the mountain, how little it cares, how tiny it is in the range you're in, how meaningless to the aggregate human consciousness, how bad your leg is going to feel when you break it and the bone punches out the skin, how good going into shock will seem. The movements, risk, psychological demands, and probability of success are personal and relevant only to the experiencer.

But something happened up there that I feel privileged to have seen. And although I hope I never witness anything like it again, it deserves description. I backed off the 14th pitch, reluctant to take the risk it required. I knew where it was steep there would be ice, none too thick, sometimes over rock, sometimes over snow. It looked like the sixth pitch, but far more difficult and sustained.

Steve grabbed the rack, fueled by desire, an unwillingness to fail, and a simmering competition between us. He groveled up a chimney to an overhang and fudged some gear in. Gingerly tapping, he swung onto a free-hanging icicle, managing three moves before it snapped. He rode it down past the first piece, which ripped without activating the Screamer, and kissed a snowslope 15 feet down with his back at the same moment the next piece took his weight. I wanted to puke. It was no place to fall off. Steve rested for a few minutes but didn't come down. I wanted him to — silently, because I also wanted to see what he'd do next.

With another piece of gear in the cave, Steve pulled onto the remaining ice, stemming and hooking toward a false salvation. Ice turned to snow. Cracks disappeared behind it. He was 25 feet out and looking at a back-breaking fall that would terminate right in front of us. Jon held the ropes and I belayed psychologically. We talked about irresponsible risk, angry with Steve for including us in his. But part of me wondered if I was seeing the future, if my mind was too small to conceive of climbing this hard in this situation, if I'm an old guy and the young guns are going to blow by me like the wind. I've fallen once in the mountains. I knew some guys who only fell the one time it took to kill them. Now I hear about guys whipping off a lot, hear them say, "It's not hard if you're not falling," and wonder why I don't share their attitude. Probably because it has no place high on an alpine wall. There are no helicopters, help, or hope up

256

here; a guy with a compound femur would bleed out before we lowered him two pitches.

I looked back up at Steve, moving less surely, Captain Ahab, committed, on the ride until it was over. Ninety minutes later he stopped at a semi-hanging stance below another mushroom and chockstone. After two pins went in I yelled up, "What do you think?"

"I can't think yet," he croaked, and continued hammering, building a five-piece, equalized anchor and a return to relative security. He fixed the rope and rapped.

"I'm sorry about that," he said uncomfortably. "That was too dangerous." I told him I respected his apology. Success breeds ambition, though. I'd like to see Steve live through his. Like I managed to live through mine at his age.

After a night on a giant mushroom, we punched for the top with no bivy gear, and no idea how far we had to go. We wanted to move fast. But the pitch around the roof and into the next system took awhile; Blitz aided off a cam, then his tools, hooks, tied-off blades, and bad nuts. The pitch ended on easier ground, though, and we started running, too quick for our own good sometimes.

Darkness again. In the brilliance of the halogen light I read relief on my friends' faces as they arrived at the 8700-foot col, where we had agreed to end our route. The black pyramid of Mount Huntington loomed nearby, and Denali, The Great One, made every other mountain look inadequate. The summit didn't matter to any of us. It was 8 p.m. and nine rappels separated us from our sleeping bags.

We landed back on the mushroom bivy at 1:30 a.m. The Northern Lights shimmered across the few degrees of sky visible between the walls enclosing our route. I wished I had a Walkman. I let out some tension, knowing that the most dangerous work was done. I should have been content with our success and how smoothly the climbing went. But I felt hollow. The three of us were friendly, but nobody's skin had worn thin enough to bare his soul. I supposed that true contact was somewhere in the future, beyond the next day's rappels and the ski back to basecamp.

There was a dark stain around the tents and I could see Steve circling, hesitant to set his pack down. I laughed loud and long when I realized that while we were on the route, the ravens had visited us. They went straight for the shit bags, the contents of which were strewn everywhere. "Pre-digested nuts, candy, grease, and meat … mmmm, good," I could hear them cacawing amongst themselves. But our feces gave them the shits and they perched on our tents and let their diarrhea flow. "Welcome home, assholes — next time leave some food out."

Jon and I talked while the first plane was flying Steve and his gear out. I was excited about climbing again and knew it would last. But, aside from Steve, I was fresh out of partners; Jon's career kept him climbing hard routes in the mountains as a lifestyle. I asked Jon where all the alpinists had gone? Life takes them away. Death takes them, too. As I age my peer group gets smaller and smaller. I understood then that the reason I won't be climbing with the new breed of mixed climbers is because they aren't comfortable in the mountains. It's why they converted an aspect of alpinism to reflect their attitude and comfort level. I realized I have nothing against them; they can't change who they are, just as I can't do much about who I am.

We dropped Jon at his sister's house in Anchorage. He and I hugged, told each other what a good time we had, and parted. I haven't spoken to him since. I'm not angry or disappointed; there just aren't any words that need to be said. Perhaps living it was enough. Steve and I talked a couple of days after we got back, but only to discuss next winter's schedule. However great winning is, I'd rather fail and learn about myself than succeed without discovering anything more than my own petty sense of competition with rivals. Sure, it may have been a hard route, but it was one of the most emotionless climbs I have ever done.

When I got home I faxed Scott the topo. I was proud and wanted to share it with him. It was the first hard alpine route I'd done without him in over four years. I missed him. Our trust had taken years to build and there was nothing like it on Mount Bradley; the three of us were simply men joined by a common goal, having fun, pushing the boat out, learning a little about each other. We weren't necessarily stronger as a team than we would have been alone. We feigned the closeness we lacked, uniting ourselves into a team by poking fun at the outsiders, anyone who wasn't where we were, doing what we were doing. And although I've known Blitz longer than Scott, the intensity of what Scott and I have been through affected me more. My fax caught Scott off guard. "It was both amazing and horrific," he said later on the phone. "I'm proud of you, but very sad I wasn't there."

The mountains won't ever feel the same without him. But his words remind me that the climbing wasn't foremost for us in the first place. Climbing mountains was just the start of it all.

First published in Climbing *No. 178, 1998.*

The Shining Mountain
Epic on Changabang,
North Face

By Andy Cave

Momentarily, I stepped outside myself. I watched my exhausted legs trying to move quickly, my feet trying to hold steady on the snow-covered moraine. I slumped against a huge slab of granite to regain a grip on reality, rested my sac against a tall cairn that Brendan had built the previous year, and took a sip of water. Minutes later, when I tried to lift the sac, a pain shot across my chest. Across the peaks and troughs of the glacier I could make out basecamp, normally about an hour away.

I jettisoned the rucsac and, in slow motion using the ski poles to stabilize my jellied limbs, edged up to the first moraine ridge. By the time I reached the top, the chest pain had returned. I was scared. The rotting-fish smell of frostbite forced me on; I had to get some medicine. I had to get there before they abandoned camp. I had to tell them what had happened.

After a full half hour I had traveled only a pitiful 700 feet. I yelled into the approaching mist. There was no reply. The thought of only making it halfway and bivying without a sleeping bag and refreezing my hands and feet frightened me enough to turn back.

After almost 12 hours of much-needed sleep, I crawled out of my snow-covered sleeping bag. I took a short piss, which turned the snow bright orange, then stuffed the sleeping bag into the rucsac with my good hand. I felt refreshed inside, but I still walked like a delirious junky.

In my head I constructed the words I would say to the others. I was convinced they would see me a long way off and would become suspicious at the sight of just one bright-red suit. As I wobbled down the final half mile, I felt intoxicated by the spring air. A small red bird that had arrived with the warm temperatures sang and hopped to the side, guiding me back to basecamp. The overnight ice had not yet melted from the edge of the stream and I staggered straight across, crunching though it in my lead-heavy boots. I was grateful for the ski poles, which let me walk in a dignified straight line. I shouted a small hello, and immediately Narinda and Vikram, our liaison officer and cook, came out of the kitchen shelter. They held out their hands warmly but nervously. It had been 18 long days. Narinda waited for my words, tears welling in his eyes.

"Mick and Steve are coming," I said. "Brendan is dead."

I appreciated that acclimatizing was a vital part of our preparation, but found it tedious. All the slopes of the neighboring cols and peaks were covered in loose snow topped by a hideous crust that made movement slow and dangerous. Consequently we plodded up to 5700 meters on a boring but relatively safe slope on the unclimbed Dunagiri Parbat. Although uninspiring in itself, the ascent gave exceptional views of our proposed route on the 5500-foot North Face of Changabang.

Last year Brendan had joined Roger Payne, Julie-Anne Clyma, and Andy Perkins in an attempt on the same face. On that trip the four climbed an impressive thin line of ice on the right side of the face. Sadly, serious gastric illness floored Perkins, and eventually they were all forced down. This year, however, that route looked almost non-existent and, besides, there were more logical and direct lines leading to the first icefield. Our group of six would approach the face in teams of two. Of three possible ice lines, Brendan and I chose the central one, as did Mick Fowler and Steve Sustad. Roger and Julie-Anne were also back, and decided on the left-hand line.

Changabang provided a perfect objective for all of us — it wasn't so high (6864 meters) but promised excellent climbing. Julie-Anne and Roger, who are married, are both seasoned Himalayan alpinists with many trips to steep and remote peaks under their belts. Their amazing organizational skills were something of a novelty to the rest of us. Mick and Steve were blown away when they learned that we were to have a table cloth for basecamp meals and delicious cakes to accompany our afternoon tea. Back in Britain Mick works as a taxman and is one of the most prolific adventure, new-route activists around. Originally from Seattle but now living in Britain, Steve is an exceptionally gifted mountaineer, although he keeps a low profile. Brendan Murphy had been on several trips to technical but relatively low-altitude objectives in recent years. We got to know each other well on a trip to climb the South Face of Gasherbrum IV in the summer of 1993. I liked his mixture of tenacity and humor.

As well as outstanding climbing there are other reasons that make Changabang special. This mountain has symbolic status. The first ascent by an

Anglo-Indian team in 1974 was followed a few years later by the monumental effort of Pete Boardman and Joe Tasker. Boardman's book *The Shining Mountain* is a gripping account of their ascent of the West Face, hailed as one of the most outrageous routes of its time. After this, Alex McIntyre and John Porter teamed up with the Poles Voytek Kurtyka and Krystof Zurek for the first ascent of the South Buttress. Many of those players have since lost their lives pushing the limits in the Himalaya, but their committing, bold journeys and quest to climb in a lightweight style continue to influence those who perform in this sphere.

I complained about the cold temperatures at such a modest height. After seeing photos and chatting to the team from an expedition the previous spring, I had expected something quite different. They had relatively mild temperatures, good quality névé, and long spells of good weather.

Brendan shook his head and said as he did so many times, "This year it really is a different mountain." How true. Out of 30 days there would be only one when it didn't snow. The long cold mornings froze our feet. I revealed how my girlfriend had threatened to telephone Brendan before the expedition and tell him I wasn't an ideal partner for such a venture — at home, I used a hot water bottle every night and protested strongly when she demanded the bedroom window remain open. Brendan just laughed.

By May 21 we were ready for action. We had good clear weather every morning but storms every afternoon. The plan was that Brendan and I would head up first. Steve and Mick would follow two days behind and Julie-Anne and Roger a day or so behind them. We would climb as independent teams, and didn't want to be too close to each other, both for fear of falling debris and limited bivouac sites.

We would climb alpine style, whatever that means. In our case the definition seemed simple enough. We had two 60-meter ropes, an alpine rack, eight to nine days' food, and 10 days' gas. The only item we had that you probably wouldn't take in the Alps was a small tent. We hoped to pitch it on a series of tiny snow aretes that dotted the bases of the various icefields.

One thing alpine style does not mean is lightweight. Despite close scrutiny of every item we carried, our sacs weighed 45 pounds. The climbing magazines and picture books often lend an air of romanticism to Himalayan climbing, but the majority of the time it is grunt work. We planned our route meticulously — one hour across the glacier, two hours for the lower slopes up to the base of the first difficulties. How naive we were.

We left at 2 a.m., spent three hours getting to the bergschrund, and, being unroped, almost fell into it. The lower slopes proved anything but a walk. By the time we arrived at what we considered the real climbing, we had broken two out of six ice screws and were about to be baptized by the daily afternoon storm.

Brendan led a meandering mixed pitch between two thundering powder chutes, eventually belaying by the left-hand chute. We searched in vain for a place to spend the night. Reluctantly I set off up the left-hand chute, which was not only extremely steep and rejected ice screws but received regular surges of powder. I finally made it onto easier ground, but by that time both my gloves were full of snow and my fingers numb. Great start, I thought, as we crawled onto a small ledge for the night. Down by the glacier, Fowler and Sustad watched our slow progress with surprise. Two days later they would experience a similar day and bivouac in the same place.

The next two days saw us edge upward, tackling pitches that would have been demanding at sea level. We'd crossed the first icefield, a giant skating rink tilted at 55 degrees with an almost impenetrable steel skin. The constant avalanches had acted like giant polishing rags on the surface of the ice, making it much tougher than we had bargained for. Getting in an ice screw took an eternity, and we now had three out of six functioning normally with one that occasionally bit if persuaded by a violent beating. We had a mixture of 1987 Polish vintage titanium screws and slightly superior 1997 Ukraine jobs. Often we were so wrecked after getting just one of these damn things halfway in we would tie it off and, together with our ice tools, declare a belay.

Dawn on day four saw us at the foot of the second icefield. This point was significant to Brendan as it was his party's high point of the previous year. The second icefield passed more quickly than anticipated and led to a choice of two steep exits. The right-hand option looked like extremely steep ice with two thin sections yet, despite our serious lack of ice screws, seemed preferable to the steep mixed line on the left.

One pitch higher and the thunderheads were building nicely. Today the ferocity of the storm would intensify to fever pitch. Brendan had just led an impressive pitch and now it was my turn.

The situation looked ugly. Even if I had 10 good ice screws I would have been worried, but with just one tied off on Brendan's belay and two more on my harness, I climbed up full of fear. Absurd quantities of powder now thundered from above, pummeling us. The wind increased tenfold and violent thunder boomed from near the summit. I had climbed beyond the point of retreat. Sixty feet above the belay I tried to place a screw. It would not bite. Tiring rapidly, I clipped into one of my tools. It held for a few seconds then ripped. Both crampons popped simultaneously and I fell onto my other tool. Then more spindrift swept upward, numbing my face. I struggled with the weight of the sac, the tip of my right tool staving off disaster. Regaining position, I managed to get the screw turning. At the halfway mark I tied it off and belayed.

We were in the eye of an angry storm. Neck, nostrils, ears, gloves packed with snow. When Brendan arrived he got the hot aches from Hell, and retched with pain. Seeing this hard little bastard wince and groan made our predicament seem even worse. Nevertheless, he hacked on, up a brittle ice-filled corner.

I began talking to myself and flapping my arms to stay warm, but I was losing. I seconded the pitch, screaming that I needed something to eat and was on the verge of hypothermia. Brendan held out a food bar and I bit into it, with the wrapper still on. Night was approaching fast as I set off on the next pitch.

The angle eased, and the storm abated. I made it to the edge of the snow arete where we could bivy. At the belay I used all the functioning ice screws, then spent 20 minutes trying to beat in one of the damaged ones. Eventually, I got it partway in and tied off my axes. I yelled a warning that the belay was shit. Normally Brendan was a super-meticulous, steady climber but, within minutes of his starting, I was yanked tight onto the belay and realized all was not well. In the dark I made out a tiny light way below. After taking a swinging, 60-foot fall, Brendan climbed a more direct route up to the belay.

"That was lucky," he said. "I could have lost my headtorch."

At 11 o'clock we crawled into our tent, psychologically and physically roasted. In 15 years in the mountains, I had never experienced such a harrowing few hours. We were both frost- nipped on the fingers and I shivered, cold to the core.

The next day we rested. It was impossible to know what was running through Brendan's mind. He was a private person, and he kept chat to a minimum.

After a day's rest I felt better. Brendan led three hard pitches that left us tantalizingly close to the groove system that cut through the final headwall. We fixed our two ropes and returned to our tent. Mick and Steve, who had set off two days behind, caught up to us at this point. We were happy to see each other and exchange stories. Mick's typical enthusiasm uplifted us, but we were all worried about the danger of being too close. We considered joining forces, thinking it might be safer. Ultimately, however, we surmised that bivouacking in the steep, upper grooves with a party of four might prove awkward, and we were also reluctant to suddenly change systems. We all agreed that teaming up for the descent might prove beneficial. At that stage, though, we had no idea what surprises lay in store.

Reaching the groove system proper involved some of the most challenging climbing yet, and Mick and Steve, seeing our slow progress, opted for a relaxing day "indoors." But this was not to be. Brendan dislodged a large rock, which beamed in on their tent like a heat-seeking missile. I feared the worst. Eventually Mick appeared and relayed that we had destroyed the back of the tent but that they were OK.

The afternoon snow began falling and filling the tent via this hole at such a rate they considered descending. We felt dreadful. We moved into the grooves which were comprised of especially hard brittle ice and succeeded in making two more holes in their tent, events which produced increasingly irate comments from below. I peered up at the next pitch. It looked long and hard. I tensioned off a knifeblade and stabbed a tool into a blob of ice at the foot of a shallow groove and then followed an intermittent seam of ice over perfect granite. In terms of quality it was one of the best pitches either of us had ever done. I reached the belay knackered but buzzing.

The next morning I woke after a fitful night, and surveyed our surroundings. We were hemmed in by walls of El Cap stature. Huge arching corners, vast blank-looking sheets of icy granite and, here and there, a lonely crack that ran into some mad-looking roof. To be up in this world, to have overcome all that had been thrown at us, now elicited feelings of pride. I began the day with a long, hard mixed pitch in a mind-blowing position.

Each pitch that day had a sting to it. The afternoon weather came in force, but we were close enough to finishing the face that we bore it with extra patience. After negotiating a hideously loose aid section, we could smell the top. But nothing came easily on this mountain. Brendan boldly persevered over granite slabs covered in powder that placed him within striking distance of the cornice. I joined him and then set to work on the final pitch to the ridge. What a pleasure to be hacking through the cornice after eight days' climbing.

The following morning, it was my birthday. To my surprise Brendan pulled out six Snickers bars. He had carried them up and never mentioned them. We couldn't be too extravagant as we had virtually no food left, but we celebrated with a whole bar each. Fortunately, Mick and Steve had over-calculated their food and had agreed to help us out during the descent. The weather that day closed in at 8 a.m. and thwarted any attempts of reaching the summit.

We passed time repitching the tent, as we had discovered that we were sleeping on a fragile snow mushroom, a section of which had disintegrated during the night leaving our feet unsupported. Throughout the day we chatted about all kinds of things. We had grown close during the climb and were like an eccentric couple. We shared one pee bottle, knew what soup or type of tea the other preferred, knew each other's aspirations and fears. Brendan however never talked without a purpose, and there was always a large part of him that seemed unknowable, that he had decided not to share.

I moaned that I was becoming too old for this sport. At 31, I had been at it 10 years. But I also loved skiing and bouldering and, after all, you couldn't carry on doing this for too long, could you? Brendan didn't say much, but he too loved his rock climbing and spoke about how he had enjoyed last summer just cragging in Britain. Philosophizing high on that twisting corniced ridge seemed like such a luxury after the grinding face. That evening we ate our last meal. We had plenty of gas and enough drinks for another two or three days, but other than two chocolate bars each, eating was officially over until we linked up with the other two.

The first day of June dawned beautifully. I came out of the tent charged with energy. We carried light sacs and conditions underfoot were good. The summit *looked* close.

"I feel like I am out for a trot in the park. Do you want me to take a bit of your gear?"

Brendan seemed to be moving slower, and handed me the two water bottles to carry. After an hour or so we were forced onto the ridge proper. We roped up, primarily for psychological reasons. But less than a minute later, an enormous section of ridge beside me snapped off and tumbled down the North Face. I teetered there, trying to control the surge of adrenaline racing through my veins. Brendan sat in a bucket seat, a leg either side of the ridge, a rope-length away.

Six pitches later the trusty afternoon cloud arrived. Our pace slowed and my earlier enthusiasm waned. A swirling mist enveloped us, robbing us of the magnificent views we had expected. The descent to the col between the horns of Changabang ate up an hour. A layer of soft snow lay over brittle ice and, at the apex of the col itself, we sank almost to our waists. Giant rocks loomed out of the mist. We climbed out from between the horns and began the final, weary 700 feet in appalling visibility. At the summit we congratulated each other, then collapsed.

"I am really chuffed," said Brendan. The lack of food was taking its toll.

As we sat there the clouds dropped below us. Nanda Devi floated in front of us, Dunagiri behind, and in the distance the unmistakable Kamet. We wanted to linger but, with the descent down the twisting ridge still to come, we turned our backs on the summit. In the top of my rucsac I found the remnants of a broken biscuit, which we shared. I was amazed that Brendan still had some of his chocolate bar left.

Voices floated up through the clouds.

"Is that you, Steve?"

A lone figure stood on the ridge far below.

"Yes. How are you?"

"Good. And you?"

"Fine."

Suddenly the mist swept in and he disappeared.

Later there were two figures, this time 200 feet lower and erecting a tent. It looked like a good spot and I chided myself for not having spotted it for ourselves. Once close enough, Mick seemed eager to catch our attention. It seemed they had arrived at this wonderful camp spot by default. Steve had tripped on his crampons and dragged the two of them down. Mick had escaped unhurt, but Steve had been less fortunate. He lay in the tent with intense pain in his ribs and chest. Assured we could do nothing to help, we returned to our tent for the last of the instant soup, if you could call that food.

Despite the fatigue, our minds were in a whirlwind. Exploring every avenue of escape we concluded that everything hinged on the extent of Steve's injuries. Mick and Steve had a rough night: Steve in pain, and Mick perturbed by his partner's irregular breathing and groaning. They were so glad that we were around to help, and we them, as we had now begun to hallucinate about eating some of their mashed-potato powder.

The weather had been so consistently bad that the arrival of another poor day evoked no response. Fortunately Steve could move, albeit with great suffering. We spent a whole day getting ourselves to the Kalanka Col. That evening Mick and Steve invited us for tea. Crammed into the back of their tent, we sat shaking with the excitement of eating. Steve prepared a wonderful dish of mashed potato, a meal that I will never forget. I even got to lick out the cooking pot. Now that was a birthday present!

If the climb had drawn Brendan and me together, now the descent would do the same for the rest of us — more than we could have imagined.

The next morning brought a biting wind. The simplest task took an eternity as I had to constantly stop and unfreeze my fingers. In near-zero visibility we started our descent, with enough food to last three or four days. For a while the sky cleared and the terrain proved straightforward. But as the weather closed in, it became difficult to find a safe route. All things considered we did extremely well to locate a tiny flat area on the edge of a vast icefield. We were all utterly exhausted, but from here just two or three abseils would see us into an easy gully and then down onto the Changabang Glacier. Mick abseiled first and I followed.

"It's too steep." Mick shouted just as I began. "Too steep for Steve."

Mick was right. Suddenly it became undercut, and a free-hanging abseil with broken ribs would have been dangerous. I climbed back out and Brendan volunteered to set up another anchor out to the right. He spent 20 minutes trying to get a screw in. There was a lot of neve but not much ice.

"I've got a bomber now." He shouted across to us.

"He reminds me of Dick Renshaw," said Steve.

I didn't know Dick but from what I had heard there were similarities: quiet,

266

determined, and tough, but always a gentleness and a disturbing modesty and selflessness.

"We used to call him the little angel," Steve continued, "because whenever there was a job to be done, a job that others didn't want to do, he would do it, without any fuss."

Seconds later a muffled noise came from above. Way up, an avalanche released and then another and another. These silent slides joined forces, and headed straight for us. Time stood still. In a panic I began screaming and yelling.

"Brendan! Brendan! Brendan!"

I beat my axe to the hilt into the slope and clipped in. The whiteness took an eternity to reach us. Brendan saw it but had no sling to clip into the ice screw. No rope. No second tool. Absolutely nothing. He tried to grab the screw. Eventually it came. So quietly and so softly it took Brendan, sweeping him away to our right. Stunned, I couldn't move at first and then started rocking my head trying to control my anguish. The avalanche had stopped now, the debris sloughing to a halt just 60 feet away. Darkness was not far off and Mick and Steve led me down to a small, safe spur where we would spend the night. Brendan had no chance of surviving, but still we shouted into the darkness. The next day we searched and shouted, and then saw the giant cliffs over which the avalanche had tracked. I shouted helplessly into the deep, empty basin.

The next two days were going to be the toughest any of us had ever dealt with. During the night, as I replayed the scene of Brendan disappearing, my frozen thumb felt like it was going to burst. The next morning it sported an ugly black blister. As long as the weather stabilized we planned to cross first the Shipton Col and then the Bagini Pass. We estimated that they were both at around 5700 meters. Our food supply, if we stuck to one meal a day, might just see us through. Although attractive, the alternative descent down through the Rishi Gorge had not been traveled for years and would take too long. We had no choice but to go for it and cross the two cols. We prayed for good snow conditions and a little luck. We had to get back to basecamp soon. Steve and I needed a doctor and Roger and Julie-Anne would be desperately worried by now, presuming they made it back to basecamp. In fact, they had spent 10 days on the face, reaching the Ice Tongue just above the second icefield and sitting out the terrible storms there before abseiling off. Visions of losing my infected thumb would drive me to leave Mick and Steve below the face, foregoing a night's rest.

We began the long climb to the Shipton Col at 1 a.m. I stared up at an unforgettable night sky. Between Nanda Devi and Changabang were whole carpets of silver galaxies. As we neared the col, the star-studded sky slowly faded and left us instead with Nanda Devi. Morning bathed the sacred mountain in a magical, golden light. I soothed myself by thinking how Brendan would rest in one of the most remote and beautiful mountain valleys on Earth. Soon the tiny spring flowers would be pushing their way through the thinning snow, carpeting the edges of the Changabang Glacier. Before reaching the col, I turned around one last time and said good-bye.

First published in Climbing *No. 171, 1997.*

What's your problem?
Why American climbers can't keep up

By Dave Pegg

YOU SUCK ...There, it's done. I've finally vented the words that have been stewing inside me for weeks. Now I'll be tarred, feathered, and deported back to England. But what the hell. I've got your attention, and we can discuss why American rock climbers have fallen so far behind their European counterparts in the last 15 years, and what, if anything, you can do about it.

Damage limitation is my only hope of surviving this assignment, so let's start by flashing back to happier times. In 1980 the hardest route in the world was Tony Yaniro's *Grand Illusion* (5.13c) at Sugarloaf, California, and the world's hardest boulder problems were Jim Holloway's *Meathook* (V12), *AHR* (V12), and *Slapshot* (V13) on the Front Range of Colorado. Back then I was thrashing my way up 5.6s on the gritstone edges of Northern England, but I devoured stories of these and other state-of-the-art American climbs — *Super Crack, Phoenix, Astroman, Midnight Lightning* — in the pages of *Mountain* magazine.

One of the first *Mountain* articles I read was "States of the Art: a celebration of American climbing," by Mark Hudon and Max Jones. In his introduction of this 1979 piece Tim Lewis, then editor of *Mountain,* wrote, "Now there can be no doubt that the growing numbers of American free rock climbers are the equal of any." Later Hudon and Jones wrote: "Climbing 5.12 and harder routes is actually a sub-sport of rock climbing. It has lost all relation to classic mountaineering. Pitches of this difficulty are not yet being led and followed regularly in one push. Most 5.12s, like a gymnastic routine, require many attempts to wire the moves, memorize the sequence, and then put all the pieces together. The route is our apparatus; climbing is our routine."

Does this sound familiar? If you forget about the grade and the natural protection we could be talking about sport climbing circa 1996. The difference of course is that the balance of power has shifted; today the breakthroughs come from Europe, and the relative standards attained by American rock climbers are a joke.

To avoid journalistic hari-kari, I'll cut the sweeping generalizations and present some facts. In 1994 Jean Baptiste Tribout conducted a survey for the French magazine *Vertical* and named 50 climbers who had redpointed 8c (5.14b) — only two Americans were on that list. Today, Tribout estimates the total is close to 100, of which seven are Americans. And that's just the B Team; consider the 15 or so 8c+ (5.14c) big boys, and not one American makes the list. Granted, Lynn Hill and Robyn Erbesfield have pushed the standards of women's free climbing, but that doesn't count because both are ex-patriots living in France.

And I'm not ignoring bold routes. The pages of Britain's *On The Edge* magazine are full of tales of palm-sweating solos and ballsy runouts on European stone, but when did you last read about a new *Bachar/Yerian* in Hot Flashes?

Then there's the European onslaught of America's hardest routes and boulder problems: *Just Do It* (5.14c) established four years ago by Tribout is still unrepeated by an American. Ditto Fred Nicole's *Crown of Aragorn* (V13), Elie Chevieux's *Shaken Not Stirred* (V12), and Jerry Moffatt's *Dominator* (V12). And the Europeans aren't just kicking your butts at first ascents: there's the Huber brothers' repeats of the *Salathé Wall;* Yuji Hirayama's ground-up on-sight of *Sphinx Crack;* Christian Brenna's recent slew of 5.13c on-sights at Rifle. I could go on...

Why is it that despite an early lead in the rock-climbing game, American climbers have fallen so far behind? Many factors have played a part, but the root of the problem is clear. American climbing had too much history; like the Dodo it was too big, too old, and too slow to adapt to a changing environment. Yaniro, Hudon, and Jones had the vision and creativity to make the sport what it is today, but their peers just didn't get it. And what happened to the "hang-dogging pioneers"? They were so reviled that for many years they simply dropped out of the sport.

"We were held back by being too conservative," says Ron Kauk, one of the few Americans who has remained consistently at the top of the sport. "In the '70s we had the freedom to do what we wanted, and the first rule was that there were no rules. All of a sudden it got all divided; that was the root of the problem. If our movement of people had stayed together, we would have gone right into it."

The Europeans had no qualms about getting right into it, says Scott Milton, a top Canadian climber who has toured extensively in Europe. "They took the

270

idea, understood it, refined it, and the first thing they said was, 'To hell with all those ethics.' They had open minds — hangdogging, rap bolting, redpointing — they were willing to do whatever it took."

By the time the Americans stopped posturing behind the mask of "good ethics" and woke up, they were so far behind that the race was already lost.

Rock has also shaped European attitudes, and in this respect Americans were handicapped from the start. The granite that dominates American crags was great for cutting edge 5.12s in the 1970s, but its most perfect sweeps are unclimbable. Limestone on the other hand — steep, rarely blank, and kind to the skin — is the perfect medium for sport climbs. Not only do the Europeans have lots of limestone, it's of the highest quality and very concentrated.

It takes a mental leap to appreciate how small Europe is, but transpose America's handful of world-class sport areas across the Atlantic and you'd find Smith Rock in London, Rifle in Madrid, and the Red River Gorge in Moscow. No wonder even the most hardened road-trippers dream of moving to the South of France where you can drive between the tendon-tweaking pockets of Buoux, the dribbling tufas of Sugiton, the blocky overhangs of Volx, and the incredible bombés of Ceüse in just five hours.

The compact European scene has also fostered the growth of climbing communities, like those in Aix-en-Provence and Sheffield. "When I went to Europe it struck me how much of a sense of security there was between small groups of people," says Verve supremo Christian Griffith. "They'd all climb, hang out, and party together."

A good example of this close-knit camaraderie is the day I arrived at Orgon Canal, France, to find Tribout, Hirayama, François Legrand, and the late Fabien Mazuer attempting the coveted first ascent of *Bronx* (F8c+, 5.14c). Snagging this project meant a lot to each of them in terms of personal satisfaction, kudos, and even money, but when one of them climbed the others stood around shouting encouragement — "Allez, François. Allez!" — sharing Beta, and generally having a good time. This group energy is common, explains Tribout: "Most of the top French climb together. They are training at a better level because of the competition between them."

While the Europeans have stood on each other's shoulders to reach the top, Americans have continued to stab each other in the back. Two recent stories illustrate my point: When Tommy Caldwell tried to repeat *The Crew* (5.14b) at Rifle, the first ascentionist Chris Knuth returned to the route and brushed off his tick marks, saying, "I wasn't going to give him a road map." In another incident, Joe Brooks worked an unclimbed route at Wild Iris. When he returned to the project after a rest day, a local had filled in two crucial pockets.

Stupid, sad, and pathetic are words which spring to mind. Just what is wrong with you people?

Part of the problem is that America doesn't have a climbing scene. Instead of drawing climbers together, the land mass has divided them into highly regional pockets of activity; small ponds where the big fish are more concerned with their territorial pissings than seeing the big picture.

"America is so spread out that it's easy to build an image without really backing it up," says Milton. "That's why locals don't want the best climbers to come to their crags. They've put up the hardest routes and want their photos in *Climbing*. If the good guys come and downrate them, it's worse not better. But you can't get away with that in the concentrated arena of Europe. If you are actually getting to the top because you're that strong, then you want other climbers to try your routes and see how they do."

Jim Karn is one American who has been willing to test himself in Europe; between 1987 and 1993 he spent more time in France than at home. Ask Karn why he's the only American man to stand on a World Cup podium, and he bristles with disaffection.

"I think the problem goes back to the attitude of everyone being for themselves," says Karn. "Every World Cup I ever went to, I was there to compete in *the World Cup.* The other Americans didn't care about their overall placing, they cared about how they placed relative to other Americans. The other countries supported each other, and the Americans were all in their little corner vibing each other out.

"That sums up the difference: In America people start competition out of insecurity; success is measured by how many logos you have on your harness, or how many free PowerBars you get. In Europe they are not insecure; they want everyone to do well, and success is measured by how you feel about your own performance."

This preoccupation with what others think has led to a new word in the climber's lexicon: *spray*. Spraying means to prattle on tediously about your achievements. It's a peculiarly American trait — after all if you climb for yourself then there is no need to spray. The cardinal rules of spray are that you first impress the sprayee with a lot of hot-aired hyperbole, and then throw in a big number to back it up.

Recently, I caught up with Tribout at Halimeh's restaurant in Rifle. I intended to catch some spray about Tribout's recent big-number sport climb *The 7 P.M. T.V. Show,* but — with typical European reserve — he seemed reluctant to blow his own horn. Instead our conversation drifted, over the course of several Buds and roll-up cigarettes, to the attitude of American climbers.

"They try routes that are too hard for them, too quickly," said Tribout. "They don't do enough foundation at the lower grades. A lot of the time I see American climbers working a .12d or .13a, but I don't think they can on-sight a .12b or .12a. And for me that is amazing; I mean, the routes they are trying

272

are too hard for them, at this moment. So they should do more routes at their level to build a base."

This scene is played out on our crags and bouldering areas everyday. The Euros are running around — climbing two, three, and four days in a row — having a great time, and generally ripping it up in a dust cloud of frenzied activity. In contrast the Americans are either spraying, or resting so that they can send and spray tomorrow. It's as if they've become so obsessed with numbers, that they've forgotten that climbing should be fun. In fact, the next time I ask an American how long he's staying at some great climbing area, and he replies, "Until I've sent *Ego Boost* 5.14a ...V10 ... blah blah blah," I think I'll scream.

"No one is as obsessed with training and nutrition as the Americans," says the German climber Udo Neumann, who (with Dale Goddard) co-authored the training tome *Performance Rock Climbing*. "Yet there's no real secret, it's just the way the Europeans move and how excited about climbing they are."

Tribout agrees, citing this as one reason why only Marc LeMenestrel of France and Jean Paul Finne of Belgium have repeated *Just Do It*. "For me the Americans are not climbing enough, that's for sure, for sure, for sure. When you see people at the cliff they are doing, let's say, four pitches in a day. For a European standard that's nothing. They should be doing 10 pitches. When I do a good day in Rifle it's 10 or 11 pitches with two warm-ups.

"I think it's the same when Americans are training inside. If you want to do good in competition you have to climb a lot. I can tell you the French [he laughs] they are climbing like crazy. Especially the women — it's unbelievable. Not always a lot of days, but very, very big sessions: six hours, let's say, between 500 and 700 moves. It's hard. You can't do that at the start. You have to train your body with lower-intensity training and then, when you become used to it, do more and more. So you become stronger ... not in one year — obviously not in one year — but in a few years. When many people are doing that, in the end, the level becomes higher. There are so many [Europeans] doing .14a and .14b that it's no big deal."

Although Tribout is talking about the highest level, this critical-mass psychology helps explain why the average European climbs harder than the average American. Example: If you don't know anyone who climbs 5.12, then 5.12 seems really hard; but if François, the pot-bellied 50-year-old who owns your local patisserie, has climbed 7b+, it becomes no big deal.

Another reason European climbers are so advanced is because there are more people to push the standards. "For the longest time we were drawing from a smaller genetic pool," says Karn. "In Europe climbing was more accepted, more people were exposed to it, so there were more chances of getting genetically strong bods. I think that's what is happening in America now. Gyms are opening up, and they're drawing in kids who are naturally strong. If they get experience and technique, and keep their psyche, there are going to be some really good climbers."

Griffiths agrees with the prophecy. "Our indoor walls will serve as the launch pad for a new generation of American climbers. I've seen a lot of the best gyms in Europe and they are laughable compared to the best gyms in the U.S."

Other things are changing. The gyms are dragging the sport into mainstream culture, and this can only help the plight of American climbers. While socialist Europe has safety nets to bail out the lifestyles of nonconformists and unfortunates, in America you have to have a real job to survive. Indeed — brought up to toe the line and equate success with material possessions — the only sports that Americans excel at are those that make money.

"It all stems from society and what's worthy," says Kauk. "We came out of the hippy generation, and then you got the yuppy generation which probably didn't think it was worth going climbing."

Fortunately, ASCF President Hans Florine says cash is on the way: "We haven't even had the money for a team coach, but we're in a transition. Mainstream culture leads to money which leads to infrastructure. In five years time, we'll have more people, more money, and more gyms — and then we'll blow the shit out of the Europeans."

The future already looks bright. This summer, 15-year-old Chris Sharma redpointed seven 5.14s in three weeks, 15-year-old Katie Brown swept the international competition circuit with wins at the X-games and the Masters in Arco, and many other youngsters — Tommy Caldwell, Kevin Branford, David Hume, and Chris Lindner to name but a few — are going full steam ahead.

Karn believes this new generation is on the right track. "I've talked to a lot of the younger climbers and they have a better attitude. Most of the complaining, bitching, and back-stabbing comes from people of my age."

The tide hasn't turned yet, but these youngsters are scrabbling at the Europeans' heels — if they get the support and direction they deserve. If they don't get sucked into the American bourgeois thing and become doctors and dentists and lawyers. If they learn to build on each others' achievements, and keep an open mind. If they climb a lot, climb for themselves, and most of all remember that climbing is fun. Then sometime in this millennium I might have the pleasure of writing an article that begins: YOU RULE.

First published in Climbing *No. 165, 1997.*

A Turn of the Cards

An epic on Half Dome's South Face

By John Middendorf

It was early spring 1986, Camp 4 parking lot, Yosemite Valley. "So what have you got in mind, Bob? I asked my friend, who'd just showed up in the Valley.

In his usual soft voice — sentences tend to trail off at their ends — Bob said, "I want to try soloing *The Prow.*"

Fresh in my mind was the memory of a recent rescue on *The Prow* (V 5.10a A3), a classic aid line on the east face of Washington Column. During it I had been given the honor of lowering down to the climbers, one of who happened to be a good friend, then jumarring back up with them.

I gave Bob a sideways look. In my two-and-a-half year tenure as a member of the Yosemite Search and Rescue team, I had been involved with dozens of lift-offs, and I was both smug and quick to dole out patronizing advice. "Just don't get rescued," I said flatly.

Bob looked nonplused, but before he had time to think, asked, "Why?" Because, I thought, rescues are serious undertakings, and getting rescued doesn't do a thing for your reputation with the Valley denizens, much of whose inner language centers around such events. "Rescue bait," they called certain less promising big-wall climbers. All I said was, "I don't know, that's just the way it is around here."

Several weeks later, two of my rescue-team friends and I would start up the *South face* of Half Dome, intending to make an early season ascent.

The *South Face* of Half Dome, one of Warren Harding's finest masterpieces, is a 2000-foot wall. Its upper half is a blank sea of white granite, void of any apparent climbable features. Remote and beautiful, the route has a history of failures, although Walt Shipley's extraordinary solo ascent two years ago and the nearby free line put up recently by Dave Schutlz and Scott Cosgrove seem to have tamed the wall's fearsome reputation. On the 1968 first-ascent attempts, Warren Harding and Galen Rowell were trapped by a severe storm for several days and had to be rescued, which in itself was a pioneering event in technical extrication, because at that time big-wall rescue technique was still in its infancy. (Their rescue was documented in *The Vertical World of Yosemite*.)

Other parties had faltered as well, for reasons ranging from lack of proper hooking gear to debilitating summer heat, often necessitating retreat. In several cases, friends on the summit have lowered ropes, gear, and provision to stranded or stalled climbers.

In fact, the *South Face* had hosted more failures than successes when my eventual partners, two Yosemite regulars, Mike Corbett and Steve Bosque, decided to go for a winter ascent. The season had been extremely mild — some called it a drought winter — so the venture seemed very feasible.

Yet from the onset of preparation, as the two made multiple six-mile uphill plods to Half Dome's base, and then fixed several pitches, they experienced setbacks. In one storm snow sloughed down the face into a 30-foot pile on the ground, forcing Steve and Mike to spend an entire day digging out their gear. Then it took another month before the long-term weather report looked good.

Normally two climbers make for the most efficient wall team, but Mike and Steve, sharing a feeling of burnout, asked me to join them. Mike and I had done a few big walls together in the past, and I always found myself charged up by his undying affinity for them. Steve's deliberate and understated approach to such adventures, which he would regularly squeeze in between periods of raising a family and working full time, always seemed impressive to me. I was really excited about our team and the chosen route. It was going to be my 40th long route (1000-plus feet) in Yosemite.

Shunning the more intelligent option of packing two separate loads to the base, I carried all my gear in a single towering 100-plus-pound haulbag, while Steve and Mike carried their light final assault loads. By the time we got up the Vernal Falls switchbacks — only two miles into the eight-mile approach — I was staggering every step. The one-shot technique works well for El Cap where the torment of the approach is halfway five minutes after you step out of your car, but this was one long, steep uphill plod. Mike and Steve periodically tried to persuade me to off some weight onto them. With too much pride in self-sufficiency, I refused. Thirty-one thousand staggers later, the grueling approach ended.

That night, it sprinkled on us, but the next day we climbed in beautiful sunny weather. The first two days took us to the end of the Arch, a huge left-facing dihedral soaring halfway up the wall, and onto the Face, a thousand feet of 75-

276

to 80-degree featured rock with very few cracks.

The eighth pitch, which we named "The Great Escape Hatch," was a contortionist's dream: a gaping bombay chimney, awkward as hell, like an aid version of the Harding Slot on *Astroman*. After that pitch, I told Mike, "You know, regardless of a wall's actual rating, every route seems to require the sum total of my aid experience." Mike understood exactly.

The third day, in T-shirts, we climbed five of the 11 remaining pitches. I eyeballed each for its free-climbing potential, realizing that we just might have discovered the most awesome free-climbable face in the Valley. I free climbed between some bat-hooking sections on my leads just to try it out. (Bat-hooking — placing specially designed hooks in shallow drilled holes — is a technique invented by Harding in order to surmount blank sections of rock.)

Up to this point the climbing and setting had been awesome, and we often commented on what an ultimate gem of a route this was. We were having a great time.

The day's fourth pitch took us to one of the Tri-Clops, three large, shallow, dark indentations in the rock that from the ground look like caves and, with some imagination, passageways into the depths of Half Dome. This evil-looking place had been Harding and Rowell's demise, and the energy of their desperation seemed to still linger. Though dusk was fast approaching, Mike had an uneasy sixth sense about the spot and decided to go for the next pitch, a steep bat-hooking stretch that ended on The Ledge, which on the topo looked like it might make a good bivy.

Darkness set in midway through Mike's lead. Then came the frightening clanging of gear and yank on the belay rope. Dead silence. "Hey, Mike, you OK?" Silence. "Hey, Corbett!"

Steve and I flashed headlamps upward but all we could see was the rope disappearing into darkness. Then from above came the explanation. Mike had popped a bat-hook and taken a 20- or 30-foot fall, fracturing his finger in an attempt to grab the previous bat-hook. But a broken finger barely slows down a guy like Mike, and he finished the lead. We set up the bivy in darkness at The Ledge, which turned out to be nothing more than a small six-inch stance formed by a protruding flake.

Sometime in the early hours of Friday morning, clouds moved in and a light rain prompted us to dig out our portaledge rainflies. Little did we know it was the start of one of Yosemite's worst storms ever. At dawn it was still pattering steadily. Mike suggested a general rest day, and Steve and I agreed. But instead of clearing, which our little box radio had promised, the weather became worse. We braced ourselves for a storm. Later, when the completeness of the radio's lie became evident, I would jettison it, as a symbolic gesture of our isolation.

On Friday evening the rain became a torrent and the winds picked up. Sometime that night, Steve's ledge collapsed, and in the minutes it took him to reconstruct it he got completely soaked. From the relative comfort of my slightly damp ledge, I listened to his struggling and cursing and felt sorry for him, but there was nothing I could do, aside from lending him my headlamp, since an exit from the ledge for even a minute meant complete saturation. It's funny about Steve; even when he has good reason to curse, he does so only as if playing a part — no semblance of actual anger exists in his tone. He is always like that.

Hours later, I felt my ledge's suspension straps begin to slip due to the wet and icy conditions. I knew what was happening: slowly, my ledge was being twisted, one outside corner sliding down, and the other twisting up, as if were trying to dump me out into the void. Any movement accelerated the slippage, but in the dark I could not see what to do to fix it. Trying not even to breathe, I cried, "Steve, I need my headlamp back, NOW!" (In the adverse conditions my headlamp was our only functioning piece of gear, and it had become a coveted item.) But in the twisted tangle of his nearly destroyed portaledge, Steve was forced into stillness; even the slightest wiggle caused his ledge's suspension to slip, then the ledge to fall apart (by this time it had collapsed several times). He tried to extend the headlamp to me, but to no avail.

So I tried to re-tension the suspension without light. My movement caused the structure to slip completely. The end-tubes dropped out of their shallow side pockets, leaving me hanging in space among an untenable assortment of tubing and fabric. Instantly, everything became soaked, as if I had jumped into the Merced River in full regalia — except that this was colder. From the haulbag I dug out my spare wool clothes and rain gear, but in the deluge they soon became drenched, too. A foot-thick sheet of water poured down from the moderately angled face above. Rain pelted us, driven sideways by the high winds. I finally retrieved my headlamp, and, with a mixture of determination and resignation, took my time reassembling the ledge. I couldn't get any wetter.

In the end the failing portaledges didn't matter, because by morning all of us were soaked to the bone anyway. Seemingly by osmosis, moisture poured through my "waterproof" ripstop rain fly. The waterproof coating mysteriously fell off the fabric in large cobweb-like sticky sheets, creating another ministorm inside.

By 10 a.m. Saturday the winds were blowing over 50 miles per hour, with gusts throwing us and the ledges about. Visibility was nil. Then the temperature dropped, the rain turned to icy BBs, and our soaked gear began to freeze solid.

"We're gonna die in these conditions," Steve said. "We've got to at least try to get out of here!" We exited our ledges and inspected each other and our gear. Instantly, fingers and toes went completely numb, and the wind and cold penetrated to the bone.

With uncanny foresight, Mike had insisted on leaving a rope fixed over the otherwise-irreversible roof below the eighth pitch. Still, that was five rappels down and several hundred feet to the left. As we discussed our situation we noticed that the ropes in front of us were frozen to the wall in solid tangles, and would need to be chopped out with an ice tool. We quickly realized that to retrieve even a short length of usable rope would be impossible. Even if we could have, our jumars would never have grabbed on the frozen cord, the ice-covered wall would have thwarted any effort to swing sideways to belay anchors, and a near-certain hang-up in the rappels would have resulted in a fatal separation from each other. Drilling our own anchors was out of the question, as it would require far more manual dexterity than our frozen fingers could provide. And in the back of my mind I remembered how miserably Rowell fared in 1968 while attempting to rappel in similar conditions from just 100 feet below our position.

All sorts of potential and likely nightmares crossed my mind, each ending with three bodies frozen to the wall. I was the first to disappear back into my portaledge.

We remained as a team, huddled in place, waiting.

All Saturday the storm beat us in a deafening roar of flapping nylon and typhoon winds. I realized how much my entire life depended on my lightweight rain fly. Violently whipping, it seemed ready to rip to shreds any minute. Earlier, Steve's fly had been torn apart, and critical corner parts of his ledge were mangled into scrap metal, rendering it useless. He was now sharing Mike's portaledge. If either of our two remaining ledges or flies failed, somebody was bound to die from exposure.

In the meantime, unbeknownst to us, a rescue effort was underway down below. In the deepening snow Werner Braun, Dan McDevitt, Sue Bonovich, and Tracy Dorton had hiked up the five miles to Lost Lake, from which they could get the Valley's closest view of the South Face, and were trying to communicate with us through a bullhorn.

In one of the frequent lulls in the storm, we suddenly became alert, hearing muffled noise. Instinctively we broke out in loud shouts to expose our position. We were able to distinguish from below, "Do you need a rescue?" We looked at each other, quickly decided that we were in dire straits, and yelled in unison for help until we were hoarse. We couldn't see who we were calling to.

Like turtles, we then retracted back into our shelters. As the hours passed, the initial hope and excitement of possible help dwindled and was replaced by renewed concentration on survival. We knew the top of Half Dome would be inaccessible: the hiking-route cables were buried and frozen over, and the storm would prohibit climbing to the top. The uncertainty of our fate made our exhausting, freezing misery that much harder. Right now, the flames of hell didn't seem so bad.

Inside my ledge, I made constant efforts to keep from being completely buried. Huge water-saturated snow piles would rise in moments; I would use all my strength to push them off one end of the ledge, then notice that at the other end snow was piling up fast. A minute of inactivity and weight of the snow would begin to crush me, tearing the fly apart at the seams, and become almost too heavy to push off. This went on for hours. Because of the angle of the wall above, and the distance in which the snow could accumulate and slide down, the snow was essentially coming down at the rate of several feet per minute.

Towards dusk, exhausted by my vigilant efforts, I dozed off, though I knew myself to be on the verge of hypothermia. It was pleasant. But then, suddenly, I was in a boxing ring, packed full of every variety of boxer and pro wrestler imaginable, each mistaking me for his training bag before a big fight. One of them was trying to crunch my skull when I snapped awake. Steve was stepping on my head.

Mike and Steve seeing that my ledge had become buried by snow, had yelled for me with no response. And thought maybe that I had died. Unable to see even where my ledge hung, Steve had kicked steps in the frozen layer of snow and ice across the near-vertical wall to investigate. In my stupor and because of the dampening effect of the thick snow cover, no sounds had penetrated — only his foot. "Glad to see you're all right, old buddy," he said before returning to his and Mike's hovel.

It was dusk, but sleep, I realized, would be fatal. I tried to keep my mind busy. I thought about new portaledge designs, and shook my head, legs, and hands rapidly for warmth in my cramped quarters, by now reduced to the size of a small doghouse. In sets of 100, I counted to 22,000, twitching with each count.

Eventually I told myself that many hours must have passed since darkness fell. I looked at my watch. It was 10 p.m.

Steve and Mike, with the marginal benefit of ensolite and double boots, sat on a single portaledge, one fly draped over their heads, beating on each other for warmth and to prevent sleep.

It occurred to me that we were experiencing some of the worst storm conditions to be found anywhere. If the route was steeper, things might have been OK. If the winds weren't accelerated by Little Yosemite Valley's venturi effect, things wouldn't have been so bad. But mostly, if the temperatures had remained either above or below freezing, we would have been sitting pretty — relatively — either in a wet rainstorm or a blizzard.

Sometime in the early hours of Sunday morning, the storm faded and the stars appeared. The absence of the deafening wind seemed strange and eerie. Steve and Mike were the first to broach the potent silence, and we briefly discussed first-light retreat plans. It soon became apparent that the clearing storm was a mixed blessing; radiation heat loss into the clear sky sucked the last bit of heat from our bodies. The most bitter of bitter cold prevailed. We struggled through each remaining moment of a long night.

In the morning, the sun finally appeared. The comparative warmth stunned us into passiveness for a while. We basked in the above-freezing temperatures and procrastinated for a few blissful moments. But we could see another storm approaching in the distance, so we started hacking out the ropes and made ready for what would be a horrendous descent. We were all functioning slowly and clumsily, but thought we could probably make it down alive. Not a bit of rock was visible; the entire wall was covered with a four-inch layer of ice.

Then came the avalanches. As the sun warmed the loosely attached stratum, hundreds of pounds of softball-sized chunks of ice began to crash down on us. Mike and Steve had helmets, while I stuffed soggy socks in my Peruvian hat for protection. Under one barrage, Mike suddenly plummeted several feet, when the bolt supporting his ledge popped. Luckily, the anchors at each side held. From above Steve and I stared for a few moments at a wide-eyed Mike, still standing upright in his ledge. Wordlessly, except for a few "Hoo-mans," we resumed our descent preparation.

The ropes were still only partially cut out of the ice when we heard it: the whop-whop-whop of a helicopter. An emotional wave swept through us. In silent disbelief, we watched the chopper pass and fly almost out of sight. "I sure hope that's for us," I thought. Then it returned, and amidst continued avalanches, locked into place hovering 100 feet above us. An angel in a pilot's suit lowered out — Petty Officer Davis from nearby LeMoore Naval Air Station. We were saved.

Mike volunteered for the first ride, and was hooped under his armpits with a "horse collar" and lifted off. Steve and I happily watched Mike and Officer Davis dangle from the helicopter as it disappeared down the valley. We tossed some haulbags and sleeping bags and endured more avalanches.

Eventually the helicopter returned, picked up Steve, and took off again. Ten years ago, helicopters that could lock into a stationary flight pattern so close to a cliff didn't exist. Despite technological advances, I was amazed at the pilot's ability to counter every gust of wind. The spinning rotor blades some-times came within a few yards of the cliff. The wind was whipping up again, and it seemed like the pilot had a more difficult time locking in place for Steve's hoist. Fearing the worst, I imagined being stranded on the wall alone, bivy gear tossed.

After what seemed like ages, the helicopter returned, but it took a couple of tries for the pilot to lock into place. Officer Davis, dangling 100 feet below the machine, darted to and fro just out of my reach, signaling to the pilot for posi-tioning. Then, with a thumb's up signal to the pilot, he stopped right in front of me. I grabbed his outstretched hand, slipped into the "horse collar," unclipped from the belay, and went for the ride of my life.

As we flew towards the valley, dazed by the view, I didn't notice that we were being winched up. Unexpectedly, the helicopter was directly above us, and I clambered into the cabin.

A huge crowd and several other helicopters greeted us in the Ahwahnee Meadow. The extent of the rescue effort astounded me, with over 30 people involved (many of who had hiked all night in waist-deep snow and were still near the base of the Half Dome cables), and four helicopters ready to go. A sudden feeling of overwhelming gratitude intoxicated me. The LeMoore Station and the Yosemite Rescue Team had coordinated the effort admirably, and it was thanks to them what we were all alive.

I stepped out of the helicopter and my legs buckled; I hadn't walked for a week. I staggered towards my friends, Jim and Tory, who whisked me away (barely escaping the pouncing paramedics) and took care of me in Jim's warm house, where I shivered uncontrollably for several hours. Meanwhile, over at the Yosemite Clinic, Mike was being poked and prodded, given IVs and warm oxygen, and splint for his finger.

At Jim's, I mindlessly leafed through the Sunday newspaper. I became entranced by a particular photo in it, nothing registered at first. Then I realized I was looking at a picture of Warren Harding in 1970 standing on The Ledge. He seemed to be smiling at me. Coincidentally, the newspaper had done a feature article about the *South Face* the same day we were fighting for our lives on it.

Later that evening, an unidentified feeling gnawed inside of me. The transition from one reality to another made both seem unreal. I realized that all my instincts insisted that I return to a soaked sleeping bag, shiver, stay awake, and generally fight for my life. It seemed we had been up on Half Dome for a lifetime, and I had developed a routine for staying alive that I could not shake.

Instead, I hobbled back to my dry VW van, pulled out a dry sleeping bag, cranked up the propane heater, and passed out — not to stand in etriers on a big wall again until the fall of 1989.

First published in Climbing *No. 120, 1990.*

Fool's Luck

Climbing the French Ridge of Mount Huntington (12,240 feet), one of Alaska's finest mountaineering prizes

By Lance Leslie

The cold was eating me slowly, feet first. It reminded me of one of those science films I'd seen in grade school, where a python laboriously swallowed a wild pig, the reptile's jaws distending to engulf the entire animal until nothing but its spindly legs stuck out. I was determined to keep my own appendages from sliding down the icy gullet.

My toes had turned into leaden clumps that no amount of wiggling and kicking could revive; still, I knew that I had to keep going through the motions. So I kicked them hard against the ends of the heavy leather double boots, in the process almost tripping backward off the narrow, placemat-size belay stance hacked into the ice of the Northeast Face of Alaska's Mount Huntington. My partner Brian McCullough, who was standing with me on the freezing perch, his helmeted head bowed against the ice wall, only grunted.

"Is he moving yet?" Brian asked dully. The question was purely rhetorical, but I answered it to give my idling brain something to do.

"Uh-uh." I pulled lightly on the rope to test it. "Come on, Keith, what are you doing out there," I mumbled into the hood of my parka. "Let's get mov ..."

A violent tug on the rope shocked me into focus. The force jerked me sideways onto the anchors as I automatically locked down the belay device.

"Whoa, Keith! You OK?" I shouted across the face, my eyes straining in the near-darkness to trace the taut rope that disappeared around a bulge and into a couloir, out of sight. I yelled again. Finally, Keith Nyitray's voice echoed faintly back. "Yeah, I'm OK. Man, I just fell! Keep me on tight till I can get something in."

I was on full alert now, tuned to the minute changes in tension on the rope.

I could feel Keith pull out slack for the clip. His "OK" drifted back, then the rope started moving slowly. The face was steep, the ice hard, and I knew that Keith was bone tired. After 20 hours on the go our wits were as dull as our tools.

I glanced at the anchors and then at Brian. We both laughed nervously. "Let's just get off this thing," Brian said, leaning out to peer down the ice and rock slabs that disappeared into the mist. We could only guess how many rappels still remained after we traversed over into the couloir behind Keith. Both of us consciously tried not to look up at the wall of seracs perched on the face directly above.

We had been on Huntington for six days, four of them climbing the *French (Northwest) Ridge* and the last two descending the upper East Ridge and then down the lower part of the Northeast Face. It was Easter Sunday morning, and since leaving our last bivy cave we had been down-climbing and rappelling this insidious slice of mountain nonstop for a day and half a night. The hours were strung together in a fatigued blur: couloirs that ended at the brink of ice-plated rock slabs, ropes frozen into unmanageable cables, and rappel anchors that gave new meaning to the word faith.

The three of us had begun the climb full of cocky assurance. At the time — this was over a decade ago — our collective experience didn't add up to much, a handful of standard routes on Alaskan peaks, nothing stellar. With a solid background of Yosemite big walls, Brian was the most technically adept. He had attempted the then unclimbed Southeast Face of Mount Saint Elias and done some smaller peaks in Alaska. I had the most alpine chops, having lived and climbed in Alaska for six years, while Keith had minimal mountain experience in the Lower 48 and had never climbed up here before.

Regardless of our self-confidence, bolstered largely by a thorough ignorance of the route, the *French Ridge* of Huntington amounted to a high-stakes game that we had entered into with darn few chips. Although we enjoyed some of the best climbing of our lives, for the most part during those six days we tiptoed the fine line of our limits. Not that getting in over your head is necessarily bad — that's how you learn — but big mountains are woefully unforgiving of naivete. If the alpinist survives his apprenticeship, it is by a margin of fool's luck.

The *French Ridge* gains elevation quickly, and is narrow, exposed, and densely corniced from beginning to end. Due to the ridge's precarious topography you must traverse below the crest much of the time, with the steep East Face sucking at your heels. To retreat from beyond the ridge's midway point in case of an emergency would be extremely difficult. In Alaska you have to be prepared to give all or nothing, and despite the misbegotten casual image that some observers have formed of, for instance, the well-worn trade routes on Denali — which still claim lives every year — it's not a place to be taken lightly. This maxim engraved itself on my consciousness during the course of our encounter with

Huntington. High on the ridge and fully committed to the route, I came eyeball to eyeball with the fact that I was a very small creature in the presence of an incredibly large predator.

In our first three days we made good time on the lower sections. Although the climbing early on had been fairly moderate, the ridge now steepened radically, the cornices become monstrously large, and the exposure was wild. We arrived at the first real crux, an 80-foot-high granite block split by a thin crack. Since we didn't have adequate rock gear to aid the crack and free climbing it in double boots, with minimal protection, was out of the question, we would have to bypass it on one side or the other.

To the right the East Face dropped away in a gut-wrenching plunge to the Tokositna Glacier, and the section of rock we now faced tilted over this void. Forget that. On the left a vertical runnel of ice curved up to a slightly overhanging cap of cornice on the knife-edged ridge for a full ropelength.

"So, you gonna lead it?" said Keith, handing over the rack of screws and pickets before I could answer. I kicked my front points more firmly into the slope, gritted my teeth, and squinted up the ridge. That, of course, was the trademark expression of the would-be hardman. We wanted desperately to be cast from the same iconic mold as Dougal Haston, Doug Scott, and Don Whillans; therefore, as we had seen our heroes do in the magazine photos, we squinted and grimaced at every opportunity. This allowed me to present a confident posture while stalling to consider my chances.

Psyching up to the appointment, I thought, "Hey, I can cruise this. Just stand back and watch the alpine master in action." Shouldering the hardware, I climbed cautiously up to the edge of the ice runnel and peered over the crest of the ridge to where the ice swept down the other side. Adrenal glands instantly flooded my central nervous system. The alpine master felt the sudden need to pee.

The ridge curled over the Northeast Face, which was corrugated with vertical ribs of snow. Mushroom-like formations clung to the face at absurd angles. Between the ribs stretched a blue-green skin of ice that looked like a Pleistocene remnant, hard as a diamond. This was no mere mountain, it was a writhing psychotic hallucination that I was being invited to share. I snugged up the leashes on my tools, took a deep breath, and glanced back at my buddies. Brian, who weighed in at 200-plus pounds, all of it muscle, presented a confident image as my belayer. "All right. Take your time," he said cheerfully, grinning through his frost-caked beard. Or maybe it was a grimace.

Traversing over onto the ice I found that my tools had all the impact of blunt kitchen implements. I twisted in a screw, clipped, and kept going before I had time to think about it too much. To my momentary relief the bulletproof stuff soon gave way to crusty snow ice. But this turned out to be almost as gripping

285

for it lay about a foot thick over the hard, brittle water ice underneath, and I was forced to hack a vertical trench in order to get even marginal tool placements.

My fingers were getting numb with cold and my forearms were fading fast as I got one more screw in, seeing that I still had about 20 feet to go to reach the overhanging wall of the cornice, which at least appeared to be firm snow.

Ten feet above the screw my body decided to relinquish all muscle control. My hands cramped and I could hardly grip the shafts of the tools. Both calves launched into an uncontrollable mambo. I looked down. The ice runnel had steered me onto the north side of the ridge and out over several thousand feet of air above the Ruth Glacier. I hung limply from my wrist loops and whimpered shamefully. I cursed myself and every snowflake that formed this infernal heap. I pleaded for forgiveness and promised God that I would quit climbing and give away all my equipment if he would get me up to the top of the ridge.

In a frenzy I beat at the ice with my tools, the blows bombarding my face with stinging particles. I eviscerated the remaining gap between myself and safety, abandoning any refined technique that I had acquired over the years. Finally reaching the underbelly of the cornice, I plunged both tools into the snow up to my elbows, I was drenched with sweat and started to shiver. Luckily, I had rounded a corner out of view from my partners — they hadn't witnessed the hardmaster's momentary seizure of performance anxiety.

After regaining composure, I excavated over the cornice wall and straddled the sharp ridgecrest. I thanked God and tried to explain what I had actually meant earlier was that I would give up really dangerous climbing like this from now on. (Since then, in the grip of fear I have forsworn climbing probably three dozen times.)

At only 12,400 feet high, Mount Huntington is not particularly big in terms of elevation, and from the air — which is your first introduction to the mountain — it may seem somewhat underwhelming, especially given its position right next to the towering bulk of Denali. However, the scale of Alaska's mountains is deceiving, and once you step onto the glacier, gawking up at thousands of feet of glistening ice, rock, and hanging glaciers the size of shopping malls, the magnitude of this place becomes real. Add to this the thousands of miles of Alaskan wilderness that surround you, and your pile of gear on the glacier seems like a tiny life raft adrift in an ocean of uncertain possibilities.

Among the popular peaks of the central Alaska Range, Huntington's fierce reputation is well deserved. It is a condensed assemblage of all the varied climbing this arctic range has to offer, and each of its 12 established routes is technical and committing. Huntington is truly "classic" in appearance, a chiseled form as memorably elegant as the Matterhorn, Ama Dablam, or K2. Shaped like a shark's tooth, Huntington has extremely steep faces on all sides, but the feature that most defines the mountain's symmetry is the serrated tendril of the *French Ridge.*

This ridge presents the most obvious line to the summit and in 1964 yielded the first ascent of the peak, to an eight-man French team lead by Lionel Terray. Mount Huntington presented a worthy objective for Terray, who had pushed extreme alpinism to a new frontier in the Himalaya and the Andes in the 1950s and 1960s and was looking for an Alaskan peak that would offer highly technical climbing at a moderate altitude. His team found a mountain that was, as Terray later wrote, "as big and majestic as the finest Himalayan peaks."

In an expedition style typical of the day, the French undertook a 17-day ascent of the ridge, fixing the ropes over much of the route and resupplying high camps from a basecamp on the West Ford of the Ruth Glacier. Terray almost lost his life when, while descending unroped, he slipped on a section of hard ice high on the ridge. Unable to self-arrest, he slid toward the precipice of the East Face, but at the very brink, a six-millimeter line that Terray was carrying to fix on a lower section, and which the rope team behind had anchored just seconds before, caught him.

At the time of our ascent the *French Ridge* had only been repeated once, by an Oregon team that had taken 41 days to complete a longer variation of the original route. Unlike the two parties before us, which had climbed and descended the same route, we intended to go for a completely alpine-style traverse of the mountain, descending the East Ridge. This plan made the most sense since it would be quicker — the East Ridge is short though very steep — and would avoid downclimbing the endless cornices of the French Ridge.

Climbing light (we didn't even carry a tent, planning to use snow caves the whole time, and carried food and fuel enough for seven days) we were able to ascend the initial 1200-foot icefall to a low saddle on the ridge at 9360 feet, then climb up the easy lower section to the start of the First Step, so named by Terray, on our first day.

The French had divided the ridge into five distinct sections. The First Step, a steep knife-edge from 9360 feet to 9680 feet, offers the route's most technical climbing, with some sections of steep ice. The Second Step presents easy snow climbing leading to a 200-foot ice headwall and knife edge above at 10,050 feet. The Third Step has an elevation gain of only about 500 feet but features the biggest, most intimidating cornices on the ridge, and is followed by the Lacework, which starts at around 11,000 and is a section filigreed with numerous smaller cornices that present short, vertical-to-overhanging ice steps. From 11,600 feet, the Fourth Step is the final stretch of real climbing before the easy summit slope, and has some steep ice and solid exposure.

We had perfect weather the entire time, although, this being early spring, it was cold and at times windy. At the end of each day we were able to locate good sites for caves, except on the Lacework, where we had to drop down onto the rocky East Face and bivy in the open on a snow ledge. We topped out late on the fourth day after completing some of the most demanding yet satisfying climbing that I have ever done. The upper ridge confronted us with a succession of ice steps, and often, in order to stay below the fracture line of cornices, we traversed along the very top of the East Face.

The air was almost dead calm as the three of us plodded wearily up to the base of the summit, a huge diving board of cornice yawning over the Northeast Face. In an act of inspired recklessness, mostly to prolong the incredible cloudless view of the entire Alaska Range for as long as possible, we bivied that night in a spacious cave dug just below the summit.

The morning greeted us with an advancing front of clouds and we hurriedly rapped off the upper headwall of the East Ridge. The wind rose, the temperature dropped, and soon we were submerged in blowing snow. Visibility dropped to barely a ropelength, just enough for us to pick our way down the steep, cornice-spiked ridge. Occasionally, through breaks in the cloud the Ruth Glacier winked up at us, still a long way below. As evening arrived, we dug a cramped cave just big enough for three bodies and squeezed in for what we hoped would be our last night on the mountain.

By morning the wind and snow had subsided, but ragged clouds lay like a torn cloak over the peaks and glaciers. The scene was somber. The sunny blue-sky days that we had enjoyed on the climb, which had perhaps blunted the sharp edge a bit, luring us in with the tease of easy victory, now seemed only a warm-up for the decisive task of making it back down in one piece. In a way the real climb was just beginning. To our dismay the ridge deteriorated into a nightmare of barely attached cornices, and we voted to head down the Northeast Face, taking the most direct line to the glacier. The only hitch in this plan was that we had little gear to leave as anchors, so we rapped off single screws and used ice bollards when we could.

The ice was brittle and often one of us would carefully chip out a perfect teardrop-shaped bollard only to have the whole thing dinnerplate out and skid down the face. Rapping off these things transported you beyond fear to a state of utter surrender. I again renounced climbing forever.

The semidarkness of Alaskan spring crept upon us while we were only two-thirds of the way down the face. Features took on indistinct proportions in the dim light, and the dying batteries of our one headlamp cast a nearly useless beam. But we had no intention of stopping, and continued down into murky couloirs and over rock walls that we blindly hoped would end before the ropes did.

The air was still and cold. Sinister wraiths of cloud glided past and preyed along the glacier below. I was starting to feel very low on the food chain again, when a thunderous boom from above stopped my heart in mid-beat. Tons of ice pulverized a couloir just 200 feet to our left and smoked down to the glacier with a deafening roar, setting the air vibrating against our bodies. Our attention was now riveted to the serac wall above that had unleashed this fury, and which now completely mortified us with cracking, popping, and a sound like shattering glass. We decided to traverse farther to the right.

"I'm not gonna let this mountain eat me without a running start," said Keith, setting up the anchor with renewed vigor. I had to laugh, seeing as we were creeping down at a glacial pace; the avalanche must have been doing 80.

By now we were down to four screws, a deadman, and two pins, with half a dozen rappels left to go until we could down-climb the rest of the face. Two of the screws were plugged solid with ice, and try as we might we couldn't beat the frozen cores loose. Finally we succeeded after first warming them under our bare armpits.

I belayed from two screws. Keith needed the other two for anchors at the next stance after he traversed over into the adjacent couloir, almost a full pitch away. That didn't leave a lot of hardware for the in-between part. "Take your time," I said, using our now official send-off. Halfway across he managed to place the deadman in a two-foot-wide blob of snow stuck to the ice. Twenty feet out from that, when one of Keith's tools popped on a patch of verglased rock, sending him for a long swinging fall, the deadman was the only thing that kept him from loading a 90-footer directly under my meager belay.

The night lurched on into daybreak, and the sun finally arrived, burning away the clouds. We postholed down an avalanche cone and onto the welcoming flatness of the glacier. Easter morning, a celebration of resurrection. The sun's warmth touched our faces, melting away the anxiety of those long hours before the dawn. The descent had been harrowing for sure, but, hey, we'd pulled it off. Maybe this business wasn't so stupid after all. Maybe I was feeling just foolish enough to take up climbing one more time.

First published in Climbing *No. 129, 1991.*

The Pornography of Death
Climbing's dark embrace

By John Thackray

Death is not a subject that mountaineers are good at handling. It is too close and at the same time too remote from consciousness. At the very least, death threatens to spoil our fun.

To write about climbing death to this audience is therefore in extremely bad taste. One's relationship to climbing deaths real and possible, abstract and concrete, is usually kept in the private closet of the psyche. Some will recover easily from the fatality of a friend by seeing the hand of fate at work ("Old Bill always was accident prone"), others will agonize, sometimes for years. But in the end all must sanitize the macabre and sweep death away — so that climbing may be resumed.

There's nothing deader than a dead climber. His mates quickly dispatch him into forgetfulness. They are not callow. It only looks that way. They are not insensitive. It only looks that way to the dear departed's family and loved ones who will insist on ceremonies of grief, tears, funeral eulogies, and all the stage props by which the living try to give death dignity and meaning. At such gatherings, the climber is an impostor with a heart of steel, his emotions and his will carefully held in check.

It takes years for wives, sweethearts, parents, and children of climbers to recognize the emotional monster in their midst. Besides, they never do entirely — right? Right. Because they cannot admit they are connected to someone so heartless and blind and obdurate towards death, they think that we need rescuing from ourselves.

Unfortunately, there are chinks in the most stoical climber's armor. We have all suffered moments of doubt, when the sheer dumb foolishness of climbing screams in the mind. And most of us have actually known climbers — good ones too — hang up their boots after an accident to themselves or a friend.

Spectral metaphors of mortality pass through our communities, subgroups, and cliques when a celebrated hero hurtles into the abyss. Be it a world-class climber, a top-rated national figure, or a local hot shot who gets the chop, there follows a wave of general sobriety. Sadness befuddles the mind, mourning generates second thoughts. But eventually the old perceptions are reconstituted. The blinkers fall into place.

The personification of Death generally wears black clothing, a chalk-white face, and a humorless dour expression. But when it comes to climbers, Death has a sense of humor. And we can, if we listen very carefully, hear his laughter behind the whirring of rockfall, the whup-whup-whup of a helicopter ferrying a body bag, deep within avalanches, and so on. Death often speaks out of climbers' mouths. Next time you hear someone say, "Well, I've as much chance of dying in a traffic accident than climbing," that's him talking death.

Death reckoning season comes in the autumn, when the survivors return from a summer's gambling with their lives and count up probability's corpses. This past autumn in the Shawangunks I bumped into an old friend, just returned from a season in Chamonix where his partner's young neck collided with a falling rock the size of a football. The parents flew over from the U.S. and my friend spent a week with them, escorting and consoling the bereaved. Then he resumed climbing. "But it wasn't a hell of a lot of fun," he confessed, "We did some good routes anyway — the *Walker Spur, Freney Pillar*." I didn't know whether to congratulate or pity him.

Congratulations certainly must go to Tom McCrumm, writing in the *Potomac Appalachian* of 1975, who while recovering from a broken back caused by a climbing fall, counted a broken wrist, 11 shoulder dislocations, two broken ankles, a hairline fracture in one leg, and three weeks in the hospital for other mountain-related problems in his 15 years of climbing. Plus 11 climbing buddies lost in accidents.

Can you top that!

That is Death joking again.

My wife says climbers are in love with death. Wrong. Climbers become in love with themselves every time they elude death. They have a narcissistic relationship to death, and preen in front of those dark mirrors. At each escape from a death dealing threat there's a little infantile voice within that shouts gleefully: "Hey, look at me! I'm terrific!" Egos feed on that magic.

In our personal myths we have all died many times: both in those years as beginners when we couldn't stop doing stupid things, and the years of maturity when most climbers quest for higher risk. Always there is resurrection from those imaginary deaths. Our minds operate like animated movies. A 50-ton weight falls onto a character's head, flattens him into cardboard, but in the next frame he's reconstituted and the chase continues. We believe in a cartoon logic. But real death stops the film. The house lights go on. The skein of illusion is broken.

Sorry about that. Bad taste again.

It is the specter of death surely that makes us so tongue-tied when asked by outsiders, "Why do you climb?" For the question really means, "Why do you tempt the gods so?" That no climber has even come up with a passable answer makes fools of us all; and forces us into evasions that paraphrase Louis Armstrong on jazz: "If you have to ask the question, you'll never know the answer."

So the death cult perpetuates itself, resistant to the sensible values of the larger human community. Of course, climbers aren't the only ones with an over-developed Freudian death wish. There are test pilots, for instance. Or bull fighters and racing-car drivers. But test pilots do it for money. So, too, bull fighters and racing-car drivers, and also perhaps for sexual allure. Climbing, however, is still largely outside the cash economy, and financially disinterested, compared to more glamorous sports. As for climbing's effect on our sex appeal, even the stars of the sport aren't surrounded by groupies. No, our problem with women is to hang onto the few who'll be halfway tolerant of our obsession.

The latest edition of the pamphlet *Accidents in North American Mountaineering* tells us that in 1978 there were 99 reported injuries and 52 fatalities in the U.S. and Canada, making a grand total of 1801 injuries and 716 deaths since 1951. Add to this the far higher statistics for Europe, the uncounted data for the Andes, Himalayas, Caucasus, and elsewhere, and in any year the names of the dead laid end to end would surely fill a page of this magazine.

Shall we find in us the capacity to pity them, and give them thanks? After all, the poor bastards did take the fall for us. Too late for regrets, caught in the ultimate downpulling embrace of gravity, the moral that flashed through most of them, which some shouted out in a final gasp, was simply — "Oh, shit!"

First published in Climbing *No. 67, 1981.*

The Wild Bunch
Yosemite Search and Rescue

By Tyler Stableford

If you want to know why we're here, go climb a big wall." Refusing to speak more, the lean 28-year-old quickly returns to arranging a mess of slings, carabiners, and pitons piled on an old picnic table, his cable-veined forearms pulsing as he sorts. Rescue member Chris Trudeau is sternly prepping for his 20-somethingth big wall. He is not happy to meet me.

A half mile farther up the valley, I enter a building near park headquarters. Rescue leader John Dill is working inside, stuffing ropes in a pack. "Hi," he says, glancing up. "Go away."

I venture upstairs to where Werner Braun is tinkering with battery chargers. He takes one look at my notebook and waves it away with his hand. "Take that and burn it," he says.

Welcome to Yosemite Search and Rescue.

A call comes in the morning of August 8. A park official radios YOSAR headquarters — he has found abandoned camping gear and an eerie 80-page letter atop the 2000-foot Glacier Point. Part of the letter allegedly reads: "At the bottom of this cliff you will find a big man named John."

Glacier Point is a popular spot for jumpers. Several years earlier the precipice had been the scene of a suicide-murder, where a man killed his wife, pushed her over the edge, and then jumped himself.

Rescue leader John Dill sends two YOSAR members with binoculars and a telescope to scan Glacier Point. True to the note, John had jumped — but he didn't make it to the bottom.

I was asked to help photograph the "clean up" for the park investigator. After rappelling nearly a thousand feet we reach Big John. Well, we find his legs. The rest of him is nowhere in sight.

Wearing sterile masks and rubber gloves, we search the ledges in the hot sun. After an hour, a rescuer announces a small find: "Good to meet you, Big John," he shouts with a grin. He holds up a large hand, pretending to shake it, before dropping it in the recovery bag.

Most rescuers say they work for YOSAR because they like to "help people." Yet if a call comes over the pagers to help carry out an obese hiker with a sprained ankle, only the team members with nothing better to do will respond. Some even joke about quickly downing a few shots of booze to make themselves ineligible for work. But, if there is promise of trauma, blood, or a cliff-bound casualty, rescue workers sprint to the scene as if their own mothers need help. In fact, so many people lined up for the suicide recovery that the selection process became competitive, and those who were left behind grumbled for days about missing the fun. One SAR member who was left out approached me that evening. With a congenial smile he said, "I'll pay you for any photos you have of the body parts."

The group's morbid curiosity extends far beyond ambulance chasing. Certain rescue workers used to pocket blood-stained rocks and whip them out back in camp as dinner-time surprises. Jim Bridwell, the YOSAR site founder, kept a small piece of a victim's skull in his tent. Carved in the bone was a lightning bolt and the words, "Cut loose and die."

But no one is more legendary for ghoulishness than Russ Walling, a YOSAR member in the 1980s. Dubbed "The Fish" for his astounding liquor tolerance, Walling was kicked off the team after a string of park offenses. "Actually," he defends, "I left right before the war crimes trial against me."

It seems Walling kept a treasured collection of body-part slides stored in a sock inside his tent. "Just to keep the dust off them," he says. When Walling's photos were mentioned in a *Playboy* magazine article on YOSAR, the rangers became red-faced with anger.

Walling's 1984 photos of an El Cap rescue also soured his standing with Yosemite officials. When the park-service film was developed, rangers discovered glossies of a grinning, yellow-helmeted rescue worker wrapping his arms around two dead Japanese climbers — another YOSAR member had hopped in the helicopter cargo net and rolled around with the frozen climbers. Walling snapped photos. "He was playing dead in the net," Walling explains. "You have to amuse yourself somehow up there."

Walling's crowning violation came in 1986 when he led a rescue in Tuolumne's high country near Mount Clark. It was in October, during the World Series, and a hiker was missing. The rangers told Walling and several others to load a helicopter and begin the search. "One ranger took me aside," says Walling, "and said, 'You know what your mission is: Follow any path or crevice and look for a crack that's big enough to hold a body.'"

When the crew arrived at Mount Clark, Walling says they quickly headed for the nearest cracks. Shutting off their radios, they climbed four new 5.10 routes. "It was within my belief that the guy could have fallen in these cracks," Walling later told the rangers.

Walling and his crew were also supposed to take overnight gear and establish a base camp for the search. Walling, however, didn't want to miss the World Series. While loading the helicopter, he surreptitiously left the camping equipment behind. "All we brought with us were box lunches and cowboy hats," he says. "We topped out on a new route, walked back down to the landing site, and radioed for a helicopter ride back in time for the ball game."

By the time the rangers fully discovered the infractions and summoned Walling to questioning, he had already packed his bags and disappeared from the park.

At the far back end of Yosemite's Sunnyside Camp ground (Camp 4, as the residents call it), down a long dirt path straddled by dusty sites and barbecue pits, sits a collection of sagging tents. Here, between the posted boundaries of the "Authorized Personnel Only" signs, is the home of the 17 YOSAR siters — the core of the rescue team.

A haphazard collection of canvas A-frames, blue tarps, and tiny pup tents crowd together in the bare dirt. An old bike lies on the ground, and empty cans of King Cobra malt liquor clutter the picnic tables. There is no electricity or running water, though some of the white canvas tents have small woodstoves for winter habitation. (Jim Bridwell tried to make the chilly nights more cozy by running an underground extension cord from the campground bathroom to an electric blanket in his tent, but when the bathroom's electrical system malfunctioned, a maintenance worker discovered the secret wiring and pulled the plug.)

Life at the YOSAR site fluctuates between weeks of relaxation and parties to sudden call-outs on treacherous rescues. During the lulls the members often get up late and eat a leisurely breakfast at the nearby Yosemite Lodge before heading to the cliffs. At dusk, they gather around the small tables outside Degnan's Deli and swill cold beer. Some siters, however, eschew the granite entirely and saunter straight from breakfast to Degnan's for the first can of Olde English 800, the cheapest buzz in the Valley.

Despite the rescue site's squalor, over 100 climbers a year apply to live there. Filling out an application is a multi-page effort, requiring numerous signatures on government liability, insurance, and wage forms. Behind the technical words of these documents is a basic agreement: In return for staying around Yosemite and being on call, the YOSAR siters are given a small plot of dirt for tenting, free showers down the road, a pager, and all the climbing time they want. When a call comes in, they get about $9 an hour for hiking rescues and $14 for technical rescues.

Over an average five-month season, YOSAR siters make about $2000. This is just enough for the frugal to subsist, but most full-timers resort to side jobs. Best Bet window washing in the valley is a popular employer, offering 9-to-3 work during summer months. Other siters like Lou Bartell often dip into winter savings. "Maybe I drink too much beer," he says with a smile.

The prestige of being on the team often causes a few aspiring applicants to lie about their climbing experience. One or two duds squeeze in each year. "We usually find that out sooner or later and show them the door," says a rescue leader. Over a dozen climbers have joined the infamous OTS (Off The Site, for good) club, booted out for some infraction of the law or for general bad behavior. The ways to get kicked off are limited only by the siters' mischievous imaginations — and the park rangers' abilities to catch them red-handed.

Drugs are a popular way to join the club. One OTS member had to be dragged out of camp in a straight jacket after overdosing, while one was booted simply for possession of a marijuana pipe. Drunk and disorderly conduct has led to a few ejections, as has BUI (pronounced buoy) — biking under the influence. Tossing full propane canisters into the campfire is also frowned upon. Last is having an uncooperative attitude, a trait that put Tucker Tech out on the streets. Rarely seen sober and unwilling to participate in team training, Tech was kicked off YOSAR in 1993. After nine years of membership, he now does odd jobs such as repairing cams outside Degnan's Deli, and occasionally finds shelter in a secret rock grotto away from prowling rangers.

Because of the benefits of SAR, most siters maintain good behavior — or try hard not to get caught. Besides the nearby rock walls and a leisurely lifestyle, another perk is a marketable image. "You work on the rescue team?" I overhear an impressed young woman ask a team member. Rescue work is a macho, daring occupation, and a well-placed mention of it draws wide eyes in the bar. Perhaps this is why Eric Rasmussen is known as Glory Boy, and why a two-foot-high wood statue bearing a wide smile and an enormous phallus stands near Rasmussen's tent.

Rescue work itself, though, is rarely glorious. Most of it involves bush-whacking through Yosemite's thick forests looking for lost hikers, or saving people who broke all the rules of common sense. An all-to-frequent rescue call involves saving a stranded swimmer who, despite posted warning signs, jumps in a river above a waterfall only to end up hugging a rock precipitously close to the edge, yelling for help. These rescues are called I.N.S. missions: Interfering with Natural Selection. "These victims aren't fit to continue their genes on this planet," says a park ranger who asked to remain anonymous. "We're doing the human race a disservice by saving them."

Yosemite Valley is blessed with some of the country's finest weather. During summer months the sky dawns a flawless blue. The air is warm and dry, and high-country thunderstorms rarely descend into the Valley. The average chance of rain for the months of June and July is less than five percent.

Ironically, it is this seductive weather that contributes to the park's tragedies, luring wall climbers into a false sense of security. Often, no one in camp can even remember the last time it rained — so why bring a rainfly on the wall?

Simple: Because when storms do sneak over the Valley rim, they pound the granite walls with ferocious intensity. A drizzle in the meadow below El Capitan can be a monsoon higher up. What's more, YOSAR's presence woos climbers into a dangerous sense of security. As the availability of rescue has become an assumed guarantee, some wall teams have cut their margins of safety well below self-sufficiency.

"Climbers on El Cap don't bring things they would in a more remote situation," says rescue leader John Dill, a 25-year fixture whose thousands of rescues have made him the world's expert on wall safety. When chance storms arrive, lightweight teams simply don't have enough gear to survive. If they are too high to rappel, they know that a few shouts for help will bring a helicopter to whisk them away. It is no small irony that YOSAR's successes have led to an increase in the number of calls for help.

And it isn't just first-timers who get into trouble. John Middendorf, founder of A5 wall gear and a climber with big-wall ascents in the United States, Patagonia, and the Karakoram, was a member of YOSAR in 1986 when he, Steve Bosque, and Mike Corbett were overtaken by a storm high on the South Face of Half Dome. Gusts up to 80 miles an hour slammed their portaledge up and down. Water leaked through their rainfly, soaking them. The temperature dropped. "When the storm turned to ice and sleet, we just froze," Middendorf says. "The storm was worse than I could ever imagine."

Being a SAR member, Middendorf's friends were keeping a close eye on him. When the weather calmed down enough to launch a helicopter, the rescue team flew in close to the wall and air-lifted the hypothermic climbers to the ground.

Accidents happen to even the best-prepared climbers, but under a new park policy, climbers who go up without proper survival gear or who are otherwise reckless will pay for their rescue. Taxpayers should not have to subsidize climbers' negligence, Dill asserts. "You can go stark naked in January," he says.

"But if we have to come rescue you, we're going to stick it to you."

Recent federal budget cuts have left YOSAR running on a fraction of its former funds, so when Dill and other rangers see an opportunity to recover costs, they take it. "It's gotten so bad that if we can pin anything on you at all," he says, "we'll throw the whole book at you."

In May 1995 two Austrian climbers were rescued in a storm from El Cap's *Shield*. They were found on an open portaledge with down sleeping bags and no rainfly. They were charged $14,000 for the rescue. "I felt sorry for them," Dill admits. "They seemed like nice guys."

The attitude toward self-reliance was different in 1964 when Tom Frost, Royal Robbins, and Yvon Chouinard started up El Cap's *North America Wall*. There was no rescue team, and the wall overhung so severely it would have been impossible for someone to throw a rope down from above. "Probably the only other person who could get up that wall was Layton Kor," Chouinard says, "and he was in Europe."

The first major accident on El Capitan came in 1966. Climbing *the Stovelegs,* a wide crack on pitch 10 of *The Nose,* Jim McCarthy slipped and broke his arm. When Chouinard and two friends learned of the accident that afternoon, they immediately set out to help him. Aiding quickly through the night, the three climbers reached McCarthy by early morning, and had him on the ground before noon.

Early Yosemite climbers looked out for each other. "If someone got hung up," Chouinard says, "other climbers would just get him down." But by 1967 so many climbers frequented the Valley that the fraternity began breaking down. That year, Jim Bridwell formed the first high-angle rescue team — YOSAR. "The key to the whole deal was the free camping," Bridwell says.

In the rescue site, climbers like Jim Bridwell, John Long, and Ron Kauk established squatter settlements. The team members, numbering no more than a dozen, were hand-picked by Bridwell for their toughness. "It was like getting on a gang," Kauk says. "You had to pass an initiation and prove yourself on all the hard-man climbs."

The 1970's climbers were an anarchistic bunch. Disliking rules as much as they coveted booze and drugs, they occasionally ran into trouble with the law. Long was one of the few who escaped punishment because his cousin was a park ranger. "I think I was the only guy on SAR who didn't spend at least one night in Yosemite jail," he says.

In the early years of SAR, every rescue was an experiment. With techniques unclear, rescuers sometimes found themselves in more of a mess than the one they were sent to fix. On a summer night in 1974, ranger Tim Setnicka roused Long from his tent. A climber was injured on Washington Column and needed help. "You're the only one big enough to lower him on your back," Setnicka said.

"How does that work?" Long asked, skeptical.

"We'll explain tomorrow morning. See you at five."

At dawn, Long strapped a saddle-shaped leather harness to his back, and was lowered on a 1000-foot rope from the top of the Column to the injured climber. With the rope connected to the saddle, the idea was for both Long and victim to be lowered in comfort to the ground.

But "the guy weighed two and a quarter," Long says, "and the goddamn harness started moving up. I could barely breath. It was cracking my ribs." About 300 feet from the ground Long was so exhausted he could no longer push away from the rock. "So I just bent my head forward," he says, "and let my helmet grind against the wall."

By the time the two touched down, Long had a hole in his helmet and two cracked ribs. "I got the guy off," he says. "There were a couple rangers who took my radio, then disappeared. I was left standing alone in the meadow thinking, 'I guess that's it.' I had a neck ache for a month."

While most YOSAR members return to the outside world after a couple seasons or years, a small band has made the canvas tents of Sunnyside their permanent home. The most legendary of these characters is a quiet, half-deaf recluse. Werner Braun, the Grand Master of rescue, is the Valley's most celebrated member — and by far the most modest. A permanent camper on the SAR site for over two decades, Braun has been on more rescues than anyone else. "I'm much more comfortable when Werner's around," says Keith Lober, a park ranger and long-time climber. "He has the best attitude of any of the SAR team members. No bullshit with him."

While John Dill stays in headquarters as the radio commander during most rescues, Braun is one of the key players on scene, rigging anchors and haul systems. "He's just as comfortable on a wall rescue as you or I are walking on the street," says a fellow SAR siter.

An electronics genius, Braun is known by almost all the park staff for his home repairs. When a stereo short circuits or a patrol car's siren fails, Braun fixes it. He has also designed radio headsets to fit rescue helmets. Because of his skills, Braun is the only SAR siter with an office in rescue headquarters — a hot, cramped corner in the attic overflowing with radios, LCD screens, wires, and pliers.

Living either in the canvas tent at the back of the SAR site or in his brown van needled with radio antennae, Braun is quiet and unassuming. Unless you asked his friends, you would never know that he has established some of the hardest crack climbs in Yosemite, or that he has climbed *Astroman* over 50 times.

I find Braun upstairs in his attic workshop, crouched with wire cutters over a small black box. He is building a home-made battery charger for headlamps and two-way radios, and is eager to explain the basic principles to me. But when I change the subject from electronics to his climbing history, Braun shuts up. Refusing to speak about himself, he fends off all inquiries with a sweep of his hand. "I don't like talking," he says.

Braun's wife, Merry, on the other hand, is one of the most gregarious members of the team. Known as the mother of the SAR site, 39-year-old Merry passes through camp each day with an unconcealable smile. She never misses a chance to chat or ask each person how he is feeling. "She's like Florence Nightengale," Dill says.

Merry's compassion plays a large role in her reason for being a rescuer. A Japanese immigrant, she arrived in America at age seven, penniless. Her upbringing in the projects of Venice Beach, she says, has bonded her to people in need. "I came to this country with nothing," she says. "In my family, we always help people because we come from the very bottom."

Unlike many rescuers who say the helicopter rides or exciting storm rescues are the highlight of their work, Braun says she is a SAR siter simply because she wants to help. "It's not about money," she says, "It's about someone's life. I don't care if they don't pay me."

The rest of the team is less people-oriented. Although the rescue site at first appears like a tightly-knit community, one where team members share occasional dinners and swap stories over picnic tables, behind the front there is a growing discontentment.

The SAR site has traditionally been a bastion of hard-man climbers, a club for the boldest and baddest wall rats. Basically, "it was a clique," says Kauk. "Even if you were the best climber from Colorado, you didn't have a hope of getting on the site. The only way was to hang around a lot. If you hadn't done a wall with someone on the site, no way."

That has changed.

The elite fraternity has wilted. Today, people who have never climbed a big wall are living on the site, and while they may be skilled in first aid, they don't climb hard. John Dill and park administrators read the applications to decide who makes the team — the days of Bridwell or other SAR siters choosing their peers are over.

"When I was on the site four years ago," gripes former ranger Jason Torlano, "nobody had climbed less than 10 El Cap routes. People who were on the SAR site were climbers for life. They weren't going to stop climbing until they died."

Today each new member arrives looking for something different. Some sign-ons are full-time climbers lured by the prospect of free camping. Some are college students looking to bolster their résumé or for a summer thrill. Others

302

simply have nowhere else to call home.

Cade Lloyd came to Camp 4 eight years ago on a climbing trip. When his money ran out he had to look for a job. YOSAR was the best offer. To supplement sporadic rescue work, Lloyd started a jewelry business outside his tent. He clamped a grindstone to a picnic table, and now spends many afternoons behind the spinning wheel. Gathering rare andalucite rocks from a secret source nearby, Lloyd polishes and drills the rocks, then strings them into necklaces.

Living in a pup tent nearby is Jeff Houston, a medical student headed into his surgery residency. He has never climbed El Cap. Adjacent to Houston lives Scott Stowe, a year-round siter who has accrued more one-day big-wall ascents than anyone can count. In another tent is a graduate student who spends half his time camping on the site, half collecting satellite transmissions at a nearby university. The neighbors rarely, if ever, eat together.

Most SAR siters follow a declining path of enthusiasm for their work. Like aging professors ranting about the end of the good old days, long-time SAR siters love to grumble. As the thrill of late-night rescues dulls, the dusty accommodations and unsteady wages become more and more unpleasant. Grouped at a stained picnic table in the canvas shanty town, SAR veterans lament the end of the golden era.

"They don't pay us enough for the work we do," says a five-year siter, a tall can of Olde English in hand.

"SAR is actually kind of lame," says one who has lived in his small tent for seven years.

"There are park service plots against SAR siters," pipes another seven-year resident. "They want us out of here."

There's no community anymore. Ask any SAR siter, old or young, and he will tell you that the binding spirit of teamwork has slowly vanished. From the grumbles permeating camp, the SAR team seems destined for a slow erosion. But perhaps it has always been this way. Climbers have constantly come and gone, the tents have continuously changed hands, and the SAR siters have constantly griped.

No matter, John Dill receives over 100 applications each year to live in one of the 17 free sites, and the old-timers have trouble leaving. "The last two years I've promised myself I wouldn't come back," Chris Trudeau says. This is his seventh season, and there are still wall routes he longs to do. Next year, when spring warms the Valley again, Trudeau will most likely return. After all, he says, "You get to live in climbing Mecca."

Published in Climbing *No. 172, 1997.*

And you call
this progress?
Finders keepers, except in climbing

By Wills Young

Dear Editor: Have you noticed? You can't even get to the routes these days, for all of the pricks that are climbing on them — it's hardly worth the trouble any more. It's a damn free-for-all.

Mike and I tried to save our local area, but it was the same old story of people going around acting like they own places when they don't even belong there. Some screwball with a lot of nerve claimed he was the first to find our new crag, about four years back. But we know it had been discovered long before that. Mike's brother, for a start, says he probably saw it once when he was out fishing with his dad when he was maybe 12! So who knows how the others think they can claim it.

Mike and I have had no end of hassle out there recently. The main thing that pissed us off was having two of our best lines stolen. We'd seen these lines long ago. They were gems, too, on a great piece of overhanging rock, way to the left of the other routes. Someone had been messing about and had the audacity to put in a few bolts, thinking as if no one had noticed the lines before!

Yeah, right. Mike and I had seen both of them the first time we ever went to the crag! I'd made a couple of the moves on the left one myself, while I was trying the low traverse. In fact, I'd stepped on and off a few times right at the start, so it was hardly new to me!

As for the other one, Mike had told me he'd seen it the same day I'd been working the traverse. Of course, now there are bolts all over it. *And we certainly didn't put them there.*

Mike just stood back, staring, and finally said, "I can't believe that!"

That's what really got our backs up. Mike never actually got a chance to try his lines before some idiot from out of town stuffed it full of bolts!

The only reason Mike hadn't pointed out his line to me months earlier was that he reckoned at the time it would never go. But the moment he pointed it out to me, the thing was obvious.

This is the basic problem, isn't it? I mean, there's always someone screwing things up for everyone else. We always do our best to get some kind of consensus, to make people see things our way and do what we tell them, but it never seems to make a bit of difference.

I mean, why do we bother?

Which brings me to what happened the last time we went to our crag. Mike was out of shape again but I figured I could count on him when it came to the crunch.

It was a frustrating day all around. We lost quite a bit of time with all the crawling through the traffic. You know what it's like: all these idiots driving along real slow right in front of you. They must have all day to do nothing.

When we finally pulled up at the parking area that day there were five vehicles in the little dirt pullout. I knew immediately that this was bad news: I didn't recognize a single car. What were they all doing there?

What really annoyed me was that these guys had taken up all the space and there wasn't even room for us to park! How would they like it if I showed up at their house and parked my car in their garage without asking? Of course they wouldn't think about it that way. Logic is not exactly their strong point.

I managed to find this tiny bit of space to the right of the other cars, so I pulled in there. It was all right for them, but we needed a lot more room for opening the doors and getting things out of the back and everything.

We ended up rushing along the track because of all the wasted time and because we were growing more eager than ever to get to our routes and find out what those idiots were doing. As we turned the final stretch of scree and boulders, two couples came into sight and I just couldn't believe it: they were actually climbing all over our lines.

Mike was in front of me and went on a little farther before stopping and turning to me with his mouth gaping open. Just at this moment, the guy on Mike's new line — the one he was waiting to get strong for — was lowering off from anchors at the top. I noticed the one bolt we had managed to take out from the left-hand route had been bypassed with a long stick clip. There was no sign of Mike's red marker he'd tied to the tree branch and both lines were caked in chalk.

Jesus! It was like a bad dream. I was just blinking and shaking my head.

When this guy coming down Mike's route gets to the ground, he turns to us, all smiles, and his girlfriend, who's belaying him, looks around and sees us and,

306

like there's nothing wrong, says, "Hi!" So we give them dead-pan stares. I just couldn't think what to say. But they carry on smiling and nod to us and the guy says: "Hey! What's up? You want to get on this one? I can leave the draws in if you want."

I felt like plugging him. It was crazy, absolutely crazy. So I turned to him and said, "As far as I'm concerned you can take your draws, your rope, and your girl and get out of here right now." I figured it best to stay calm, not try to create a confrontation for no reason.

He dropped his jaw, looking stupid as hell, and didn't say anything.

Mike said, "Is that your route?"

What could the clown say?

He started to mumble something about how he didn't know whose route it was and that it had always been there as far as he knew. Which was a dead give-away right there. Anyone who knew anything about the place would have known it was a new line — or at least had been. It was obvious from then on that whatever he said didn't really mater, because the fact was he didn't belong there.

While he untied the knot, the girl said something about calming down and started pulling the rope. Then the guy on the other route, to the left, got lowered and both these guys stood staring at us, like gorillas or something.

I still wonder if they were deliberately rude just to provoke us. I wished I could have just nailed them then and there. Just who did they think they were? But there was nothing we could do about it because there were three of them and only two of us.

It would have been nice if we could have done our routes — or at least pulled the bolts. But with all those hostile out-of-towners it wasn't worth it.

I'll tell you right now, I'm not about to share my crag with people who have no respect for other people's property. So we turned away and walked back along the trail, madder than hell. Just one more day wasted by selfish climbers with no concept of right and wrong.

And you call this progress?

First published in Climbing *No. 151, 1995.*

Doin' the Dog
On Half Dome with Royal Robbins

By Dick Dorworth

All climbers know Royal Robbins. Even non-climbers know about Half Dome. Been here a while, and it's hard too. No need to introduce either.

Royal thinks he owns Half Dome. He's written that he wants it, and the truth lies closer to the entire valley. Every route on the north wall in all the photographs belongs to Robbins. There were three. One hasn't had a repeat and one has had one. Robbins territory.

Warren Harding, too, has survived the years with good reason; and in early, hot July he finally bathooked his way up the South Face of Half Dome. There's a connection between Harding, Robbins, and Half Dome (causing consideration of "Bathook and Robbins" as a title); but the link is lost in the mists of Yosemite big-wall mythology, which they both love. So I wondered what Robbins thought about Harding hooking up, so to speak, the backside of Royal's rock.

Don't know, but a few days after Harding finished his route I was beaching with my lady, Jane, at Tenaya Lake, soaking up sun, rest, and pleasure when Robbins plops down in the sand with a proposition in his mind: a new route on Half Dome.

Five seconds passed before the answer could surface. The delay had several sources. I had never done a Grade VI, except a jumared one; the dry summers plague Yosemite walls between June and September; I'd never pounded pitons with the finesse required for what is known as an A4 pin, could not conceive the delicacy of an A5er. Who knew what minuscule cracks were there? Not me. I'd only climbed 10 days in a year. Would I flame out? Was I experienced enough? Ready for a major route? A new one? What if I couldn't do it? What if I died?

Comfy beach. Nice lady.

But, what the hell. Only one way to know, and there's really nothing better to do than find out. Is there? And Robbins is such fun to climb with. He is so good. Plays so hard. Besides, he's my friend, and he asked. You gotta go with the times, grow with them. Time to find out about those walls. What the hell.

Twenty four hours later we were at the base of the wall after a five-hour frontal approach, an interesting adventure itself. Heaps of man signs there: tin cans, glass bottles, paper, empty plastic water bottles, webbing slings, and old clothes. Others had come before.

Our luck found water trickling from the wall, saving a two-hour walk to the spring. I asked Royal how much water we would take. "Quartandahalfperdayperman," he said, looking as if I'd questioned the Trinity. I hoped July heat might necessitate, at least allow, more survival than the classic Yosemite formula. Not so. Not so. I held out for 10 Sportade packets, a bag of lemon drops, a water bottle of fruit cocktail, and some ginseng. I didn't know, but I knew my own system.

Sustained by minimum food and water, and armed with dozens of nuts, clogs, and pitons, we leapt upon the northwest face of Half Dome at four in the afternoon. Royal first. He led 30 feet before aiding himself. Precious little went for free after that. The rope ran out regularly. I played diligent belayer, shouting out the remaining rope at appropriate intervals. When no extra rope between us remained, he asked if I'd move up a bit. I climbed 10 feet to a tiny foothold and watched the loose rope climb higher. I moved up again. It was a difficult place and my arms and hands were tired long before the rope pulled taut. It had begun.

I cleaned and banged up to a timely ledge. Hot and much too tired for only having climbed a long and a short pitch. Bad sign. Got to live cleaner. The incredible Valley Yosemite below. A Hobbit world of elf forms, dark Strider shadows, rich green separated from pale blue sky by orange yellow sunset giving way to night. Robbins, making his seventh ascent on the face, had never seen so few lights in the Saturday night valley. Good sign. My partner gave me his ensolite pad to sleep upon.

The Sabbath is the day of rest, but we were honest and I set off first. Rotten. Crumbly. Unclimbable without nuts. Flaky. Dirty. Terrible. Shitty! A boulder balanced on a flake right in the way. Knock it off or throw it down? Succumbing to ego rather than chancing faith, I told the belayer to move to one side of the ledge. Then I tossed the boulder down on top of the water bottles, on the other side of the ledge. Less than a quart lost, but it thinned the already skinny formula. I was aided up the rest of the pitch by some dry Robbins humor.

At the end of my rope was a terrifying belay. Royal came up, complimented my pitch, complained of my anchors, and commented that a fair amount of suffering might be ahead.

We gardened another pitch each. I felt terrible, alien, as dry as the rock, in a world unfit for humans. Candy and food wrappers littered every ledge and many cracks. I thought we must be on an often-climbed route, but Royal assured me it was just tourist garbage thrown from above. Hikers on top of Half Dome seem fascinated with throwing rocks, pebbles, boulders, and even beer cans down the face. You hear them coming, turning over in the air, making a sound like a heavy prop gone mad. You shrink inside and scrunch against the rock. You get a hand or arm over your head, and don't question what good that might really do. You exhaust your obscenity repertoire. You understand something of the soldier in combat. You are outraged at people's ignorance. You are pissed.

After two more insane pitches, we found ourselves inside a huge chimney on a chockstone big enough to stand two or curl one. It was my tiredest moment.

"What shall we name the route?" I asked.

"The Dog," he said. Sometime later Royal invented another Greek or Roman name which I kept forgetting. The spontaneity of the first christening somehow sticks in mind, and *The Dog* it is to me.

It was my turn, but darkness was near so the faster Robbins took over and made a brilliant lead up the chimney. He finished in the dark and slept on a tiny ledge. I curled up in the bottom of what I call, for personal reasons, "Mad Dog Chimney," for the most uncomfortable, miserable, suffering night of my life. I was drowning in my own thirst, and my intestines stuck together like last night's noodles. My mouth and throat were too dry to eat, and there wasn't enough water. Ration it. Sip it. Hold it in the mouth until it turns to brine, and then swallow. No comfort there. Sleep eluded. I tossed all night in the bottom of Mad Dog Chimney.

Why had I left Tenaya Lake and Jane?

Discomfort greeted the morning with a mixture of longing and despair. I cleaned the pitch and joined Royal for some fruit cocktail. Happiness is fruit cocktail after a night in Mad Dog Chimney in mid-July.

Some easy climbing brought us to the bolt ladder on the regular route. We had started a hundred feet right of the regular route, and now we would climb this old line until we could cross to the left. Two pitches found us at the big ledges at the base of the Robbins Chimney. No less than 20 empty plastic water bottles and uncountable tins and paper wrappings littered the ledge. Fleeing the pollution, I nutted up a diminishing crack left of the old route. An exhilarating pitch on better rock. I belayed off a tiny ledge on which I found an unmistakable Bridwell topo of Half Dome's regular route.

"You sure we're the first ones up here?"

"Yeah, Man, I'm sure."

From there we were in left-facing dihedrals, whereas the lower part of the climb had been in right-facing ones, which caught the last bits of sun. Cooler now. Cracks filled with vegetation — lush, growing things smelling of rich, green life, and water. During belays I buried my nose in these hardier forms of mountain greenery, breathing in the fragrance of organic growth and water. A single leaf of some determined bush held all the wonder and beauty and sadness and creation of the universe. I promised myself that I would lie naked in a meadow by a stream and breathe in the fragrance of paradise, known as earth.

Robbins led up some overhangs to a belay in slings in a dihedral about 50 feet below a huge overhanging flake. Then I followed a thin crack to a point where I placed a marginal Leeper just below the flake. I stood as high as possible to tap the flake. Good. Harder. Solid. I put a long dong behind the flake and hit it twice. A terrifying and indescribable sound stopped everything. Bits of sand fell out from behind the flake.

In a couple of minutes my heart worked enough for me to retreat to the Leeper.

Time to confer with Master Royal.

A tension traverse right got me to another crack. A few pins later the crack thinned to an eighth of an inch wide, twice that deep, crumbling, and looking worse above. Time to bolt, one way or another.

"Why don't I have a look at it," my friend said.

"Right on."

I was too far up to be lowered, so unclipped from the pins in the right crack and began a small pendulum back to the left dihedral. The Leeper pulled as soon as I began, and the next 20 feet down were faster than anticipated.

Royal lowered me, assured us both I was okay, joked with arid humor about my adventure up there, exchanged belay for lead, and went to it. He took two hours to finish the lead without a bolt, using tiny wired nuts mashed to stay in microscopic cracks. I cleaned a pitch of climbing education, or superb climbing, depending.

The sun galloped down as we rappelled a hundred feet into a chimney with two sitting ledges. It looked like rain, but it never materialized. I wanted the sky to drop an ocean, but it gave not a drop. Our high point was about a hundred feet left of where psyche flake used to be, and we thought we'd be off the next night. Just two quarts of water for the next day. Body cells collapsed and sticky, mouth cauterized, brain devoted to basics.

Ready by the first morning light after a sleepless night. We jumared to our high point. I led off, tensioning left around a corner to a lovely dirt-moss-grass-filled crack a half-inch deep and just as wide. After half an hour of severe kidney strain, we exchanged leads. In 10 minutes Robbins found just the right combination and carried on. Royal led all the last day, except the easy free climbing to the summit. Hard, intricate climbing. Problems following puzzles, solved through an array of tricks and talents possessed only by a master. Robbins is a supreme rock climber, artist, and craftsman. Still competing, but very generous and considerate. A man who, while climbing, knows what he is about, able to concentrate on the immediate detail and the keeping going what must go; to the extent that his being appears as a mystic or a mad scientist, depending.

We reached the summit late in the afternoon, met not by Harding, but a beggar chipmunk. Suffering suddenly left. The experience adds to confidence, and the suffering is forgotten in the face of the memory of adventure. No doubt we will suffer again.

On the way down we passed six girls with packs, climbing the cables to sleep a night on Half Dome. One was fat and puffing; all clutched the cables like life itself; their adventure was no less than ours. We wished them good night. Further down we ran across three spacy looking fellows with a vicious dog that tore Royal's pants trying to bite him. The owner sidled over, begging pardon, for the dog had had a hard day.

"So have we," Robbins answered, putting his hammer back in its holster.

First published in Climbing *No. 7, 1971.*

Coonyard Mouths Off — Part II
Affairs of the states

By Yvon Chouinard

There is a spontaneous and light-hearted quality in a sport which vanishes as the sport matures."
— Sir Arnold Lunn

Between 1915 and 1932, the Swiss guide Hans Lauper knocked off 18 major first ascents in the Alps, including the North Faces of the Monch, Jungrau, and Kamm, and the East Face of the Eiger. During the 1930s most of the great north faces in the Alps were climbed, including the "last great problem," the Eigerwand in 1938.

In 1947, John Salathé and Anton Nelson, wearing sneakers and driving pitons directly into decomposed granite, climbed the *Lost Arrow Chimney.* They placed expansion bolts on the smooth summit knob.

In 1957, the first Grade VI in North America was put up on the North Face of Half Dome, and if you found a Vibram track on any trail in America, you knew it was made by a climber, who was a friend of a friend of a friend.

By 1960, gas was 25 cents a gallon and for 50 bucks you could get a decent car. With a couple of hundred dollars more you could spend April to November climbing all over the country. This was the beginning of the age of specialization. You climbed and that was it. Robbins was the only one we knew who also skied and we never really trusted him because of that. In Yosemite you climbed cracks or you were a face climber. The first 5.10s were put up beginning in 1960, and by the end of the decade it was possible to effect a rescue on El Cap from the top.

In November 1964, finding 15 inches of snow on the summit after making the first ascent of the *North American Wall,* Robbins, Pratt, Frost, and I threw off a duffel bag and watched helplessly as someone jumped out of a car, ran to the base of the wall, and made off with all our down jackets and bivouac gear.

In May 1970, *Climbing* No. 1 was hot off the press, definitely slanted toward Colorado climbing; but the Northwest had *Off Belay,* Southern California had *Summit,* and the Gunks had the *Vulgarian Digest.* The free standard was now 5.11, and the *Dawn Wall* was marathoned in 29 days for the ultimate in big-wall living; they blew it, though — two days more and they could have inked a big promo deal with Baskin-Robbins.

More and more people were getting into climbing and backpacking, but you couldn't leave your gear at the base of a wall or even in your tent any more. The *Wall Street Journal* advised corporate America to invest in the "high growth" specialty outdoor industry. The Park Service was busy setting up reservation systems for backcountry use. The Yosemite Master plan was being formulated to eliminate automobiles in the Valley by the year 1990.

In 1972, the Chouinard Equipment Catalog came out with the "Whole Natural Art of Protection," and almost overnight the game changed, most of America switching over to natural protection. People attempted to de-piton routes in Europe, like the *Walker Spur* but democracy wouldn't allow it; the lowest common denominator prevailed, and within weeks they were pegged up again.

Sometime around 1973 the rate of growth in outdoor sports peaked. Some companies diversified into soft goods, some didn't even see the change until was too late. Gas prices shot upward and suddenly there was less fat in the system to support those on the bottom end of the social spectrum. The draft card burners of the 1960s were getting older, having kids, and looking to upgrade their lifestyles.

Enter the 1980s. You can't "out-rebel" your parents — they were the wigged-out, drug-crazed hippies of the 1960s. So change the rules. Drive them crazy by going to law school. Join the Boy Scouts, don't take any risks, and, above all, it's very uncool to be passionate about anything. Instead of marathon weekend drives to the Valley, you jog around the block every day and put in a nice 10-miler on the weekend, with maybe a little session of Nautilus or aerobics here and there. The heroes are Eastwood and Stallone, who both chickened out of going to the Cannes Film Festival for fear of being terrorized.

It's the "me-now" generation, and narcissism is the game. You can't even get your picture in the British mags without your shirt off (and I've never seen a day in the Isles when I've even wanted to take off my sweater)! Pink hair, pierced noses, lycra with codpieces, its all good fun and doesn't hurt anybody. After all, we used to wear all white on the walls.

But the mountains are strangely empty. Backpackers are now car camping, and the only ones you see in the woods are redneck survivalists who jump out of the trees to scare the shit out of you before they "camo" back into the bushes. The only people in the Winds are kids or executives, sent there to wrest some sort of character building or moral out of confronting the wilderness.

The Valley now has a video store and the Merced is open for commercial boating. Many of the environmental gains of the 1960s are wiped out by an over-zealous Secretary of the Interior who believes that "Jesus wants us to drill for oil in the wilderness."

The dominant environmental policy of the 1980s is that we should drill all our oil, cut down the forests, and dam the rivers right now. Go for the short-term goals, and let the future generations worry about reforestation of acid-rain killed forests, cleaning up dead rivers, and bringing back extinct species. Like in Vietnam, we may have to destroy the earth in order to save it.

Climbers are polarized into socio-geographical areas: Eldorado, Joshua Tree, Hueco Tanks. In the Tetons, they are all on the Grand, sometimes 100 a day on the top, but the other peaks are empty. Everest is in vogue with overachieving attorneys, doctors, and businessmen. Oh, there are still a few geeks around like Stump and Lowe doing risky alpine climbing, but the system doesn't recognize, understand, or reward this kind of abnormal behavior. Which is why they do it, I guess.

Ice climbing is dead — the tools are so efficient anyone can climb vertical ice on their first day. So what do you do the next day? Sport rock climbing is the rage, but is has as much spiritual relationship to the mountains as modern agriculture has to the earth — the dirt holds the chemicals and plants in place so they don't fall to middle earth.

It's tough making a name in climbing today. So you climbed the *Nose* and Half Dome in one day? Didn't even make the sports page in the Fresno Bee. You can try and follow Bachar but there's too good a chance of getting snuffed. It's a lot easier to be an asshole. Make a name by being "controversial." Piss off the locals and they won't forget who you are. Infamy is better than no recognition at all.

On the positive side there is less specialization. Climbers ski, kayakers climb — the unbalanced ones are the specialists who have only one trick, the 5.13 climbers who can only look forward to a self-destructing body with its muscle tears and inflamed ligaments.

Now, for 1987 and beyond. The recent elections sent a clear message to those turkeys in Washington. The people would rather have clean rivers and be able to drink out of the tap than have MX missiles. The freshman in some schools are now considerably more liberal than the sophomores. Reagan and his lamer-than-lame trickle-down economy is in deep shit. The mood is changing.

Risk sports which thrive only during politically liberal times may be on their way back. There could be a resurgence in the geek sports like alpine climbing, backcountry skiing, and whitewater kayaking. Alpine touring is coming on especially strongly.

Americans have no background in true winter climbing. The Europeans made winter ascents of all their north faces back in the 1950s and 1960s, while our best alpine climb, the North Face of the Grand Teton, has had only one winter ascent. American climbers in the Himalaya have a real gap in their experience because they've missed out on this winter-climbing stage. Our mountains are not as accessible as the Alps, and perhaps this new interest in backcountry skiing will give access to the thousands of American mountains awaiting first winter ascents.

Hangdogging, chipping holds, placing bolts on rappel, climbing competitions — the great debate continues. Who is right and who is wrong? I say it's pretty simple. There are ethics and there is style. Ethics are so you don't screw it up for the next guy, and style is so you don't delude yourself into thinking you're so hot. Here's all you need to know about ethics:

The Climber's Bill of Rights: You have the right to climb anywhere in any style you wish, as long as it doesn't alter the medium or infringe on the next person's experience. It's simple. You use chalk, place a bolt, leave fixed pro, shit on El Cap Tower, it's all bad ethics. I don't care if Everest is climbed by an expedition of 100 Rotary Club members all sucking O's from basecamp, as long as the mountain is not altered and it doesn't bother the other groups on the mountain.

Style is another story, and it's mostly a matter of degree. We need to establish a cornerstone.

Let's call it:

Perfect Climbing Style: A naked human free soloing a new route on sight. If you put on shoes you get docked one point, chalk one to three points depending on the climb, the heat, and the humidity. Previewing or reading a guide book another point, placing one piece of pro, another point, and so on into infinity. The farther you get away from this Perfect Style, the less proud you should be of yourself. With this criteria, the best climber in the world today is probably Berndt Arnold of Dresden, with his nearly bare feet, no chalk, and long runouts.

Is climbing, as a passion and as a sport, better off now that it was in the past? We can do harder climbs now in faster times — techniques are more refined and equipment more sophisticated — but are we really any better off?

On the plus side we have the free climber soloing rock that was unclimbable 10 years ago, the alpine climber in Europe who is so incredibly competent and fit that he needs to knock off three or four big north faces to feel like he's had a good day, and those applying alpine techniques to Alaskan and Himalayan walls. There is still a lot of room in these games for adventure, spontaneity, soul, and art.

On the negative side we have the ice climber hacking his way up the *Black*

Ice Couloir with his three tools, the El Cap climber with his full rack of chocks, full racks of pitons, and a full rack of Friends, and the specialist sport climber who chooses to become better and better at less and less. I'd say we are small winners.

As a sport matures, it doesn't necessarily get better. Look at alpine skiing. In the 1936 Olympics they painted your skis to make sure you used the same pair in the slalom as in the downhill. Now you can't tell the winners without the aid of electronic timers accurate to the millisecond. The specialists are the ones who take the soul out of any sport.

It's a great thing to run a marathon. You train a bit, maybe change your diet, give up smoking, and you knock it off in three-plus hours. If you want to do one in two-plus hours, that's another story, and if you want to do one in sub-two hours, you have to kiss off sex, your job, your friends, all the "non-essentials," and devote your entire life to the effort.

I say the last 10 percent of the way to perfection takes so much of your life that it isn't worth the effort. This overzealous attitude is what creates religious fanatics, body nazis, and athletes who are exceedingly dull to converse with, unless you want to talk about their particular specialty or their bodies.

Specialization, when indulged in by true geniuses like Mozart, Babe Ruth, or Berndt Arnold can create great art that elevates mankind above the lowly beasts. But you and I can evolve more quickly by putting that energy into more than one direction.

It's unrealistic to think we can go back to what climbing was in the 1930s, but we do need to constantly change the rules of the game to keep the sport evolving. When basketball players are all over seven feet tall, you need to raise the height of the basket. When the thrill is gone from alpine skiing, you just free up the heels and re-invent the telemark turn. Any activity, whether sport, business, or love, needs constant change, even revolution to keep it from degenerating.

Hangdoggers think they are the revolutionaries who are going to save climbing. But bad ethics in the name of raising the standards or making American rock climbers more internationally competitive is twisted zeal. Remember, these are really the arch-conservatives of the 1980s, because they want to minimize the risk factor in climbing at the expense of the rock. They are the super-patriots that believe American climbers shouldn't be second to anyone. And like James Watt, they are the ones who believe the old Christian ethic of having dominion over the beasts and fishes (and rocks).

In the greater scope of things, how important is it that Americans climb 5.14? The grading system has to be flawed anyway, when an out-of-shape, 48-year-old surfer can now do some 5.11a's, when in 1960 he could barely do 5.10a's — and that when he was in his prime and could do one-arm pullups!

319

At this rate he will be a 5.13 climber when he's 90!

It's bloody tough to beat anyone at their own game. Climbing and similar individual sports like solo around-the-world sailing are a strong European tradition. They have much more accessible rock, many more climbers, and greater public acceptance of the sport. The Europeans don't have the National Safety Council and insurance companies not allowing them to take risks. It's crazy for us to think we can beat them at their own game. Do you see the French sending over a team to play in the Super Bowl?

I say change the rules! Let's play our own game. In America, we have one thing going for us that the Europeans used to have, but they've already used it up. We still have a bit of wilderness left, a few grizzlies, a couple of condors, and some still-virgin mountains and rocks. We also have a strong tradition, going back to Thoreau, Muir, and Bob Marshall, of loving and wanting to preserve wilderness.

Are we going to allow a few "me-now" hangdoggers to be the spokesmen for American climbing? Are we willing to compromise our ethics and style, all for the sake of raising the standards? If so, the climbers coming after us will have to grind off our chipped holds, plug up our bolt holes, and wash away our chalk marks in order to raise their own standards. It seems to me that climbing would be better off if we just learned to hold back a bit, and take an attitude of "each climb has its time."

First published in Climbing *No. 100, 1987.*

Letters From Herbert
The friends we have

By Don Lauria

The envelope was wrinkled, as if the postman had carried it in his hip pocket all the way from the writer's home in Coarsegold. It had been addressed to me, but a line was stricken through "Don," and "Anna" Lauria was the addressee. The scrawl was unmistakable — a letter from TM Herbert:

"Dearest:

We must never let the clod know how close we are. OK, now here's the plan; you and the kids will come up with Don next weekend. We will, of course, be together almost all the time; however, I will pretend that I am all hot to go climbing with him (or as we would say, "IT"). Now there are places to slide around in the snow near Rixon's Pinnacle for the kids and Squaw while I entertain the clod. Later on we'll have drinks and music and I will do an impersonation of someone who is dumb and ugly — you won't believe it! So cancel all rinky-dink Brownie and Cub Scout goodies and order all those brats to prepare for a weekend with HERBERT!

See you next weekend,

TM Valentino

P.S. Have you thought of a way to break the news about our overnight snow caving to IT?"

Letters from Herbert arrived frequently during the spring months of Yosemite's transitional years — 1967 through 1975. I saved them, as vehicles of his personality, his humor. I will not apologize for TM's choice of words, because those who know him realize that to edit Herbert is to mute Beethoven — you lose the essence. His letters are gems, his humor is scathing, yet harmless; coarse, yet witty. He uses vulgarity to amuse. His lack of propriety occurs only among his peers — those whom he cannot offend. TM is really quite shy outside of his milieu.

The following are excerpts from assorted letters:

(on his physical prowess) "I now weigh 103 pounds. And yet I can still lift the front end of a D-9 tractor. And also I can hold a full lever on a high bar with my wee-wee."

(on having a good time) "If climbing at Joshua Tree is out, how about a get-together at your place — break windows and furniture and leave the place in flames."

(on remembering climbing routes) "Some guy wrote me about that Baja Rock. Shit! I can easily remember my name and age, but things like what route we did — no way! Maybe what model and year car I have — would he accept that, do you think?"

(on next weekend) "Then Friday morning we cut out to Ventura and climb somewhere Saturday for thousands of heroic glorious feet. Then Saturday night we drink and take powerful artificial drug stimulants and cruise the boulevard for young girls — you will pose as my uncle who is driving. We will stash your old lady and kids. Our old-bag wives will pose as our mothers."

(on family living) "Can you come to the Valley over Easter vacation? Or are your kids gonna play jacks. And your wife is probably entering the local knitting contest ... Are you a man or a mouse? Order all those dip-shits into the car and tell them to head for the Valley, where your wife and I have special hideaways while you stay home and spray the aphids and pull crab grass."

(on becoming more masculine) "Now why don't you quit hanging around with those pacifist, long-haired queers down there — come up and we'll kick the shit out of a couple of bars. The ones where the shit stompers hang out. Then head over to Hornitos and take on some dudes on the pool table. Then a bunch of clawing scratching women will be fightin' for us."

Herbert was so frustrated by his inability to arouse a written response from me that he often sent a multiple-choice reply for my convenience. Here is a sampling, shortened for lack of space:

"Don,

I'm doing some correspondence psychology work; could you fill out this form so's I can see what kind of a weird perverted mother-fucker you really are? Check appropriate boxes.

- I'm fairly well-adjusted.
- Well, I'm not so adjusted as I'd like.
- Oh, I'm all fucked up.
- Creepin' green Chinese crud, I've got a sabre up my ass!
- None of the above.

322

- Some of the above.
- Every other one of the above.
- I'll kill anyone or anything that even looks at me.
- I wanna fuck a sheep, an' a cow, an' a dog, an' a big clawing Bengal tiger."

The following note came to me in the aftermath of a bawdy, outrageous party held in old Camp 4. Joy Herman and Mick Burke had been dancing to a blaring Stones album in my campsite when the rangers arrived. Tourists had peered from the surrounding Winnebagos, unable to hide their disgust. Herbert had gathered his family and fled into the night, leaving his lantern and stove on my table.

"We came back to Camp 4 at about 8:15 a.m., but you had already gone. You should have seen us sneak in ... we parked our car many tables away and whisked our stoves and stuff off as we walked by. Many evil eyes were upon us, so I had to disguise myself. When you next see me I will be in the form of a large sugar pine.

See you, TM."

First published in Climbing *No. 120, 1990.*

Running Stairs

Say, coach, there I was
dying high on an Asian
mountain and do you know
what I thought of?

By Mark Jenkins

*He who fights with monsters should be careful lest he
thereby become a monster.*

— *Fredrich Nietzsche*

I have not bathed in 73 days. I know this will disgust you, Coach. I can see
your veiny blue face bulging, spitting obscenities. But we're sweating so
hard from Day One, sweating like horses sweat, so everyone smells the
same. After two weeks you reach a state of equilibrium: body oiled and content
in its own animal smell, heat rash where the pack straps go over your shoulders, hair malleably greasy.

I believe I've lost 20 pounds. I trained hard before all this, going to the stadium every day, so I didn't have that much to lose. Feeling my corporeal self
inside my sleeping bag, beneath my foul long underwear, I find things missing. For example I no longer have triceps. They have vanished leaving my
shrunken biceps the only muscle fastening elbow to shoulder. And my lats, the
wings of the back, they too are gone. And my pecs, once shallow plaques of
masculinity, gone.

Of course any fat was dispatched long ago. The little slip of suet below one's
chin, the invisible pads between the legs, the pleasing wrap around one's
waist, all the physical manifestations of affluence and boredom, dished up and
devoured. Strange sort of metaphor, consuming oneself outside in.

I see now that arms and chest were inconsequential. All I really needed was
legs and lungs. Big lungs and ceaseless legs. Legs that keep kicking even when
it's all over.

I grope down inside my bag and squeeze the muscles above my feet. (I won't
touch my feet. I'm afraid to touch my feet.) Quads, glutes, calves. Each is sculpted,
hard as marble, proud of itself for surviving. Coach, you would be impressed.

I take a deep breath. Even up here, where we gulp at the air as if we are drowning, I can still do that. My skin is stretched taut around my chest. Every bone protrudes. I feel the curve of each rib, the small lumps and dents from injuries I acquired decades ago, perhaps the year you knew me. When I lie flat on my back I can feel the nodes of every vertebrae. My hip bones poke up ridiculously into the goose down of my sleeping bag.

Ah, I hear you. Snorting phlegm up your throat, popping your knuckles like walnuts. Self-indulgence offends you. Ordinarily, I wouldn't mention all this, but today is unusual: I have taken a rest day. Not by choice. This is my 17th consecutive day above 21,000 feet. Everyone said I should go down and rest, that I was tempting fate, but I kept on until I couldn't. So now I'm tent bound. Perhaps if …

I'm back. I don't know. I just fell asleep.

I should tell you. I'm living on the edge of a terminal drop. I'm living on a ledge, like a hermit, my hair curling into my beard, my skin peeling off in strips. The ledge is far up in the sky. It took us a month to get this high.

I'm inside a tiny red tent on this tiny ledge. I imagine the tent as a kite, a kite that cut loose and soared so high it disappeared above the clouds, then crashed into the side of the Himalaya like a plane. Sometimes I dream that it is just hanging here by strings frozen into the ice.

I have taken a rest day because of last night. Because of last night I can go nowhere. I am not sure I can walk.

I know I should not even think it, let alone speak it, but Coach, I am weak. I realize that is blasphemous. Even the word itself is anathema to you, the sound of it in some poor body's throat would make you vomit like a sick bull. I know.

This morning it took all I had to piss out the tent zipper. I got up on my knees, still in my sleeping bag. The slice of light that came through the tent flap stabbed my eyes. I got dizzy for a moment.

Dizziness is death up here. Vertigo is death. If I had fallen forward I would have fallen off the edge. A flight of 2000 feet.

But I didn't have vertigo. I never do on a mountain. If I've been living the horizontal life for several months and happen to get to the top of a building, and look over, I get vertigo. I think it's due to the suddenness of a mortal perspective. The horizontal life provides primarily oblique panoramas. Too many things in the way for you to see whatever it is you're really looking for. From above, things look fairly clear. But going up mountains, especially a mountain this size, is slow business. Believe it or not, you get used to living on little bird ledges and hanging in midair. You get used to looking down and having to search the glacier for a speck you know is a tent. It's almost like being in a plane. Who gets vertigo in a plane?

After pissing I felt better. I collapsed back inside and must have fallen asleep because when I opened my eyes my cheek was frozen to the tent floor. I got myself deep in my sleeping bag and decided to read, then decided not to.

I have already read my section of *Moby Dick,* page 263, "Of the Less Erroneous Pictures of Whales, and the True Pictures of Whaling Scenes," to page 429, "Measurement of the Whale's Skeleton." Read it twice. Like all the books, we ripped it into four pieces and distributed them amongst us. We swap with each other once we've finished out sections, which of course means I can't read the book in order, which you might think would be disagreeable. Actually, I enjoy it. Makes me see how nicely things fit together; how the present is no more than a small extension of the past; how the future is but an interesting turn on the present; everything already right there from very early on; we just don't usually see it.

I know you don't have any idea what I'm talking about. I know you don't give a damn, either.

Anyway, I've done everything I must do, everything I can do, so I decided to write you. I see that my handwriting started out erect and smooth but has already degenerated. Cold does that. It's like cancer.

I know you don't know anything about mountain climbing — it's not much like football — most people don't. Most people think that it's just cold that makes you cold. But at 23,000 feet, the real problem is dehydration. Melting snow is so time consuming you get tired and don't boil up as much water as you need. So you get dehydrated and your blood turns to syrup and can't get into the capillaries. That's how you lose fingers and toes.

About half this team has had something amputated. Joe, the leader of this expedition, he lost his big toes when he was about my age. They were snipped off irregularly in some hinterland hospital, leaving rough gnarls of skin that catch when he tries to pull on his wool socks. He says it has never bothered him, but I watch him, slowly picking his way down through the glacier using his ski poles for balance. He goes slow. Like a dog with three legs. He could go faster, but without big toes you lose forever.

Sorry, fell asleep again.

You know you feel safe inside sleep. I dreamed of green again. We're all dreaming of green, have been for weeks. We live in a world of unbearable, blinding, burning white — so we dream of green. We dream of it like we once dreamed of sex. Carnal green. Voluptuous green. Velvety wet warm green. We wake up and tell each other of dreaming of sleeping naked with green. Of green cottonwoods growing straight up out of the glacier.

Of course that's not all we talk about. At dinner, when we're not too tired, lying on our sides in our bags with our noses in cups of steaming hot chocolate, we talk about sports that make sense. Snorkeling, in warm green Caribbean water. Or lawn tennis in England. Funny no one has mentioned golf yet, all that endless soft flowing green trimmed short as a woman's pubic hair.

Does it sound like I'm with somebody right now? I'm not. Of course you can sometimes think you're with somebody even when you're not. Just like when you're in an old house at night and the floors start to creak as if someone is walking around and you get up to have a look, maybe grabbing a butcher knife from the kitchen on the way. You do that sort of thing here, too. Listen too closely and you start to hear life outside the snapping tent, voices and sometimes yells and footsteps crunching in the snow coming close and then going away and then coming back again, so you dress slowly and yank on your headlamp and step outside onto the tiny platform and look around and the beam of your headlamp barely pierces all the horrid black white wiping clean the face of the earth — and nothing. Of course, nothing. Just like at home because after you've been here long enough it is home.

But none of this is really what I wanted to talk to you about. I seem to be getting off on tangents, which as you probably don't know is likely due to hypoxia.

I'll explain briefly. Hypoxia is a lack of oxygen to the brain. At this altitude you get about half the oxygen you would at sea level. Affects everybody differently. Some climbers get nauseous and vomit regularly; there's a frozen yellow glob just outside the tent. Some get searing headaches. Some get loose concentration and float a little. You have to be careful with this one. Just because your mind is floating, you can sometimes start thinking your body can too and forget about gravity. But you can never forget about gravity. If mountain climbing is anything at all, it is dancing with gravity. Dark and beautiful and seductive she is. She has eyes that take your clothes off. She wants to lie down with you. She slowly slips from her dress and you see her and her flesh and she smiles and reaches up and takes your arm and her grip is suddenly not soft and delicate but heavy, so unimaginably heavy, and she won't let go and you have to willing to kick her because she's a sorceress, a widowmaker, an executioner.

You learn this quickly or you don't live long climbing mountains. Like I said, this ain't football.

Anyway, what I wanted to tell you about was what happened yesterday.

It started out as just another day. I was alone, kicking the points of my crampons into the blue ice, slowly juggling the lines up the ice wall. I don't suppose you can imagine it but it's not that different from climbing the ropes in gym, except we have spikes on our feet and wear big gloves.

Yesterday was the sixth day in a row I'd gone up on the face carrying loads. Every day the same: up at 3 a.m., boil something, down it, walk up the glacier in the dark under the stars brilliant as fireworks which is magic every single time, then start up the wall. On a good day, even with a heavy load, I would be up to this camp by noon.

But yesterday I felt different almost from the beginning. Uneasy. Like how you feel when you think something bad is going to happen to someone you're close to, but you don't know who, or how, and you can't do anything about it and it makes you feel raw and upset but since you can't do anything you just do what you would normally.

To my surprise, I started dragging about halfway up the wall. At first I tried to ignore it — which I've had more practice at since you knew me — but when it's really bad, I don't care what you used to say, Coach, it's bad. In disbelief, I was suddenly barely moving. Each step was shrinking, rising only a few inches above the last. It seemed to require extraordinary energy to move at all. I felt like I was diminishing, as if I were being absorbed by something too vast and perhaps even too kind to fight. I had to stop for every breath. I kept craning my neck around like a baby bird, looking up, looking for this little red nest on a ledge. Then I was stopping more than going. Just standing there a thousand feet in the air, straight up above the glacier, hanging onto a rope balancing on four tiny metal teeth shoved into the ice. I kept looking up. Then I was just stopped. I don't know for how long. Just stopped. The air was getting colder. I could feel it freezing the snow on my face. I thought I saw some sparrows flitting above me, darting, diving, swooping playfully in the dusk. Then it was getting dark. I couldn't believe it. Quite calmly it occurred to me that I might not make it. I couldn't see the ledge and I couldn't lift my legs anymore and I couldn't feel my toes. Everything was starting to move in slow motion and my thoughts were coming slower and slower like when you are given anesthetic and can't seem to control ...

I said something to myself out loud. It took a while to sink in. "Fuck," I whispered, my mouth barely capable of forming around the word. My lips felt unattached. I started consciously breathing the word over and over very slowly, forcing myself to speak loudly. "Fuck. Fuck. Fuck."

Then something snapped or I don't know what and I was lucid for a moment. I thought: how dumb, I'm going to die. I'm going to freeze stiff as a strip of jerky hanging on a wall between two camps on a big mountain in the middle of the sky in the middle of the night in the middle of Asia.

Then you know what I thought of? You won't believe it: running stairs. I couldn't believe it myself. Here I was, couldn't even feel my damn feet and I'm thinking of running stairs. It was a visceral thought. My body thought of it, not me.

Right after that I thought of you and I started moving again. Hate has a lot of energy.

I'm sorry. I can barely hold the pen. I have to sleep now.

Back again.

You won't remember but it was because of you I learned how to run stairs.

I was a skinny kid, sinewy. I set the junior-high record (it might still be up on the gymnasium wall) for doing 1589 sit-ups in a half hour. You made us do all the physical fitness tests on the bare hardwood floor. Setting that record left me with a three-inch bleeding gash in the middle of my back, but anything was worth it for a piece of pride when we were 12. You knew that.

Actually, Coach, you can't take all the credit. I learned how to run stairs partly because of a boy named Weichman.

It was during a game of Murder Ball.

This was back when boys and girls did not have gym class together. There was a boys gym and girls gym, both enormous three-story mausoleums with dusty yellow light coming through a thousand panes of old warped glass and bleachers running all the way to the ceiling.

Now that I think about it, once a month, only once a month, by some stroke of erotic temptation, we'd have "coed day," which meant boys and girls would get to bounce on trampolines in the same gym. Coach, I recall you would stand along the edge of the girl's tramp and look up their skirts. We knew you were sick. Every other day, in the scary, sacred, gigantic boys gym, Murder Ball was enacted.

Murder Ball was an elementary game that I don't think you thought up, although it's precisely the kind of game you would have if you could have. Perhaps theatrically named, I think now it had some very adult, real-world veracity. Take a class of 30 gangly, all-sized, ruddy-cheeked boys — some shy to the point of fainting at VD health movies, some already so abused they could take a punch from a full-grown man, and a large bunch of us just trying to be normal and stay out of the way — randomly divide it in half, divide the gymnasium in half, put a team on either side, slowly roll five or 10 hard red rubber balls down the half-court line.

Rules were simple; you barked them: "Don't git hit; if you do, yer ass is out. Don't ever go too far and step over the line."

The beginning was always tense. I remember this was the part you relished. Your eyes would roll in your head and you'd clench your jaw so much we could see the muscles in your blue cheeks. The balls would be gliding silently down that line following one after another and several brave boys from both sides would have to race to the line swerving and ducking, snatch up a ball and throw it as hard as they could at somebody doing the same thing three feet away. Some kid always got it good.

Thereafter both teams commenced to pummel each other. The fat kids or slow kids or dumb kids always went out first, often getting hit with two or three balls at once, which would send them to the floor screaming.

Although I was reasonably quick and strong, I hated this game. I think every boy hated this game except maybe the large, vicious kids who could really throw a ball and the few kids whose dads wanted them to be World Series pitchers and had taught them how to throw hard and accurate.

330

Anyway, one day I hit this kid Weichman in the face. I almost always threw with the fury of fear amidst a pell-mell dash, absolutely no aim, my eyes mostly closed. The ball flew out wildly hooking to the far left just when Weichman was stumbling forward narrowly avoiding another hissing peril. He happened to be looking up. I saw his eyes in his fat face, and when it hit I could tell it hurt bad and for a split second I wanted to yell out, "Sorry. Hey, I'm sorry," or something foolish like that before I realized I was close to the line and about to be hurt and threw myself backwards zigzagging like a shell-shocked rabbit.

When the bell rang I innocently thought Weichman had forgotten all about it although even from across the gym I could see his face was still red and welted. He jumped me in the locker room. He was much bigger but I was much quicker so all in all we punched and scraped and banged each other up against the metal lockers until Weichman's face was bleeding and a crowd was gathered. Then you broke through and dragged us off to your office.

We knew what could happen. The bruises and blood were nothing now. We'd seen the perfect pattern of blisters in a rectangle of black on several of the tough boys who said it didn't hurt but didn't sit down even putting on their shoes for a month.

I was scared but inside I was feeling good too because fat Weichman twice my size hadn't killed me, and when I started to think about it I must have just somehow smiled again because you got purple in the face like you did yelling at your football team that I'd quit after the second week.

"Why you goddamn little smartass!" you said. You shoved Weichman out of your office bellowing: "Better quit yer fuckin' cryin'! Shower that blood off yer fat face." You slammed your office door and the pin-up girl tacked to the inside waved.

You cornered me. "Paddlin's somethin' pretty funny to smartfarts like you ain't it. Well get th'fuck out. Tomorrow'll be somethin' fer you." And you slapped me in the face and kicked me right in the anus and opened the door and shoved me out of your office.

So I was scared all the rest of the day and through that night when things can get real bad for a boy. The next day during roll call you roared at me to step forward.

"Saw you step yer ass cross the line yesterday, boy!" you said.

A strange sound went through the kids in class. It was like a breeze that changes its shape as it moves. At first it sounded like a snicker but then it sickened and turned into a faint groan and ended in an inaudible gasp like what happens when someone is punched in the stomach. I knew what was about to happen and began to tremble and immediately forced myself to stop it and to put on a blank look. I was biting my tongue.

"Asshole! Go stand yer ass against that wall."

Coach, you were smiling. I know now that you lived for this kind of thing. I know now you aren't the only vicious person on earth.

I walked rigidly across the gym floor trying to think about making my knees work, stopped at the wall, and turned around.

You cursed and all the boys lined up on the half court line. Your voice was kind of high-pitched, like an over-excited dog. The boys charged and scuffled and cuffed and of course the balls ended up in the hands of the meanest, most accurate throwers in the class. One of them gave Weichman a ball.

I decided one thing. I decided to just make sure Weichman's ball didn't hit me.

Then you blew your whistle and all the itchy kids with strong arms and frenzied faces hurled at once but I was concentrating hard watching Weichman and I was fast and dodged and a firestorm descended and I dodged and suffocated and dove and got away and one caught me hard in the ear and one caught me in the nuts and I dropped fast and felt hot and swallowed hot vomit and heard off in the distance that blurry snickersickgroan and saw what I thought were sparrows flitting above me, darting and diving and swooping playfully but couldn't figure out how they got inside the gymnasium when your black leather shoes shoved up under my face.

"Well, smartfart, git up."

I looked up.

"Don't you! Don't you give me that fuckin' ..." and I saw your leather feet twitch and shuffle as if you were going to kick me in the face.

Then everything was quiet for a minute.

"You got stairs for one whole fuckin' month. Startin today. Now git on it." Coach, you dragged me to my feet by my ears because my hair was too short and shoved me off and kicked me in the anus.

That's when I knew you liked me and all the kids knew I was lucky enough to get stairs because I'd managed not to get killed by Weichman and had even given him a bloody nose and managed somehow not to get the paddle either by not crying.

I've been running stairs ever since. Three months before every expedition I start visiting the stadium. It is a mile away and I run there every day. It is a ritual. I stand in the middle of the football field and stare up and listen to all the crowds whistling and hooting at football games I never go to. Then I take off. I run them until I can't. Until I puke.

Coach, I have to sleep again now.

First published in Climbing *No. 152, 1995.*

Sex and the
Single Jellyfish
The worst month of my life

By John Sherman

I was obviously learning little at photo school, so on the advice of my college counselor, I dropped out after just a semester. I then sold most of my possessions, and hopped on the only flight I could find to Australia. All the other flights were booked that December, except for one on Christmas Day. Well, not exactly Christmas Day, because you lose a day crossing the international dateline when flying west, so when I landed in Sydney there were only a few hours of Christmas left. Waiting for me at the airport was the woman who had enticed me over there to go traveling. Waiting with her was her boyfriend of one week. I didn't know it at the time, but the first domino in a long line had just tipped over. The worst month of my life had begun.

I had to get out of Sydney. I took refuge in an American friend's rented flat for a few days until I rounded up a used car. It was a Ford Cortina, kind of a shrunken Maverick, with a Kahlua-and-cream paint job. It blasted through red lights pretty well and had only minor trouble staying on the left side of the road. It wasn't hard finding climbers eager to drive along to Mount Arapiles.

A year and a half before, I had had the time of my life hanging out at the *Piles.* I hadn't climbed since, though, due to a fierce case of tendinitis spawned by that very trip. My elbows were still shot, so I had no intention of climbing this time, but I liked the local pub at Natimuk, and more importantly it was 600 miles away from Sydney. About 300 miles into the drive, though, the Cortina started lurching. I'd been had twice that week.

My friends and I limped into Arapiles, the engine hacking like a three-pack-a-day smoker. None of us knew squat about car engines, but a Yank in the campground professed to such knowledge. In friendly fashion he tinkered around under the hood. In friendlier fashion he offered to share his tent that night. The way he kept asking sounded like he wanted to tinker under another hood. Holding fast to my phobias, I spent a cramped night inside my car, listening to the rain pelt the roof.

I wanted out of Arapiles, but the car was still sick. HB, a local climber and holder of the Natimuk-to-Arapiles speed driving record, took a crack at the engine. In a few minutes he had the carburetor apart and was swapping the jets about to improve the car's high-end performance. The valiant effort was for naught. Nevertheless, the Cortina survived the all-day drive south to Melbourne, where I reluctantly agreed to have a rebuilt engine installed.

I got the Cortina back from the auto shop and drove over to Camp Hog's Melbourne headquarters. The beers and bullshit flowed in equal measure that night and I slept well knowing that my car problems were over.

The next morning I went outside to stash gear in my car. I was pretty sure I'd parked the car on that block, but it wasn't there. I checked the next block and the next and even walked to a friend's house a mile away on the off chance that I'd done something really stupid and driven it over there drunk. No dice. It was stolen.

Within 48 hours I had it back. The Melbourne police explained that when it rains, people get sick of waiting for the bus and pilfer cars to drive home. Judging by the empties and trash adorning the interior, the bandits had had a fine 100-kilometer joy ride. Judging by the car's further performance, they hadn't driven at recommended new-engine break-in speeds. Moreover, they had relieved the glove box of my passport and credit cards.

I was starting to feel unlucky. I'd been in Australia less than two weeks and already I needed a change of scenery. At the time, my brother Brad lived in Perth, on the west coast. I hadn't seen him in years, and there was a U.S. consulate there. I still had traveler's checks, and bought a plane ticket. Of course the petty bureaucrat behind the ticket desk would not give me the mandatory foreigner's discount because I had no proof, other than a string of red, white, and blue American expletives, that I was not an Australian citizen. This, however, was just a warm-up for the bureaucracy I was to experience at the hands of the Australian customs and immigration department in Perth.

A pretty big crowd of Yanks had gathered in Perth to watch Dennis Connor retrieve the America's Cup from its embarrassing year of captivity Down Under. The U.S. Ambassador was one of them, and the consulate had its hands full entertaining him. Doubtless this was much more fun than helping U.S. citizens who'd lost their passports. I had plenty of time to kill. This was supposed to be a vacation, so I headed to the beach.

Warm Indian Ocean water lapping at the sugar-white sands makes the

334

beaches at Perth particularly inviting. I swim about as well as John Kruk steals bases, but I ventured a short way past the shorebreak anyway. Given the distance from the shore and the depth of the water, I wasn't as nervous as I would usually be. Suddenly, a highway flare ignited in my swim trunks. A tentacle from a box jellyfish, the local version of the Portuguese Man-O-War, had slithered up the leg of my trunks and was stroking a tender appendage. Understandably panicked, I worsened the situation by thrashing about with my hands in an attempt to remove the incendiary device, wiping the stinging cells over more sensitive skin. I set personal swimming and running records as I churned through the surf, sprinted up the beach, and high-tailed it to the nearest grocery store. I bought a jug of vinegar, found some privacy, and poured it down my shorts.

Days later but still smarting, I upped my humiliation level. When I'd started climbing back in high school, I'd developed the habit of tossing handjams, fingerlocks and the like into cracks in buildings as I walked by. Back then it was worthwhile practice, the stark parallelism of the cracks requiring honest technique to gain a stick. This day, strolling back to my brother's house from the grocery store, I passed an eight-foot-tall brick wall. Coming up quick on my right was an inch-and-an-eighth vertical fissure begging for a thumb-index stack. I shifted the bag of groceries to my left hand, nonchalantly tossed in the technical jam with my right and strode by. Ordinarily, it's all you can do to make such a jam hold; this day, however, my fingers were positioned so well that instead of spitting them out, the jam held fast, accompanied by the twig-snapping sound of a knuckle being broken.

The consulate was still dragging its heels and I was still stuck at my brother's without a passport. Other than genes, my brother and I don't have a whole lot in common. This seemed like a good chance to change that. My brother is a scuba diver and that sounded like fun, so I went down to a local dive shop and signed up for a course that would start in a few days. A day shy of the start of the course the guy at the shop called up and told me that due to slim enrollment, the class was cancelled. Not keen on spending another week at my brother's twiddling my thumbs, I called around until I found another course. I felt lucky to get in on such short notice, and hurried down to the new shop to pay my non-refundable course fee. Minutes after I got back to my brother's, the phone rang.

"Is this John?"

"Speaking."

It was the guy from the first dive shop. "I've got great news for you. The class isn't cancelled after all. A planeload of Swedish stewardesses just came in and signed up."

My brother doesn't own guns and it's a good thing. I would have taken my index, fingered the trigger, then bent my swollen knuckle for all it was worth.

There were no Swedish stewardesses in my class, but at least one gal took a liking to me. Long hair, far-away eyes — her slightly parted lips waited breathlessly for mine. Her name was Resusci-Annie.

"Don't fret," my brother said. "Your course ends Friday, you'll be certified, and you can go diving with us this weekend. The underwater photography club is going to Penguin Island and there will be scads of single women trolling for you."

Yeah, right.

Her name was Jennie and she leaned against the rail at the stern of the dive boat, the wind flipping her long auburn hair behind her shoulders. I was mesmerized by her face — straight nose, high cheekbones, a hint of strength to the jaw. Add to that the redhead's light dust of freckles and my knees turned to mercury. A conservative one-piece black swimsuit did little to avert the poorly concealed stares of the men on board. The face, the curves, she made the Victoria's Secret models look like trolls.

The presence of such a goddess intimidated me. All I could say to her was, "Could I borrow some sunscreen?" I was dancing on the thin line between pleasure and torture, convinced that somehow the latter was meant to be. It was a relief when the boat stopped and we all swam our different ways.

Late that afternoon I strolled about the island by myself, agonized by my shyness. This was worse than having my car stolen. Nematocysts to the gonads were a delight in comparison. Break all my fingers; I don't care.

I walked up the trail and crested a low hill. Walking up the trail was Jennie, camera bouncing off her breasts. Somehow I managed to say "Hi," and we started talking about photography. We walked and talked and watched the seabirds sweep past the cliffs. She was a marine biologist and just as her swimsuit couldn't hide her figure, neither did her peaceful smile and lovely face hide her intelligence. What a pair of cerebral hemispheres! I was smitten.

We strolled down to the beach. Reddish-orange stripes licked the horizon as the persimmon sun disappeared. It was unbearably romantic, the kind of sunset adoring couples pose in front of on Trojan boxes. The gods were playing a sick joke on me. They had scoured my dreams, created the perfect woman, then sent her down to earth to torture me. I could not hold her hand, lest she slap me; hug her, lest she scream; kiss her, lest she vomit. Still, I could not leave her side and we continued walking in the dark.

We were sitting in the sand when we first kissed. This was no dream. My luck had changed.

I went back to her place after the weekend. I was convinced I should quit climbing (not a whole lot around Perth), move to Australia, and become an underwater photographer. I thought of spending the rest of my life with her. After a few days I dropped back in on my brother. I was wearing the kind of

336

lip-stretching smile that is usually only seen on those doing mushrooms. My brother's girlfriend stated the obvious, "John's in love."

That day my jaw felt sore. Was it from the shit-eating grin? Holding a regulator in my mouth? All the necking? The extracurricular activities?

The next morning I couldn't eat. My jaw wouldn't close far enough for my teeth to touch. My cheeks looked like a chipmunk's and my saliva glands refused to work. No amount of water could slake the terrible cottonmouth. I went to the doctor.

"John, you've got the mumps."

I thought only kids got them. The doctor then told me about certain side effects the disease can cause in adults.

"That's OK, doc. I never wanted to have kids anyway."

"Trust me, John. This is not the way you want to get sterilized."

My brother freaked. He wanted kids bad, and was on the verge of kicking me out.

A day later I looked like Mr. Potatohead with a bad growth of stubble, but at least I was in love. Jennie gave me some token sympathy, then gave me the boot. She assured me she had had the mumps as a kid, so I was left with one suspect — Rususci-Annie.

I could swear that the gods had sent not just Jennie to torture me, but a host of bit players too. At customs they made me fill out forms for three hours to receive a box of gear sent from the States. After I handed over the forms they said come back tomorrow to fill out the rest of the forms. Immigration treated me likewise. At the consulate they ran me through a two-on-one rapid-fire interrogation to verify I was who I said I was. They asked for exact street addresses of long-ago domiciles and even queried me on the basketball team's record where I went to grade school. They knew more about me than I could remember myself. It was kind of scary, but they finally coughed up a passport and with that I had my freedom.

There was one way to change my luck and one way only. I jetted back to Melbourne, packed up the loathsome Cortina and drove to Arapiles. We did a short approach to a simple climb named *Skink* and I started up. Stabbing pains shot through my elbows as I pulled over a bulge into a small but exposed dihedral. I had no confidence in my protection and my legs vibrated violently. Out of control and against all sense, I continued up the orange sandstone wall, gripped out of my gourd. At last, life was good.

First published in Climbing *No. 152, May, 1995.*